# Study Guide

for

## Kail and Cavanaugh's

# Human Development
## A Life-Span View
### Fourth Edition

**Dea K. DeWolff**

**Terri A. Tarr**
*Indiana University*
*Purdue University Indianapolis*

THOMSON
★
™
WADSWORTH

Australia • Brazil • Canada • Mexico • Singapore • Spain • United Kingdom • United States

Printed in the United States of America

2 3 4 5 6 7 10 09 08 07

Printer: Thomson West

ISBN-13: 978-0-495-13056-7
ISBN-10: 0-495-13056-7

Cover Images (clockwise from top left): Seiya Kawamoto/Getty Images; Nancy Honey/Getty Images; Ken Weingart/Getty Images; Getty Images; John Terrence Turner/Getty Images; Tim Hall/Getty Images

**Thomson Higher Education**
**10 Davis Drive**
**Belmont, CA 94002-3098**
**USA**

For more information about our products, contact us at:
**Thomson Learning Academic Resource Center**
**1-800-423-0563**

For permission to use material from this text or product, submit a request online at
**http://www.thomsonrights.com.**
Any additional questions about permissions can be submitted by email to **thomsonrights@thomson.com.**

# TABLE OF CONTENTS

# THE STUDY OF HUMAN DEVELOPMENT

This chapter includes tips on how to use the textbook, a discussion of developmental theories and research, a look at common influences and issues in development, and the methods that developmentalists use to make discoveries.

# 1.1 HOW TO USE THIS BOOK

- Skim the text, paying attention to chapter outlines and outline headings.

- Before reading each section in the textbook, read the *Learning Objectives* at the beginning of the section.

- After reading each section, try to answer the *Test Yourself* questions at the end of each section in the textbook.

- Now turn to the *Study Guide*.

- Read **To Master the Learning Objectives** for each section and try to answer each question on a separate piece of paper.

- Complete each section of the study guide. On **Know the Terms** sections, try to figure out the answers before looking at your choices.

- At the end of each chapter, integrate the chapter information by completing the **Summary**.

- Test yourself using the **Multiple-choice** and **Essay** questions.

- Check your answers and re-read the pages that are associated with each question that you could not answer correctly.

# 1.2 THINKING ABOUT DEVELOPMENT

## TO MASTER THE LEARNING OBJECTIVES:

**What fundamental issues of development have scholars addressed throughout history?**

- Explain how one's genes (nature) and one's environment (nurture) interact with each other to influence development.

- Explain the difference between continuous and discontinuous development, and be able to give examples of both types of development.

- Explain the difference between context-specific and universal development.

**What are the forces in the biopsychosocial framework? How does the timing of these forces make a difference in their impact?**

- Define the biopsychosocial framework. Give examples of biological, psychological, sociocultural, and life-cycle forces in development, and know how they interact to shape development.

## 1.2 KNOW THE TERMS

Biological forces

Biopsychosocial framework

Continuity-discontinuity

Human development

Life-cycle forces

Nature-nurture

Psychological forces

Sociocultural

Universal versus context-specific

1. _____ is the multidisciplinary study of how people change and how they remain the same over time.

2. The _____ issue addresses the degree to which genetic influences and environmental influences determine the type of person you are.

3. The _____ issue is concerned with whether a particular developmental phenomenon follows a smooth progression throughout the life span or a series of abrupt shifts.

4. The issue of whether there is one path of development or several is addressed by the _____ issue.

5.  The _____ on development include all genetic and health-related factors that affect development.

6.  The _____ on development include all internal perceptual, cognitive, emotional, and personality factors that affect development.

7.  Interpersonal, societal, cultural, and ethnic factors are the _____ forces that influence development.

8.  Differences in how the same event may affect people of different ages are called _____ .

9.  The _____ is used to organize biological, psychological, and sociocultural influences on development.

# 1.2 KNOW THE DETAILS OF THINKING ABOUT DEVELOPMENT

1.  Any one particular feature of development is caused exclusively by either genes or experience.
    TRUE or FALSE

2.  The continuity-discontinuity issue addresses the question of whether development occurs in a smooth progression throughout the lifespan or in a series of abrupt shifts.
    TRUE or FALSE

3.  A developmentalist who takes a universal view of development would say that development occurs in fundamentally different ways depending on the context.
    TRUE or FALSE

4.  Biological forces in development include all genetic and health-related factors that affect development.
    TRUE or FALSE

5.  A person's thoughts and beliefs are psychological forces that can affect development.
    TRUE or FALSE

6.  Life-cycle forces cause the same event to have different effects on people of varying ages.
    TRUE or FALSE

7.  Puberty and menopause are examples of sociocultural forces.
    TRUE or FALSE

8.  The biopsychosocial framework emphasizes that biological forces explain more of human development than any of the other basic forces.
    TRUE or FALSE

9.  All biological forces are determined by our genetic codes.
    TRUE or FALSE

# 1.3 DEVELOPMENTAL THEORIES

## TO MASTER THE LEARNING OBJECTIVES:

**How do psychodynamic theories account for development?**

- Describe how one moves through Erikson's stages of psychosocial development.

**What is the focus of learning theories of development?**

- Explain the operant conditioning principles of reinforcement and punishment.

- Explain how imitation (or observational learning) and self-efficacy influence behavior.

**How do cognitive-developmental theories explain changes in thinking?**

- Describe how Piaget would explain the process of development.

- Describe how information processing theory explains development.

- Describe Vygotsky's theory and the importance of social context to development.

**What are the main points in the ecological and systems approach?**

- Explain the roles of the microsystem, mesosystem, exosystem, and macrosystem in development according to Bronfenbrenner's ecological theory.

- Describe the competence-environmental press framework.

**What are the major tenets of life-span and life course theories?**

- Describe the life-span perspective, including the idea of selective optimization with compensation.

- Describe the life-course perspective.

## 1.3 KNOW THE TERMS

| | |
|---|---|
| Ecological theory | Operant conditioning |
| Epigenetic principle | Punishment |
| Exosystems | Psychodynamic |
| Information-processing theory | Psychosocial |
| Life course perspective | Reinforcement |
| Life-span perspective | Selective optimization with compensation |
| Macrosystems | Self-efficacy |
| Mesosystems | Social cognitive theory |
| Microsystems | Theory |
| Observational | |

1.  In human development, a _____ is an organized set of ideas that is designed to explain development.

2.  _____ theories propose that human behavior is guided by motives and drives that are internal and often unconscious.

3.  Erikson's _____ theory proposes that personality development is the result of the interaction of an internal maturational plan and societal demands.

4.  The _____ of Erikson's theory means that each psychosocial stage has its own period of importance.

5.  According to B.F. Skinner, in _____ the consequences of a behavior determine whether a behavior is repeated in the future.

6.  A _____ is a consequence that increases the likelihood that a behavior will be repeated in the future.

7.  A _____ is a consequence that decreases the likelihood that a behavior will be repeated in the future. This could include spanking and withdrawal of privileges.

8.  Learning by simply watching other people is called imitation or _____ learning.

9.  _____ suggests that people are actively trying to understand the world through reinforcement, punishment, and imitation.

10. People's beliefs about their own abilities or talents is called _____ . This belief may determine when people will imitate others.

11. The _____ proposes that human cognition consists of mental hardware and software.

12. According to _____ , human development cannot be separated from the environmental contexts in which a person develops (see figure).

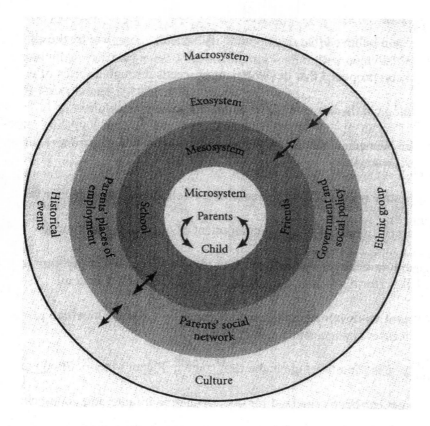

13. According to Bronfenbrenner, one's _____ includes the people, such as parents, and objects in one's immediate environment.

14. Bronfenbrenner's _____ include the interrelations between one's microsystems.

15. Bronfenbrenner's _____ are social settings that influence one's development even though one does not experience them first hand.

16. According to Bronfenbrenner, the _____ includes the cultures and subcultures in which the microsystems, mesosystems, and exosystems are embedded.

17. The _____ is the view that development is determined by many forces and cannot be understood within a single framework.

18. The basic assumption of the _____ model is that the processes of selection, compensation, and optimization form a system that generates and regulates development and aging.

19. The _____ describes the ways in which various generations experience the forces of development in their respective historical contexts.

# 1.3 KNOW THE DETAILS OF DEVELOPMENTAL THEORIES

1. Learning theories suggest that human behavior is caused mainly by internal, unconscious motives and drives.
   TRUE or FALSE

2. According to psychodynamic theorists, human development takes place in a series of universal stages.
   TRUE or FALSE

3. Bandura, Erikson, and Piaget all proposed psychodynamic theories of development.
   TRUE or FALSE

4. Erikson believed that development is basically complete by the end of adolescence.
   TRUE or FALSE

5. Erikson proposed that development proceeds through a series of eight stages.
   TRUE or FALSE

6. Ecological theories are based on the epigenetic principle.
   TRUE or FALSE

7. John Watson, a behaviorist, believed that genes have a stronger influence than experience on development.
   TRUE or FALSE

8. Negative reinforcement increases the likelihood that a behavior will occur in the future.
   TRUE or FALSE

9. Observational learning is a component of operant conditioning.
   TRUE or FALSE

10. Bandura believes that self-efficacy plays a major role in determining whether someone will attempt a task.
    TRUE or FALSE

11. Cognitive-developmental theorists focus on the ways in which people think and how these processes change over time.
    TRUE or FALSE

12. The sensorimotor stage is the first stage in Piaget's theory of cognitive development.
    TRUE or FALSE

13. Piaget has been criticized for overestimating infants' and young children's abilities.
    TRUE or FALSE

14. Kohlberg's theory of moral reasoning is based on information-processing theory.
    TRUE or FALSE

15. According to Piaget, human cognition consists of mental hardware and mental software.

    TRUE or FALSE

16. Information-processing theory proposes that human cognition develops in a series of stages.

    TRUE or FALSE

17. Vygotsky views development as an apprenticeship.

    TRUE or FALSE

18. According to ecological theory, human development is inseparable from the environmental contexts in which a person develops.

    TRUE or FALSE

19. In Bronfenbrenner's theory, the mesosystem refers to the broadest environmental context, such as the culture, in which an individual develops.

    TRUE or FALSE

20. The exosystem refers to social settings that a person may not experience first hand but that still influence development.

    TRUE or FALSE

21. The competence-environmental press theory postulates that how well people adapt is a function of the match between a person's abilities and the demands put on them by the environment.

    TRUE or FALSE

22. According to the life-span perspective, human development is determined primarily by biological forces.

    TRUE or FALSE

23. Multidirectionality, plasticity, historical context, and multiple causation are key features of the life span perspective.

    TRUE or FALSE

24. Elective selection, loss-based selection, and compensation are three processes featured in the information-processing approach.

    TRUE or FALSE

25. The life course perspective describes how biological, psychological, and sociocultural forces of development affect generations differently within their own historical contexts.

    TRUE or FALSE

# 1.4 DOING DEVELOPMENTAL RESEARCH

## TO MASTER THE LEARNING OBJECTIVES:

**How do scientists measure topics of interest in studying human development?**

- Define systematic observation, structured observation, naturalistic observation, sampling behavior with tasks, self reports, reliability, validity, populations, and samples.

**What general research designs are used in human development research? What designs are unique to human development research?**

- Know the differences between correlational and experimental studies.

- Explain what positive correlations, negative correlations, and the strength of a correlation coefficient mean.

- Explain the difference between independent and dependent variables.

- Describe the advantages and disadvantages of cross-sectional, longitudinal, and sequential research designs.

**What ethical procedures must researchers follow?**

- Know the ethical procedures that researchers should follow.

## 1.4 KNOW THE TERMS

| | |
|---|---|
| Cohort effects | Naturalistic observation |
| Correlational study | Population |
| Correlation coefficient | Reliability |
| Cross-sectional | Sample |
| Dependent variable | Self reports |
| Experiment | Sequential |
| Independent variable | Structured observations |
| Longitudinal | Systematic observation |
| Meta-analysis | Validity |
| Naturalistic observation | |

1. _____ involves watching people and carefully recording what they do or say.

2. In _____ , people are observed as they behave spontaneously in some real-life situation.

3. In _____ , a researcher creates a setting that is particularly likely to elicit the behavior of interest.

4. _____ are people's answers to questions about the topic of interest.

5. The _____ of a measure is the extent to which it provides a consistent index of a characteristic.

6. The _____ of a measure refers to whether it really measures what researchers think it measures.

7. A _____ is a broad group of people who are of interest to researchers.

8. A subset of the population of interest is called a _____ .

9. In a _____ , investigators look at relations between variables as they exist naturally in the world.

10. A _____ expresses the strength and direction of a relation between two variables.

11. An _____ is a systematic way of manipulating key factors that a researcher thinks causes a particular behavior.

12. The factor that is manipulated by the researcher in an experiment is called the _____ .

13. The behavior that is observed after other variables are manipulated is called the _____ .

14. _____ research designs involve testing or observing the same people at different points in their lives.

15. A _____ research design involves testing people of different ages in a study.

16. _____ are differences between age groups (cohorts) that are the result of environmental events.

17. _____ studies are more complex research designs that are based on cross-sectional and longitudinal approaches to research.

18. _____ is a tool that allows researchers to synthesize the results of many studies to estimate the relations between variables.

# 1.4 KNOW THE DETAILS OF DOING DEVELOPMENTAL RESEARCH

1. Systematic observation involves watching people and carefully recording what they say or do.
   TRUE or FALSE

2. In naturalistic observations, the researcher creates a setting that is particularly likely to elicit the behavior of interest.
   TRUE or FALSE

3. A limitation of self reports is that they may be invalid because of response bias.
   TRUE or FALSE

4. A weakness of physiological measures is that they are not specific in what they measure.
   TRUE or FALSE

5. The reliability of a measure depends on whether it really measures what researchers think it measures.
   TRUE or FALSE

6. A measure can be valid but not reliable.
   TRUE or FALSE

7. A correlational study involves looking at relations between variables as they exist naturally in the world.
   TRUE or FALSE

8. When a correlation is less than 0, two variables are completely unrelated.
   TRUE or FALSE

9. A strength of correlational studies is that they can be used to determine cause and effect.
   TRUE or FALSE

10. In a correlational study, investigators systematically manipulate the key factors that they think cause a particular behavior.
    TRUE or FALSE

11. The factor that is manipulated in an experimental design is called the independent variable.
    TRUE or FALSE

12. Researchers interested in the stability of a behavior should use a longitudinal design rather than a cross-sectional design.
    TRUE or FALSE

13. A cross-sectional study involves studying the same individuals repeatedly at different points in their lives.
    TRUE or FALSE

14. Cohort effects are more of a problem for cross-sectional studies than for longitudinal studies.
    TRUE or FALSE

15. Sequential designs are simpler and less expensive than either cross-sectional or longitudinal designs.
    TRUE or FALSE

16. Meta-analysis involves comparing the results of many studies.
    TRUE or FALSE

17. To conduct research ethically, investigators must submit their research proposals to review panels after they collect their data but before they submit their report to a scientific journal.
    TRUE or FALSE

# SUMMARY

## 1.2 THINKING ABOUT HUMAN DEVELOPMENT

1. **Recurring Issues in Human Development**

   Three main issues are prominent in the study of human development. The _____ issue involves the degree to which genetics and the environment influence human development. In general, theorists and researchers view nature and nurture as mutually _____ influences; development is always shaped by both. The continuity-discontinuity issue focuses on whether the _____ explanations (continuity) or _____ explanations (discontinuity) must be used to explain changes in people over time. In the issue of universal versus context-specific development, the question is whether development follows the _____ general path in all people or is fundamentally _____ depending on the sociocultural context.

2. **Basic Forces in Human Development: The Biopsychosocial Framework**

   Development is based on the combined impact of four primary forces. _____ forces include all genetic and health-related factors that affect development. Some biological forces, such as puberty and menopause, are universal and affect people across generations, while others, such as diet or diseases, affect people in specific generations or occur only in a small number of people. _____ forces include all internal perceptual, cognitive emotional, and personality factors that influence development. Like biological forces, psychological forces may affect all individuals, only specific generations, or only a few individuals. _____ forces include interpersonal, societal, cultural, and ethnic factors that affect development. _____ refers to the knowledge, attitudes, and behavior associated with a group of people. Overall, sociocultural forces provide the context or backdrop for development. The _____ framework emphasizes that the forces are mutually interactive, and that development cannot be understood by examining forces in isolation. Furthermore, the same event can have different effects depending on when it happens. _____ forces provide a context for understanding how people perceive their current situation and its effects on them.

## 1.3 DEVELOPMENTAL THEORIES

1. Developmental theories _____ knowledge in order to provide _____ explanations of human behaviors and the ways in which they change over time. Current approaches to developmental

theory focus on specific aspects of behavior. At present, there is no single unified theory of human development.

2. **Psychodynamic Theories**

   Psychodynamic theories propose that behavior is determined by _____ motives. Erikson proposed a life-span theory of _____ development, consisting of eight universal stages, each characterized by a particular struggle.

3. **Learning Theory**

   Learning theory focuses on the development of _____ behavior. Operant conditioning is based on the notions of environmental control of behavior, _____ which increases the likelihood that a behavior will be repeated, and punishment which _____ the likelihood that a behavior will be repeated. _____ theory proposes that people learn by observing others.

4. **Cognitive-Developmental Theory**

   Cognitive-developmental theory focuses on thought processes. Piaget proposed a four-stage sequence of _____ development. Information-processing theory argues that people deal with information like a _____ and development consists of increased _____ in handling information. Vygotsky emphasized the influence of _____ on development.

5. **The Ecological and Systems Approach**

   Bronfenbrenner proposed that development occurs in the context of several interconnected systems of increasing complexity. These systems include the _____ , the mesosystem, the _____ , and the macrosystem. The _____ framework postulates that there is a "best fit" between one's abilities and the demands placed on a person by the _____ .

6. **Life-Span Perspective, Selective Optimization with Compensation, and Life Course Perspective**

   According to the life-span perspective, human development is characterized by multidirectionality, plasticity, historical context, and multiple causation. All four forces are key. _____ refers to the developmental trends to focus one's efforts and abilities in successively fewer domains as one ages and to acquire ways to compensate for normative losses. The life-course perspective refers to understanding human development within the context of the _____ period in which a generation develops, which creates unique sets of experiences.

# 1.4 DOING DEVELOPMENTAL RESEARCH

1. **Measurement in Human Development Research**

   Research typically begins by determining how to measure the topic of interest. _____ observation involves recording people's behavior as it takes place either in a _____ setting (naturalistic observation) or a _____ setting (structured observation). Researchers sometimes create tasks to obtain samples of people's behavior. In _____ , people answer questions posed by the experimenter. Researchers must determine that their measures are _____ and _____ ; they must also obtain a sample that is _____ of some larger population.

2. **General Designs for Research**

   In correlational studies, investigators examine relations among variables as they occur _____ . This relation is often measured by a correlation coefficient, r, which can vary from -1 (strong inverse relation) to 0 (no relation) to +1 (strong _____ relation). Correlational studies cannot determine cause and effect, so researchers do experimental studies in which an _____ variable is manipulated, and the impact of this manipulation on a dependent variable is recorded. Experimental studies allow conclusions about cause and effect, but the strict control of other variables that is required often makes the situation artificial. The best approach is to use both experimental and correlational studies to provide converging evidence.

3. **Designs for Studying Development**

   To study development, some researchers use a _____ design in which the same people are observed repeatedly as they grow. This approach provides evidence concerning actual patterns of individual growth but has several shortcomings as well: it is time-consuming, some people _____ of the project, and repeated testing can affect performance. An alternative, the _____ design, involves testing people of _____ ages. This design avoids the problems of the longitudinal design but provides no information about individual _____ . Also, what appear to be age differences may be _____ effects. The best approach is to use both designs to provide converging evidence.

4. **Integrating Findings from Different Studies**

   Meta-analysis provides a way for researchers to look for trends across _____ studies to estimate the relations among variables.

5. **Conducting Research Ethically**

   Planning research also involves selecting methods that preserve the rights of research _____ .
   Experimenters must _____ the risks to potential research participants, describe the research
   so that potential participants can decide if they want to participate, avoid _____ , and keep
   results anonymous or confidential.

6. **Communicating Research Results**

   Once research data are collected and _____ , investigators _____ the results in
   scientific outlets such as journals and books. Such results form the foundation of knowledge about
   human development.

# TEST YOURSELF

## MULTIPLE-CHOICE QUESTIONS

1. Venus and her sister Serena are both outstanding athletes. Do they have similar athletic abilities
   because their parents reared them the same way, or because they both inherited athletic talent from their
   parents? Developmental theorists refer to this question as the _____ issue.
   a. continuity versus discontinuity
   b. nature versus nurture
   c. universal versus context-specific development
   d. life-cycle

2. An example of _____ in development occurs when a quiet, shy child becomes a quiet, shy adult.
   a. universality
   b. context-specificity
   c. continuity
   d. discontinuity

3. The universal versus context-specific development issue addresses the question of whether
   a. there is one path of development or several different paths.
   b. genes or environment most influence development.
   c. individuals play an active role in their own development.
   d. development occurs in a smooth progression or in a series of abrupt shifts.

4. Internal perceptual, cognitive, emotional, and personality factors that affect development are referred to
   as _____ forces.
   a. sociocultural
   b. biological
   c. life-cycle
   d. psychological

5. The _____ framework emphasizes that human development involves more than just biological, psychological, or sociocultural forces considered in isolation.
   a. universal
   b. discontinuity
   c. life-cycle
   d. biopsychosocial

6. A child's school is a _____ force that influences development.
   a. psychological
   b. life-cycle
   c. sociocultural
   d. biological

7. Arturo's age is a _____ factor that might influence the impact his parents' divorce has on his development.
   a. life-cycle
   b. biological
   c. psychological
   d. sociocultural

8. _____ theorists propose that internal drives and unconscious motives drive much of behavior.
   a. Cognitive
   b. Learning
   c. Psychodynamic
   d. Ecological

9. The psychodynamic perspective has its roots in
   a. Watson's theory.
   b. Freud's theory.
   c. Locke's view.
   d. Piaget's theory.

10. Erikson's theory is based on the _____ principle, which suggests that each psychosocial issue has a period of time during which it is of most importance.
    a. early experience
    b. epigenetic
    c. ecological
    d. egocentrism

11. Erikson's theory
    a. considers development to be complete by adolescence.
    b. takes a cognitive-developmental approach.
    c. proposes a series of eight stages of development.
    d. emphasizes self-efficacy.

12. According to the principles of _____, the consequences of a behavior determine whether a behavior is repeated in the future.
    a. cognitive-developmental theory
    b. competence-environmental press theory
    c. information-processing theory
    d. operant conditioning

13. _____ is a consequence that decreases the likelihood that a particular behavior will occur in the future.
    a. Punishment
    b. Negative reinforcement
    c. Positive reinforcement
    d. Self-efficacy

14. Observational learning is an important component of
    a. operant conditioning.
    b. information processing theory.
    c. psychodynamic theory.
    d. social learning theory.

15. People's beliefs about their own abilities and talents is known as
    a. observational learning.
    b. the epigenetic principle.
    c. self-efficacy.
    d. operant conditioning.

16. Social-cognitive theory is associated with
    a. Freud
    b. Skinner
    c. Piaget
    d. Bandura

17. According to _____, children act like little scientists and create theories about the world.
    a. Erikson
    b. Piaget
    c. Bandura
    d. Bronfenbrenner

18. Piaget's theory is associated with which perspective?
    a. psychodynamic
    b. learning
    c. cognitive-developmental
    d. life course

19. Kohlberg developed a theory of
    a. psychosexual development.
    b. operant conditioning.
    c. information-processing.
    d. moral reasoning.

20. The computer is used as a metaphor for human thinking in
    a. Piaget's theory.
    b. Kohlberg's theory.
    c. systems theory.
    d. information-processing theory.

21. According to _____ theory, you cannot separate human development from the context in which it occurs.
    a. ecological
    b. Piaget's
    c. information-processing
    d. Freud's

22. Hannah lives with her mother, father, and younger sister. Bronfenbrenner would say that Hannah's immediate family are part of her
    a. mesosystem.
    b. exosystem.
    c. macrosystem.
    d. microsystem.

23. The concept of "best fit" or "best match" is of central importance in _____ theory.
    a. psychodynamic
    b. information-processing
    c. competence-environmental press
    d. life-cycle

24. According to the life-span perspective,
    a. development is essentially complete by adolescence.
    b. every period of a person's life can be understood apart from its origins.
    c. human development is multiply determined.
    d. all behavior is consistent across the life span.

25. The idea that new skills can be learned even in late life is related to the concept of
    a. multidirectionality.
    b. plasticity.
    c. historical context.
    d. multiple causation.

26. Ivory decided to stop working overtime because her children have begun to need her at home nearly every evening, and on weekends to help them with homework and drive them to activities. This is an example of
    a. elective selection.
    b. loss-based selection.
    c. compensation.
    d. optimization.

27. The _____ describes the ways in which various generations experience the biological, psychological, and sociocultural forces of development in their respective historical contexts.
    a. ecological approach
    b. psychodynamic perspective
    c. cognitive approach
    d. life course perspective

28. In a _____, people are observed as they behave spontaneously in some real-life situation.
    a. structured observation
    b. naturalistic observation
    c. self report
    d. sampling of behavior with tasks

29. Dr. Peters has decided to use class attendance as a measure of student motivation. Her colleague, Dr. Martin, expresses concern that attendance may be due to health rather than motivation. Dr. Martin is questioning the _____ of Dr. Peter's measure of motivation.
    a. reliability
    b. validity
    c. representativeness
    d. artificiality

30. When scores on a test are very inconsistent from one administration to another, there is reason to be concerned about the test's
    a. correlation coefficient.
    b. cohort effects.
    c. validity.
    d. reliability.

31. In a life span development course, a correlation of .90 was found between the amount of time students spent studying for the first exam and their scores on the exam. This means that
    a. students who studied more received lower scores.
    b. students who studied more received higher scores.
    c. students who studied less received 90's.
    d. the amount of time spent studying was not related to scores on the exam.

32. A weakness of correlational designs is that they
    a. are expensive to conduct.
    b. cannot be used to determine cause and effect.
    c. are often laboratory-based, so tend to be artificial.
    d. cannot be used to study the stability of behavior.

33. In a(n) _____ study, key factors are manipulated to determine what causes a particular behavior.
    a. correlational
    b. experimental
    c. sequential
    d. longitudinal

34. An investigator interested in the effect of noise on recall memory randomly assigns college students to either a quiet or a noisy condition and asks them to study a list of words for five minutes. They are tested later to determine the number of words on the list they can recall. In this study, the independent variable is _____, and the dependent variable is _____.
    a. the amount of time they were allowed to study the list; the amount of noise
    b. college students; the number of words recalled
    c. the number of words recalled; the amount of noise
    d. the amount of noise; the number of words recalled

35. Dr. Wong assessed the memory skills of the same group of children when they were 3, 5, 7, and 9 years of age. Dr. Wong conducted a _____ study.
    a. longitudinal
    b. cross-sectional
    c. sequential
    d. confounded

36. A disadvantage of longitudinal studies is
    a. cost.
    b. an inability to answer questions about the stability of behaviors.
    c. only correlational methods can be used.
    d. cohort effects complicate the interpretation of age differences.

37. An investigator studied friendship formation in 5-, 8-, 11-, and 15-year-olds by observing students new to a school during the first month of the 2006-07 school year. The researcher used a _____ design.
    a. longitudinal
    b. sequential
    c. cross-sectional
    d. confounded

38. When a cross-sectional design study is repeated over regular intervals, the research design is
    a. longitudinal.
    b. sequential.
    c. experimental.
    d. correlational.

39. Dr. Jefferson wants to compare the findings of many studies that measured the relation between parental divorce and academic achievement. What method would be most appropriate for him to use?
    a. sequential
    b. meta-analysis
    c. correlational
    d. experimental

## ESSAY QUESTIONS

1. You are talking to a friend who says, "Development is the result of the genes that you inherit, and those genes put you on a developmental path which stays the same throughout your life. This path also is the same for everybody." What can you tell your friend about the issues of nature versus nurture, continuity versus discontinuity, and universal versus context-specific development?

2. Your sister Kumi is having problems with her 2-year-old daughter. Your niece, Kayla, has been throwing tantrums to get what she wants. As you watch Kumi and Kayla interact, you see that Kumi will say "no" to Kayla, Kayla will cry and scream, and then Kumi will give in to her. What can you tell Kumi about the principles of operant conditioning that might help her deal with the situation?

3. A researcher is interested in determining if personality changes or stays the same as a person matures from young adulthood to old age. Should the researcher use a longitudinal or a cross-sectional research design? State the advantages and disadvantages of each type of research design.

# SOLUTIONS

## 1.2 KNOW THE TERMS

1. Human development (1)
2. nature-nurture (5)
3. continuity-discontinuity (6)
4. universal versus context-specific (6)
5. biological forces (7)
6. psychological forces (7)
7. sociocultural (7)
8. life-cycle forces (7)
9. biopsychosocial framework (7)

## 1.2 KNOW THE DETAILS OF THINKING ABOUT DEVELOPMENT

1. F, 5
2. T, 6
3. F, 6
4. T, 8
5. T, 8
6. T, 7
7. F, 8
8. F, 8
9. F, 8

## 1.3 KNOW THE TERMS

1. theory (11)
2. Psychodynamic (11)
3. psychosocial (11)
4. epigenetic principle (13)
5. operant conditioning (14)
6. reinforcement (14)
7. punishment (14)
8. observational (14)
9. Social cognitive theory (15)
10. self-efficacy (15)
11. information-processing theory (17)
12. ecological theory (18)
13. microsystem (18)
14. mesosystems (19)
15. exosystems (19)
16. macrosystems (19)
17. life-span perspective (20)
18. selective optimization with compensation (21)
19. life course perspective (22)

## 1.3 KNOW THE DETAILS OF DEVELOPMENTAL THEORIES

1. F, 14
2. T, 11
3. F, 11
4. F, 11
5. T, 11
6. F, 13
7. F, 14
8. T, 14
9. F, 14
10. T, 15
11. T, 15
12. T, 16
13. F, 16
14. F, 16
15. F, 15
16. F, 17
17. T, 17
18. T, 18
19. F, 19
20. T, 19
21. T, 19
22. F, 20
23. T, 20
24. F, 22
25. T, 22

## 1.4 KNOW THE TERMS

1. Systematic observation (28)
2. naturalistic observation (28)
3. structured observations (28)
4. Self reports (29)
5. reliability (30)
6. validity (30)
7. population (30)
8. sample (30)
9. correlational study (31)
10. correlation coefficient (31)
11. experiment (32)
12. independent variable (32)
13. dependent variable (32)
14. Longitudinal (33)
15. cross-sectional (34)
16. Cohort effects (34)
17. Sequential (36)
18. Meta-analysis (34)

## 1.4 KNOW THE DETAILS OF DOING DEVELOPMENTAL RESEARCH

1. T, 25
2. F, 25
3. T, 26
4. F, 27
5. F, 27
6. F, 27
7. T, 28
8. F, 28
9. F, 29
10. F, 29
11. T, 30
12. T, 31
13. F, 32
14. T, 32
15. F, 33
16. T, 34
17. F, 34

## SUMMARY

### 1.2 THINKING ABOUT HUMAN DEVELOPMENT

1. nature-nurture (5); interactive (5); same (6); different (6); same (6); different (6)
2. Biological (8); Psychological (8); Sociocultural (8); Culture (8); biopsychosocial (9); Life-cycle (10)

### 1.3 DEVELOPMENTAL THEORIES

1. organize (11); testable (11)
2. unconscious (11); psychosocial (11)
3. observable (14); reinforcement (14); decreases (14); Social learning (14)
4. cognitive (16); computer (17); efficiency (17); culture (17)
5. microsystem (18); exosystem (19); competence-environmental press (19); environment (19)
6. Selective optimization with compensation (21); historical time (22)

### 1.4 DOING DEVELOPMENTAL RESEARCH

1. Systematic (25); natural (25); structured (25); self reports (26); reliable (27); valid (27); representative (28)

23

2. naturally (28); positive (28); independent (30)

3. longitudinal (31); drop out (32); cross-sectional (32); different (32); growth (32); cohort (32)

4. multiple (34)

5. participants (34); minimize (35); deception (35)

6. analyzed (35); publish (35)

# TEST YOURSELF

## MULTIPLE-CHOICE QUESTIONS

| | | |
|---|---|---|
| 1. B, 5 | 14. D, 14 | 27. D, 22 |
| 2. C, 6 | 15. C, 15 | 28. B, 28 |
| 3. A, 6 | 16. D, 15 | 29. B, 30 |
| 4. D, 7 | 17. B, 15 | 30. D, 30 |
| 5. D, 9 | 18. C, 15 | 31. B, 28 |
| 6. C, 8 | 19. D, 16 | 32. B, 29 |
| 7. A, 10 | 20. D, 16 | 33. B, 30 |
| 8. C, 11 | 21. A, 18 | 34. D, 30 |
| 9. B, 11 | 22. D, 18 | 35. A, 31 |
| 10. B, 13 | 23. C, 19 | 36. A, 32 |
| 11. C, 13 | 24. C, 20 | 37. C, 32 |
| 12. D, 14 | 25. B, 20 | 38. B, 33 |
| 13. A, 14 | 26. A, 22 | 39. B, 34 |

## ESSAY QUESTIONS

1. You can tell your friend that both nature and nurture interact with each other to influence development. Virtually no features of development are shaped only by heredity or only by environment. While nature and nurture interact to direct development, both continuous changes and discontinuous changes occur throughout development. Some aspects of development will show a more continuous pattern while others will show discontinuous patterns. Finally, some aspects of development seem to apply to different people across cultures (universal) while other aspects seem to be specific to a particular culture or context. In other words, your friend's statement was incorrect, and perhaps he should take a course in life-span development to learn more about human development. (5)

2. You should tell Kumi that reinforcers increase the likelihood that behaviors will be repeated in the future. Reinforcers could include getting a toy, getting to play with something that you want even if your mother said "no," etc. By giving in to Kayla, Kumi is reinforcing her tantrums and increasing the likelihood that Kayla will throw another tantrum. Instead, Kumi should be punishing Kayla's tantrums because punishment decreases the likelihood that a behavior will be repeated. Punishments can include things such as spankings, being sent to one's room, having privileges taken away, or having a toy taken away. Kumi should stop giving in to Kayla which only reinforces her tantrums. (14)

3. In a longitudinal study a measure of personality might be administered to a group of young adults at one point in time. When this group of adults is middle-aged, the personality measure would be administered again. Finally, when this group of adults reaches old age, the personality measure would be administered again. The main advantage of longitudinal studies is that they allow researchers to observe the stability or instability of behaviors such as personality. One disadvantage of longitudinal studies is the high cost associated with keeping up with a sample of people over a long period of time. A second disadvantage of longitudinal studies is that it is difficult to maintain the constancy of the sample over the course of the study. The people who drop out of the study may be significantly different from those people who stay in the study. This inconsistent sample may influence a researcher's results. A third disadvantage is that subjects in longitudinal studies may become "test-wise." In other

words, people may show improvement over time because they become more familiar with the test each time they participate in the study. In a cross-sectional study, a measure of personality would be administered to a group of young adults, a group of middle-aged adults, and a group of older adults. The answers of the three groups would be compared to see if people of different ages show differences in personality. The main advantages of cross-sectional designs is that they avoid the costs of longitudinal designs and they avoid the problems of sample constancy and "test-wise" subjects. The major disadvantage of cross-sectional designs is that cohort effects may be present which make it difficult to draw conclusions about developmental change. Differences in personality between the three age groups may not be the result of age but may be the result of cohort effects. (31-33)

# BIOLOGICAL FOUNDATIONS

2.1 In the Beginning: 23 Pairs of Chromosomes

2.2 From Conception to Birth

2.3 Influences on Prenatal Development

2.4 Labor and Delivery

This chapter discusses the role of heredity in shaping development, the stages of prenatal development, the influences on prenatal development, and the process of labor and delivery.

# 2.1 IN THE BEGINNING: 23 PAIRS OF CHROMOSOMES

## TO MASTER THE LEARNING OBJECTIVES:

**What are chromosomes and genes? How do they carry hereditary information from one generation to the next?**

- Describe what happens to the red blood cells in sickle cell anemia and why these changes have negative effects.

- Explain the difference between autosomes and sex chromosomes.

- Know the difference between genes and chromosomes.

- Know the difference between genotype and phenotype.

- Explain the difference between being homozygous and heterozygous for a particular trait.

- Explain the difference between dominant alleles, recessive alleles, and incomplete dominance.

- Explain how the effects of heredity and environment can be studied using twins and adopted children.

**What are common problems involving chromosomes, and what are their consequences?**

- Describe how phenylketonuria and Huntington's disease are inherited.

- Describe the disorders associated with extra autosomes or abnormal sex chromosomes.

**How is children's heredity influenced by the environment in which they grow up?**

- Describe behavioral genetics and polygenic inheritance.

- Describe how twin studies, adoption studies, and the isolation of DNA segments are used to determine the role of heredity and environment.

- Describe the 4 general properties that describe the relation between genes and environment, including the concepts of reaction range, niche-picking, and non-shared environmental influences.

# 2.1 KNOW THE TERMS

| | |
|---|---|
| Alleles | Huntington's disease |
| Autosomes | Incomplete dominance |
| Behavioral genetics | Monozygotic |
| Chromosomes | Niche-picking |
| Deoxyribonucleic acid (DNA) | Non-shared environmental influences |
| Dizygotic | Phenotype |
| Dominant | Phenylketonuria |
| Gene | Polygenic inheritance |
| Genotype | Reaction range |
| Heterozygous | Recessive |
| Homozygous | Sex chromosomes |
| Sickle-cell trait | |

1.  _____ are the threadlike structures in the nuclei of the sperm and egg that contain genetic material.

2.  The first 22 pairs of chromosomes are called _____ .

3.  The 23rd pair of chromosomes determines the sex of the child and are called the _____ .

4.  Each chromosome consists of one molecule of _____ .

5.  A _____ consists of a group of compounds that provide a specific set of biochemical instructions.

6. The complete set of genes makes up a person's heredity and is known as the person's _____ .

7. One's _____ includes physical, behavioral, and psychological features that are the result of the interaction between one's genes and environmental influences.

8. Different forms of genes are called _____ .

9. An individual is _____ if both alleles in a pair of chromosomes are the same.

10. An individual is _____ if the alleles in a pair of chromosomes differ from each other.

11. When an allele is _____ , its chemical instructions are followed.

12. When an allele is _____ , its chemical instructions are ignored when the allele is combined with a dominant allele.

13. The situation where one allele does not completely dominate another is called _____ .

14. _____ occurs in individuals who have one dominant allele for normal blood cells and one recessive sickle-cell allele. These individuals typically only have problems when they are seriously deprived of oxygen, such as when they engage in vigorous exercise or when they are at high altitudes.

15. _____ is an inherited disorder in which babies are born lacking an important liver enzyme.

16. _____ is a fatal disease characterized by the progressive degeneration of the nervous system.

17. The branch of genetics that deals with inheritance of behavioral and psychological traits is called _____ .

18. _____ occurs when phenotypes are the result of the combined activity of many separate genes.

19. _____ twins are also called identical twins because they are the result of a single fertilized egg that split in two to form 2 new individuals.

20. Fraternal twins, or _____ twins, are the result of the fertilization of 2 separate eggs by two sperm.

21. _____ refers to the fact that a particular genotype can interact with various environments to produce a range of phenotypes.

22. The process of deliberately seeking environments that are compatible with one's heredity is called _____ .

23. _____ are forces within a family that make children different from one another.

# 2.1 KNOW THE DETAILS

1. The first 22 pairs of chromosomes are called autosomes.
   TRUE or FALSE

2. The autosomal chromosomes determine the sex of the child.
   TRUE or FALSE

3. Chromosomes are composed of deoxyribonucleic acid.
   TRUE or FALSE

4. Phenotypes are determined solely by genotypes.
   TRUE or FALSE

5. When the alleles in a chromosome pair differ, the pair is heterozygous.
   TRUE or FALSE

6. In a heterozygous chromosome pair, the chemical instructions of the recessive allele are followed and those of the dominant allele are ignored.
   TRUE or FALSE

7. Incomplete dominance occurs in a chromosome pair when the chemical instructions of one allele are followed and those of the other allele are completely ignored.
   TRUE or FALSE

8. Infants born with phenylketonuria are missing an important liver enzyme.
   TRUE or FALSE

9. Most inherited disorders are carried by dominant alleles rather than by recessive alleles.
   TRUE or FALSE

10. Down Syndrome is typically caused by a dominant allele that carries the disorder.
    TRUE or FALSE

11. Klinefelter's syndrome and Turner's syndrome are both disorders associated with abnormal sex chromosomes.
    TRUE or FALSE

12. Behavioral genetics is the branch of genetics that deals with the inheritance of behavioral and psychological traits.
    TRUE or FALSE

13. A polygenic pattern of genetic inheritance occurs when many different genes determine a characteristic.
    TRUE or FALSE

14. Monozygotic twins have identical genotypes.

TRUE or FALSE

15. Fraternal twins are called dizygotic twins and come from two separate eggs fertilized by two separate sperm.

TRUE or FALSE

16. The term reaction range refers to the fact that children may deliberately pick environments that fit their heredity.

TRUE or FALSE

17. The forces within a family that make children different from one another are referred to as nonshared environmental influences.

TRUE or FALSE

# 2.2 FROM CONCEPTION TO BIRTH

## TO MASTER THE LEARNING OBJECTIVES:

**What happens to a fertilized egg in the first two weeks after conception?**

- Describe the timing and the major events associated with the period of the zygote.

- Describe in vitro fertilization and how reproductive technologies are related to eugenics.

**When do body structures and internal organs emerge in prenatal development?**

- Describe the timing and the major events associated with the period of the embryo.

- Know which layers of the embryo will become which bodily system.

- Know the location and functions of the amnion, amniotic fluid, umbilical cord, and placenta.

- Know the difference between cephalocaudal and proximodistal growth.

**When do body systems begin to function well enough to support life?**

- Describe the timing and major events associated with the period of the fetus.

- Describe the behavior of the fetus and how it is related to later behavior.

## 2.2 KNOW THE TERMS

Age of viability                           Implantation

Amnion                                      In vitro fertilization

Amniotic fluid

Cephalocaudal

Cerebral cortex

Ectoderm

Embryo

Endoderm

Eugenics

Germ disc

Mesoderm

Period of the fetus

Placenta

Prenatal development

Proximodistal

Umbilical cord

Vernix

Zygote

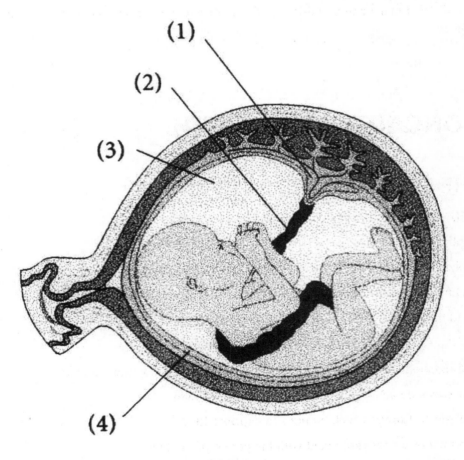

1.  The many changes that transform the fertilized egg into a newborn human are known as _____ .

2.  The technique of _____ involves fertilizing eggs with sperm in a petri dish and then transferring several of the fertilized eggs to the mother's uterus where they might implant in the lining of the wall of the uterus.

3. _____ is the effort to improve the human species by letting only certain people mate and pass along their genes.

4. The fertilized egg is called a _____ .

5. _____ occurs when the zygote burrows into the uterine wall and establishes connections with a woman's blood vessels.

6. The _____ is a small cluster of cells near the center of the zygote that will eventually become the baby.

7. Nutrients and wastes are exchanged between mother and the developing organism through the _____ (see #1 on figure).

8. Once the zygote is completely embedded in the uterine wall it is called an _____ .

9. The outer layer of the embryo which will become the hair, outer layer of skin, and the nervous system is called the _____ .

10. The middle layer of the embryo which will become the muscles, bone, and circulatory system is called the _____ .

11. The inner layer of the embryo which will become the lungs and the digestive system is called the _____ .

12. The embryo will rest in a sac called the _____ (see #4 on figure).

13. The amnion is filled with _____ , which cushions the embryo and maintains a constant temperature (see #3 on figure).

14. The _____ houses blood vessels that join the embryo to the placenta (see #2 on figure).

15. The _____ principle states that growth proceeds from the head to the base of the spine.

16. The _____ principle states that growth occurs in body parts near the center of the body before it occurs in parts that are more distant.

17. The _____ is the longest period of prenatal development and begins at the 9th week after conception and lasts until birth.

18. The thick, greasy substance that protects the fetus is called _____ .

19. The _____ is the wrinkled surface of the brain that regulates many important human behaviors.

20. A 7-month-old fetus is at the _____ because most of its bodily systems will be functioning well enough that it is likely to survive.

# 2.2 KNOW THE DETAILS OF PRENATAL DEVELOPMENT

1. The average full-term pregnancy lasts 38 weeks from conception to birth.
   TRUE or FALSE

2. After one sperm has penetrated the cellular wall of an egg, no other sperm are able to do so.
   TRUE or FALSE

3. In vitro fertilization involves injecting sperm into the fallopian tubes.
   TRUE or FALSE

4. The period of the zygote ends when the zygote becomes embedded in the uterine wall.
   TRUE or FALSE

5. The germ disc eventually becomes the placenta.
   TRUE or FALSE

6. Once the zygote is completely embedded into the uterine wall, it is called a fetus.
   TRUE or FALSE

7. The ectoderm becomes hair, the outer layer of skin, and the nervous system.
   TRUE or FALSE

8. The mesoderm develops into the digestive system and the lungs.
   TRUE or FALSE

9. An 8-week-old embryo looks basically the same as a 3-week-old embryo.
   TRUE or FALSE

10. The umbilical cord connects the developing individual to the placenta.
    TRUE or FALSE

11. The period of the fetus is the longest phase of prenatal development.
    TRUE or FALSE

12. The age of viability is reached at about 12 weeks after conception.
    TRUE or FALSE

13. Newborns can recognize some of the sounds they heard while in the womb.
    TRUE or FALSE

# 2.3 INFLUENCES ON PRENATAL DEVELOPMENT

## TO MASTER THE LEARNING OBJECTIVES:

**How is prenatal development influenced by a pregnant woman's age, her nutrition, and the stress that she experiences while pregnant?**

- Explain how maternal age can affect prenatal development.

- Describe how maternal nutrition is related to prenatal development.

- Explain how maternal stress affects prenatal development.

**How do disease, drugs, and environmental hazards sometimes affect prenatal development?**

- Describe the effects of thalidomide on prenatal development.

- Describe the effects of cigarette smoking on prenatal development.

- Explain the effects associated with alcohol consumption by the mother during pregnancy.

- Know the effects associated with the consumption of aspirin, caffeine, cocaine, heroin, marijuana, and nicotine by the mother during pregnancy.

- Know the effects associated with contracting AIDS, cytomegalovirus, genital herpes, rubella, and syphilis during pregnancy.

- Know the effects of exposure to lead, mercury, and X-rays during pregnancy.

- Describe how ingesting PCBs affects development.

**What general principles affect the ways prenatal development can be harmed?**

- List the 4 general principles concerning the effects of teratogens on prenatal development.

**How can prenatal development be monitored? Can abnormal prenatal development be corrected?**

- Describe how genetic counseling can help prevent some inherited disorders.

- Describe the procedures used in ultrasound, amniocentesis, and chorionic villus sampling and the kind of information each provides about prenatal development.

- Describe how various problems of prenatal development can be treated with administration of drugs to the fetus, fetal surgery, and genetic engineering.

## 2.3 KNOW THE TERMS

**Amniocentesis**

**Chorionic villus sampling**

**Spina bifida**

**Stress**

| | |
|---|---|
| **Fetal** | **Teratogen** |
| **Fetal alcohol syndrome** | **Ultrasound** |

1. Consuming inadequate amounts of folic acid during pregnancy can result in _____ , a disorder in which the embryo's neural tube does not close properly during prenatal development.

2. A person's physical and psychological responses to threatening or challenging situations are known as _____ .

3. An agent that causes abnormal prenatal development is called a _____ .

4. _____ often occurs in babies whose mothers consumed large amounts of alcohol while they were pregnant with them.

5. The prenatal diagnostic technique called _____ uses sound waves to generate a picture of the fetus.

6. _____ is a prenatal diagnostic technique that involves withdrawing a sample of amniotic fluid through the abdomen, using a syringe.

7. _____ is a prenatal diagnostic technique that involves taking a sample of tissue from part of the placenta.

8. The field of medicine that is concerned with treating prenatal problems before birth is called _____ medicine.

## 2.3 KNOW THE DETAILS OF THE EFFECTS OF TERATOGENS AND PRENATAL DIAGNOSIS

1. Insufficient folic acid during pregnancy is associated with increased risk of spina bifida in the baby.
   TRUE or FALSE

2. Poor maternal nutrition during pregnancy is associated with an increased risk of prematurity, low birth weight, and problems with nervous system development.
   TRUE or FALSE

3. Stress during pregnancy has not been found to have any negative consequences on the developing baby.
   TRUE or FALSE

4. Women in their 40s are just as likely as women in their 20s to have healthy babies.
   TRUE or FALSE

5. A teratogen is any supplement that pregnant women should take to improve their chances of having a healthy baby.

   TRUE or FALSE

6. Thalidomide, alcohol, aspirin, caffeine, and nicotine are all known teratogens.

   TRUE or FALSE

7. Exposure to second-hand smoke during pregnancy is associated with having smaller babies.

   TRUE or FALSE

8. Pregnant women who consume large quantities of alcoholic beverages often give birth to babies with Down Syndrome.

   TRUE or FALSE

9. AIDS can be passed from the mother to an embryo or fetus through the placenta or as the baby passes through the birth canal.

   TRUE or FALSE

10. Pregnant women who work at computer monitors or video-display terminals have an increased risk of giving birth to a baby with a birth defect.

    TRUE or FALSE

11. Prenatal exposure to polychlorinated biphenyls (PCBs) harms children's verbal and memory skill.

    TRUE or FALSE

12. The impact of teratogens on prenatal development is the same for all developing organisms.

    TRUE or FALSE

13. Exposure to teratogens during the period of the embryo is most likely to result in major defects in bodily structure.

    TRUE or FALSE

14. Damage from teratogens is always evident at birth.

    TRUE or FALSE

15. The prenatal diagnostic procedure called chorionic villus sampling involves inserting a needle through the mother's abdomen to obtain a sample of the fluid surrounding the fetus.

    TRUE or FALSE

16. Amniocentesis and chorionic villus sampling increase the risk of miscarriage.

    TRUE or FALSE

# 2.4 LABOR AND DELIVERY

## TO MASTER THE LEARNING OBJECTIVES:

**What are the different phases of labor and delivery?**

- List and describe the events associated with the 3 stages of labor.

**What are "natural" ways of coping with the pain of childbirth? Is childbirth at home safe?**

- List some of the benefits associated with prepared childbirth classes.
- Know the circumstances under which home delivery is safe.

**What are some complications that can occur during birth?**

- Describe the problems associated with anoxia, prematurity, and low birth weight.
- Know the causes of and possible preventions of the high infant mortality rate in the United States.

## 2.4 KNOW THE TERMS

Cesarean section

Crowning

Doula

Extremely low birth weight

Hypoxia

Infant mortality

Low birth weight

Preterm

Very low birth weight

1. The appearance of the top of the baby's head during labor is known as _____ .

2. A person who is familiar with childbirth and who provides emotional and physical support throughout labor and delivery is called a _____

3. Lack of oxygen during delivery is called _____ . This situation may occur if the umbilical cord becomes pinched or tangled during delivery or if the infant's lungs do not work properly.

4. Making an incision in the abdomen to remove a baby from the mother's uterus is called _____ .

5. Babies born before the 36th week after conception are _____ .

6. _____ newborns weigh less than 2500 grams (5.5 pounds) at birth.

7. Newborns who weigh less than 1500 grams (3.3 pounds) are considered _____ babies.

8. Babies who weigh less than 1000 grams (2.2 pounds) are considered to be _____ .

9. _____ is the number of infants out of 1,000 births who die before their first birthday.

## 2.4 KNOW THE DETAILS OF LABOR AND DELIVERY

1.  Contractions enlarge the cervix during Stage 1 of labor.

    TRUE or FALSE

2.  The placenta is expelled during Stage 2 of labor.

    TRUE or FALSE

3.  Stage 3 is usually the longest stage of labor.

    TRUE or FALSE

4.  Pain-relieving drugs do not impair the childbirth process or affect the baby.

    TRUE or FALSE

5.  There is no difference between women who do or do not attend childbirth classes in the amount of anesthetic used during childbirth.

    TRUE or FALSE

6.  Birth problems are more common in babies delivered at home than in babies delivered in a hospital, even when the woman is healthy and her pregnancy has been problem free.

    TRUE or FALSE

7.  Hypoxia during childbirth can cause mental retardation.

    TRUE or FALSE

8.  Babies born before the 36th week after conception are considered premature.

    TRUE or FALSE

9.  Most premature babies are developmentally delayed throughout childhood.

    TRUE or FALSE

10. Babies weighing less than 1500 grams (3.3 pounds) at birth often do not survive or have developmentally delayed intellectual and motor skills.

    TRUE or FALSE

11. Infant mortality refers to the number of infants out of 1000 births who die before their first birthday.

    TRUE or FALSE

12. Infant mortality rates in the United States are the lowest in the world.

    TRUE or FALSE

# SUMMARY

## 2.1 IN THE BEGINNING: 23 PAIRS OF CHROMOSOMES

1.  **Mechanisms of Heredity**

    At conception, the 23 chromosomes in the sperm merge with the 23 chromosomes in the egg. Each chromosome is one molecule of _____ ; a section of DNA that provides specific biochemical instructions is called _____ . All of a person's genes make up a _____ ; the _____ refers to the physical, behavioral, and psychological characteristics that develop when the genotype is exposed to a specific environment. Different forms of the same gene are called _____ . A person who inherits the same allele on a pair of chromosomes is _____ . A person who inherits different alleles on a pair of chromosomes is _____ . If an individual is heterozygous, the instructions of the _____ allele are followed whereas those of the recessive allele are ignored.

2.  **Genetic Disorders**

    Most inherited disorders are carried by _____ alleles. Examples include sickle-cell disease and _____ in which toxins accumulate and cause mental retardation. Sometimes fertilized eggs do not have 46 chromosomes (44 autosomes and 2 sex chromosomes). Usually they are aborted spontaneously soon after conception. An exception is _____ syndrome, in which individuals usually have an extra 21st chromosome. Down-syndrome individuals have a distinctive appearance and are _____ .

3.  **Heredity, Environment, and Development**

    Behavioral and psychological phenotypes that reflect an underlying continuum (such as intelligence) often involve _____ inheritance. In polygenic inheritance, the phenotype reflects the activity of many distinct genes. Polygenic inheritance is often examined by studying twins and _____ children, and by identifying DNA markers. These studies indicate substantial influence of heredity in intelligence, psychological disorders, and personality. The impact of a gene on behavior depends on the environment in which the genetic instructions are carried out. This demonstrates the concept of _____ , where the outcome of heredity depends upon the environment in which development occurs. Niche-picking occurs when individuals actively seek environments related to their genetic makeup. Family environments affect siblings differently, which is known as nonshared environmental influences

## 2.2 FROM CONCEPTION TO BIRTH

1. **Period of the Zygote**

   Prenatal development consists of three periods. The first period of prenatal development lasts _____ weeks. It begins when the egg is fertilized by the sperm and ends when the fertilized egg has _____ in the lining of the wall of the uterus. By the end of this period, cells have begun to _____ .

2. **Period of the Embryo**

   The second period of prenatal development begins two weeks after conception and ends eight weeks after conception. This is a period of _____ in which most of the major body _____ are created. Growth in this period is cephalocaudal and _____

3. **Period of the Fetus**

   The third period of prenatal development begins 8 weeks after conception and lasts until birth. The highlights of this period are a remarkable increase in the _____ of the fetus and change in body systems that are necessary for life. By _____ , most body systems function well enough to support life. This is known as the age of viability.

## 2.3 INFLUENCES ON PRENATAL DEVELOPMENT

1. **General Risk Factors**

   Parents' age can affect prenatal development. _____ often have problem pregnancies mainly because they rarely receive adequate prenatal care. After age 35, pregnant women are more likely to _____ or give birth to a child with mental retardation. Prenatal development can also be harmed if a pregnant mother has inadequate _____ , or experiences considerable stress.

2. **Teratogens: Drugs, Diseases, and Environmental Hazards**

   Teratogens are agents that cause _____ prenatal development. Many drugs that adults take are teratogens. For most drugs, scientists have not established amounts that can be consumed safely by pregnant women. Several diseases are teratogens. Only by avoiding these diseases entirely can a pregnant woman escape their harmful consequences. _____ teratogens are particularly dangerous because a pregnant woman may not know that these substances are present in the environment.

3. **How Teratogens Influence Prenatal Development**

   The impact of teratogens depends upon the _____ of the organism, the period of prenatal development when the organism is exposed to the teratogen, and the _____ of exposure. Sometimes the impact of a teratogen is not evident until later in life.

4. **Prenatal Diagnosis and Treatment**

   Many techniques are used to track the progress of prenatal development. A common component of prenatal care is _____ , which uses sound waves to generate a picture of the fetus. This picture can be used to determine the _____ of the fetus, its sex, and if there are any gross physical deformities. When genetic disorders are suspected, _____ and chorionic villus sampling are used to determine the genotype of the fetus. Fetal medicine is a new field in which problems of prenatal development are corrected medically, with surgery, or using genetic engineering.

## 2.4 LABOR AND DELIVERY

1. **Stages of Labor**

   Labor consists of three stages. In Stage 1, the muscles of the uterus _____ . The contractions, which are weak at first and gradually become stronger, cause the opening of the cervix to enlarge. In Stage 2, the baby moves through the _____ . In Stage 3, the _____ is delivered.

2. **Approaches to Childbirth**

   Natural or prepared childbirth is based on the assumption that parents should understand what takes place during pregnancy and birth. In natural childbirth, pain-relieving medications are avoided because this medication prevents women from _____ during labor and because it affects the fetus. Instead women learn to cope with pain through _____ , imagery, and with the help of a supportive coach. Most American babies are born in hospitals, but many European babies are born at home. Home delivery is safe when the mother is _____ , pregnancy and birth are trouble-free, and a health-care professional is present to deliver the baby.

3. **Adjusting to Parenthood**

   Following the birth of a child, a woman's body undergoes several changes: her breasts become filled with milk, her uterus becomes smaller, and hormone levels drop. Both parents adjust psychologically and sometimes fathers feel left out. After giving birth, some women experience postpartum depression: they are _____ have a poor appetite and disturbed _____ and are apathetic.

4. **Birth Complications**

   During labor and delivery, the flow of blood to the fetus can be disrupted, either because the _____ is squeezed shut or because the placenta becomes detached from the wall of the uterus. This causes a lack of oxygen to the fetus that is called _____ Some babies are born prematurely and others are small for date. Premature babies develop more _____ at first but catch up by 2 or 3 years of age. Small-for-date babies often do not fare well, particularly if they weigh less than 1500 grams and if their _____ is stressful.

5. **Infant Mortality**

   Infant mortality is relatively _____ in the United States, primarily due to low birth weight and inadequate _____ .

# TEST YOURSELF

## MULTIPLE-CHOICE QUESTIONS

1. Egg and sperm cells each contain _____ chromosomes.
   a. 23
   b. 26
   c. 43
   d. 46

2. Which sex chromosome pair would produce a male?
   a. XX
   b. YY
   c. XY
   d. YO

3. Physical, behavioral, and psychological features are referred to as a person's
   a. chromosomes.
   b. reaction range.
   c. phenotype.
   d. genotype.

4. When the alleles in a gene pair are the same, the pair is
    a. heterozygous.
    b. homozygous.
    c. a phenotype.
    d. a genotype.

5. Inheritance of cheek dimples operates on the dominant-recessive principle. The gene for dimples (D) is dominant, and the gene for no dimples (d) is recessive. Who would *not* have cheek dimples?
    a. Amy, who is Dd
    b. John, who is DD
    c. Sarah, who is dd
    d. neither Amy nor Sarah would have cheek dimples

6. Intelligence is determined by a number of different genes. Therefore, intelligence follows a _____ pattern of inheritance.
    a. dominant-recessive
    b. sex-linked
    c. polygenic
    d. codominant

7. Barry and Larry are twins that came from a single fertilized egg that split in two. They are _____ twins.
    a. Monozygotic
    b. dizygotic
    c. codominant
    d. polygenic

8. Which of the following disorders is carried by dominant alleles?
    a. Huntington's disease
    b. phenylketonuria
    c. sickle-cell disease
    d. Down syndrome

9. Seth was born with extra chromosomes. He
    a. will not survive long past birth.
    b. is likely to develop more rapidly than average.
    c. is likely to have normal development.
    d. may survive but is likely to have disturbed development.

10. If a trait is strongly influenced by genetic factors, one would expect to find that, with respect to that trait,
    a. dizygotic twins are more alike than monozygotic twins.
    b. dizygotic twins are more alike than siblings.
    c. adopted children resemble their adoptive parents more than their biological parents.
    d. adopted children resemble their biological parents more than their adoptive parents.

11. When a genotype can lead to a wide variety of phenotypes depending on the environment, that genotype has a relatively large
    a. polygenic inheritance.
    b. reaction range.
    c. dominance.
    d. niche-picking.

12. Etta, who inherited musical ability from her father, often seeks out opportunities to exercise her singing talent. Etta's behavior is a good example of
    a. a reaction range.
    b. codominance.
    c. polygenic inheritance.
    d. niche-picking.

13. The forces within a family that make children different from each other are called
    a. nonshared environmental influences.
    b. niche-picking.
    c. polygenic inheritance.
    d. a reaction range.

14. _____ is being performed when a human egg is fertilized by sperm while both are in a petri dish.
    a. Artificial insemination
    b. In vitro fertilization
    c. Implantation
    d. Eugenics

15. Attempting to improve the human species by allowing only certain select people to reproduce is called
    a. eugenics.
    b. viability.
    c. niche picking.
    d. implantation.

16. Which of the following shows the periods of prenatal development in their correct sequence from first to last?
    a. zygote, embryo, fetus
    b. fetus, embryo, zygote
    c. zygote, fetus, embryo
    d. embryo, zygote, fetus

17. A fertilized egg is first known as a(n)
    a. embryo.
    b. Zygote
    c. germ disc.
    d. fetus.

18. When the zygote has burrowed into the uterine wall and established connections with a woman's blood vessels, _____ has just occurred.
    a. in vitro fertilization
    b. ovulation
    c. fertilization
    d. implantation

19. Implantation is complete
    a. when fertilization occurs.
    b. at the end of the period of the embryo.
    c. at the end of the period of the zygote.
    d. at the end of the period of the fetus.

20. Nutrients and waste are exchanged between the mother and the fetus through the
    a. placenta.
    b. endoderm.
    c. ectoderm.
    d. mesoderm.

21. In prenatal development, most body structures and internal organs are formed during the period of the
    a. fetus.
    b. embryo.
    c. zygote.
    d. germ disc.

22. The muscles, bones, and circulatory system are formed from the
    a. ectoderm.
    b. endoderm.
    c. mesoderm.
    d. amnion.

23. The embryo rests in a sac called the
    a. placenta.
    b. germ disc.
    c. umbilical cord.
    d. amnion.

24. The thick, greasy substance that protects the fetus' skin is called
    a. vernix.
    b. amniotic fluid.
    c. cortex.
    d. cartilage.

25. The age of viability is reached _____ weeks after conception.
    a. 8 to 10
    b. 12 to 15
    c. 22 to 28
    d. 32 to 38

26. Maternal stress during pregnancy is associated with _____ in babies.
    a. central nervous system damage
    b. chromosomal abnormalities
    c. increased vulnerability to illness
    d. premature birth and low birth weight

27. Which of the following women is most likely to have a child whose development was harmed prenatally?
    a. Mindy, who had the flu while she was pregnant
    b. Suzanne, who had a cold while she was pregnant
    c. Carol, who drank alcohol heavily throughout her pregnancy
    d. Jasmine, who worked long hours at a video display terminal throughout her pregnancy

28. When a developing organism is exposed to a teratogen during the period of the zygote, the usual result is
    a. major defects in bodily structure.
    b. minor defects in bodily structure.
    c. improperly functioning bodily systems.
    d. spontaneous abortion.

29. _____ is a prenatal diagnostic procedure in which tissue is obtained from part of the placenta.
    a. Ultrasound
    b. Amniocentesis
    c. Fetal medicine
    d. Chorionic villus sampling

30. Katie is seven weeks pregnant with her fourth child and is gaining weight much more quickly than she did during her first three pregnancies. She suspects she might be carrying twins. Which of the following procedures could determine whether she is pregnant with twins the earliest with the least risk of causing a miscarriage?
    a. a blood test
    b. ultrasound
    c. amniocentesis
    d. chorionic villus sampling

31. Crowning occurs during stage _____ of labor.
    a. 1
    b. 2
    c. 3
    d. 4

32. Which of the following events occurs during stage 3 of labor?
    a. The cervix enlarges to 10 centimeters.
    b. Crowning occurs.
    c. The placenta is expelled.
    d. The baby is delivered.

33. Which of the following strategies would you *least* expect to find as part of a childbirth class?
    a. teaching pregnant women ways to relax during labor
    b. encouraging pregnant women to maximize the use of pain-relieving drugs during birth
    c. showing pregnant women how to use visual imagery to take their minds off pain
    d. having pregnant women bring a supportive "coach" with them to class

34. A pregnant woman with high blood pressure, protein in her urine, and swelling in her extremities has symptoms of
    a. a prolapsed umbilical cord.
    b. a baby in an irregular position.
    c. cephalopelvic disproportion.
    d. preeclampsia.

35. Premature babies are those who arrive before the _____ week of gestation.
    a. 38th
    b. 36th
    c. 30th
    d. 25th

36. Hannah gave birth to a baby who weighed 3 pounds. Her baby would be classified as
    a. normal weight.
    b. low birth weight.
    c. very low birth weight.
    d. extremely low birth weight.

37. Which of the following countries has the highest rate of infant mortality?
    a. United States
    b. Switzerland
    c. Canada
    d. Netherlands

## ESSAY QUESTIONS

1. Your friends Fred and Wilma are expecting their first child. Both Fred and Wilma have dark, curly hair but they hope that their baby will have straight, blond hair because they have always hated their dark, unruly curls. Using the table in your text on page 49, what can you tell Fred and Wilma about genetic inheritance and the likelihood that they will get their wish?

2. You and a friend were talking about the role of heredity and environment, and your friend said, "Genes are destiny. Whenever you inherit genes for bad diseases there is nothing about the environment that

can change the negative effects." What can you tell your friend about the interaction of heredity and environment in cases such as those involving individuals with phenylketonuria?

3.  Your friend Lafon is pregnant, and she told you that she knows the three stages of prenatal development--the first trimester, the second trimester, and the third trimester--but she wasn't exactly sure about what happens during each of the stages. What can you tell Lafon about the 3 stages of prenatal development and the major events that occur during each of the stages?

4.  Lafon also is concerned that her baby will be okay when it is born, and she is wondering if there is anything that she can do to help ensure that she has a healthy baby. What can you tell her about the effects of teratogens that can help her make some informed decisions during her pregnancy?

5.  Your pregnant friend Lafon is in her 6th month of pregnancy, and she isn't sure if she should take the prepared childbirth classes that are being offered at the local hospital. The class meets for 3 hours every Monday night for 6 weeks, and that looks like a big commitment of time to Lafon. What can you tell Lafon about the benefits of prepared childbirth classes?

6.  Lafon had her baby 2 weeks ago and she is worried that she isn't a good mother. Right after her son was born she was thrilled and excited, but now she finds her son's crying irritating, she resents the fact that she barely has time for simple things like taking a shower, and she frequently bursts into tears. What can you tell Lafon about adjusting to parenthood and postpartum depression that might help her?

7.  Recently one of your friends told you that prenatal care is a waste of time for a mother who is young and healthy. What can you tell your friend about prenatal care in teenage mothers and about infant mortality in the United States that would contradict his statement?

# SOLUTIONS

## 2.1 KNOW THE TERMS

1. Chromosomes (46)
2. autosomes (46)
3. sex chromosomes (47)
4. deoxyribonucleic acid (DNA) (47)
5. gene (47)
6. genotype (48)
7. phenotype (48)
8. alleles (48)
9. homozygous (48)
10. heterozygous (48)
11. dominant (48)
12. recessive (48)
13. incomplete dominance (49)
14. Sickle-cell trait (49)
15. Phenylketonuria (50)
16. Huntington's disease (50)
17. behavioral genetics (51)
18. Polygenic inheritance (52)
19. Monozygotic (53)
20. dizygotic (53)
21. Reaction range (54)
22. niche-picking (55)
23. Nonshared environmental influences (56)

## 2.1 KNOW THE DETAILS

1. T, (46)
2. F, (47)
3. T, (47)
4. F, (48)
5. T, (48)
6. F, (48)
7. F, (49)
8. T, (50)
9. F, (50)
10. F, (50)
11. T, (51)
12. T, (53)
13. T, (52)
14. T, (53)
15. T, (53)
16. F, (54)
17. T, (56)

## 2.2 KNOW THE TERMS

1. prenatal development (57)
2. in vitro fertilization (58)
3. Eugenics (59)
4. zygote (58)
5. Implantation (58)
6. germ disc (58)
7. placenta (59)
8. embryo (59)
9. ectoderm (59)
10. mesoderm (59)
11. endoderm (59)
12. amnion (59)
13. amniotic fluid (59)
14. umbilical cord (59)
15. cephalocaudal (60)
16. proximodistal (60)
17. period of the fetus (61)
18. vernix (61)
19. cerebral cortex (61)
20. age of viability (61)

## 2.2 KNOW THE DETAILS OF PRENATAL DEVELOPMENT

1. T, (57)
2. T, (57)
3. F, (58)
4. T, (59)
5. F, (58)
6. F, (59)
7. T, (59)
8. F, (59)
9. F, (59)
10. T, (59)
11. T, (61)
12. F, (61)

13. T, (62)

## 2.3 KNOW THE TERMS

1. spina bifida (63)
2. stress (64)
3. teratogen (66)
4. Fetal alcohol syndrome (66)
5. ultrasound (72)
6. Amniocentesis (72)
7. Chorionic villus sampling (73)
8. fetal (73)

## 2.3 KNOW THE DETAILS OF THE EFFECTS OF TERATOGENS AND PRENATAL DIAGNOSIS

1. T, (63)
2. T, (64)
3. F, (64)
4. F, (65)
5. F, (66)
6. T, (66)
7. T, (66)
8. F, (66)
9. T, (67)
10. F, (68)
11. T, (68)
12. F, (69)
13. T, (70)
14. F, (71)
15. F, (72)
16. T, (73)

## 2.4 KNOW THE TERMS

1. crowning (75)
2. doula (76)
3. hypoxia (79)
4. cesarean section (79)
5. preterm (79)
6. Low birth weight (79)
7. very low birth weight (79)
8. extremely low birth weight (79)
9. Infant mortality (80)

## 2.4 KNOW THE DETAILS OF LABOR AND DELIVERY

1. T, (75)
2. F, (75)
3. F, (75)
4. F, (76)
5. F, (77)
6. F, (77)
7. T, (79)
8. T, (79)
9. F, (79)
10. T, (79)
11. T, (80)
12. F, (80)

## SUMMARY

### 2.1 IN THE BEGINNING: 23 PAIRS OF CHROMOSOMES

1. DNA (47); gene (47); genotype (48); phenotype (48); alleles (48); homozygous (48); heterozygous (48); dominant (48)

2. recessive (50); phenylketonuria (50); Down (50); mentally retarded (50)

3. polygenic (52); adopted (53); reaction range (54)

## 2.2 FROM CONCEPTION TO BIRTH

1. two (57); implanted (59); differentiate (59)

2. rapid growth (59); structures (59); proximodistal (60)

3. size (61); 22-28 weeks (61)

## 2.3 INFLUENCES ON PRENATAL DEVELOPMENT

1. Teenagers (64); miscarry (65); nutrition (64)

2. abnormal (66); Environmental (67)

3. genotype (69); amount (70)

4. ultrasound (72); position (72); amniocentesis (72)

## 2.4 LABOR AND DELIVERY

1. contract (75); birth canal (75); placenta (75)

2. pushing (76); relaxation (76); healthy (77)

3. irritable (77); s leep (77),

4. umbilical cord (79); hypoxia (79); slowly (79); environment (79)

5. high (80); prenatal care (80)

# TEST YOURSELF

## MULTIPLE-CHOICE QUESTIONS

1. A, (46)
2. C, (47)
3. C, (48)
4. B, (48)
5. C, (48)
6. C, (52)
7. A, (53)
8. A, (50)
9. D, (50)
10. D, (53)
11. B, (54)
12. D, (55)
13. A, (56)
14. B, (58)
15. A, (58)
16. A, (58)
17. B, (58)
18. D, (58)
19. C, (59)
20. A, (60)
21. B, (59)
22. C, (59)
23. D, (59)
24. A, (61)
25. C, (61)
26. D, (64)
27. C, (66)
28. D, (70)
29. D, (72)
30. B, (72)
31. B, (75)
32. C, (75)
33. B, (76)
34. D, (78)
35. B, (79)
36. C, (79)
37. A, (80)

## ESSAY QUESTIONS

1. You can tell Fred and Wilma that both dark hair and curly hair are dominant traits. That means that an individual who is heterozygous with one dominant allele and one recessive allele will display the dominant trait. Given that both Fred and Wilma show the dominant traits, they both must have at least one allele for the dominant trait, so it is not likely that their child will NOT inherit the dominant alleles for dark hair and curly hair. (48-49)

2. You can tell your friend that genes are not destiny. One can inherit a particular genotype, but that genotype can interact with a particular environment to change the phenotype. In the case of phenylketonuria (PKU), an individual may inherit the gene for PKU. In the usual case, the individual cannot break down phenylalanine. This condition leads to damage of the nervous system and mental retardation. However, if the environment is

changed so that the amount of phenylalanine in the individual's diet is reduced, then the damage to the nervous system does not occur and the mental retardation does not occur. In other words, the same genotype for PKU can interact with 2 different environments (either a regular diet or a low-phenylalanine diet) to lead to 2 very different outcomes (either normal intelligence or mental retardation). So, even in the case of a negative, inherited disorder the environment can still play an important role in shaping development. (50; 54)

3. Tell Lafon that the 3 stages of prenatal development do not correspond to the trimesters of pregnancy. The first stage of prenatal development is called the period of the zygote, and it lasts from conception until 2 weeks after conception. During this period, the cells of the new individual are dividing rapidly. This period ends when the zygote (fertilized egg) implants in the lining of the wall of the uterus. The second period of prenatal development is called the period of the embryo, and it lasts from the third week until the eighth week after conception. During this period of prenatal development most of the organs and systems of the body are formed. The third period of prenatal development, the period of the fetus, lasts from 9 weeks until 38 weeks after conception. During this period the fetus grows from a few ounces to its birth weight of 7 or 8 pounds. Refinement of the structures that were formed during the period of the embryo and their functions also occur during this period. (57-62)

4. You can tell Lafon that there are a number of teratogens that she can try to avoid while she is pregnant. One of the most common is alcohol. Women who drink at least 3 ounces of alcohol per day while they are pregnant are likely to have babies born with Fetal Alcohol Syndrome. These babies usually have deformed faces, heart problems, retarded growth, and are mentally retarded. Lafon should also avoid diseases such as AIDS, cytomegalovirus, genital herpes, rubella, and syphilis. Common results of exposure to these diseases are blindness, deafness, neurological damage, and mental retardation. Finally, there are environmental hazards that Lafon should avoid. For example, one environmental hazard is PCBs which can be ingested if one eats fish that come from PCB-contaminated waters. Children whose mothers ate a large amount of PCB-contaminated fish while they were pregnant showed some deficits in verbal skill and memory skill at 4 years of age. The 4-year-olds who showed the greatest deficits had the greatest prenatal exposure to PCBs. (65-69)

5. The purpose of prepared childbirth classes is to teach a pregnant woman and her coach the basic facts about labor and delivery. Women learn relaxation techniques such as deep breathing and visualizing pleasant things These techniques help them to relax and control the pain during contractions, and the coach learns how to offer support and encouragement to the mother-to-be through labor. Research has shown that mothers who do attend these childbirth classes feel more positively about labor and birth and use less medication during delivery than mothers who do not attend these classes. So, while the classes may be a big time commitment for Lafon, she will probably have a better idea of what to expect during labor and delivery and may be able to relax and control her pain more during labor. (76-77)

6. Lafon should know that her behavior isn't unusual and it does not make her a bad mother. Approximately half of all new mothers feel irritation, resentment, and have crying spells. Caring for a new baby is very time consuming and stressful. Also, Lafon may be experiencing many physiological and hormonal changes as her body recovers from pregnancy and labor. About 10 to 15 percent of new mother may experience postpartum depression. Postpartum depression may last for months after the birth of a baby and the feelings of sadness and irritability may be accompanied by feelings of low self-worth, disturbed sleep, poor appetite, and apathy. Postpartum depression is a serious problem that can have harmful effects on the baby and the mother, so if Lafon's 'baby blues' last longer than a few weeks, she should seek help. Home visits by health-care professionals may teach Lafon new ways to cope with her baby. Breast-feeding also may have a positive effect on her mood perhaps because it causes the release of hormones that are anti-depressants (77-78).

7. You can tell your friend that prenatal care is important. Evidence supporting the importance of prenatal care is the infant mortality rate in the United States. Compared to other industrialized countries, the United States has one of the highest infant mortality rates. Part of the reason for this high infant mortality rate is the high number of low-birth-weight babies born in the United States. Low birth weight can usually be prevented with good prenatal care. In almost all of the countries with low infant mortality rates, extensive prenatal care is provided to pregnant women at little or no cost. So, good prenatal care contributes to the birth of healthy babies. (64; 80-81)

# TOOLS FOR EXPLORING THE WORLD

This chapter describes the newborn, covers physical growth, investigates the development of motor skills, discusses perception in the newborn, and presents information on the developing sense of self.

# 3.1 THE NEWBORN

## TO MASTER THE LEARNING OBJECTIVES:

**How do reflexes help newborns interact with the world?**

- Know the name and significance of each newborn reflex.

**How do we determine if a baby is healthy and adjusting to life outside the uterus?**

- List the components of the Apgar scale and describe what the scale tells us about the newborn.

- Describe the information about the newborn that can be learned from the Brazelton Neonatal Behavioral Assessment.

**What behavioral states are common among newborns?**

- List and describe the 4 newborn states.

- Describe the 3 different types of crying found in newborns.

- Describe the pattern of REM and non-REM sleep found in the newborn.

- Describe sleep disturbances such as nightmares, night terrors, sleep walking, and bedwetting.

- List and describe the factors associated with Sudden Infant Death Syndrome.

**What are the different features of temperament? Do they change as children grow?**

- Describe the dimensions of temperament.

- Describe cross-cultural differences in temperament.

- Explain how temperament is influenced by heredity and environment.

- Explain the stability of temperament across childhood.

# 3.1 KNOW THE TERMS

| | |
|---|---|
| **Alert inactivity** | **Reflexes** |
| **Basic** | **REM (irregular)** |
| **Crying** | **Sleeping** |
| **Mad** | **Sleepwalking** |
| **Nightmares** | **Sudden infant death syndrome (SIDS)** |
| **Night terrors** | **Temperament** |
| **Non-REM (regular)** | **Waking activity** |
| **Pain** | |

1. _____ are unlearned responses that are triggered by specific stimulation.

2. When newborns are in the state of _____ , their eyes are open, they are attentive, and they seem to be deliberately inspecting the environment.

3. When newborns are in the state of _____ , their eyes are open but unfocused, and their arms and legs move in bursts of uncoordinated movements.

4. In the _____ state, newborns cry vigorously and move in an uncoordinated way.

5. In the _____ state, newborns alternate from being still and breathing regularly to moving gently and breathing irregularly.

6. When babies are hungry or tired they often use a _____ cry that starts softly and gradually becomes more intense.

7. A _____ cry is a more intense version of a basic cry.

8. A _____ cry begins with a sudden, long burst of crying followed by a long pause and gasping.

9. During _____ sleep, an infant's eyes will dart rapidly beneath her eyelids, she may move her arms and legs, and she may grimace.

10. During _____ sleep, heart rate, breathing, and brain activity are steady, and newborns lie quietly.

11. _____ are vivid, frightening dreams that occur toward morning and usually wake a child.

12. _____ occur when children appear to wake in a panicked state and are often breathing rapidly and perspiring heavily.

13. The sleep disturbance called _____ occurs during deep sleep when children get out of bed and walk.

14. In _____ , a healthy baby dies suddenly, for no apparent reason.

15. _____ refers to a consistent style or pattern to an infant's behavior.

# 3.1 KNOW THE DETAILS OF NEWBORN BEHAVIOR

1. Newborn reflexes are learned responses to stimulation in the environment.
   TRUE or FALSE

2. The Babinski reflex occurs when a baby throws its arms out then inward in response to a loud noise or when its head falls.
   TRUE or FALSE

3. The rooting reflex occurs when a baby responds to its cheek being stroked by turning its head toward the cheek that was stroked and opening its mouth.
   TRUE or FALSE

4. Babies who practice the stepping reflex often learn to walk earlier than those who don't practice this reflex.
   TRUE or FALSE

5. Reflexes can be used to determine whether the newborn's nervous system is working properly.
   TRUE or FALSE

6. The lower the Apgar score, the healthier the newborn is.
   TRUE or FALSE

7. The Neonatal Behavioral Assessment Scale is a more comprehensive evaluation of newborn functioning than the Apgar.
   TRUE or FALSE

8. A baby with open, unfocused eyes, who is moving its arms in an uncoordinated manner, is in a state of alert inactivity.
   TRUE or FALSE

9. Babies cry differently when they're mad than when they're in pain.
   TRUE or FALSE

10. Newborns sleep 16 to 18 hours daily.
    TRUE or FALSE

11. Brains are more active during REM sleep than during non-REM sleep.
    TRUE or FALSE

12. REM sleep becomes more frequent as infants grow.
    TRUE or FALSE

13. Most babies who die of SIDS are between 2 and 4 months of age.
    TRUE or FALSE

14. The positive affect dimension of temperament refers to the amount of time a child devotes to an activity.
    TRUE or FALSE

15. Temperament characteristics are equally common across cultures.
    TRUE or FALSE

16. Temperament is entirely due to experience.
    TRUE or FALSE

17. Temperament tends to change greatly between infancy and later childhood.
    TRUE or FALSE

# 3.2 PHYSICAL DEVELOPMENT

## TO MASTER THE LEARNING OBJECTIVES:

**How do height and weight change from birth to 2 years of age?**

- Describe the pattern of growth that is seen in children from birth to 2 years of age.

- Know how average size and normal size differ from each other.

**What nutrients do young children need? How are they best provided?**

- Describe the advantages of bottle feeding and breast feeding.

- Describe how children's eating habits change during the first two years of life.

**What are the consequences of malnutrition?  How can it be treated?**

• Describe the effects of malnutrition on growth in young children.

• Explain why it is important to combine changes in diet and parent training when treating malnutrition in children.

**What are nerve cells and how are they organized in the brain?**

• List and describe the parts of neurons.

• Describe the structure and various functions of parts of the brain such as the cerebral cortex, hemispheres, and the corpus callosum.

**How does the brain develop?  When does it begin to function?**

• Describe the development of the brain throughout prenatal development and the first few years after birth.

• Describe the functions of the left and right hemispheres and the frontal lobe of the brain.

• Describe the various methods that are used to study the functions of the brain.

• Describe neuroplasticity.

# 3.2 KNOW THE TERMS

| | |
|---|---|
| Axon | Hemispheres |
| Cell body | Neural plate |
| Cerebral cortex | Neuron |
| Corpus callosum | Neurotransmitters |
| Dendrite | Neuroplasticity |
| Electroencephalogram (EEG) | Malnourished |
| Frontal cortex | Myelin |
| Functional magnetic resonance imaging | Synaptic pruning |
| | Terminal Button |

1. Being small for one's age may indicate that a child is _____ , or receives an inadequate diet.

2. The basic unit of the brain and nervous system that specializes in receiving and transmitting information is called a _____ .

3.

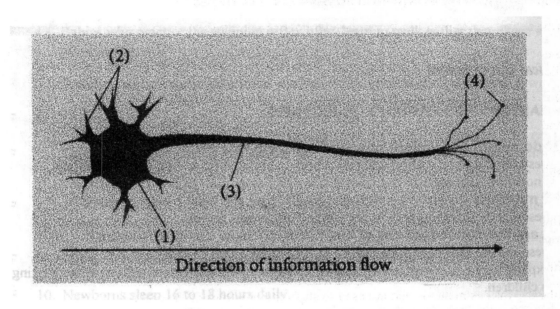

Direction of information flow

The _____ is in the center of the neuron, and it keeps the neuron alive (see #1 above).

4. The _____ is the part of the neuron that receives information, and it looks like a tree with many branches (see #2 above).

5. The _____ is a tube-like structure that emerges from the one end of the cell body, and it transmits information to other neurons (see #3 above).

6. The small knob at the end of the axon is called the _____ (see #4 above).

7. _____ are the chemical messengers that carry information to nearby neurons.

8. The wrinkled surface of the brain is called the _____

9. The right and left halves of the cortex are called _____ .

10. The _____ connects the 2 hemispheres with a thick bundle of neurons.

11. Personality and the ability to carry out plans are controlled by the _____ .

12. During prenatal development, the flat group of cells that will become the brain and spinal cord is called the _____ .

13. The fatty sheath that allows neurons to transmit information more rapidly is called _____ .

14. The gradual disappearance of neurons that begins in infancy is called _____ .

15. The pattern of brain waves that comes from electrodes that are placed on the scalp is known as an _____ .

16. The use of magnetic fields to track the flow of blood in the brain is called _____ .

17. _____ is the extent to which brain organization is flexible.

## 3.2 KNOW THE DETAILS OF PHYSICAL GROWTH

1. Growth is more rapid during infancy than during any other period of life after birth.
   TRUE or FALSE

2. The bodies of infants and children have the same proportions as those of adults.
   TRUE or FALSE

3. Infants require more calories per pound of body weight than adults.
   TRUE or FALSE

4. Bottle-feeding is the best way to make sure babies get the nourishment they need.
   TRUE or FALSE

5. The American Academy of Pediatrics recommends that children be breast fed for the first year.
   TRUE or FALSE

6. The rate of development is not affected by malnourishment.
   TRUE or FALSE

7. Children who are malnourished during infancy have been found to score lower on intelligence tests during childhood.
   TRUE or FALSE

8. A dendrite looks like a tree with many branches and is the receiving end of the neuron.
   TRUE or FALSE

9. The neurotransmitters are tube-like structures that emerge from the side of the cell body and transmit information to other neurons.
   TRUE or FALSE

10. The wrinkled surface of the brain is the cerebral cortex.
    TRUE or FALSE

11. The corpus callosum is a thick bundle of nerves that links the left and right hemispheres of the brain.
    TRUE or FALSE

12. Personality and the ability to make and carry out plans are largely controlled by areas of the brain at the rear of the cortex.
    TRUE or FALSE

13. Recognition of emotions is primarily controlled by neurons in the right hemisphere of the brain.

    TRUE or FALSE

14. The neural plate is a group of cells that form a flat structure that is present in the embryo approximately 3 weeks after conception.

    TRUE or FALSE

15. Myelin is a fatty wrap that reduces the speed at which neurons transmit information.

    TRUE or FALSE

16. Functional magnetic resonance (F-MRI) detects the pattern of brain waves.

    TRUE or FALSE

17. The left hemisphere of the brain is specialized for language processing.

    TRUE or FALSE

18. Neuroplasticity is a method of tracking the flow of blood in the brain.

    TRUE or FALSE

# 3.3 MOVING AND GRASPING— EARLY MOTOR SKILLS

## TO MASTER THE LEARNING OBJECTIVES:

**What are the component skills involved in learning to walk? At what age do infants master them?**

- Describe some of the important developments that lead to the ability to maintain one's balance and eventually walk.

- Know dynamic systems theory and the difference between differentiation and integration.

- Describe how practice is related to motor development.

- Describe the development of running and hopping.

**How do infants learn to coordinate the use of their hands?**

- Describe the development of fine motor skills from simple grasping in the newborn to the ability to eat with a spoon in a 2-year old.

- Describe the development of handedness from about 6 months of age until kindergarten.

**How do maturation and experience influence mastery of motor skills?**

- Explain how both heredity and environment influence the development of handedness.

# 3.3 KNOW THE TERMS

| | |
|---|---|
| **Differentiation** | **Locomote** |
| **Dynamic systems theory** | **Motor skills** |
| **Fine motor skills** | **Toddlers** |
| **Integration** | **Toddling** |

1. Coordinated movements of the muscles and limbs are called _____ .

2. To _____ is the ability to move around in the world.

3. _____ are associated with grasping, holding, and manipulating objects.

4. The early, unsteady form of walking is called _____ .

5. Young children who are inexperienced walkers are called _____ .

6. According to _____ , motor development involves many distinct skills that are organized and reorganized over time to meet the demands of specific tasks.

7. The mastery of complex motions involves _____ of individual motions.

8. Mastery of complex motions also involves the _____ of the individual motions into a coherent, coordinated whole.

# 3.3 KNOW THE DETAILS OF MOTOR DEVELOPMENT

1. Walking is an example of a fine motor skill.
   TRUE or FALSE

2. By about 4 months of age, most babies will be able to roll over and sit with support.
   TRUE or FALSE

3. Most infants can sit alone by 7 months of age.
   TRUE or FALSE

4. By 24 months, most children can climb steps, walk backwards, and kick a ball.
   TRUE or FALSE

5. According to dynamic systems theory, motor development occurs naturally when necessary muscles and neural circuits mature.
   TRUE or FALSE

6. Infants' bodies tend to be unstable because they are bottom-heavy.
   TRUE or FALSE

7. Differentiation refers to the combination of component skills into a coherent, working whole.
   TRUE or FALSE

8. By about 12 to 15 months of age, infants typically master the component skills needed to walk.
   TRUE or FALSE

9. Infants from traditional African cultures have been found to reach motor milestones later than infants growing up in Europe and North America.
   TRUE or FALSE

10. By 2 years of age, most children run easily, bending their knees when they run, and can quickly change directions or speed.
    TRUE or FALSE

11. Most infants can successfully reach for objects at about 4 months of age.
    TRUE or FALSE

12. Most infants begin to use their thumbs to hold objects at about 7 or 8 months of age.
    TRUE or FALSE

13. Infants are able to coordinate the motions of both hands as soon as they are able to use them.
    TRUE or FALSE

14. Most infants begin to be able to pick up "finger foods" at about one year of age.
    TRUE or FALSE

15. At about one year of age, most infants are ready to begin trying to eat with a spoon.
    TRUE or FALSE

16. A preference for one hand over the other does not typically appear until children enter school.
    TRUE or FALSE

17. Hereditary factors, not sociocultural factors, are the sole determinant of handedness.
    TRUE or FALSE

# 3.4 COMING TO KNOW THE WORLD: PERCEPTION

## TO MASTER THE LEARNING OBJECTIVES:

**Are infants able to smell, to taste, and to experience pain?**

• Describe the newborn's sense of smell and taste.

- Describe the newborn's sense of touch and pain and how we infer these feelings.

**Can infants hear?  How do they use sound to locate objects?**

- Describe infants' hearing, perception of music, perception of pitch, differentiation of speech sounds, and localization of sound.

**How well can infants see?  Can they see color and depth?**

- Know how infants' visual acuity is assessed.

- Describe the development of color perception.

- Describe the differences in the reactions of non-crawling and crawling infants when they are placed on the "deep" side of the visual cliff.

- Describe the various cues that are used to infer depth, include kinetic cues, visual expansion, motion parallax, retinal disparity, pictorial cues, linear perspective, and texture gradient.

- Describe how infants perceive objects.

**How do infants coordinate information between different sensory modalities, such as between vision and hearing?**

- Explain how researchers can tell if infants can integrate information from vision and touch.

- Know the importance of intersensory redundancy in infants' perception.


# 3.4 KNOW THE TERMS

| | |
|---|---|
| **Cones** | **Pictorial cues** |
| **Kinetic cues** | **Retinal disparity** |
| **Intersensory redundancy** | **Texture gradient** |
| **Linear perspective** | **Visual acuity** |
| **Motion parallax** | **Visual cliff** |
| **Perception** | **Visual expansion** |

1.  The processes by which the brain receives, selects, modifies, and organizes incoming nerve impulses that are the result of physical stimulation are called _____ .

2.  The smallest pattern that one can distinguish reliably defines visual clarity, or _____ .

3.  The specialized neurons in the back of the eye, along the retina, that sense color are called _____ .

4.  A glass-covered platform that appears to have a "shallow" side and a "deep" side is called a _____ .

5. _____ use motion to estimate depth.

6. _____ refers to the fact that as an object moves closer, it fills an ever-greater proportion of the retina.

7. _____ refers to the fact that objects that are close move across our visual fields faster than objects that are in the distance.

8. _____ is one way to infer depth when the retinal images in the left and right eyes differ.

9. Cues for depth that are the same as the cues that artists use to convey depth in drawings and paintings are called _____

10. _____ occurs when parallel lines come together at a single point in the distance.

11. The cue of depth where the texture of near objects is coarse but distinct and the texture of distant objects is finer and less distinct is called _____

12. The simultaneous presentation of information to different sensory modes is called _____ .

## 3.4 KNOW THE DETAILS OF PERCEPTION

1. Newborns can differentiate between their mother's odor and another woman's odor.
   TRUE or FALSE

2. Infants are not able to differentiate between salty, sour, bitter, and sweet tastes.
   TRUE or FALSE

3. Newborns seem to have a preference for sour tastes.
   TRUE or FALSE

4. The newborn infant's nervous system is not capable of transmitting pain.
   TRUE or FALSE

5. Infants can hear as well as adults.
   TRUE or FALSE

6. Infants can use sound to locate objects.
   TRUE or FALSE

7. Infants prefer looking at patterned stimuli over plain, unpatterned stimuli.
   TRUE or FALSE

8. Newborns' visual acuity is about 20/400.
   TRUE or FALSE

9. Specialized neurons called cones are responsible for depth perception.
   TRUE or FALSE

10. Newborns perceive color in the same way adults do.
    TRUE or FALSE

11. The visual cliff is used to measure infant visual acuity.
    TRUE or FALSE

12. One-and-a-half-month-old infants notice a difference between the deep and shallow sides of a visual cliff.
    TRUE or FALSE

13. Infants do not use retinal disparity as a depth cue.
    TRUE or FALSE

14. Newborns visually scan objects in the same way as older infants.
    TRUE or FALSE

15. Infants are able to integrate information between vision and touch and between vision and hearing.
    TRUE or FALSE

# 3.5 BECOMING SELF-AWARE

## TO MASTER THE LEARNING OBJECTIVES:

**When do children begin to realize that they exist?**

- Know when self-recognition appears and how it is measured.
- Know how saying "mine" while playing with toys is related to self-awareness.

**What are toddlers' and preschoolers' self-concepts like?**

- Describe the characteristics of young children's self-concepts.

**When do preschool children begin to acquire a theory of mind?**

- Define theory of mind and know the three phases of theory of mind in preschool children.

## 3.5 KNOW THE DETAILS OF SELF-AWARENESS

1. By 9 months of age, infants obviously recognize themselves in a mirror.
   TRUE or FALSE

2. Self awareness emerges between 18 and 24 months.
   TRUE or FALSE

3. Preschoolers tend to define themselves in terms of their possessions and physical characteristics.
   TRUE or FALSE

4. In the earliest phase of the theory of mind, 2-year-olds understand that people have desires and that desires can cause behavior.
   TRUE or FALSE

5. At age 3, children are not 2able to clearly distinguish the mental world from the physical world.
   TRUE or FALSE

6. By age 4, children understand that behavior is often based on a person's beliefs about events and situations, even when those beliefs are wrong.
   TRUE or FALSE

7. False belief tasks can be used to assess a child's theory of mind.
   TRUE or FALSE

# SUMMARY

## 3.1 THE NEWBORN

1. **The Newborn's Reflexes**

   Babies are born with a number of reflexes. Some help them _____ to life outside of the uterus, some help _____ them from danger, and some serve as the basis for later voluntary motor behavior.

2. **Assessing the Newborn**

   The _____ measures five vital signs to determine a newborn baby's physical well being. The Neonatal Behavioral Assessment provides a comprehensive evaluation of a baby's _____ and physical status.

3. **The Newborn's States**

   Newborns spend their day in one of four states: _____ , waking activity, crying, and sleeping. A newborn's crying includes a basic cry, a _____ cry, and a pain cry. The best way to calm a crying baby is by putting it on the shoulder and rocking. Newborns spend approximately two-thirds of every day asleep and go through a complete sleep-wake cycle once every 4 hours. By 3 or 4 months, babies sleep through the night. Newborns spend about half of their time asleep in _____ sleep, an active form of sleep that may stimulate growth of the nervous system. Sleep-related problems include nightmares, night terrors, sleep walking, and bed wetting. Some healthy babies die from sudden infant death syndrome. Factors that contribute to SIDS are prematurity, _____ , and parental smoking. Also, babies are more vulnerable to SIDS when they sleep on their _____ and when they are overheated. The goal of the Back to Sleep campaign is to prevent SIDS by encouraging parents to have infants sleep on their backs.

4.  **Temperament**

Temperament refers to a consistent style or _____ to an infant's behavior. Modern theories include 2-6 dimensions of temperament, including, for example, activity level, positive affect, and _____ . Temperament is influenced by both heredity and environment and is a reasonably stable characteristic of infants and young children.

## 3.2 PHYSICAL DEVELOPMENT

1.  **Growth of the Body**

Physical growth is particularly _____ during infancy, but babies of the same age differ considerably in their heights and weights. Size at maturity is largely determined by heredity. Infants and young children have disproportionately larger _____ . Infants must consume a large number of _____ relative to their body weight, primarily because of the energy that is required for growth. Breast feeding and bottle feeding both provide babies with adequate nutrition. _____ is a worldwide problem that is particularly harmful during infancy, when growth is so rapid. Treating malnutrition adequately requires improving children's diet and training their parents to provide _____ environments.

2.  **The Emerging Nervous System**

A nerve cell, called a _____ , includes a cell body, a dendrite, and an _____ . The mature brain consists of billions of neurons organized into nearly identical left and right hemispheres connected by the _____ The cerebral cortex controls most of the functions that we think of as distinctively human. The _____ cortex is associated with personality and goal-directed behavior. The left hemisphere of the cortex is associated with _____ , and the right hemisphere is associated with processes such as perceiving music and regulating emotions. The brain specializes early in development. The brain is moderately _____ . On the one hand, most brains are organized in much the same way. On the other hand, following brain injury, cognitive processes are sometimes _____ to undamaged neurons.

## 3.3 MOVING AND GRASPING--EARLY MOTOR SKILLS

1. **Locomotion**

   Infants acquire a series of motor skills during their first year, culminating in walking a few months after the first birthday. Like most motor skills, learning to walk involves _____ of individual skills, such as maintaining balance and using the legs alternately, and then _____ these skills into a unified, coordinated whole.

2. **Fine-Motor Skills**

   Infants first use only one hand at a time, then both hands independently, then both hands in common actions, and, finally, at about 5 months of age, both hands in different actions with a common purpose. Most people are right handed, a preference that emerges after the _____ and that becomes well established during the preschool years. Handedness is determined by heredity but can also be influenced by _____ .

## 3.4 COMING TO KNOW THE WORLD: PERCEPTION

1. **Smell and Taste**

   Newborns are able to recognize their mothers' odors. They also taste, preferring _____ substances and responding negatively to bitter and sour tastes.

2. **Touch and Pain**

   Infants respond to touch. They probably experience pain, because their _____ to painful stimuli are similar to those of older children.

3. **Hearing**

   Babies can hear. More importantly, they can distinguish different sounds and can use sound to _____ objects in space.

4. **Seeing**

   A newborn's visual acuity is relatively poor, but 1-year-olds can see as well as adults with normal vision. Color vision develops as different sets of _____ begin to function, a process that seems to be complete by 3 or 4 months of age. Infants perceive depth, based on _____ , kinetic cues, and pictorial cues. They also use motion to recognize objects. Infants are particularly attached to _____ , but whether this reflects certain processing mechanisms is uncertain.

5. **Integrating Sensory Information**

Infants coordinate information from different senses. They can recognize, by _____ , an object that they have felt previously. They look at a woman's face when they hear a woman's voice or look at an object that is becoming more distant when a sound becomes _____ .

## 3.5 BECOMING SELF AWARE

1. **Origins of Self Concept**

Beginning at about 15 months, infants begin to _____ themselves in the mirror, which is one of the first signs of self-recognition. They also begin to prefer to look at pictures of themselves, begin to refer to themselves by name, and sometimes know their age and _____ . Evidently, by two years most children are self aware. Preschoolers often define themselves in terms of observable characteristics, such as possessions, _____ characteristics, preferences, and _____ . During the elementary-school years, self-concept begins to include observable characteristics, such as a child's possessions and preferences.

2. **Theory of Mind**

Theory of mind, which refers to a person's ideas about connections between thoughts, _____ , intentions, and behavior, develops rapidly during the preschool years. Most 2-year-olds know that people have desires and that desires can cause _____ . By age 3, children distinguish the _____ world from the physical world, but still emphasize desire in explaining others' actions. By age 4, however, children understand behavior is based on _____ about the world, even when those beliefs are wrong.

# TEST YOURSELF

## MULTIPLE-CHOICE QUESTIONS

1. When a baby throws its arms out and then draws them inward in response to a loud noise or when its head falls, the baby is displaying the _____ reflex.
   a. Babinski
   b. palmar
   c. rooting
   d. Moro

2. Kelly has noticed that whenever she places an object in her newborn son's hand, he grasps it tightly. He is demonstrating the _____ reflex.
   a. Moro
   b. palmar
   c. Babinski
   d. rooting

3. Mariko's newborn baby received an Apgar score of 10. This means that her baby
   a. was stillborn.
   b. has a life-threatening condition.
   c. needs special attention and care.
   d. is in good physical health.

4. The Neonatal Behavioral Assessment Scale (NBAS)
   a. is a prenatal diagnostic procedure.
   b. provides a quick, approximate assessment of the newborn's status.
   c. involves a comprehensive evaluation of a broad range of newborn abilities and behaviors.
   d. assesses the risk an infant has of dying from sudden infant death syndrome.

5. Two-month-old Stephen is calm and his eyes are open and attentive. He seems to be inspecting the room he is in. Stephen is in a(n) _____ state.
   a. alert inactivity
   b. waking activity
   c. crying
   d. sleeping

6. Newborns spend most of their time in which of the following states?
   a. Sleep
   b. alert inactivity
   c. waking activity
   d. crying

7. Most babies sleep through the night by
   a. 2 or 3 weeks of age.
   b. 3 or 4 months of age.
   c. 5 or 6 months of age.
   d. 7 or 8 months of age.

8. Sudden infant death syndrome (SIDS) is more likely
   a. when infants sleep on their backs than when they sleep on their stomachs.
   b. in the spring or fall than in the winter.
   c. in infants whose parents smoke.
   d. when infants are under-dressed and get cold.

9. Alex is shy and withdrawn when he meets people. Alex is high on which temperament dimension?
   a. negative affect
   b. positive affect
   c. persistence
   d. inhibition

10. An infant's weight typically _____ between birth and one year of age.
    a. doubles
    b. triples
    c. quadruples
    d. quintuples

11. The correlation between the average of two parents' height and their child's height at 2 years of age is about
    a. -.9
    b. 0.0
    c. .2
    d. .7

12. Which of the following comparisons of breast feeding and bottle feeding is FALSE?
    a. Breastfed infants are more prone to diarrhea and constipation.
    b. Breast milk contains more antibodies that help to fight disease.
    c. Breastfed infants are less likely to develop allergies.
    d. Breastfed infants are less likely to make the transition to solid foods easily.

13. Malnourishment is most harmful during
    a. infancy.
    b. early childhood.
    c. later childhood.
    d. adolescence.

14. Malnourished children
    a. tend to be overly active.
    b. are often unresponsive and lethargic.
    c. are usually very attentive.
    d. need to be in environments with low levels of stimulation.

15. The _____ is the basic unit in the brain and the rest of the nervous system and is a cell that specializes in receiving and transmitting information.
    a. terminal button
    b. dendrite
    c. axon
    d. neuron

16. The _____, in the center of the neuron, contains the basic biological machinery that keeps the neuron alive.
    a. axon
    b. dendrite
    c. cell body
    d. terminal button

17. _____ are chemical messengers that transmit information to other neurons.
    a. Neurotransmitters
    b. Terminal buttons
    c. Dendrites
    d. Axons

18. Personality and deliberate goal-oriented behavior seem to be controlled in the _____ of the brain.
    a. left hemisphere
    b. right hemisphere
    c. corpus callosum
    d. frontal cortex

19. Language is controlled largely by the _____ of the brain.
    a. left hemisphere
    b. right hemisphere
    c. corpus callosum
    d. frontal cortex

20. The bundle of nerves that connects the right and left hemispheres of the brain is called the
    a. corpus callosum
    b. frontal cortex
    c. neural plate
    d. terminal button

21. _____ is a fatty wrap that allows neurons to transmit information more rapidly.
    a. The cerebral cortex
    b. Myelin
    c. The neurotransmitter
    d. The terminal button

22. Unnecessary connections between neurons disappear between infancy and adolescence, a process called
    a. neuroplasticity
    b. synaptic pruning
    c. neural transmission
    d. functional magnetic resonance

23. The extent to which brain organization is flexible is referred to as
    a. synaptic pruning.
    b. functional magnetic resonance.
    c. neural transmission.
    d. neuroplasticity.

24. By what age are most infants able to sit alone?
    a. 3 months
    b. 5 months
    c. 7 months
    d. 12 months

25. Most infants learn to walk alone at about _____ months of age.
    a. 6 to 8
    b. 9 to 10
    c. 12 to 15
    d. 20 to 24

26. Which of the following is NOT an essential skill for locomotion?
    a. the ability to maintain an upright posture
    b. the ability to continuously adjust posture to avoid falling down
    c. the ability to alternately move the legs
    d. the ability to move legs at different speeds

27. Taiji has just started being able to coordinate the motions of his hands. He now can hold a toy car in one hand and explore it with his other hand. Taiji is probably about _____ months of age.
    a. 2
    b. 5
    c. 8
    d. 12

28. Right or left hand preference is usually clear
    a. when the child enters school.
    b. during the late preschool years.
    c. by age 2 years.
    d. at birth.

29. Newborns have
    a. highly developed senses of taste and smell.
    b. a highly developed sense of smell but not taste.
    c. a highly developed sense of taste but not smell.
    d. poorly developed senses of taste and smell.

30. Which of the following statements about infant hearing is true?
    a. Newborns are not sensitive to sound.
    b. Six-month-old infants can hear sounds but cannot distinguish different pitches.
    c. Infants can detect the direction from which a sound is coming but are not able to judge the nearness of the sound.
    d. Six- to seven-month-old infants are able to distinguish different pitches and differentiate many speech sounds.

31. A typical newborn can see at 20 feet what adults with normal vision can see at _____ feet.
    a. 10
    b. 20
    c. 50 to 100
    d. 200 to 400

32. The ability to see color is
    a. fully developed in newborns.
    b. similar to that of adults by 3 or 4 months of age.
    c. similar to that of adults starting at about one year of age.
    d. not fully developed until about three years of age.

33. The ability to perceive color is most closely associated with
    a. cones.
    b. retinal disparity.
    c. visual acuity.
    d. the visual cliff.

34. The visual cliff is used to assess
    a. color perception.
    b. visual acuity.
    c. depth perception.
    d. retinal disparity.

35. By the time infants are able to crawl, when their mothers try to coax them across the deep side of a visual cliff, the infants typically will
    a.  show fear of the deep side and refuse to cross.
    b.  show interest in the deep side and readily cross it.
    c.  appear to not detect the difference between the deep and shallow sides of the visual cliff.
    d.  experience heart rate deceleration.

36. Retinal disparity is used
    a.  as a depth cue.
    b.  as a color cue.
    c.  to assess visual acuity.
    d.  to integrate sight and sound.

37. Infants are
    a.  able to integrate information between sight and touch and between sight and sound.
    b.  able to integrate information between sight and touch but not between sight and sound.
    c.  able to integrate information between sight and sound but not between sight and touch.
    d.  not able to integrate information between sight and other senses.

38. A mother surreptitiously places a red mark on her 1-year-old daughter's nose, then places the infant in front of a mirror. What would you expect the infant to do?
    a.  Not notice the red mark on the infant in the mirror.
    b.  Touch the red mark on the face in the mirror.
    c.  Reach up and touch her own nose.
    d.  Cry and turn her face away from the mirror.

39. Self-awareness is well established in most children by age
    a.  6 months.
    b.  1 year.
    c.  2 years.
    d.  6 years.

40. According to the theory of mind, 2-year-olds
    a.  understand that behavior is often based on a person's beliefs about events and situations, even when those beliefs are wrong.
    b.  often use "mental verbs" like "think," "believe," "remember," and "forget."
    c.  understand that people have desires and that desires can cause behavior.
    d.  clearly distinguish the mental world from the physical world.

41. By about _____ years of age, children begin to understand that behavior is often based on a person's beliefs about events and situations, even when those beliefs are false.
    a.  2
    b.  4
    c.  6
    d.  8

42. Which child is in the highest phase of children's theory of mind?
    a. Jill, who understands that behavior is often based on a person's beliefs even when those beliefs are wrong
    b. Callie, who talks about thoughts and beliefs, but emphasizes desires when trying to explain why people act as they do
    c. Sienna, who is aware of desires and often speaks of her wants and likes
    d. Annabelle, who can clearly distinguish the mental world from the physical world

## ESSAY QUESTIONS

1. Lafon has just had a baby boy named Anthony. In the hospital and during the first few weeks at home, Lafon noticed that when Anthony cries he stops as soon as she picks him up. Even when she accidentally poked him with a diaper pin, he stopped crying very quickly after she picked him up. Lafon was wondering if Anthony's behavior is any indication that he will be an easy baby and child. What can you tell Lafon about temperament and the stability of temperament?

2. Your friend, Shayda, just had a baby boy named Kyle who weighed 7 pounds 6 ounces at birth. While you and Shayda are out shopping for clothes for Kyle, you notice that she is filling the cart with lots of 0-3 month size clothes. You ask Shayda if she thinks that it's a good idea to buy so many small-sized clothes given how quickly infants grow. Shayda's response is that Kyle is so small now there's no way that he will outgrow all of these clothes so quickly. What can you tell Shayda about infant growth that may persuade her to put some of the clothes back?

3. You have been hired by a local charitable agency that plans to battle malnutrition in your city. You have been to a few meetings and you have heard people mention the fact that good nutrition will help these malnourished children so they will do better in school. Based on what you know about battling malnutrition, what other aspect should be added to your program?

4. Your friend Elena has noticed that her 7-month-old daughter, Mariana, has been picking up toys with her left hand and will bat at the objects that are hanging above her in her infant gym. Elena and her husband are both right-handed, and they do not want their daughter to become left handed because so many items are made for right-handed people (e.g., door handles, desk seats, scissors, etc.). What can you tell Elena about the development of handedness and the role of heredity and environment on the development of handedness?

5. Your friend Cole has noticed that his 3-week-old son Nate seems to drink more from his bottle when it contains sugar water than when it contains formula. Cole even thinks that he saw Nate lick his lips when he was given a bottle of sugar water. Cole thinks that he is crazy because he doesn't think that the senses are really functioning in babies who are so young. What can you tell Cole that may help him feel better?

6. Your friend Sunmi keeps leaving her 3-month-old son on the edge of the bed or couch. You told her that you don't think that this is a very safe practice but she said that 3-month-old babies can detect depth and they are afraid of falling, so her son will be okay. What can you tell Sunmi about depth perception and fear (as measured by experiments using a visual cliff) that may change her mind?

# SOLUTIONS

## 3.1 KNOW THE TERMS

1. Reflexes (88)
2. alert inactivity (90)
3. waking activity (90)
4. crying (90)
5. sleeping (90)
6. basic (90)
7. mad (90)
8. pain (90)
9. REM (irregular) (91)
10. non-REM (regular) (91)
11. Nightmares (92)
12. Night terrors (92)
13. sleepwalking (92)
14. sudden infant death syndrome (92)
15. Temperament (93)

## 3.1 KNOW THE DETAILS OF NEWBORN BEHAVIOR

1. F, (88)
2. F, (89)
3. T, (89)
4. T, (88)
5. T, (88)
6. F, (89)
7. T, (89)
8. F, (90)
9. T, (90)
10. T, (91)
11. T, (91)
12. F, (91)
13. T, (92)
14. F, (94)
15. F, (94)
16. F, (94)
17. F, (95)

## 3.2 KNOW THE TERMS

1. malnourished (99)
2. neuron (100)
3. cell body (100)
4. dendrite (100)
5. axon (100)
6. terminal button (100)
7. Neurotransmitters (100)
8. cerebral cortex (100).
9. hemispheres (100)
10. corpus callosum (101)
11. frontal cortex (101)
12. neural plate (101)
13. myelin (101)
14. synaptic pruning (102)
15. electroencephalogram (103)
16. functional magnetic resonance imaging (103)
17. Neuroplasticity (104)

## 3.2 KNOW THE DETAILS OF PHYSICAL GROWTH

1. T, (96)
2. F, (96)
3. T, (97)
4. F, (98)
5. T, (98)
6. F, (99)
7. T, (99)
8. T, (100)
9. F, (100)
10. T, (100)
11. T, (101)
12. F, (101)
13. T, (101)
14. T, (101)
15. F, (101)
16. F, (103)
17. T, (104)
18. F, (104)

## 3.3 KNOW THE TERMS

1. motor skills (105)
2. locomote (106)
3. Fine motor skills (106)
4. toddling (107)
5. toddlers (107)
6. dynamic systems theory (107)
7. differentiation (108)
8. integration (108)

## 3.3 KNOW THE DETAILS OF MOTOR DEVELOPMENT

1. F, (106)
2. T, (107)
3. T, (107)
4. T, (107)
5. F, (107)
6. F, (107)
7. F, (108)
8. T, (108)
9. F, (108)
10. F, (109)
11. T, (109)
12. T, (109)
13. F, (110)
14. F, (110)
15. T, (110)
16. F, (111)
17. F, (111)

## 3.4 KNOW THE TERMS

1. perception (112)
2. visual acuity (114)
3. cones (115)
4. visual cliff (115)
5. Kinetic cues (116)
6. Visual expansion (116)
7. Motion parallax (116)
8. Retinal disparity (116)
9. pictorial cues (116).
10. Linear perspective (116)
11. texture gradient (116).
12. intersensory redundancy (121)

## 3.4 KNOW THE DETAILS OF PERCEPTION

1. T, (112)
2. F, (112)
3. F, (112)
4. F, (113)
5. F, (113)
6. T, (114)
7. T, (114)
8. T, (115)
9. F, (115)
10. F, (115)
11. F, (115)
12. T, (116)
13. F, (116)
14. F, (118)
15. T, (121)

## 3.5 KNOW THE DETAILS OF SELF-AWARENESS

1. F, (123)

2.  T, (123)
3.  T, (123)

4.  T, (124)
5.  F, (124)

6.  T, (124)
7.  T, (124)

# SUMMARY

## 3.1 THE NEWBORN

1.  adjust (88); protect (88)
2.  Apgar (89); behavioral (89)
3.  alert inactivity (90); mad (90); REM (91); low birth weight (92); stomach (92)
4.  pattern (93); negative affect (94)

## 3.2 PHYSICAL DEVELOPMENT

1.  rapid (96); heads and trunks (97); calories (97); Malnutrition (99); stimulating (100)
2.  neuron (100); axon (100); corpus callosum (101); frontal (101); language (101); plastic (104); transferred (104)

## 3.3 MOVING AND GRASPING--EARLY MOTOR SKILLS

1.  differentiation (108); integration (108)
2.  first birthday (110); cultural values (110)

## 3.4 COMING TO KNOW THE WORLD: PERCEPTION

1.  sweet (112)
2.  responses (113)
3.  locate (114)
4.  cones (115); retinal disparity (116); faces (118)
5.  sight (121); softer (121)

## 3.5 BECOMING SELF AWARE

1.  recognize (123); gender (123); physical (123); competencies (123)
2.  beliefs (124); behavior (124); mental (124); beliefs (124)

# TEST YOURSELF

## MULTIPLE-CHOICE QUESTIONS

1.  D, (89)
2.  B, (89)
3.  D, (89)
4.  C, (89)
5.  A, (90)
6.  A, (91)
7.  B, (91)
8.  C, (92)
9.  D, (94)
10. B, (96)
11. D, (96)

12. A, (98)
13. A, (99)
14. B, (100)
15. D, (100)
16. C, (100)
17. A, (100)
18. D, (101)
19. A, (101)
20. A, (101)
21. B, (101)
22. B, (102)

23. D, (104)
24. C, (106)
25. C, (108)
26. D, (107)
27. B, (110)
28. C, (111)
29. A, (112)
30. D, (113)
31. D, (115)
32. B, (115)
33. A, (115)

| 34. C, (115) | 37. A, (121) | 40. C, (124) |
| 35. A, (116) | 38. B, (123) | 41. B, (124) |
| 36. A, (116) | 39. C, (123) | 42. A, (124) |

## ESSAY QUESTIONS

1.  Temperament includes two to six different dimensions which include positive affect (the extent to which the child expresses pleasure, enthusiasm, and contentment), activity (the amount of physical and motor activity), and negative affect (the extent to which a child is irritable, easily distressed, and prone to anger). Anthony's behavior seems to indicate his level of negative affect. He doesn't seem to become upset easily and he returns to a calm state quickly. Research on the stability of temperament indicates that temperament is somewhat stable during the infant and toddler years. For example, newborns who cry under moderate stress are more likely to cry in stressful situations as 5-month-olds and inhibited 2-year-olds tend to be shy 4-year-olds. The stability is not perfect though, so while it is likely that Anthony will be a fairly calm, easily-soothed child, it isn't possible to predict perfectly his future behavior. (93-95)

2.  Shayda should know that growth during infancy is more rapid than at any other time during one's life. In fact, the average infant will double his birth weight by the time he is 3 months old. So, Kyle will probably weigh around 15 pounds in just 12 weeks. By the time Kyle is 1 year old, he will probably weigh about 22 pounds. After presenting these facts to Shayda, you might want to ask her if she thinks that she will get her money's worth out of all of those expensive outfits that Kyle will have outgrown in a few short weeks. Fortunately, this rapid growth does taper off and Shayda might want to buy more expensive clothes when Kyle is older and not growing as rapidly. (96-97)

3.  Malnourished children tend to be listless and inactive. They also tend to be very quiet and uninterested in their environments. This behavior often leads parents to conclude that their children are unresponsive, and the parents may start providing fewer experiences to their children. These experiences could be important for stimulating the child, so the child loses because of the direct effects of malnutrition and because of the indirect effects of receiving less stimulation. So, effective programs that treat malnutrition need to include not only dietary supplements but parental training. Parents need to be encouraged to stimulate their children even though they may think they are unresponsive. Parents also may need to be taught which experiences are appropriate stimulation for their children. Children who are in programs that combine dietary supplements with parent training often catch up with their peers both physically and intellectually. In other words, the children in your program probably won't do much better in school just because they are better nourished, so parental training should be included in your program. (99-100)

4.  Most children who are Mariana's age (6-9 months old) will use their left and right hands interchangeably, so it is unlikely that Mariana's use of her left hand is predictive of her later hand preference. It isn't until most children are about 1-year old that they start to show a preference for one hand over the other. Throughout the preschool years, preference for one hand becomes stronger and more consistent so that by the time a child enters kindergarten hand preference is well established and difficult to reverse. Heredity does influence handedness. Identical twins are more likely than fraternal twins to have the same handedness. Given that both Elena and her husband are right-handed, it is likely that Mariana will be right-handed also. However, experience does play a role, too. Evidence of the influence of culture comes from the United States where teachers used to encourage left-handed children to use their right hands. When this practice stopped, the incidence of left-handedness increased. Given that Mariana has 2 right-handed parents who are likely to encourage right-handed behavior, she will probably become right-handed, but it is too early to tell. (111)

5.  Infants have a highly developed sense of taste. They can easily tell the difference between sweet, salty, bitter, and sour tastes. In fact, infants seem to react to these different tastes in ways that are similar to the reactions of adults. For example, most infants seem to have a sweet tooth because they react to sweet substances by licking their lips, smiling, and sucking on the bottle longer. Infants also show negative reactions to bitter and sour tastes. So, Cole is not going crazy--Nate probably does have a sweet tooth and is reacting positively to the sugar water. (112-113)

6.  When 1 ½-month-old infants are placed on the deep side of a visual cliff their heart rates will drop, indicating that they perceive the depth but they only find it interesting, not frightening. However, by the time infants are

old enough to crawl (around 7 months of age), their heart rates increase when they are placed on the "deep" side of the visual cliff, indicating that they perceive the depth and are frightened by it. So, Sunmi should know that, yes, her son can detect the drop off the bed or couch, but he probably isn't old enough to be afraid of the drop, and he is likely to fall. (115-116)

# THE EMERGENCE OF THOUGHT AND LANGUAGE

4.1 The Onset of Thinking: Piaget's Account

4.2 Information-Processing During Infancy and Early Childhood

4.3 Mind and Culture: Vygotsky's Theory

4.4 Language

This chapter focuses on language development and theories of cognitive development such as Piaget's theory, information processing theories, and Vygotsky's theory.

# 4.1 THE ONSET OF THINKING: PIAGET'S ACCOUNT

## TO MASTER THE LEARNING OBJECTIVES:

**According to Piaget, how do assimilation, accommodation, and organization provide the foundation for cognitive development throughout the life span?**

- Explain Piaget's concepts of scheme, assimilation, accommodation, and equilibration and explain how they are related to each other.

**How do schemes become more advanced as infants progress through the six stages of sensorimotor thinking?**

- Describe the development from reflexive behavior to active experimentation.

- Describe the infant's understanding of objects.

- Explain what "using symbols" means and why it is an important achievement for cognitive development.

**What are the distinguishing characteristics of thinking during the preoperational stage?**

- Describe how the three-mountains problem demonstrates egocentrism in preoperational children.

- Describe animism in preoperational children.

- Describe how centration is demonstrated in the conservation of liquid quantity task.

- Explain how preoperational children confuse appearance and reality.

- Describe changes in children's ability to use scale models.

**What are some of the shortcomings of Piaget's account of cognitive development?**

- Describe the implications of Piaget's theory for teaching practices.

- Explain how the phrasing of questions is related to young children's performance on conservation problems.

- Explain how Baillargeon's research involving possible events and impossible events conflicts with Piaget's description of the timing of object permanence.

- Describe what Piaget would say about consistent performance across different tasks. Does research support Piaget's view?

- Describe children's naive theories of physics and biology.

# 4.1 KNOW THE TERMS

| | |
|---|---|
| Accommodation | Egocentrism |
| Animism | Equilibration |
| Assimilation | Object permanence |
| Centration | Schemes |
| Core knowledge hypothesis | Sensorimotor |

1. According to Piaget, psychological structures that organize experience are called _____ .

2. _____ occurs when new experiences are readily incorporated into existing schemes.

3. _____ occurs when schemes are modified based on experience.

4. The process of reorganizing one's schemes to return to a state of equilibrium is known as _____ .

5. The _____ period is the first of Piaget's four stages of cognitive development. This period lasts from birth to approximately 2 years.

6. Piaget's term for understanding that objects exist independently is _____

7. The young child's difficulty in seeing the world from another's outlook is called _____ .

8. Crediting inanimate objects with life and life-like properties is called _____ .

9.  Narrowly focused thought that characterizes preoperational thought is called _____ .

10. A rudimentary knowledge of the world that is elaborated based on children's experiences is called

    _____ .

# 4.1 KNOW THE DETAILS OF PIAGET'S THEORY

1.  According to Piaget, thinking changes quantitatively but not qualitatively with age.
    TRUE or FALSE

2.  Piaget believed that during infancy most schemes are based on conceptual categories, not actions.
    TRUE or FALSE

3.  Assimilation occurs when a scheme is changed because of a new experience.
    TRUE or FALSE

4.  Disequilibrium has occurred when a child spends more time accommodating than assimilating schemes.
    TRUE or FALSE

5.  Children can go through Piaget's periods in many different sequences.
    TRUE or FALSE

6.  Infants are in Piaget's concrete operational period of cognitive development.
    TRUE or FALSE

7.  According to Piaget, newborns respond reflexively rather than intentionally.
    TRUE or FALSE

8.  Infants lack object permanence in the first six months of life.
    TRUE or FALSE

9.  According to Piaget, infants are able to use symbols by the end of the sensorimotor period.
    TRUE or FALSE

10. Children in Piaget's preoperational period generally understand that other people have different ideas and emotions than their own.
    TRUE or FALSE

11. Preoperational thinkers often confuse appearance and reality.
    TRUE or FALSE

12. Piagetian theory suggests that the teacher's role is to create environments where children can discover for themselves how the world works.
    TRUE or FALSE

13. Piagetian theory suggests that teachers can speed up children's cognitive growth by pointing out inconsistencies in children's thinking rather than letting children figure out inconsistencies themselves.

    TRUE or FALSE

14. Children's performance on conservation problems appears to be due partly to language development, not just because of the concepts Piaget used to explain their thinking.

    TRUE or FALSE

15. Research evidence suggests that infants do not understand object permanence until a much older age than Piaget's theory suggests.

    TRUE or FALSE

16. Piaget's theory has been criticized because children often perform less consistently on Piagetian tasks than Piaget's theory suggests they would.

    TRUE or FALSE

17. In contrast to Piaget's view that children develop general theories of the world, more recent views of children's cognitive development propose that children develop more specialized theories about narrow areas.

    TRUE or FALSE

18. By the preschool years, children's naive theories of biology include the idea that animals can move themselves, but inanimate objects can only be moved by other objects or by people.

    TRUE or FALSE

# 4.2 INFORMATION-PROCESSING DURING INFANCY AND EARLY CHILDHOOD

## TO MASTER THE LEARNING OBJECTIVES:

**What is the basis of the information-processing approach?**

- Describe the information-processing approach to human thinking. What constitutes a person's hardware and software?

**How well do young children pay attention?**

- Define attention, orienting response, and habituation.

- Describe what can be done to help children pay attention to relevant information.

**Do infants and preschool children remember?**

- Describe infants' learning in classical conditioning, operant conditioning, and imitation.

- Describe the 3 important features of infant's memories that were found by Carolyn Rovee-Collier.

- Describe the improvements in memory as children become toddlers.

- Define autobiographical memory and describe how parents, language skill, and a sense of self contribute to it.

**What are the shortcomings of preschoolers' eyewitness testimony? What can we do to make it more reliable?**

- Describe preschoolers' eyewitness memory and its relation to source monitoring.

- Describe the 3 guidelines that should be followed to help improve the reliability of child witnesses

**Can infants discriminate different quantities?**

- Describe a young infant's ability to distinguish different numbers of objects.

**How do preschoolers count?**

- Describe young children's counting ability, including the 3 counting principles that most children master by age 3.

## 4.2 KNOW THE TERMS

| | |
|---|---|
| **Attention** | **One-to-one** |
| **Autobiographical memory** | **Operant conditioning** |
| **Cardinality** | **Ordinality** |
| **Classical conditioning** | **Orienting response** |
| **Habituation** | **Software** |
| **Hardware** | **Stable-order** |

1.  The term mental _____ refers to mental and neural structures that are built in and that allow the mind to operate.

2.  The term mental _____ refers to mental programs that are the basis for performing particular tasks.

3.  _____ determines which information will be processed further by an individual.

4.  An _____ occurs when a person starts, fixes his eyes on a stimulus, and shows changes in heart rate and brain wave activity.

5.  The diminished response to a stimulus as it becomes more familiar is called _____ .

6. _____ occurs when a neutral stimulus elicits a response that was originally produced by another stimulus.

7. _____ focuses on the relation between the consequences of behavior and the likelihood that the behavior will occur.

8. People's memory for the significant events and experiences of their own lives is called _____ .

9. _____ refers to the fact that numbers can differ in magnitude; some values are greater than others.

10. The counting principle that states that there must be one and only one number name for each object counted is known as the _____ principle.

11. The counting principle that states that number names must always be counted in the same order is known as the _____ principle.

12. The understanding that the last number name denotes the number of objects one is counting is called the _____ principle.

## 4.2 KNOW THE DETAILS OF INFORMATION PROCESSING

1. In the information-processing view, human cognition is thought to be based on mental hardware and mental software.
   TRUE or FALSE

2. Information-processing theorists believe that as children develop, their mental software becomes more complex, more powerful, and more efficient.
   TRUE or FALSE

3. An orienting response is the diminished response to a stimulus as it becomes more familiar.
   TRUE or FALSE

4. Young children direct their attention as effectively as adults.
   TRUE or FALSE

5. Infants and toddlers are not capable of learning through classical conditioning.
   TRUE or FALSE

6. Operant conditioning focuses on the relation between the consequences of behavior and the likelihood that the behavior will reoccur.
   TRUE or FALSE

7.  Young babies cannot remember events for more than one day.
    TRUE or FALSE

8.  Structures in the brain that are responsible for retrieving memories develop much later than those responsible for the initial storage of information.
    TRUE or FALSE

9.  Autobiographical memory emerges during infancy.
    TRUE or FALSE

10. Law-enforcement officials and child-protection workers can almost always accurately judge whether children are telling the truth about child abuse.
    TRUE or FALSE

11. Children's testimony is more accurate when they are encouraged to trust the interviewer and told that the interviewer will not try to trick them.
    TRUE or FALSE

12. Children's testimony is more reliable when they are asked questions that have them evaluate alternative hypotheses rather than questions that ask for a single correct answer.
    TRUE or FALSE

13. Child witnesses are more reliable when they are questioned repeatedly on a single issue.
    TRUE or FALSE

14. By 2 years of age, children usually know some number words and have begun to count.
    TRUE or FALSE

15. The cardinality principle refers to the principle that there must be one and only one number name for each object that is counted.
    TRUE or FALSE

16. The Chinese, Japanese, and Korean number systems are more regular than the English system, helping to explain why children learn to count sooner in Asian countries than in the U.S.
    TRUE or FALSE

# 4.3 MIND AND CULTURE: VYGOTSKY'S THEORY

## TO MASTER THE LEARNING OBJECTIVES:

**What is the zone of proximal development? How does it help explain how children accomplish more when they collaborate with others?**

- Describe Vygotsky's zone of proximal development.

**What is a particularly effective way of teaching youngsters new tasks?**

- Describe how "teachers" use scaffolding to aid learning.

- How does scaffolding differ in different cultures?

**When and why do children talk to themselves as they solve problems?**

- Describe the process by which private speech becomes inner speech. What function does private speech serve?

# 4.3 KNOW THE TERMS

**Private speech**                                           **Zone of proximal development**

**Scaffolding**

1. The difference between what someone can do with assistance and what she can do by herself is called _____ .

2. A teaching style in which teachers gauge the amount of assistance that they offer to the learner's needs is called _____ .

3. Comments that are not intended for others but serve the purpose of helping children regulate their behavior are known as _____ .

# 4.3 KNOW THE DETAILS OF VYGOTSKY'S THEORY

1. According to Vygotsky, children progress faster developmentally when they collaborate with more skilled persons than when they learn on their own.
   TRUE or FALSE

2. The zone of proximal development is the area between children's capability when working alone and their performance when working with the guidance of a more skilled person.
   TRUE or FALSE

3. Vygotsky proposed that cognition is initially under the child's independent control and then gradually begins functioning in a social setting as well.
   TRUE or FALSE

4. Children require more scaffolding with a familiar task than with a novel task.
   TRUE or FALSE

5. Private speech is an intermediate step toward self-regulation of cognitive skills.
   TRUE or FALSE

6.  As children gain greater skill, private speech becomes "inner speech."
    TRUE or FALSE

# 4.4 LANGUAGE

## TO MASTER THE LEARNING OBJECTIVES:

**When do infants first hear and make speech sounds?**

- Define phonemes.

- Describe how habituation is used to determine if infants can distinguish different speech sounds.

- Describe how an infant's ability to discriminate speech sounds that are not found in her language environments changes as she approaches her first birthday.

- Explain how infants identify words.

- Define infant-directed speech and describe how the features of this type of speech might aid language development.

**When do children start to talk? Why?**

- Define cooing, babbling, and intonation and describe how each changes during the first year of life.

- Describe some early words that are found in young children's vocabularies.

- Explain why recognizing words as symbols is important for language development.

**How do youngsters learn the meanings of words?**

- Define fast mapping and describe the rules that children use to learn new words.

- Know the difference between overextensions and underextensions.

- Define phonological memory.

- Describe the importance of the child's language environment.

- Describe how bilingual children differ from monolingual children.

- Know the difference between referential and expressive word learning styles.

- Explain how parents and television are related to children's language growth.

**How do young children progress from two-word speech to more complex sentences?**

- Define telegraphic speech, grammatical morphemes, and overregularization and explain how they are related to each other.

- Explain behaviorist, linguistic, cognitive, and social-interaction explanations of children's mastery of grammar.

**How well do youngsters communicate?**

- Explain how turn-taking changes in 1- to 3-year-olds.

- Describe how preschoolers adjust their messages to listeners' different needs.

- Describe how listening skills change over the preschool and elementary school years.

# 4.4 KNOW THE TERMS

| | |
|---|---|
| **Babbling** | **Overregularization** |
| **Cooing** | **Phonemes** |
| **Expressive** | **Phonological memory** |
| **Fast mapping** | **Referential** |
| **Grammatical morphemes** | **Telegraphic** |
| **Infant-directed** | **Underextension** |
| **Overextension** | |

1. Unique speech sounds that can be used to create words are called _____ .

2. Speech that adults use with babies that is slow, loud, and has exaggerated changes in pitch is called _____ speech.

3. Early vowel-like sounds that babies produce are known as _____ .

4. Speech-like sounds that consist of a vowel-consonant combination are known as _____ .

5. The fact that children make connections between new words and referents so quickly that they can't be considering all possible meanings is known as _____ .

6. An _____ occurs when children define a word too broadly.

7. An _____ occurs when children define a word too narrowly.

8. The ability to remember speech sounds briefly is called _____

9. Vocabularies of children who use a(n) _____ language style are dominated by names of objects, persons, or actions.

10. Vocabularies of children who use a(n) _____ language style include many social phrases that are used like a single word.

11. Young children often use _____ speech, which contains only the words that are directly relevant to meaning, and nothing more.

12. Words or endings of words that make a sentence grammatical are known as _____ .

13. Applying grammatical rules to words that are exceptions to the rules is known as _____ .

# 4.4 KNOW THE DETAILS OF LANGUAGE DEVELOPMENT

1. Infants can distinguish speech sounds by as early as one month after birth.
   TRUE or FALSE

2. Young infants can discriminate speech sounds that do not occur in their native language, but they later lose this ability.
   TRUE or FALSE

3. When using infant-directed speech, adults speak quickly and in a monotone voice.
   TRUE or FALSE

4. Infants begin to babble before they are able to coo.
   TRUE or FALSE

5. Infants typically understand many words before they can say them.
   TRUE or FALSE

6. Fast mapping refers to the fact that children make connections between new words and referents so rapidly that they cannot be considering all possible meanings for the new word.
   TRUE or FALSE

7. Toddlers are more likely to learn the name of an object when adults look at the object while saying its name instead of looking elsewhere.
   TRUE or FALSE

8. When children are learning new words, they usually follow the rule that if an unfamiliar word is heard in the presence of objects that already have names and those that don't, the word refers to one of the objects that doesn't already have a name.
   TRUE or FALSE

9. When children define a word too narrowly, it is referred to as an underextension.
   TRUE or FALSE

10. Children with an expressive language learning style have vocabularies that are dominated by words that are the names of objects, persons, and actions.
    TRUE or FALSE

11. Preschool children who often watch Sesame Street typically have larger vocabularies in kindergarten than do preschoolers who watch Sesame Street less often.
TRUE or FALSE

12. Phonemes are words or endings of words that make a sentence grammatical.
TRUE or FALSE

13. Overregularization occurs when children apply rules to words that are exceptions to the rule.
TRUE or FALSE

14. Parents do not usually encourage conversational turn-taking until their children have said their first words.
TRUE or FALSE

15. By the time they are preschoolers, children have begun to adjust their speech to match the listener and the context.
TRUE or FALSE

16. Preschoolers are able to recognize when a message is ambiguous and will ask for clarification.
TRUE or FALSE

# SUMMARY

## 4.1 THE ONSET OF THINKING: PIAGET'S ACCOUNT

1. **Basic Principles of Cognitive Development**

   In Piaget's view, children construct their own understanding of the world by creating _____ , categories of related events, objects, and knowledge. Infants' schemes are based on _____ , but older children's and adolescents' schemes are based on functional, _____ , and abstract properties. Schemes change constantly. In _____ , experiences are readily incorporated into existing schemes. In _____ , experiences cause schemes to be modified. When accommodation becomes more common than assimilation, this is a sign that children's schemes are inadequate, so children reorganize them. This reorganization produces four different phases of mental development from infancy through adulthood.

2. **Sensorimotor Thinking**

   The first two years of life constitute Piaget's sensorimotor period. Over these two years, infants begin to adapt to and explore their environment, understand objects, and begin to use _____

3. **Preoperational Thinking**

From 2 to 7 years of age, children are in Piaget's preoperational stage. Although now capable of using symbols, their thinking is limited by _____ , the inability to see the world from another's point of view. Preoperational children also are _____ in their thinking and sometimes confuse appearance with _____ .

4.  **Evaluating Piaget's Theory**

    One important contribution of Piaget's theory is the view that children _____ try to understand their world. Another contribution is specifying conditions for cognitive development. However, the theory has been criticized because children's performance on tasks is sometimes better explained by ideas that are not part of his theory. Another shortcoming is that children's performance from one task to the next is not as _____ as the theory predicts it to be.

5.  **Extending Piaget's Account:  Children's Naive Theories**

    In contrast to Piaget's idea that children create a comprehensive theory that integrates all knowledge, the modern view is that children are _____ , generating naive theories in particular domains, including physics and biology. Infants understand many properties of objects; they know how objects move, what happens when objects collide, and that objects fall when not supported. Infants understand the difference between animate and inanimate objects. As preschoolers, children know that, unlike inanimate objects, animate objects move themselves, grow, have distinct internal parts, resemble their parents, and repair through healing.

## 4.2 INFORMATION-PROCESSING DURING INFANCY AND EARLY CHILDHOOD

1.  **General Principles of Information Processing**

    According to the information-processing view, mental development involves changes in mental _____ and in mental software.

2.  **Attention**

    Infants use habituation to filter unimportant stimuli. Compared to older children, preschoolers are less able to pay _____ to task-relevant information. Their attention can be improved by making irrelevant stimuli less noticeable.

3.  **Learning**

    Infants are capable of many different forms of learning, including classical conditioning, operant conditioning, and _____ .

4. **Memory**

Infants can remember and can be reminded of events that they seem to have forgotten. _____ emerges in the preschool years, in part, due to parents' _____ children about past events. Preschoolers are sometimes asked to testify in cases of child abuse. When they are questioned repeatedly, preschoolers often have difficulty distinguishing what they really _____ from what others may suggest that they have experienced. Inaccuracies of this sort can be minimized by following certain guidelines when interviewing children, such as warning children that interviewers may try to _____ them.

5. **Learning Number Skills**

Infants are able to distinguish small quantities, such as "twoness" from _____ . By 3 years of age, youngsters can count small sets of objects, and in so doing, adhere to the _____ , stable-order, and _____ principles. Learning to count to larger numbers involves learning rules about unit and decade names. This learning is more difficult for English-speaking children compared to children from Asian countries, because names for numbers in English are irregular.

## 4.3 MIND AND CULTURE: VYGOTSKY'S THEORY

1. **The Zone of Proximal Development**

Vygotsky believed that cognition develops first in a social setting and only gradually comes under the child's independent control. The difference between what children can do with assistance and what they can do alone constitutes the _____ .

2. **Scaffolding**

Control of cognitive skills is most readily transferred to the child through scaffolding, a teaching style in which teachers let children take on _____ of a task as they master its different components. Scaffolding is common worldwide, but the specific techniques for scaffolding children's learning _____ from one cultural setting to the next.

3. **Private Speech**

Children often talk to themselves, particularly when the task is difficult or after they have made a mistake. Such _____ is one way that children help to regulate their own behavior and represents an intermediate step in the transfer of control of thinking from the others to the self.

## 4.4 LANGUAGE

1. **The Road to Speech**

    _____ are the basic units of sound from which words are constructed. Infants can hear phonemes soon after birth. They can even hear phonemes that are not used in their native language, but this ability _____ after the first birthday. Infant-directed speech refers to adults' speech to infants that is _____ and that has greater variation in pitch and loudness. Infants prefer infant-directed speech, perhaps because it gives them additional language clues. Newborns' communication is limited to crying, but at about 3 months of age, babies _____ . Babbling soon follows, consisting of a single syllable; over several months, infants' babbling includes longer syllables and _____ .

2. **First Words and Many More**

    After a brief period in which children appear to understand other's speech but do not speak themselves, most infants will begin to speak around the _____ . The first use of words is triggered by the realization that words are _____ . Soon after, vocabulary expands rapidly. Most children learn the meanings of words much too rapidly for them to consider all plausible meanings systematically. Instead, children use a number of rules to determine probable meanings of new words. The rules do not always lead to the correct meaning. An _____ is a child's meaning that is narrower than an adult's meaning, and an overextension is a child's meaning that is broader. Individual children differ in the size of their vocabularies. These differences are attributable to _____ and the quality of the language environment. Bilingual children learn language readily and have a better understanding of the _____ nature of words. Some youngsters use a referential style that emphasizes words as names and that views language as an intellectual tool. Other children use an _____ style that emphasizes phrases and that views language as a social tool. Children's vocabulary is stimulated by experience. Both parents and television can foster the growth of vocabulary: The key ingredient is actively involving children in language-related activities.

3. **Speaking in Sentences: Grammatical Development**

    Soon after children speak, they create two-word sentences that are derived from their own experiences. Moving from two-word to more complex sentences involves adding grammatical _____ . Children first master grammatical morphemes that express simple relations, then those that denote complex relations. Mastery of grammatical morphemes involves learning rules as well as the

_____ to the rules. Some linguists claim that grammar is too complex for children to learn solely from their experience; instead, the brain must be pre-wired to learn language. However, language experience is important. Children try to infer grammatical rules from speech that they hear, and parents provide children with _____ concerning these tentative rules.

4. **Communicating with Others**

Parents encourage _____ even before infants talk and, later, demonstrate both the speaker and listener roles for their children. By 3 years of age, children spontaneously take turns and prompt one another to take their turn. Preschool children adjust their speech in a rudimentary fashion to fit the listener's _____ . However, preschoolers are unlikely to identify the shortcomings in another's speech; instead, they are more likely to assume that they knew what the speaker meant.

# TEST YOURSELF

## MULTIPLE-CHOICE QUESTIONS

1. In Piaget's theory, psychological structures that organize experience are called
   a. schemes.
   b. scripts.
   c. scaffolding.
   d. mental software.

2. According to Piaget, intellectual adaptation occurs through
   a. the processes of accommodation and assimilation.
   b. the process of maturation.
   c. the formation of associations between stimuli and responses.
   d. imitation of others.

3. When new experiences are easily fit into existing schemes, Piaget would say that _____ is taking place.
   a. fast mapping
   b. assimilation
   c. accommodation
   d. overextension

4.  Two-year-old Joey played with many soft and furry stuffed animals, picking them up by their ears and dragging them around the house. Joey's parents gave him a real live soft and furry puppy for his birthday. Joey tried to pick her up by her ears and drag her around the house. The puppy wiggled and whimpered. Joey decided he was going to have to change his scheme for playing with soft and furry objects. Piaget would say that this is an example of
    a.  overregularization.
    b.  assimilation.
    c.  accommodation.
    d.  habituation.

5.  Which of the following shows Piaget's periods of cognitive development in their proper sequence?
    a.  preoperational, concrete operational, sensorimotor, formal operational
    b.  sensorimotor, preoperational, formal operational, concrete operational
    c.  sensorimotor, preoperational, concrete operational, formal operational
    d.  preoperational, sensorimotor, formal operational, concrete operational

6.  The end of the sensorimotor period is marked by
    a.  reflexive responding.
    b.  the ability to use mental symbols.
    c.  the absence of object permanence.
    d.  unintentional behavior.

7.  Piaget's concept of egocentrism is *best* illustrated by which of the following?
    a.  5-year-old Katie preening in front of a mirror
    b.  4-year-old Kelly holding a picture in front of the television so Big Bird can see it
    c.  6-year-old Kaitlin calling her friend Kara every day to see if she can play
    d.  3-year-old Kaylie believing that she becomes a princess when she puts on a crown

8.  Which of the following statements *best* demonstrates Piaget's concept of animism?
    a.  "Greg hates cats."
    b.  "Brian is terribly bull-headed."
    c.  "Gary claimed the ball was tired and just didn't want to go in the basket."
    d.  "Carson flew like a bird down to the end of the court."

9.  Which of the following is *not* a characteristic of preoperational thinking?
    a.  ability to distinguish between appearance and reality
    b.  egocentrism
    c.  animism
    d.  centration

10. Confusion between appearance and reality is a characteristic of
    a.  sensorimotor thinking.
    b.  concrete operational thinking.
    c.  preoperational thinking.
    d.  formal operational thinking.

11. Which of the following is *not* a criticism of Piaget's theory of cognitive development?
    a. Piaget's theory is too narrow and would be more useful if it were more comprehensive.
    b. Alternative explanations may give better explanations for children's performances on Piaget's tasks.
    c. Children's performance across several of Piaget's tasks is less consistent than it should be according to Piaget's theory.
    d. Infants have some understanding of the permanence of objects at a much younger age than Piaget's theory would predict.

12. The idea that infants are born with rudimentary knowledge of the world, with the knowledge being elaborated based on the children's experience, is known as
    a. adaptation.
    b. equilibration.
    c. scaffolding.
    d. the core knowledge hypothesis.

13. Preschool children's naive theories of biology include all of the following EXCEPT
    a. thinking that inanimate objects can move by themselves.
    b. understanding that living things have offspring that resemble their parents.
    c. believing that animals get bigger but inanimate objects do not grow.
    d. thinking that only living things have offspring that resemble their parents.

14. The information processing view
    a. proposes that cognitive development occurs in a sequence of four stages.
    b. considers adaptation to be the primary mechanism for development.
    c. compares human cognition to computer hardware and software.
    d. is based on behavioral learning theory.

15. Mental programs that are the basis for performing particular tasks are called mental
    a. hardware.
    b. software.
    c. adaptations.
    d. scaffolding.

16. When Michael first saw the shiny red car, he couldn't take his eyes off it. After seeing it several times, he paid less attention to it. His diminished response is due to
    a. attention.
    b. habituation.
    c. an orienting response.
    d. operant conditioning.

17. Gayle wants to teach her 4-year-old daughter, Molly, to write her name. However, every time they sit down at the kitchen table to practice, Gayle cannot get Molly to pay attention long enough to write anything. What advice would be most appropriate to give Gayle?
    a. Give up on trying to get Molly to write her name for now. Molly is not yet capable of paying attention for any length of time.
    b. Try to make the work area more interesting and attractive by adding lots of pictures, bright colors, and manipulative objects.
    c. Don't keep telling Molly to practice her name. Let her try it only when she chooses.
    d. Try working in a quieter, less distracting area with fewer people around.

18. Gabby learned that when her mother showed her a bottle that was an indication that she would soon be fed, so she would get excited whenever she saw a bottle. This is best explained through the process called
    a. habituation.
    b. the orienting response.
    c. classical conditioning.
    d. operant conditioning.

19. In her work on infant memory, Carolyn Rovee-Collier found that 3-month-old infants who learned to kick a mobile to make it move
    a. were able to remember to kick to make the mobile move a few days later.
    b. were able to remember to kick to make the mobile move several weeks later only if they were given cues.
    c. were never able to remember to kick to make the mobile move any time after the day they were taught.
    d. never forgot that kicking made the mobile move.

20. Joshua remembers many details about his 6th birthday party. This would be considered
    a. an autobiographical memory.
    b. an orienting response.
    c. habituation.
    d. attention.

21. Which of the following guidelines concerning the reliability of child witnesses is supported by research?
    a. Use questions with a single, correct answer instead of questions that evaluate alternative hypotheses.
    b. Question children repeatedly on a single issue.
    c. Warn children that interviewers may sometimes try to trick them or suggest things that didn't happen.
    d. Always trust what the child says. In a courtroom situation, children are unlikely to say something happened unless it actually did happen.

22. The cardinality principle states that
    a. there must be one and only one number name for each object that is counted.
    b. number names must be counted in the same order.
    c. the last number name differs from the previous ones in a counting sequence in denoting the number of objects.
    d. numbers can differ in magnitude; some values are greater than others.

23. Sonja understands that number names must be counted in the same order. Sonja has mastered the
    a. one-to-one principle.
    b. cardinality principle.
    c. ordinality principle.
    d. stable-order principle.

24. Learning to count beyond 10 is most complicated in
    a. China.
    b. Japan.
    c. Korea.
    d. the United States.

25. Vygotsky provided
    a. a complete theory of cognitive development from birth through adolescence.
    b. definitive accounts of cognitive change in specific domains.
    c. a view of development as an apprenticeship.
    d. a perspective of human thinking based on mental hardware and mental software.

26. Five-year-old Winnie was unable to arrange the furniture in her dollhouse by herself. However, she was able to completely arrange the furniture when her mother helped her sort the furniture by room and then suggested that she work on one room at a time. The difference between what Winnie was able to do on her own and what she could do with her mother's help is called
    a. her zone of proximal development.
    b. scaffolding.
    c. equilibration.
    d. habituation.

27. Scaffolding refers to
    a. the difference between what someone can do with and without assistance.
    b. a style in which teachers gauge the amount of assistance that they offer to match a learner's needs.
    c. comments children make that are not intended for others, but, instead, are designed to help them regulate their own behavior.
    d. cognition that is under the child's independent control.

28. Children are more likely to use private speech
    a. after a correct response than after a mistake.
    b. on difficult tasks than on easy tasks.
    c. when they are skilled rather than unskilled at a task.
    d. when their behavior is being regulated by speech from other people.

29. The sound of "p" in the word "put" and the sound of "a" in "cat" are both
    a. morphemes.
    b. phonemes.
    c. underextensions.
    d. overextensions.

30. _____ involves speaking more slowly and with exaggerated changes in pitch and loudness.
    a. An overextension
    b. Babbling
    c. Cooing
    d. Infant-directed speech

31. At two months of age, babies start making vowel-like sounds such as "ooooooo" and "ahhhhhh," which are called
    a. babbling.
    b. intonation.
    c. cooing.
    d. infant-directed speech.

32. Infants' babbling
    a. has the same pattern of intonation regardless of the language spoken by their caregivers.
    b. is influenced by the characteristics of the speech that they hear.
    c. is the same in deaf and hearing infants.
    d. first consists of consonant sounds and then progresses to include vowel sounds.

33. Infants
    a. say their first words at about the same time that they can understand them.
    b. usually understand words before they are able to say them.
    c. usually say words before they understand them.
    d. differ in whether they first understand or say words.

34. A child's ability to make connections between new words and referents so rapidly that they cannot be considering all possible meaning for the new word is referred to as
    a. overregularization.
    b. underextension.
    c. overextension.
    d. fast mapping.

35. Which of the following is a correct statement concerning the rules children use to learn new words?
    a. If an unfamiliar word is heard in the presence of objects that already have names and objects that don't, the word refers to one of the objects that doesn't have a name.
    b. A name refers to a part of an object, not the whole object.
    c. A name refers to one particular object, not to all objects of the same type.
    d. If an object already has a name and another name is presented, the new name is incorrect.

36. Eighteen-month-old Shannon saw an older woman with gray hair and called her "Grandma" even though she was not her grandmother. Shannon made a mistake common to young children which is called
    a. telegraphic speech.
    b. overregularization.
    c. an overextension.
    d. an underextension.

37. Children whose vocabularies are dominated by words that are the names of objects, persons, or actions have a(n) _____ language learning style.
    a. expressive
    b. overextension
    c. underextension
    d. referential

38. Children whose vocabularies include some names but also many social phrases that are used like a single word have a(n) _____ language learning style.
    a. expressive
    b. referential
    c. overextension
    d. underextension

39. Which of the following should parents do to expand their children's vocabulary?
    a. When reading stories, simply read the story and don't ask children any questions.
    b. Speak to their children infrequently.
    c. Name objects that are the focus of the children's attention.
    d. Do not allow children to watch Sesame Street on television.

40. Two-year-old Tyler speaks in sentences such as "Me go" instead of "I want to go," and "She sleep" instead of "She is sleeping." Tyler is using
    a. telegraphic speech.
    b. overregularization.
    c. fast mapping.
    d. grammatical morphemes.

41. Language is learned through imitation and reinforcement according to
    a. linguistic theorists.
    b. cognitive theorists.
    c. social-interaction theorists.
    d. behavioral theorists.

42. Professor Rubenstein stated that children are born with neural circuits in their brains that allows them to learn language. What viewpoint is Professor Rubenstein conveying?
    a. social-interaction
    b. cognitive
    c. linguistic
    d. behaviorist

## ESSAY QUESTIONS

1. The other day your friend Jamal and his 3-year-old daughter, Kia, were at the local shopping mall, and they saw an older woman who looked like the witch in The Wizard of Oz. Kia pointed at the woman and said, "Look, Dad, there's a witch. She's really mean." Jamal tried to explain to Kia that the woman wasn't a witch and, in fact, she probably is very nice, but Kia insisted that the woman was a witch and

that she is very mean. Jamal would like to convince Kia that you "can't judge a book by its cover," but Kia is adamant every time he brings up the subject. What can you tell Jamal about preoperational children's ability to distinguish appearance and reality that might make him feel better?

2. Your 7-month-old son, Matt, loves to play with the remote control for the television. He loves to hear people shout when he changes the channel or turns off the TV in the middle of a show. You remember from your college developmental psychology class that Piaget said that 7-month-olds do not have object permanence. In other words, "out of sight, out of mind." You decide that you will thwart your son and hide the remote control because he doesn't have object permanence. Your spouse, however, has seen new research that suggests that object permanence develops much earlier than Piaget suggested and thinks that Matt will look for the control if you hide it behind a pillow on the couch. Describe the research that demonstrates that object permanence may occur much earlier than Piaget suggested.

3. A teacher at your child's daycare center recently has been accused of child molestation by a 3-year-old girl at the daycare. You are talking with one of the other parents and this other parent said, "It must have happened because no child would make up a story like that." What can you tell this other parent about testimony by young children, and what should be done to ensure more reliable testimony from them?

4. Your brother Pretesh is concerned that his 2-year-old daughter's counting ability is below average. When she counts, his daughter will say, "one, two, c, door...door balls" when counting the four balls in a picture book. What can you tell Pretesh about the mastery of the principles of counting that will reassure him that his daughter can count perfectly well for someone her age?

5. You have been watching your friend Collum trying to teach his son Sean how to do a puzzle. Sean has done this puzzle many times, and he usually just needs help with the pieces that are in an area that is all black. Collum is trying to help Sean, but his instructions would be appropriate for someone who has never done the puzzle before. What can you tell Collum about Vygotsky's theory, in general, and scaffolding, in particular, that might help him teach Sean in more effective ways?

6. Your brother and his wife just had a baby and they are wondering when their baby will begin talking. They hope it's soon, and they have begun saying "mama" and "dada" to their baby. What can you tell them about the course of language development during the first year of life?

7. The other day Superna was in the store with her 13-month-old son, Rahul. As they passed a man in the store, Rahul pointed at the man and said, "Daddy." Superna did not know this man and was very embarrassed, and now she is worried that Rahul does not know who his father is. What can you tell Superna about young children's errors in learning the meanings of words that might make her feel better?

# SOLUTIONS

## 4.1 KNOW THE TERMS

1. schemes (132)
2. Assimilation (132)
3. Accommodation (133)
4. equilibration (133)
5. sensorimotor (134)
6. object permanence (134).
7. egocentrism (135)
8. animism (136)
9. centration (137)
10. core knowledge hypothesis (144)

## 4.1 KNOW THE DETAILS OF PIAGET'S THEORY

1. F, (132)
2. F, (132)
3. F, (132)
4. T, (133)
5. F, (134)
6. F, (134)
7. T, (134)
8. T, (134)
9. T, (135)
10. F, (135)
11. T, (138)
12. T, (140)
13. F, (141)
14. T, (142)
15. F, (142)
16. T, (143)
17. T, (144)
18. T, (145)

## 4.2 KNOW THE TERMS

1. hardware (147)
2. software (147)
3. Attention (147)
4. orienting response (147)
5. habituation (147)
6. Classical conditioning (148)
7. Operant conditioning (148)
8. autobiographical memory (150)
9. Ordinality (153)
10. one-to-one (153)
11. stable-order (153)
12. cardinality (153)

## 4.2 KNOW THE DETAILS OF INFORMATION PROCESSING

1. T, (147)
2. T, (147)
3. F, (147)
4. F, (148)
5. F, (148)
6. T, (148)
7. F, (149)
8. T, (150)
9. F, (150)
10. F, (151)
11. F, (152)
12. T, (152)
13. F, (152)
14. T, (153)
15. F, (153)
16. T, (154)

## 4.3 KNOW THE TERMS

1. zone of proximal development (155)

2. scaffolding (155)    3. private speech (156)

## 4.3 KNOW THE DETAILS OF VYGOTSKY'S THEORY

1. T, (155)    3. F, (155)    5. T, (156)
2. T, (155)    4. F, (156)    6. T, (156)

## 4.4 KNOW THE TERMS

1. phonemes (158)    6. overextension (164)    11. telegraphic (167)
2. infant-directed (159)    7. underextension (164)    12. grammatical morphemes (167)
3. cooing (160)    8. phonological memory (165)    13. overregularization (168)
4. babbling (160)    9. referential (165)
5. fast mapping (162)    10. expressive (166)

## 4.4 KNOW THE DETAILS OF LANGUAGE DEVELOPMENT

1. T, (158)    7. T, (163)    13. T, (168)
2. T, (158)    8. T, (163)    14. F, (169)
3. F, (159)    9. T, (164)    15. T, (171)
4. F, (160)    10. F, (165)    16. F, (171)
5. T, (161)    11. T, (166)
6. T, (162)    12. F, (167)

## SUMMARY

### 4.1 THE ONSET OF THINKING: PIAGET'S ACCOUNT

1. schemes (132); actions (132); conceptual (132); assimilation (132); accommodation (133)
2. symbols (135)
3. egocentrism (135); centered (137); reality (138)
4. actively (140); consistent (143)
5. specialists (144)

### 4.2 INFORMATION-PROCESSING DURING INFANCY AND EARLY CHILDHOOD

1. hardware (147)
2. attention (148)
3. imitation (149)
4. Autobiographical memory (150); questioning (151); experienced (151); trick (152)
5. threeness (153); one-to-one (153); cardinality (153)

### 4.3 MIND AND CULTURE: VYGOTSKY'S THEORY

1. zone of proximal development (155)

2. more (156); vary (156)   3. private speech (156)

## 4.4 LANGUAGE

1. Phonemes (158); diminishes (158); slower (159); coo (160); intonation (160)

2. first birthday (161); symbols (161); underextension (164); phonological memory (165); arbitrary (165); expressive (166)

3. morphemes (167); exceptions (168); feedback (169)

4. turn-taking (170); needs (171)

# TEST YOURSELF

## MULTIPLE-CHOICE QUESTIONS

| | | |
|---|---|---|
| 1. A, (132) | 15. B, (147) | 29. B, (158) |
| 2. A, (132) | 16. B, (147) | 30. D, (159) |
| 3. B, (132) | 17. D, (148) | 31. C, (160) |
| 4. C, (133) | 18. C, (148) | 32. B, (160) |
| 5. C, (133) | 19. A, (149) | 33. B, (161) |
| 6. B, (135) | 20. A, (150) | 34. D, (162) |
| 7. B, (135) | 21. C, (152) | 35. A, (163) |
| 8. C, (136) | 22. C, (153) | 36. C, (164) |
| 9. A, (138) | 23. D, (153) | 37. D, (165) |
| 10. C, (138) | 24. D, (153) | 38. A, (166) |
| 11. A, (140) | 25. C, (155) | 39. C, (166) |
| 12. D, (144) | 26. A, (155) | 40. A, (167) |
| 13. A, (145) | 27. B, (155) | 41. D, (168) |
| 14. C, (147) | 28. B, (156) | 42. C, (168) |

## ESSAY QUESTIONS

1. Preoperational children cannot distinguish between what something "looks like" and what something "really is." For example, if someone "really is" angry but she "looks like" she is happy, preoperational children will say that she "looks like" she is happy and she "really is" happy. Difficulty in distinguishing appearance and reality is a deep-seated characteristic of preoperational thought. So, Jamal should take some comfort in the fact that Kia is like other children her age, and no matter how much he discusses the issue, he isn't likely to change her mind. (138-139)

2. Piaget said that object permanence is not fully developed until about 18 months of age. Piaget said that at 4 or 5 months, infants would search for hidden objects, but even at 9 months infants aren't very effective searchers. Piaget believed that this ineffective searching indicated their poor object permanence. More recent research by Renée Baillargeon indicates that object permanence that does not involve searching is consistently evident in 4 ½-month-olds. Baillargeon showed infants a screen that rotated back and forth. After familiarizing the infants with this display, the infants saw either an impossible event or a possible event. The possible event involved placing a box behind the rotating screen. When the screen touched the box, it stopped. The impossible event again involved placing the box behind the screen, but this time the rotating screen rotated back until it was flat--an impossible event if the box is behind the screen. If a baby does not have object permanence, this event is no different from the rotating screen without the box that they saw at the beginning of the experiment. If a baby does have object permanence, then he should look longer at the impossible event because it defies his expectations. So, Matt should have object permanence but may give up his search for the remote if you hide it well enough. (142-143)

3.  Young children also tend confuse the source of memories and thoughts so that they are unsure if they are remembering an actual event or an event that someone has suggested may have happened. Preschoolers also are more likely to agree with authority figures if they are confused about events. So, the questioning that is part of a child abuse investigation can confuse a child and can lead the child into believing that what really happened is the event that the questioning adults think happened. Unfortunately, research has shown that many professionals who become involved in child abuse cases cannot distinguish children who are telling the truth from those who are not. Before being interviewed, children should be warned that the interviewer may try to trick them or may suggest things that did not happen. The interviewers should test many alternative hypotheses and not use a series of questions that imply a single, correct answer. Interviewers also should avoid repeatedly questioning a child on a single issue which often implies that one gave the wrong answer the first time. (151-152)

4.  You can reassure your brother that your niece is doing well in the area of counting. Most children begin counting around their second birthday and have mastered the counting principles around 5 years of age. Your niece has mastered the one-to-one principle in which she assigns one and only one number name to each object to be counted. She also has mastered the stable-order principle in which the same names for numbers are used in a consistent order. Your niece also seems to understand that the last number name denotes the number of items in the set (the cardinality principle). In other words, your niece's mastery of counting principles is more advanced than most two-year-olds. Tell your brother to relax. Your niece has plenty of time to learn the real number names. (153-154)

5.  According to Vygotsky's principle of zone of proximal development, Sean will do better on the puzzle if he is assisted by someone who has more puzzle-building expertise than he does. However, according to the concept of scaffolding, a skilled teacher will gauge his instruction to the learner's needs. In other words, a beginner should get more instruction than someone who is close to mastering a task. Sean is close to mastering this puzzle, and Collum should stop providing so much instruction and should only provide help on the section where Sean needs help. (155-156)

6.  Your brother and sister-in-law will have a few months to wait because most babies do not say their first words until around their first birthdays. However, during the next year, they should see their baby producing many different sounds. Around 3 months of age, their baby should start producing vowel-like sounds called cooing. Around 4 or 5 months, the baby should start combining these vowel-like sounds with consonants to produce babbling syllables. At first, these syllables will be produced alone (e.g., "ma" or "ba"), and later, these syllables will be repeated (e.g., "mamamama" or "bababa") and combined (e.g., "damaba"). Later, infants' babbling sounds more like speech because they vary the pitch. This intonation will mimic the intonation found in the language that the child hears. Finally, around the first birthday, the baby will say her first word. (160-161)

7.  When children are learning the meanings of many new words it is not uncommon for them to make errors. Two common errors are underextensions and overextensions. When children underextend word meanings they use a much narrower than accepted meaning of the word. For example, the child might have learned the word "dog" in the context of his parents referring to the family dog. When the child underextends the meaning of "dog" he might not realize that other 4-legged, furry, animals that bark are also dogs, but might mistakenly believe that the word "dog" refers only to his dog. Similarly, when children overextend word meanings they use a much broader meaning of the word than is normally accepted. In Rahul's case, he learned that "Daddy" refers to an adult male. Rahul does not realize yet that the word "Daddy" is usually used when referring to one's father. So, when Rahul called the unfamiliar adult male "Daddy" he was only overextending the meaning of the word "Daddy." Superna should realize that even though Rahul's behavior was embarrassing, it was typical of a child his age who overextends the meaning of words. (164-165)

# ENTERING THE SOCIAL WORLD

5.1 Beginnings: Trust and Attachment

5.2 Emerging Emotions

5.3 Interacting with Others

5.4 Gender Roles and Gender Identity

This chapter discusses the development of attachment, the development of emotions, the development of social relationships, and the development of gender roles.

# 5.1 BEGINNINGS: TRUST AND ATTACHMENT

## TO MASTER THE LEARNING OBJECTIVES:

**What are Erikson's first three stages of psychosocial development?**

*   Describe Erikson's trust versus mistrust crisis and explain why establishing trust is important for later development.

*   Describe Erikson's autonomy versus shame and doubt crisis and explain how the resolution of this crisis is related to the development of will.

*   Describe how purpose comes from the resolution of initiative versus guilt.

**How do infants form an emotional attachment to mother, father, and other significant people in their lives?**

*   Explain the importance of attachment according to evolutionary psychology.

*   Describe the development of attachment starting with preattachment.

*   Describe the differences in how mothers and fathers interact with their infants.

**What are the different varieties of attachment relationships, how do they arise, and what are their consequences?**

- Explain the differences between secure attachment, avoidant attachment, resistant attachment, and disorganized attachment.
- Describe evidence that supports the view that secure attachment relationships are related to better social relationships later in childhood.
- Describe how parental responsivity and sensitivity are related to the quality of attachment.
- Explain how the temperament of the infant and the personality of the mother are related to the quality of attachment.

**Is attachment jeopardized when parents of infants and young children are employed outside of the home?**

- Describe the effects of day care on attachment.
- Describe the factors that one should look for when searching for quality daycare.

## 5.1 KNOW THE TERMS

| | |
|---|---|
| **Attachment** | **Internal working model** |
| **Avoidant** | **Purpose** |
| **Disorganized** | **Resistant** |
| **Evolutionary psychology** | **Secure** |
| **Hope** | **Will** |

1. _____ , an openness to new experience tempered by wariness, occurs when trust and mistrust are in balance.

2. _____ , the knowledge that a young child has that she can act on the world intentionally, which occurs when autonomy, shame, and doubt are in balance.

3. A balance between individual initiative and the willingness to cooperate with others is _____ .

4. _____ suggests that many human behaviors represent successful adaptation to the environment.

5. _____ is an enduring social-emotional relationship between an infant and an adult.

6. As measured by the Strange Situation, young children who have a _____ attachment relationship with their mothers will want to be near the mother when they are reunited following a brief separation.

7. Infants who ignore or turn away from their mothers when they are reunited following a brief separation have _____ attachment relationships.

8. Infants who remain upset or angry and are difficult to console when they are reunited with their mothers following a brief separation have _____ attachment relationships.

9. Infants who don't seem to understand what's happening when they are separated and subsequently reunited with their mothers have _____ attachment relationships.

10. An _____ is a set of expectations about parents' availability and responsiveness, generally and in times of stress.

# 5.1 KNOW THE DETAILS OF ATTACHMENT

1. According to Erikson, infants must deal with the crisis of initiative versus guilt during the first year of life.
   TRUE or FALSE

2. Erikson stated that, with a proper balance of trust and mistrust, infants can acquire hope.
   TRUE or FALSE

3. During Erikson's second psychosocial stage, children are striving for independence or autonomy from others.
   TRUE or FALSE

4. At 3 to 5 years of age, children face the crisis of identity versus role confusion.
   TRUE or FALSE

5. John Bowlby's work on attachment is based on ecological theory.
   TRUE or FALSE

6. According to John Bowlby, forming an attachment to an adult makes a child more likely to survive.
   TRUE or FALSE

7. An infant's first attachment figure is usually the mother.
   TRUE or FALSE

8. Infants usually become attached to only one parent.
   TRUE or FALSE

9. Infants usually single out an attachment figure by 7 or 8 months of age.
   TRUE or FALSE

10. Fathers typically spend more time playing with infants than taking care of them.
    TRUE or FALSE

11. When infants are distressed, they prefer being with their mother to being with their father.
    TRUE or FALSE

12. Babies who are securely attached typically ignore the mother when she returns after a brief separation.
    TRUE or FALSE

13. Babies who are securely attached usually become upset when the mother leaves the room and remain upset or angry when she returns after a brief separation.
    TRUE or FALSE

14. The Strange Situation procedure has been criticized for its emphasis on separation and reunion for measuring attachment because the appropriate response may vary by culture.
    TRUE or FALSE

15. Infants who form secure attachments are more likely to have skilled social interactions later in childhood
    TRUE or FALSE

16. An internal working model is a set of expectations infants develop about parents' availability and responsivity.
    TRUE or FALSE

17. Insecure attachment is more likely when parents are sensitive and responsive.
    TRUE or FALSE

18. Temperament has not been found to be related to the quality of attachment.
    TRUE or FALSE

19. Early child care experience does not appear to have an overall effect on mother-infant attachment.
    TRUE or FALSE

# 5.2 EMERGING EMOTIONS

## TO MASTER THE LEARNING OBJECTIVES:

**At what ages do children begin to express basic emotions?**

- Know the basic emotions.
- Describe how physiological responses, facial expressions, and emotions are related to each other.
- Describe the development of positive emotions, such as happiness, and negative emotions, such as anger and fear.

**What are complex emotions and when do they develop?**

- Explain why complex emotions don't emerge until the very end of infancy.

- Describe how the cultural setting influences complex emotions.

**When do children begin to understand other people's emotions? How do they use this information to guide their own behavior?**

- Describe infants' ability to distinguish facial expressions.

- Describe social referencing.

- Describe the development of the ability to regulate one's emotions.

## 5.2 KNOW THE TERMS

| | |
|---|---|
| **Basic emotions** | **Social smiles** |
| **Social referencing** | **Stranger wariness** |

1. The _____ are experienced by people worldwide. They consist of a subjective feeling, a physiological change, and an overt behavior.

2. Around 2 months of age, infants smile when they see another human face. These smiles are called _____ .

3. _____ occurs around 6 months of age when infants become wary in the presence of an unfamiliar adult.

4. Infants use _____ in an unfamiliar or ambiguous situation by looking at their parents as if searching for cues that will help them interpret the situation.

## 5.2 KNOW THE DETAILS OF EMERGING EMOTIONS

1. Joy, anger, and fear are all considered to be basic emotions.
   TRUE or FALSE

2. Infants' facial expressions often reflect the infants' underlying emotional states.
   TRUE or FALSE

3. Social smiles usually first appear when infants are about 8 months old.
   TRUE or FALSE

4. Anger is usually first seen in infants when they are between 4 and 6 months of age.
   TRUE or FALSE

5. Fear is common in newborns.
   TRUE or FALSE

6. Infants tend to be more fearful of strangers in a familiar environment than in an unfamiliar environment.
   TRUE or FALSE

7. Unlike complex emotions, basic emotions have a self-evaluative component in them.
   TRUE or FALSE

8. Guilt, embarrassment, and pride are complex emotions.
   TRUE or FALSE

9. Preschoolers are often afraid of the dark and of imaginary creatures.
   TRUE or FALSE

10. Culture has no influence on emotions.
    TRUE or FALSE

11. Social referencing occurs when infants look to their parents to get cues to help them interpret an unfamiliar or ambiguous situation.
    TRUE or FALSE

12. Emotion regulation begins in infancy.
    TRUE or FALSE

# 5.3 INTERACTING WITH OTHERS

## TO MASTER THE LEARNING OBJECTIVES:

**When do youngsters first begin to play with each other? How does play change during infancy and the preschool years?**

- Describe how peer interactions change during infancy and the preschool years.
- Describe how culture influences make-believe play.
- Describe the benefits of make-believe play.
- Explain how children with imaginary companions differ from those who do not have imaginary companions.
- Know the differences between healthy and unhealthy solitary play.
- Explain how different play styles in boys and girls are related to children choosing same-sex playmates.
- Describe how parents influence children's peer interactions.

**What determines whether preschool children cooperate with one another?**

- Describe how a child's age influences cooperation.

- Describe how observing cooperative behavior and another child's response to cooperative behavior influence cooperative behavior.

- Describe cultural differences in cooperation and competition.

**What determines whether children help one another? What experiences make children more inclined to help?**

- Describe how perspective-taking and empathy are related to altruistic behavior.

- Describe how feelings of responsibility, feelings of competence, mood, and costs of altruism are related to altruistic behavior.

- Explain how parents' disciplinary practices, modeling altruistic behavior, and providing opportunities to behave prosocially are related to children's altruistic behavior.


## 5.3 KNOW THE TERMS

| | |
|---|---|
| **Altruism** | **Enabling** |
| **Constricting** | **Parallel play** |
| **Cooperative** | **Prosocial** |
| **Empathy** | **Simple social play** |

1. _____ occurs when children play alone, but they are aware of and are interested in what another child is doing.

2. Around 15-18 months toddlers will engage in similar activities and will talk and smile at each other. This is called _____ .

3. Around the second birthday, children's play will be organized around a theme, and each child will take on special roles based on the theme during _____ play.

4. Girls' interactions with others typically are _____ because their remarks and actions tend to support others and sustain the interaction.

5. Boys' interactions are often _____ because one boy usually tries to emerge as the victor by threatening, contradicting, or exaggerating.

6. _____ behavior refers to any behavior that benefits another person.

7. _____ refers to behavior such as helping and sharing in which the individual does not benefit directly from her behavior.

8. Actually experiencing another person's feelings is called _____ .

# 5.3 KNOW THE DETAILS OF INTERACTING WITH OTHERS

1. The first signs of peer interaction usually appear at about 6 months of age.
   TRUE or FALSE

2. Parallel play occurs when a distinct theme organizes children's play, and the children take on special roles based on the theme.
   TRUE or FALSE

3. When children play hide-and-seek they are engaged in cooperative play.
   TRUE or FALSE

4. One- to two-year-olds spend most of their time in cooperative play.
   TRUE or FALSE

5. Children who spend much time in make believe play tend to be delayed in their cognitive development.
   TRUE or FALSE

6. Children can learn to overcome some of their fears through the use of make-believe play.
   TRUE or FALSE

7. Children who have imaginary playmates tend to be less sociable and have fewer friends.
   TRUE or FALSE

8. Wandering aimlessly and hovering are healthy forms of solitary play.
   TRUE or FALSE

9. A preference for same-sex peers is common in preschoolers and elementary school children in the United States, but it is unusual in other parts of the world.
   TRUE or FALSE

10. Girls have a more enabling play style than do boys.
    TRUE or FALSE

11. Children play more cooperatively and longer when parents are present than when they are not.
    TRUE or FALSE

12. Cooperation is valued more highly in the Chinese culture than in the North American culture.
    TRUE or FALSE

13. Behavior that is driven by feelings of responsibility toward other people, such as helping and sharing, in which individuals do not benefit directly from their actions, is referred to as prosocial behavior.
    TRUE or FALSE

14. Empathy is positively related to prosocial behavior.
    TRUE or FALSE

15. Parents who use reasoning as a disciplinary style are more likely to have altruistic children.
    TRUE or FALSE

# 5.4 GENDER ROLES AND GENDER IDENTITY

## TO MASTER THE LEARNING OBJECTIVES:

**What are our stereotypes about males and females? How well do they correspond to actual differences between boys and girls?**

- Define social roles.

- Define gender stereotypes and describe how children learn them.

- Describe sex differences in verbal ability, mathematics, spatial ability, social influence, aggression, and emotional sensitivity.

**When do young children understand that gender is fixed? How does this understanding influence their learning about roles for girls and boys?**

- Describe the ways in which parents treat sons and daughters similarly and differently.

- Explain how peers contribute to gender typing.

- Define gender identity and explain how children develop gender identity.

- Explain how the knowledge of gender and gender-typed activities are related to each other.

- Describe the influence of gender schema on behavior and activities.

- Describe the biological influences on gender roles and gender identity.

**How are gender roles changing? What further changes might the future hold?**

- Describe how different aspects of gender stereotyping are influenced by parents and society.

## 5.4 KNOW THE TERMS

Congenital adrenal hyperplasia

Gender constancy

Gender identity

Gender labeling

Gender-schema theory

Gender stability

Gender stereotypes

Relational aggression

Social role

1. A set of cultural guidelines about how one should behave especially with other people is called a
_____ .

2. _____ are beliefs and images about males and females that may or may not be true.

3. Trying to hurt someone by damaging their relationships with peers is called _____ .

4. A sense of oneself as male or female is called _____ .

5. Children's understanding that they are either boys or girls and their ability to label themselves accordingly is called _____ .

6. Children's understanding that boys become men and girls become women is called _____ .

7. The understanding that maleness and femaleness do not change over situations or according to personal wishes is called _____ .

8. According to _____ , children first decide if an activity is associated with males or females, then use this information to determine if they should learn more about the activity.

9. _____ is a genetic disorder in which the adrenal glands secrete large amounts of androgen during prenatal, and later, development.

## 5.4 KNOW THE DETAILS OF GENDER ROLES AND GENDER IDENTITY

1. Gender stereotypes are beliefs and images about males and females that may or may not be true.
TRUE or FALSE

2. Research suggests that males and females often do not differ in the ways specified by cultural stereotypes.
TRUE or FALSE

3. On average, females have higher verbal abilities than males.
TRUE or FALSE

4. Males tend to get higher grades on math achievement tests, but girls often get better grades in math courses.
TRUE or FALSE

5. Females tend to have better spatial ability than males.
TRUE or FALSE

6. Females are typically more compliant and more readily influenced by others than males.
   TRUE or FALSE

7. Males and females typically have similar levels of physical aggression.
   TRUE or FALSE

8. Mothers are more likely than fathers to treat sons and daughters differently.
   TRUE or FALSE

9. Once children learn rules about gender-typical play, they often punish peers who violate those rules.
   TRUE or FALSE

10. Children begin to label themselves as either boys or girls between 5 and 7 years of age.
    TRUE or FALSE

11. Gender constancy refers to the understanding that maleness and femaleness do not change over situations or according to personal wishes.
    TRUE or FALSE

12. In gender schema theory, children first decide if an object, activity, or behavior is female or male, then use this information to decide whether they should learn more about the object, activity, or behavior.
    TRUE or FALSE

13. Congenital adrenal hyperplasia is a genetic disorder in which adrenal glands secrete large amounts of androgen.
    TRUE or FALSE

# SUMMARY

## 5.1 BEGINNINGS: TRUST AND ATTACHMENT

1. **Erikson's Stages of Early Psychosocial Development**

   In Erikson's theory of psychosocial development, individuals face various psychosocial crises at different phases in development. The crisis of infancy is to establish a balance between _____ and mistrust of the world, producing hope. One- to three-year-olds must blend autonomy and _____ to produce will. Three- to five-year-olds must balance initiative and guilt to achieve _____ .

2. **The Growth of Attachment**

   Attachment is an enduring _____ relationship between infant and parent. For both adults and infants, many of the behaviors that contribute to the formation of attachment are biologically programmed. Bowlby's theory of attachment is rooted in _____ and describes four stages in the development of attachment: _____ attachment in the making, true attachment, and

_____ Research with the Strange Situation, in which infant and mother are separated briefly,

reveals four primary forms of attachment. Most common is a _____ attachment, in which

infants have complete trust in the mother. Less common are three types of attachment relationships

in which this trust is lacking. In avoidant relationships, infants deal with this lack of trust by

_____ the mother; in resistant relationships, infants often seem angry with the mother; in

disorganized relationships, infants seem to not _____ the mother's absence. Children who

have had secure attachment relationships during infancy often interact with their peers more readily and

more _____ . Secure attachment is most likely to occur when mothers respond _____

and consistently to their infant's needs.

3.  **Attachment, Work, and Alternate Caregiving**

    Many U.S. children are cared for at home by a father or other relative, in a day-care provider's home, or

    in a day care center. Infants and young children are not harmed by such care as long as the care is

    _____ and parents remain _____ to their children.

## 5.2 EMERGING EMOTIONS

1.  **Experiencing and Expressing Emotions**

    Scientists often use infants' facial expressions to judge when different emotional states emerge in

    development. Basic emotions, which include _____ , anger, and _____ emerge in the

    first year. Fear first appears in infancy as _____ . Complex emotions usually appear between

    18 and 24 months, have an _____ component, and include guilt, _____ , and pride.

    These require more sophisticated _____ skills than basic emotions like happiness and fear.

    Cultures differ in the rules for expressing emotions and the situations that elicit particular emotions.

2.  **Recognizing and Using Others' Emotions**

    By 6 months of age, infants have begun to recognize the emotions associated with different

    _____ . They use this information to help evaluate _____ situations. Beyond

    infancy, children understand the causes and consequences of different emotions and that people can feel

    multiple emotions simultaneously, and the rules for displaying emotions appropriately.

3.  **Regulating Emotions**

Infants use simple strategies to regulate emotions such as fear. As children grow, they become better skilled at regulating their emotions. Children who do not regulate emotions well tend to have problems interacting with others.

## 5.3 INTERACTING WITH OTHERS

1. **The Joys of Play**

   Even infants notice and respond to one another, but the first real interactions, at about 12 to 15 months, take the form of _____ play, in which toddlers play alone while watching each other. A few months later, simple social play emerges, in which toddlers engage in similar activities and interact with one another. At about 2 years of age, _____ play organized around a theme becomes common. Make-believe play is also common and provides one way in which children can examine _____ topics. Most forms of solitary play are harmless.

2. **Learning to Cooperate**

   Cooperation becomes more common as children get _____ . Children will more readily cooperate if they are shown that cooperation is _____ and if peers respond to their cooperation with further cooperation. Cooperation is also influenced by societal values; it is more _____ in cultures that prize cooperation more highly than competition.

3. **Helping Others**

   Prosocial behaviors, such as _____ or sharing, are more common in children who understand (perspective-taking) and who experience (empathy) another's feelings. Prosocial behavior is more likely when children feel _____ for the person in distress, when they believe that they have the skills needed to help, when they are feeling _____ or successful, and when the perceived costs of helping are small. Parents can foster prosocial behavior in their children by behaving _____ themselves, by encouraging their children to help at home and elsewhere, and by using _____ in their discipline.

## 5.4 GENDER ROLES AND GENDER IDENTITY

1. **Images of Men and Women: Facts and Fantasy**

   _____ are beliefs about males and females that are often used to make inferences about a person, simply based on his or her gender. Studies of sex differences find that girls have greater _____ and get better grades in math courses but boys have greater spatial skill and get higher scores on math achievement tests. Girls are better able to interpret emotions and are more prone to social influence, but boys are more _____ . These differences can vary on the basis of a number of factors, including the historical period.

2. **Gender Typing**

Parents treat sons and daughters similarly, except in sex-typed activities. _____ may be particularly important in gender typing, because they are more likely to treat sons and daughters differently. In Kohlberg's theory, children gradually learn that gender is stable over time and cannot be changed according to personal _____ . After children understand gender stability, they begin to learn gender-typical behavior. According to gender-schema theory, children learn about gender by _____ to behaviors of members of their own sex and ignoring behaviors of members of the other sex. Girls with congenital adrenal hyperplasia are more likely than other girls to prefer _____ and male playmates.

3. **Evolving Gender Roles**

Gender roles are changing. However, studies of nontraditional families indicate that some components of gender stereotypes are more readily changed than others. For example, children in nontraditional families still engage in _____ activities and choose same-sex playmates but they have fewer _____ about occupations and fewer sex-typed attitudes about use of _____ .

# TEST YOURSELF

## MULTIPLE-CHOICE QUESTIONS

1. Infants under one year of age are in Erikson's first stage of psychosocial development, which involves a crisis of
   a. autonomy versus shame and doubt.
   b. initiative versus guilt.
   c. basic trust versus mistrust.
   d. industry versus inferiority.

2. According to Erikson, a balance between autonomy versus shame and doubt leads to the development of
   a. hope.
   b. purpose.
   c. will.
   d. self.

3. John Bowlby's theory of attachment is based on
   a. psychodynamic theory.
   b. social learning theory.
   c. ecological theory.
   d. evolutionary theory.

4. Most infants develop an attachment to a specific individual by about
   a. 3 to 4 months of age.
   b. 7 to 8 months of age.
   c. 12 to 15 months of age.
   d. 18 to 24 months of age.

5. Which of the following statements concerning infants' relationships with their mothers and fathers is true?
   a. Infants usually form attachments to their mothers and fathers simultaneously.
   b. Fathers usually spend more time taking care of their infants than they do playing with them.
   c. Infants usually become attached only to their mothers.
   d. Infants generally prefer playing with their father over playing with their mother.

6. Mary Ainsworth used _____ to assess the quality of attachment in infants.
   a. the Strange Situation procedure
   b. habituation
   c. interviews with the caregivers
   d. a visual cliff

7. When 15-month-old Marie was reunited with her mother after a 3-minute separation from her, Marie turned away from her mother and ignored her. Marie's behavior suggests that she has a(n) _____ attachment relationship with her mother.
   a. secure
   b. avoidant
   c. resistant
   d. disorganized (disoriented)

8. Eighteen-month-old Eric responded to a brief separation from his mother by holding up his arms to be held when they were reunited and then happily returning to his play activities after a minute or two. Eric behaved as if he had a(n) _____ attachment relationship with his mother.
   a. Secure
   b. avoidant
   c. resistant
   d. disorganized (disoriented)

9. The security of an infant's attachment is
   a. unrelated to the quality of future social relationships.
   b. related to the sensitivity and responsivity of the caregiving received.
   c. based purely on biological forces.
   d. stronger when parents typically wait a long time before responding to infant cries.

10. The set of expectations that infants develop about parents' availability and responsivity are referred to as
    a. empathy.
    b. ethology.
    c. social referencing.
    d. an internal working model.

11. Which of the following statements about the impact of day care on infants or children is most accurate?
    a. Children with extensive experience in day care are more likely to have behavioral problems.
    b. Children who begin day care early are more likely than children who begin day care later to have an insecure attachment.
    c. An insecure attachment is more likely when a child has less sensitive parenting and is in low quality day care.
    d. A secure mother-infant attachment is less likely when the child-care arrangements are changed frequently.

12. High quality child care has
    a. a high ratio of children to caregivers.
    b. high staff turnover.
    c. effective communication between parents and day-care workers.
    d. inexperienced staff.

13. Basic emotions contain each of the following elements except
    a. a self-evaluative component.
    b. a subjective feeling.
    c. a physiological change.
    d. an overt behavior.

14. Social smiles first appear at
    a. birth.
    b. 2 months of age.
    c. 6 months of age.
    d. 12 months of age.

15. Seven-month-old Stephen looked away and began to fuss when his aunt, whom he was seeing for the first time, tried to pick him up. Stephen is showing signs of
    a. insecure attachment.
    b. prosocial behavior.
    c. social referencing.
    d. stranger wariness.

16. Who is experiencing a complex emotion?
    a. Nate, who is embarrassed
    b. Pat, who is happy
    c. Gregory, who is surprised
    d. Mark, who is angry

17. When a clown approached Emily at a circus, Emily looked at her mother to see how she was reacting to the clown. After Emily's mother smiled and said hello to the clown, Emily smiled at the clown, too. Emily was showing
    a. a complex emotion.
    b. insecure attachment.
    c. social referencing.
    d. parallel play.

18. When infants look away from something that frightens them, they are using
    a. social referencing.
    b. a complex emotion.
    c. emotion regulation.
    d. stranger wariness.

19. Sarah and Beth are coloring pictures in separate coloring books but often look to see what the other is doing. They are engaged in
    a. solitary play.
    b. parallel play.
    c. cooperative play.
    d. make-believe play.

20. One- and two-year-olds spend most of their time in _____ play whereas three- and four-year-olds most often engage in _____ play.
    a. make-believe; parallel
    b. cooperative; make-believe
    c. cooperative; parallel
    d. parallel; cooperative

21. Four-year-old Mitchell has an imaginary friend. Mitchell
    a. is likely to have developmental problems.
    b. is one of very few children his age who has an imaginary companion.
    c. is probably quite sociable and is likely to have more real friends than children without imaginary companions.
    d. is likely to have more difficulty distinguishing between reality and fantasy than do preschoolers without imaginary companions.

22. Which of the following statements concerning gender differences in play is true?
    a. During the elementary school years, children interact primarily with same-sex peers.
    b. Boys' interactions are more likely than girls' to be enabling.
    c. Children segregate by gender only when encouraged to do so by their parents.
    d. Boys and girls do not differ in the ways that they play.

23. Cooperative behavior
    a. becomes less common as children grow older.
    b. increases when a child observes a successful model of cooperation.
    c. increases when the child gets a negative response to a cooperative overture.
    d. is more common among children in North America than among those in China.

24. Which of the following is the best example of altruistic behavior?
    a. Jennie, who gave some of her prize tokens to a friend who had not won any.
    b. Christine, who said, "Ouch!" when her friend tripped and fell.
    c. Valerie who gave a friend the apple from her lunch in exchange for the candy bar from the friend's lunch.
    d. Stephanie, who fed her dog every day because that was her assigned chore.

25. When a child actually experiences another child's feelings, the child is displaying
    a. social referencing.
    b. Prosocial behavior.
    c. altruism.
    d. empathy.

26. Altruistic behavior is least likely to occur when a child
    a. feels responsible for the person in need.
    b. feels competent to help the person in need.
    c. is happy or feeling successful.
    d. has to make a major sacrifice in order to help the person in need.

27. A _____ is a set of cultural guidelines regarding how a person should behave, particularly with other people.
    a. social role
    b. gender stereotype
    c. gender identity
    d. gender stability

28. Females _____ than males.
    a. tend to be more physically aggressive
    b. have better spatial ability
    c. are less compliant
    d. have stronger verbal abilities

29. In math,
    a. males outperform females on math achievement tests and usually get better grades in math courses.
    b. females outperform males on math achievement tests and usually get better grades in math courses.
    c. males outperform females on math achievement tests, but females often get better grades in math courses.
    d. females outperform males on math achievement tests, but males often get better grades in math courses.

30. As a group, males _____ than females.
    a. have higher verbal ability
    b. have better spatial ability
    c. are more readily influenced by others
    d. are less aggressive

31. Which of the following statements concerning parents' treatment of their children is true?
    a. Fathers encourage gender-related play more than mothers.
    b. Mothers and fathers punish sons and daughters equally.
    c. Parents tend to assign sons and daughters the same household chores.
    d. Mothers are more likely than fathers to treat sons and daughters differently.

32. Children typically understand that they are either boys or girls, and label themselves accordingly, by age
    a. 1 year.
    b. 2 to 3 years.
    c. 4 years.
    d. 5 to 7 years.

33. When James saw his friend Timmy dress up in a woman's clothing, he pointed at him and said, "Timmy's a girl!" James does not appear to have acquired the concept of
    a. gender constancy.
    b. gender stereotypes.
    c. gender labeling.
    d. gender stability.

34. According to Kohlberg's theory of how gender identity develops,
    a. gender stability must be acquired before knowledge of gender-stereotyped activities is learned.
    b. knowledge of gender-stereotyped activities must be acquired before gender stability will be understood.
    c. gender schemas influence interest in activities.
    d. gender schemas have no influence on interest in activities.

35. In _____, children first decide if an object, activity, or behavior is female or male, then use this information to decide whether they should learn more about the object, activity, or behavior.
    a. Kohlberg's theory
    b. social learning theory
    c. gender-schema theory
    d. the internal working model

36. Results of the Family Lifestyles Project, in which children were reared by parents who were members of the counterculture of the 1960s and 1970s and who tried to rear their children without traditional gender stereotypes, suggest that children who experience this kind of upbringing
    a. are likely to have many opposite-sex friends.
    b. are not likely to prefer sex-typed activities.
    c. have few stereotypes about occupations.
    d. do not show any aspects of gender stereotyping.

## ESSAY QUESTIONS

1. You and a friend have just visited some other friends who have an 8-month-old baby. When you get home, your friend comments on how differently the mother and the father interacted with their baby. The father seemed rough with the baby, and your friend wonders if that is normal behavior. What can you tell your friend about the differences in how mothers and fathers interact with their babies?

2. Your friend Marta has a 9-month-old baby, and she said that she isn't concerned about the effects of day care on attachment because attachment only lasts a few years and doesn't affect other later behavior. What can you tell Marta about the relation between attachment and later social behavior?

3. Your friend Ben has a 12-month-old daughter, Sadie. Recently, they saw one of Ben's coworkers whom Sadie did not know. When this stranger approached them, Ben thought that Sadie looked at him to gauge his reaction to the stranger and then smiled after she saw Ben smile and greet the stranger in a friendly manner. When Ben told this story to his wife, she laughed and told him that he was giving Sadie more credit than a 1-year-old should get. Is Ben or his wife correct? Explain your answer.

4. Your 6-year old niece does not like to play with boys. Your brother thinks that this is okay, but his wife thinks that your niece should play with both boys and girls. What can you tell your sister-in-law about sex differences in interaction styles and how that is related to the selection of same-sex playmates?

5. Your friend Jason told you that he would like his young son, Erik, to grow up and be a nice, helpful person. What can you tell Jason about factors that have been shown to be related to altruistic behavior?

6. Your friend Gretchen is an elementary school teacher. She told you one day that she has noticed that the boys that she has had in class seem to have more language problems than do the girls. She's also noticed that fewer of the girls need to go to the reading teacher to get extra help. The girls in Gretchen's class also seem to get higher math grades than the boys. Gretchen wonders if sex differences in verbal and math ability are substantiated by research or if she has had unusual students. What can you tell Gretchen about sex differences in math and verbal ability?

# SOLUTIONS

## 5.1 KNOW THE TERMS

1. Hope (179)
2. Will (179)
3. purpose (179)
4. Evolutionary psychology (179)
5. Attachment (180)
6. secure (181)
7. avoidant (182)
8. resistant (182)
9. disorganized (182)
10. internal working model (183)

## 5.1 KNOW THE DETAILS OF ATTACHMENT

1. F, (178)
2. T, (179)
3. T, (179)
4. F, (179)
5. F, (180)
6. T, (180)
7. T, (180)
8. F, (180)
9. T, (180)
10. T, (181)
11. T, (181)
12. F, (181)
13. F, (181)
14. T, (182)
15. T, (183)
16. T, (183)
17. F, (183)
18. F, (184)
19. T, (185)

## 5.2 KNOW THE TERMS

1. basic emotions (187)
2. social smiles (188)
3. Stranger wariness (188)
4. social referencing (190)

## 5.2 KNOW THE DETAILS OF EMERGING EMOTIONS

1. T, (187)
2. T, (187)
3. F, (188)
4. T, (188)
5. F, (188)
6. F, (189)
7. T, (189)
8. T, (189)
9. T, (189)
10. F, (189)
11. T, (190)
12. T, (191)

## 5.3 KNOW THE TERMS

1. Parallel play (193)
2. simple social play (193)
3. cooperative (193)
4. enabling (195)
5. constricting (195)
6. Prosocial (197)
7. Altruism (197)
8. empathy (198)

## 5.3 KNOW THE DETAILS OF INTERACTING WITH OTHERS

1.  T, (193)
2.  F, (193)
3.  T, (193)
4.  F, (193)
5.  F, (194)

6.  T, (194)
7.  F, (195)
8.  F, (195)
9.  F, (195)
10. T, (195)

11. T, (196)
12. T, (197)
13. F, (197)
14. T, (198)
15. T, (200)

## 5.4 KNOW THE TERMS

1.  social role (202)
2.  Gender stereotypes (202)
3.  relational aggression (204)
4.  gender identity (206)

5.  gender labeling (206)
6.  gender stability (206)
7.  gender constancy (206)
8.  gender-schema theory (206)

9.  Congenital adrenal hyperplasia (207)

## 5.4 KNOW THE DETAILS OF GENDER ROLES AND GENDER IDENTITY

1.  T, (202)
2.  T, (203)
3.  T, (203)
4.  T, (203)
5.  F, (203)

6.  T, (203)
7.  F, False (204)
8.  F, (205)
9.  T, (205)
10. F, (206)

11. T, (206)
12. T, (206)
13. T, (207)

# SUMMARY

## 5.1 BEGINNINGS: TRUST AND ATTACHMENT

1.  trust (178); shame (179); purpose (179)

2.  social-emotional (180); evolutionary psychology (179); preattachment (180); reciprocal relationships (180); secure (181); ignoring (182); understand (182); skillfully (183); sensitively (184)

3.  high quality (185); responsive (185)

## 5.2 EMERGING EMOTIONS

1.  joy (187); fear (187); stranger wariness (188); evaluative (189); embarrassment (189); cognitive (189)

2.  facial expressions (190);          3.
    unfamiliar (190)

## 5.3 INTERACTING WITH OTHERS

1.  parallel (193); cooperative (193); 2.  older (197); effective (197);  3.  helping (197); responsible (199);
    frightening (194)                      common (197)                         happy (199); altruistically (200);
                                                                                reasoning (200)

## 5.4 GENDER ROLES AND GENDER IDENTITY

1.  Gender stereotypes (202); verbal  2.  Fathers (205); wishes (206);    3.  sex-typed (208); stereotypes
    ability (203); aggressive (204)        paying attention (206);              (208); objects (208)
                                           masculine activities (207)

# TEST YOURSELF

## MULTIPLE-CHOICE QUESTIONS

| | | |
|---|---|---|
| 1. C, (178) | 13. A, (187) | 25. D, (198) |
| 2. C, (178) | 14. B, (188) | 26. D, (200) |
| 3. D, (180) | 15. D, (188) | 27. A, (202) |
| 4. B, (180) | 16. A, (189) | 28. D, (203) |
| 5. D, (181) | 17. C, (190) | 29. C, (203) |
| 6. A, (181) | 18. C, (191) | 30. B, (203) |
| 7. B, (182) | 19. B, (193) | 31. A, (205) |
| 8. A, (181) | 20. D, (193) | 32. B, (206) |
| 9. B, (183) | 21. C, (194) | 33. A, (206) |
| 10. D, (183) | 22. A, (195) | 34. A, (206) |
| 11. C, (185) | 23. B, (197) | 35. C, (206) |
| 12. C, (185) | 24. A, (197) | 36. C, (208) |

## ESSAY QUESTIONS

1.  You can tell your friend that the differences in the ways that fathers and mothers interact with their children are very different in many cultures. In many other countries, as well as in the United States, mothers do most of the caregiving and fathers fill the role of "playmate." Mothers are more likely to read and talk to their babies, show their babies toys, and play quiet games like pat-a-cake and peek-a-boo. Fathers are more likely to engage in physical, rough-and-tumble physical activities with their children. Infants are more likely to choose their fathers as playmates and their mothers as a source of comfort when distressed. (180-181)

2.  Attachment does last longer than a few years, and a secure attachment relationship is related to better social relationships later in life. There is much evidence that children who are securely attached have higher quality friendships and fewer conflicts in their friendships. School-age children are less likely to have behavior problems if they have secure attachment relationships. Even children who are at high risk for poor social relationships (e.g., they've been maltreated or they have a parent with a psychiatric disorder) have better social relationships if they were securely attached. (182)

3.  You can tell Ben that Sadie was engaging in social referencing. Social referencing occurs when infants encounter unfamiliar or ambiguous situations and involves looking at a parent to find cues to interpret the situation. The approach of the stranger would be an ambiguous situation to Sadie who is old enough to use social referencing. In

this ambiguous situation, Sadie looked at Ben to see how he reacted, and when Ben was friendly to the stranger, Sadie smiled. In other words, Ben's ideas about Sadie's behavior are correct. (190-191)

4. Around the world, girls generally play with girls and boys generally play with boys. Even when parents encourage boys and girls to play together most children will resist. Part of this resistance seems to come from the fact that girls and boys have very different styles of interacting. Boys tend to prefer more rough-and-tumble play and generally are more competitive and dominating in interactions. Girls seem to find this style of interaction aversive. Girls' interactions tend to be enabling. In other words, girls' remarks and behavior tend to provide support for each other. Boys' interactions tend to be constricting. Boys will try to dominate each other by using intimidation, threats, and exaggeration. When boys and girls interact, girls find that their supportive, compromising style is not very effective with boys. So, your niece is not unusual, and your sister-in-law's efforts to get her to play with boys are not likely to be successful. (195-196)

5. Research has found 3 factors that are related to altruistic behavior in children. First, parents who are warm and supportive, set guidelines, provide feedback, and use reasoning in their disciplinary style tend to have children who are more altruistic. Second, parents whose children are more altruistic show more warmth and concern for others and model altruistic behavior. Third, children and adolescents are more likely to act prosocially when they are given regular opportunities to help and cooperate with others. Experiences such as participating in community service sensitize children to others' needs. So, by modeling altruistic behavior, by using a disciplinary style that uses reasoning, by providing opportunities to act prosocially, Jason will increase the likelihood that Erik will engage in altruistic behavior. (200-201)

6. Research does show that females tend to have better verbal ability than males. For example, females tend to have larger vocabularies and read, write, and spell better than males. Girls also have fewer reading and other language-related problems than do boys. Girls also tend to obtain higher grades in math courses but boys tend to get higher scores on math achievement tests. So, you can tell Gretchen that the students that she has seen conform to the patterns found for the average boy and girl. (203)

# OFF TO SCHOOL

This chapter discusses cognitive development in school-age children, intelligence testing and the factors that influence IQ scores, the characteristics and needs of special children, the acquisition of academic skills, and physical development during childhood.

# 6.1 COGNITIVE DEVELOPMENT

## TO MASTER THE LEARNING OBJECTIVES:

**What are the distinguishing characteristics of thought during Piaget's concrete-operational and formal-operational stages?**

• Describe thought in concrete operational children.

• Describe the types of jokes that children entering the concrete operational period would find funny.

• Describe thinking in formal operational children and describe how their problem-solving approach differs from that of concrete operational children.

**What are some of the limitations of Piaget's account of thinking during the formal-operational stage?**

• Describe the circumstances under which adolescents are most likely to use deductive reasoning.

**How do children use strategies to improve learning and remembering?**

• Describe how working memory and long-term memory are related.

• Describe when simple memory strategies appear, and describe how memory strategies change with age.

**What is the role of monitoring in successful learning and remembering?**

• Define metacognition, metamemory, metacognitive knowledge, and cognitive self-regulation.

• Explain how monitoring changes with age.


## 6.1 KNOW THE TERMS

Cognitive self-regulation

Deductive reasoning

Elaboration

Long-term memory

Mental operations

Metacognitive knowledge

Metamemory

Organization

Working memory


1. Concrete operational children can reverse _____ , which are actions that can be performed on objects or ideas and that consistently yield a result.

2. Formal operational adolescents can draw conclusions from facts using _____ .

3. _____ is the type of memory where a small number of thoughts and ideas are held for a brief period of time.

4. _____ is a permanent storehouse of knowledge that has unlimited capacity.

5. _____ is a memory strategy in which related information is placed together.

6. Embellishing to-be-remembered information to make it more memorable is called _____

7. _____ is a child's intuitive understanding of memory.

8. Knowledge and awareness of cognitive processes is called _____

9. Successful students are good at _____ which involves identifying goals, selecting effective strategies, and monitoring accurately.


## 6.1 KNOW THE DETAILS OF COGNITIVE DEVELOPMENT

1. Children are in Piaget's concrete operational stage from approximately 7 to 11 years of age.
   TRUE or FALSE

2. Concrete operational thinkers are egocentric.

   TRUE or FALSE

3. Concrete operational thinkers are able to reverse their thinking.

   TRUE or FALSE

4. Concrete operational thinking is limited to the tangible and real.

   TRUE or FALSE

5. The formal operational period begins at adulthood.

   TRUE or FALSE

6. Formal operational thinkers are not able to reason abstractly.

   TRUE or FALSE

7. Combinatorial reasoning is characteristic of formal operational thinking.

   TRUE or FALSE

8. Formal operational thinkers do not use deductive reasoning.

   TRUE or FALSE

9. One of the shortcomings of Piaget's theory is that he has not addressed developmental changes in cognition that occur during late adolescence and adulthood.

   TRUE or FALSE

10. Working memory can store an unlimited amount of information.

    TRUE or FALSE

11. Long-term memory stores information permanently.

    TRUE or FALSE

12. Children begin to use simple strategies for remembering information, such as rehearsal, by the age of 7 or 8.

    TRUE or FALSE

13. Younger children are more likely than older children to choose an inappropriate strategy for remembering information.

    TRUE or FALSE

14. The ability to monitor progress toward the goal of a memory task improves with age.

    TRUE or FALSE

15. Cognitive self-regulation is a characteristic of successful students.

    TRUE or FALSE

# 6.2 APTITUDES FOR SCHOOL

## TO MASTER THE LEARNING OBJECTIVES:

**What is the nature of intelligence?**

- Describe Carroll's hierarchical theory of intelligence.
- Describe Gardner's theory of multiple intelligences and its application in the school setting.
- Describe Sternberg's theory of successful intelligence.

**Why were intelligence tests first developed?  What are their features?**

- Explain why the first intelligence test was developed by Binet and Simon.
- Explain the concept of mental age.
- Describe what Terman meant by intelligence quotient.

**How well do intelligence tests work?**

- Explain what is meant by the reliability and validity of a test.
- Describe how intelligence tests are validated.
- Describe how well intelligence tests predict success inside and outside of school.
- Explain the difference between dynamic testing and traditional intelligence testing.

**How do heredity and environment influence intelligence?**

- Explain how twin studies provide evidence that heredity influences intelligence.
- Describe what studies of adopted children tell us about the impact of heredity on intelligence.
- Describe the aspects of the environment that are related to higher levels of intelligence.
- Describe the effects of intervention programs like the Carolina Abecedarian Project.

**How and why do test scores vary for different racial and ethnic groups?**

- Describe the factors that influence racial and ethnic differences in IQ test scores.
- Explain what is meant by culture-fair intelligence tests.
- Explain how test-taking skills and stereotype threat are related to scores on intelligence tests.

## 6.2 KNOW THE TERMS

| | |
|---|---|
| Analytic ability | Mental age |
| Creative ability | Practical ability |
| Culture-fair | Psychometricians |

**Dynamic testing**                          **Savants**

**Emotional intelligence**                   **Stereotype threat**

**Intelligence quotient**

1.  Psychologists who specialize in measuring psychological characteristics such as intelligence and personality are called _____ .

2.  _____ are individuals with mental retardation who are extremely talented in one domain.

3.  The ability to use one's own and others' emotions effectively for solving problems and living happily is called _____

4.  _____ involves analyzing problems and generating different solutions.

5.  _____ involves dealing adaptively with novel situations and problems.

6.  _____ involves knowing what solution or plan will actually work.

7.  In intelligence testing, _____ refers to the difficulty of the problems that a child can solve correctly.

8.  Scores on the Stanford-Binet were converted into an _____ which was a ratio of mental age to chronological age, multiplied by 100.

9.  _____ involves measuring a child's learning potential by having the child learn something new in the presence of the examiner with the examiner's help.

10. To avoid cultural bias in intelligence tests, _____ intelligence tests include test items that are based on experiences common to many cultures.

11. _____ occurs when knowledge of stereotypes leads to anxiety and reduced performance consistent with a negative stereotype.

# 6.2 KNOW THE DETAILS OF INTELLIGENCE TESTING

1.  Psychometricians are psychologists who specialize in measuring psychological characteristics such as intelligence and personality.
    TRUE or FALSE

2.  Hierarchical theories of intelligence include both general and specific components.
    TRUE or FALSE

3. According to Gardner's more recent theory of multiple intelligences, intelligence includes nine distinct components.
   TRUE or FALSE

4. Musical intelligence, spatial intelligence, and intrapersonal intelligence are subtheories of Sternberg's triarchic theory of intelligence.
   TRUE or FALSE

5. Gardner believes that schools should focus on linguistic and logical-mathematical intelligences.
   TRUE or FALSE

6. Sternberg's theory of successful intelligence focuses on analytic, creative, and practical abilities.
   TRUE or FALSE

7. The purpose of the intelligence test developed by Binet and Simon was to identify children who would be unable to learn in school without special instruction.
   TRUE or FALSE

8. Chronological age refers to the difficulty of the problems children can solve correctly.
   TRUE or FALSE

9. On Terman's early version of the Stanford-Binet, intelligence quotients were derived using the formula IQ= CA/MA x 100.
   TRUE or FALSE

10. Today, IQ scores are determined by comparing children's test performance to that of others their age.
    TRUE or FALSE

11. The average IQ score is 120.
    TRUE or FALSE

12. Modern intelligence tests are not very reliable.
    TRUE or FALSE

13. Intelligence tests predict school performance reasonably well.
    TRUE or FALSE

14. Dynamic testing involves having children learn something new in the presence of the examiner.
    TRUE or FALSE

15. Identical twins have been found to have more similar IQs than fraternal twins, suggesting that genes influence intelligence.
    TRUE or FALSE

16. The influence of environment on intelligence has been shown by intervention programs which have been able to increase children's intelligence test scores by enriching the children's environment.
    TRUE or FALSE

17. On most intelligence tests, there are no ethnic differences in average scores.
    TRUE or FALSE

18. The Stanford-Binet is an example of a culture-fair intelligence test.
    TRUE or FALSE

# 6.3 SPECIAL CHILDREN, SPECIAL NEEDS

## TO MASTER THE LEARNING OBJECTIVES:

**What are the characteristics of gifted and creative children?**

• Describe the typical characteristics of gifted children.

• List and describe the prerequisites of exceptional talent in children.

• Define convergent and divergent thinking and explain the difference between the two.

• Describe the types of home and school environments that nurture creativity in children.

**What are the different forms of mental retardation?**

• Describe how adaptive behaviors are used to assess mental retardation.

• Define organic mental retardation and familial retardation and explain how the two differ.

• Describe the typical living situations and functioning of profoundly, severely, moderately, and mildly (educable) retarded individuals.

**What is a learning disability?**

• Describe what is meant by learning disability and describe some of the different types.

**What are the distinguishing features of hyperactivity?**

• Describe the 3 symptoms of ADHD and describe the incidence of ADHD in boys and girls.

• Describe the treatments for ADHD.

## 6.3 KNOW THE TERMS

| | |
|---|---|
| Convergent thinking | Learning disability |
| Divergent thinking | Mental retardation |
| Familial | Organic |

1. Using information to arrive at a standard, correct answer is called _____ .

2. Thinking in novel and unusual directions is called _____ .

3. _____ refers to substantially below average intelligence and problems adapting to an environment that emerge before the age of 18.

4. Mental retardation that can be traced to a specific biological or physical problem is called _____ mental retardation.

5. People with _____ mental retardation have not suffered physical damage but their intelligence merely represents the low end of the normal distribution of intelligence.

6. Someone with normal intelligence who has difficulty mastering at least one academic subject has a _____ .

# 6.3 KNOW THE DETAILS OF CHILDREN'S SPECIAL NEEDS

1. The traditional definition of giftedness was a score of 130 or greater on an intelligence test.
   TRUE or FALSE

2. Today's definitions of giftedness include exceptional talent in a variety of areas, such as art, music, creative writing, and dance.
   TRUE or FALSE

3. If a child is exceptionally talented, the talent will grow even in the absence of environmental support and encouragement.
   TRUE or FALSE

4. Gifted children tend to have emotional problems and difficulty getting along with other children.
   TRUE or FALSE

5. Intelligence is associated with divergent thinking; creativity is related to convergent thinking.
   TRUE or FALSE

6. Mental retardation that can be traced to a specific biological or physical problem is known as familial mental retardation.
   TRUE or FALSE

7. The more extreme forms of mental retardation are usually due to organic causes, the less extreme forms are more likely to be familial.
   TRUE or FALSE

8. Individuals with profound and severe mental retardation may develop the intellectual skills of a nonretarded 7- or 8-year-old.
   TRUE or FALSE

9. Mildly mentally retarded individuals can master academic skills and often lead independent lives as adults.
   TRUE or FALSE

10. Children classified as learning disabled have below normal intelligence.
    TRUE or FALSE

11. Many more boys than girls have an attention-deficit hyperactivity disorder.
    TRUE or FALSE

12. Overactivity, inattention, and impulsivity are symptoms of a learning disability.
    TRUE or FALSE

13. Most children with ADHD grow out of it in adolescence or young adulthood.
    TRUE or FALSE

14. Research consistently indicates that there is a connection between food allergies and ADHD.
    TRUE or FALSE

# 6.4 ACADEMIC SKILLS

## TO MASTER THE LEARNING OBJECTIVES:

**What are the components of skilled reading?**

- Describe the components of reading.

- Describe the cues that aid word recognition.

- Describe the factors that contribute to improved reading comprehension.

**As children develop, how does their writing improve?**

- Describe the factors that contribute to improved writing in children.

**When do children understand and use quantitative skills?**

- Describe the strategies that children use to add and subtract.

- Compare the math skills of students in the United States to students in other countries and the differences in schools and culture that contribute to the differences.

**What are the hallmarks of effective schools and effective teachers?**

- Describe the characteristics of schools where students typically succeed.

- Describe the functions that computers serve in the classroom.

- Describe the characteristics of effective teachers.

## 6.4 KNOW THE TERMS

Comprehension

Knowledge-telling

Knowledge-transforming

Phonological awareness

Propositions

Word recognition

1.  The process of identifying a unique pattern of letters is _____ .

2.  The process of extracting meaning from a sequence of words is called _____ .

3.  The ability to hear the distinctive sounds of letters is called _____ .

4.  Children derive meaning from written material by combining words to form _____ or ideas.

5.  The _____ strategy involves writing down information as it is retrieved from memory.

6.  The _____ strategy involves deciding what information to include and how best to organize it for the reader.

## 6.4 KNOW THE DETAILS OF ACADEMIC SKILLS

1.  *Word recognition* refers to the process of identifying a unique pattern of letters.
    TRUE or FALSE

2.  Knowledge of letter names is one of the best predictors of success in learning to read.
    TRUE or FALSE

3.  Phonological awareness has not been found to be related to success in learning to read.
    TRUE or FALSE

4.  As children become more experienced readers, they tend to sound out fewer words and retrieve more from memory.
    TRUE or FALSE

5.  Children derive meaning when reading by combining words to form propositions and then combining propositions.
    TRUE or FALSE

6.  A *knowledge-transforming* strategy of writing refers to writing down information on a topic as it is retrieved from memory.
    TRUE or FALSE

7.  Children often count on their fingers as they begin to learn to add.
    TRUE or FALSE

8. In math, the very best students in Asian countries such as Korea and Singapore perform only at the level of average students in the U.S.
   TRUE or FALSE

9. Students in Taiwan and Japan spend more time on homework and value homework more the student in the U.S.
   TRUE or FALSE

10. The safety and nurturance of the school climate is related to whether students are likely to succeed or fail.
    TRUE or FALSE

11. Student success in schools is unrelated to parent involvement in the school.
    TRUE or FALSE

12. Students interact with each other less when computers are introduced into the classroom.
    TRUE or FALSE

13. Students tend to learn the most when teachers are effective classroom managers.
    TRUE or FALSE

14. Students tend to learn the most when teachers assume that students are responsible for their own learning.
    TRUE or FALSE

15. Peer tutoring is not an effective way for students to learn.
    TRUE or FALSE

# 6.5 PHYSICAL DEVELOPMENT

## TO MASTER THE LEARNING OBJECTIVES:

**How much do school-age children grow?**

- Describe the growth rate of school-age children.

- Describe ethnic differences in height and weight.

**How do motor skills improve during the elementary school years?**

- Describe changes in gross and fine motor skills.

- Know the gender differences in motor skills.

**Are American children physically fit?**

- Know the benefits of physical fitness.

**What are the consequences of participating in sports?**

- Know the benefits of participating in sports.
- Know the characteristics of good and bad coaches.

# 6.5 KNOW THE DETAILS OF PHYSICAL DEVELOPMENT

1. Boys are more likely than girls to have entered puberty by the end of the elementary school years.
   TRUE or FALSE

2. The average 7- to 10-year-old needs to consume about 2,400 calories per day.
   TRUE or FALSE

3. During elementary school years, children's motor skills improve as they get bigger and stronger.
   TRUE or FALSE

4. During the elementary school years, girls tend to have better handwriting than boys.
   TRUE or FALSE

5. During the elementary school years, girls tend to be stronger than boys but boys tend to be more flexible and have better balance.
   TRUE or FALSE

6. The average school-age child in the United States is physically fit.
   TRUE or FALSE

7. Children are most likely to maintain interest in sports when coaches emphasize winning.
   TRUE or FALSE

# SUMMARY

## 6.1 COGNITIVE DEVELOPMENT

1. **More Sophisticated Thinking: Piaget's Version**

   In progressing to Piaget's stage of concrete operations, children become less _____ , rarely confuse appearances with reality, and are able to _____ their thinking. They now solve perspective-taking, _____ , and class-inclusion problems correctly. Thinking at this stage is limited to the _____ and the real. With the onset of formal-operational thinking, adolescents can think hypothetically and reason _____ . In deductive reasoning, they understand that conclusions are based on _____ , not on experience. Critics of Piaget's account of formal-operational thinking point to two shortcomings. First, in everyday thinking, adolescents' reasoning is often _____ sophisticated than would be expected of formal-operational thinkers. Second, Piaget assumed that after the formal-operational stage is reached, thinking never again changes _____ .

2. **Information-Processing Strategies for Learning and Remembering**

Rehearsal and other memory strategies are used to transfer information from _____ memory, a temporary store of information, to long-term memory, a permanent store of knowledge. Children begin to rehearse at about 7 or 8 years of age and begin to use other strategies as they get older. Effective use of strategies for learning and remembering begins with an analysis of the _____ of any learning task. It also includes _____ one's performance to determine if the strategy is working. Collectively, these processes define an important group of study skills.

## 6.2 APTITUDES FOR SCHOOL

1. **Theories of Intelligence**

Psychometric approaches to intelligence include theories that describe intelligence as a general factor as well as theories that include specific factors. Hierarchical theories include both general intelligence as well as various specific skills, such as verbal and spatial ability. Gardner's theory of multiple intelligences proposes seven distinct intelligences. Three are found in psychometric theories ( _____ , logical-mathematical, spatial), but six are new ( _____ , bodily-kinesthetic, interpersonal, intrapersonal, naturalistic, and existential intelligence). The theory has implications for education, suggesting, for example, that schools should adjust teaching to each child's unique intellectual strengths. According to Robert Sternberg, intelligence is defined using abilities to achieve short-term and long-term goals and depends on three abilities: _____ to analyze problems and generate solutions, creative ability to deal adaptively with novel situations, and _____ to know what solutions will work.

2. **Binet and the Development of Intelligence Testing**

Binet created the first intelligence test in order to identify students who would have difficulty in school. Using this work, Terman created the Stanford-Binet in 1916; it remains an important intelligence test. The Stanford-Binet introduced the concept of the _____ , which was MA/CA x 100.

3. **Do Tests Work?**

Intelligence tests are reasonably valid measures of achievement in school. They also predict people's performance in the workplace. Dynamic tests are designed to improve validity by measuring children's _____ for future learning.

4. **Hereditary and Environmental Factors**

   Evidence for the impact of heredity on IQ comes from the finding that (a) siblings' IQ scores become more alike as siblings become more similar genetically, and (b) adopted children's IQ scores are more _____ their biological parents' test scores than their adoptive parents' scores. Evidence for the impact of the environment comes from the finding that children who live in _____ home environments tend to have higher IQ scores, as do children who participate in intervention projects.

5. **Impact of Ethnicity and Social Class**

   The average IQ score for African Americans is _____ than the average score for European Americans. This difference has been attributed to the fact that more African American children live in poverty and that the test assesses knowledge based on _____ experiences. IQ scores are valid predictors of school success, however, because middle-class experience is often a prerequisite for school success.

## 6.3 SPECIAL CHILDREN, SPECIAL NEEDS

1. **Gifted and Creative Children**

   Traditionally, gifted children have been those with high scores on _____ tests. Modern definitions of giftedness have been broadened to include exceptional talent in, for example, the arts. _____ is associated with divergent thinking, in which the aim is to think in novel and unusual directions. Tests of divergent thinking can predict which children are most likely to be creative. Creativity can be fostered by experiences that encourage children to think _____ and to explore alternatives.

2. **Children with Mental Retardation**

   Individuals with mental retardation have IQ scores of _____ or lower and deficits in adaptive behavior. Organic mental retardation, which is severe but _____ common, can be linked to specific biological or physical causes; familial mental retardation, which is less severe but more common, reflects the _____ end of the normal distribution of intelligence. Most retarded persons are classified as mildly or educably retarded; they attend school, work, and have families.

3. **Children with Learning Disability**

Children with a learning disability have _____ intelligence but have difficulty mastering specific academic subjects. The most common is _____ disability, which often can be traced to inadequate understanding and use of language sounds.

4. **Attention-Deficit Hyperactivity Disorder**

Children with ADHD are distinguished by being overactive, _____ , and impulsive. They often have _____ problems and do poorly in school. Children with ADHD are often administered _____ that calm them. They also can be taught more effective ways of regulating their behavior and attention.

## 6.4 ACADEMIC SKILLS

1. **Reading**

Reading includes a number of component skills. Pre-reading skills include knowing letters and the _____ associated with them. _____ is the process of identifying a word. Beginning readers more often accomplish this by sounding out words; advanced readers more often retrieve a word from long-term memory. _____ , the act of extracting meaning from text, improves with age due to several factors: working memory capacity _____ , readers gain more world knowledge, and readers are better able to monitor what they read and to match reading strategies to the goals of the reading task.

2. **Writing**

As children develop, their writing improves, reflecting several factors: They know more about the world and so they have more to say; they use more effective ways of _____ their writing; they master the mechanics (e.g., handwriting, spelling) of writing; and they become more skilled at _____ their writing.

3. **Math Skills**

Children first add and subtract by counting, but then use more effective strategies such as retrieving sums _____ from memory. In mathematics, American students lag behind students in most other industrialized nations. This difference can be traced to cultural differences in the time spent in schoolwork and homework, and in parents' _____ towards school, effort, and ability.

4. **Effective Schools, Effective Teachers**

Schools influence students' achievement in many ways. Students are more likely to achieve when their school emphasizes _____ , has a safe and nurturing environment, _____ pupils' and teachers' progress, and encourages _____ to be involved. Students achieve at higher levels when their teachers manage classrooms effectively, take _____ for their students' learning, teach _____ of material, pace material well, value tutoring, and show children how to _____ their own learning.

## 6.5 PHYSICAL DEVELOPMENT

1. **Growth**

   Elementary-school children grow at a steady pace, more so in their _____ than in the trunk. Boys and girls tend to be about the _____ size for much of these years, but there are large individual and ethnic differences. School-age children need approximately _____ calories daily, preferably drawn from the 5 food groups. Children need to eat breakfast because this meal should provide about _____ of their daily calories and without breakfast, they often have trouble concentrating in school.

2. **Development of Motor Skills**

   Fine and gross motor skills improve substantially over the elementary-school years, reflecting children's greater size and strength. Girls tend to excel _____ skills that emphasize dexterity as well as gross-motor skills that require flexibility and balance; boys tend to excel in gross-motor skills that emphasize _____ Although some of the differences reflect differences in body make-up, they also reflect differing _____ regarding motor skills for boys and girls.

3. **Physical Fitness**

   Fewer than half of American school children meet all standards for physical fitness. Part of the explanation for the lack of fitness is that physical education in elementary school are not taught _____ and involve too little activity. Television may also contribute. Physical education in schools needs to be more frequent and more oriented toward developing _____ exercise. Families can become more active, thereby encouraging children's fitness.

4. **Participating in Sports**

Adult coaches often can help children improve their skills but they sometimes overemphasize

_____ they are so controlling that children have little opportunity to experience leadership,

and they overemphasize drills, strategy, and _____

# TEST YOURSELF

## MULTIPLE-CHOICE QUESTIONS

1. During Piaget's concrete operational stage, children
   a. are more egocentric than they were during the preoperational period.
   b. often confuse appearances with reality.
   c. are unable to reverse their thinking.
   d. are able to perform mental operations.

2. Who is most likely to laugh at a joke that depends on the listener's having an understanding of conservation?
   a. Janine, who is in Piaget's sensorimotor stage
   b. Raven, who is in Piaget's preoperational stage
   c. Maureen, who is in Piaget's concrete operational stage
   d. Paula, who is in Piaget's formal operational stage

3. Connie is a concrete operational thinker whereas Forrest is a formal operational thinker. Which of the following statements is *most* likely to be true?
   a. Forrest is better than Connie in abstract reasoning.
   b. Connie is better than Forrest in combinatorial reasoning.
   c. Forrest is more likely than Connie to focus on the tangible and real aspects of a task.
   d. Connie is better than Forrest at hypothetical reasoning.

4. By the time they reach Piaget's _____ stage, children are able to draw logical conclusions even when the conclusion contradicts what experience tells them is really true.
   a. preoperational
   b. formal operational
   c. concrete operational
   d. sensorimotor

5. The ability to draw appropriate conclusions from facts is referred to as
   a. deductive reasoning.
   b. divergent thinking.
   c. performing a mental operation.
   d. concrete thinking.

6. Piaget's theory has been criticized because
   a. adolescents don't always reason at the formal operational level even though they are capable of it.
   b. adolescents are not able to use contrary-to-fact reasoning.
   c. it suggests that qualitative changes in thinking continue to occur throughout adulthood.
   d. it did not provide a comprehensive view of cognitive development.

7. Most thought takes place in the _____, according to information processing theorists.
   a. sensorimotor
   b. working memory
   c. long-term memory
   d. intelligence quotient

8. The _____ is a permanent storehouse of knowledge that has an unlimited capacity.
   a. sensorimotor
   b. working memory
   c. long-term memory
   d. intelligence quotient

9. If 7-year-old Kevin performs like a typical young child on a memory task, he will
   a. use rehearsal to try to remember the to-be-recalled information.
   b. accurately judge the objective of a memory task.
   c. usually pick the best strategy to use to remember the to-be-recalled information.
   d. successfully monitor how much of the information he can recall.

10. Which of the following shows the correct sequence in which the events should take place for effective learning to occur?
    a. analyze the task, select an appropriate strategy, monitor progress toward the goal
    b. monitor progress toward the goal, analyze the task, select an appropriate strategy
    c. select an appropriate strategy, analyze the task, monitor progress toward the goal
    d. analyze the task, monitor progress toward the goal, select an appropriate strategy

11. Natsuki has an extensive vocabulary and excels at using language to convey ideas to others. According to Gardner's theory of multiple intelligences, Natsuki is high in the _____ component.
    a. intrapersonal intelligence
    b. logical-mathematical intelligence
    c. linguistic intelligence
    d. spatial intelligence

12. In Sternberg's theory of successful intelligence, _____ ability involves investigating problems and generating different solutions; _____ ability involves dealing adaptively with novel situations; and _____ ability involves knowing what solution or plan will actually work.
    a. analytic; creative; practical
    b. creative; analytic; practical
    c. creative; practical; analytic
    d. analytic; practical; creative

13. The difficulty of the problems that a child can solve on an intelligence test determines the child's
    a. chronological age.
    b. mental age.
    c. mental operations.
    d. divergent reasoning.

14. Which of the following is the formula that Terman originally used to determine an intelligence quotient?
    a. IQ = MA/CA x 100
    b. IQ = CA/MA x 100
    c. IQ = MA x CA x 100
    d. IQ = CA/100 x MA

15. Who has the highest IQ?
    a. a 4-year-old with a mental age of 4
    b. a 10-year-old with a mental age of 12
    c. a 6-year-old with a mental age of 10
    d. a 5-year-old with a mental age of 3

16. _____ refers to the extent that a test really measures what it claims to measure.
    a. Reliability
    b. Stability
    c. Variability
    d. Validity

17. If intelligence is influenced by genes, then the IQ scores of identical twins should be
    a. less similar than those of fraternal twins.
    b. less similar than those of children and their adopted siblings.
    c. less similar than those of children and their biological parents.
    d. more similar than those of other pairs of siblings.

18. Which of the following statements about the impact of the Carolina Abecedarian Project on children's achievement is *true*?
    a. Intervention had no impact on children's achievement test scores.
    b. Children who received intervention had higher IQ, reading, and math scores throughout the 15 years of the project.
    c. IQ scores were affected, but not reading, math, or language scores.
    d. Intervention increased reading scores, but not math or written language scores.

19. If you wanted to get a culture-fair assessment of intelligence, which of the following tests would be best to use?
    a. Kaufman Assessment Battery for Children (K-ABC)
    b. Raven's Progressive Matrices
    c. Stanford-Binet
    d. Wechsler Intelligence Scale for Children-III (WISC-III)

20. Gifted children
    a. tend to have more emotional problems than their nongifted peers.
    b. often have difficulty getting along with other children.
    c. tend to be more mature than their nongifted peers.
    d. will flourish even if their talents are not nurtured by others.

21. Which of the following is *not* a prerequisite for exceptional talent?
    a. The child must love the subject and have an almost overwhelming desire to master it.
    b. The child must be instructed at an early age by an inspiring and talented teacher.
    c. The child must receive support and help from parents who are committed to promoting their child's talent.
    d. The child must demonstrate outstanding reading or math skills in an academic setting.

22. Which question requires divergent thinking?
    a. What is 3,928 + 2,432?
    b. How many different ways can you think of to use a paper clip?
    c. What is the chemical composition of water?
    d. Who was the thirty-fifth president of the United States?

23. Who is *most* likely to be described as having familial mental retardation?
    a. Sam, who has Down Syndrome and an IQ of 45
    b. Stella, who suffered oxygen deprivation during birth and has an IQ of 20
    c. Susan, who was born 15 weeks prematurely, has an IQ of 85, and is visually impaired
    d. Sunny, who has an IQ of 65 and no obvious biological or physical problems

24. Approximately 90 percent of all mentally retarded individuals are classified as _____ mentally retarded.
    a. mildly
    b. moderately
    c. severely
    d. profoundly

25. A child with a learning disability has
    a. difficulty in one or more academic subjects.
    b. below average intelligence.
    c. difficulty learning due to a visual impairment.
    d. learning problems due to poor teaching.

26. Clyde is unusually energetic, has difficulty concentrating in school, and often acts without thinking. Clyde shows many of the characteristics of
    a. a learning disability.
    b. attention-deficit hyperactivity disorder.
    c. mild mental retardation.
    d. moderate mental retardation.

27. Children with attention-deficit hyperactivity disorder
    a.  can be successfully treated with depressant drugs.
    b.  are not usually capable of learning to regulate their own behavior.
    c.  are most successfully treated by reducing the amount of sugar and food additives in their diets.
    d.  are most successfully treated with treatments that address the biological, psychological, and sociocultural contributions to the disorder.

28. The ability to hear the distinctive sounds of letters is a skill known as
    a.  phonological awareness.
    b.  letter recognition.
    c.  word recognition.
    d.  knowledge-telling.

29. Which of the following is NOT a factor related to improved reading comprehension as children get older?
    a.  increases in working memory capacity
    b.  acquiring more knowledge of the physical, social, and psychological world
    c.  using more appropriate reading strategies
    d.  doing less monitoring of comprehension

30. Before he started to write, Billy decided what information he wanted to include and thought about how he could best organize it to get his point across. What strategy was Billy using?
    a.  a knowledge-telling strategy
    b.  a knowledge-transforming strategy
    c.  a prepositional strategy
    d.  a phonological strategy

31. Compared to students in other countries, U.S. students have
    a.  the highest math achievement scores in the world.
    b.  the lowest math achievement scores in the world.
    c.  substantially lower math achievement than students in the nation with the highest level of math achievement.
    d.  math achievement scores very close to those in the nation with the highest math achievement scores.

32. Which of the following comparisons between students in the U.S., Japan, and Taiwan is true?
    a.  Students in Japan and Taiwan spend 50 percent more time in school than students in the U.S.
    b.  Students in the U.S. spend more time on homework than student in Japan and Taiwan.
    c.  Parents in the U.S. have much higher standards for their children's achievement than do parents in Japan and Taiwan.
    d.  Parents in the U.S. believe more strongly than parents in Japan and Taiwan that effort, not native ability, is the key factor in school success.

33. In which of the following schools would students be most likely to fail?
    a.  In School A where the school climate is safe and nurturant
    b.  In School B where parents are involved
    c.  In School C where the progress of students, teachers, and programs is monitored
    d.  In School D where many nonacademic activities are included in the school day

34. Who is likely to be the most effective teacher?
    a. Ms. Allen, who believes she is responsible for her students' learning
    b. Mr. Brown, who often lectures and then has students do worksheets
    c. Mr. Curry, who presents material at a very rapid pace
    d. Ms. Diamond, who spends a lot of time disciplining students

35. During the elementary school years,
    a. boys grow faster than girls for most years.
    b. growth occurs at a steady pace.
    c. most of the growth occurs in the trunk not the legs.
    d. growth slows down, so children need to consume fewer calories than in the preschool years.

36. _____ children tend to be taller than _____ children, who tend to be taller than _____ children.
    a. European American; African American; Asian American
    b. African American; European American; Asian American
    c. African American; Asian American; European American
    d. Asian American; African American; European American

37. In regard to elementary school aged children's motor skills,
    a. boys outperform girls on skills that require strength.
    b. boys outperform girls on skills that require balance.
    c. boys outperform girls on skills that require flexibility.
    d. there are no gender differences in performance levels.

38. Gender differences in motor skills during the elementary school years are due in part to
    a. differences in experience.
    b. girls' bodies having less fat.
    c. girls' bodies having more muscle.
    d. beliefs that physical fitness is less important for boys than for girls.

39. Participation in sports during the elementary school years
    a. is more informal today than in years past.
    b. gives children a chance to learn valuable social skills.
    c. is most beneficial when coaches emphasize competition rather than skill development.
    d. is detrimental to cognitive skill development.

40. Guidelines for enhancing children's enjoyment of youth sports include
    a. critiquing children's efforts.
    b. having high expectations for children's performances.
    c. emphasizing the seriousness of sports.
    d. developing children's respect for their opponents and other individuals involved.

## ESSAY QUESTIONS

1. Your friend Sam took his children to a hands-on science museum when they were on vacation in Florida. Sam noticed that his 8-year-old son and his 12-year-old son interacted with some of the displays in

very different ways. One display involved opening doors to safes by determining the combination. Each safe had 3, 4, or 5 buttons that had to be pressed in a particular order to open the door. Sam's 8-year-old son randomly pushed the buttons and gave up before the door opened. Sam's 12-year-old son approached the task in a very systematic manner--trying all possible combinations until the doors opened. Sam wonders if his sons are typical. What can you tell Sam about the differences between concrete operational and formal operational thought that might explain his sons' behavior?

2.  Your friends Mick and Mia are both above average in intelligence, and they are concerned that their new son Mike will be intelligent also. They want to know how they can shape Mike's environment so that it will increase his chances of being above average in intelligence. What can you tell them about the effects of environment and heredity on intelligence?

3.  Your friend Lola would like her 5-year-old daughter, Lisa, to become a piano virtuoso at a young age. She has seen 12- and 13-year-olds winning national instrumental competitions on television, and Lola is wondering what she should be doing to increase the likelihood that Lisa will be one of those adolescents in a few short years. What can you tell Lola about the prerequisites for exceptional talent?

4.  Your friend Antonio wonders if his son Claudio, who is very active, has attention-deficit hyperactivity disorder. What can you tell Antonio about the symptoms of ADHD that might help him decide if he should seek treatment for his son?

5.  Your friend, Jin-pyo, is a concerned father, and he would like to do all that he can to help his 4-year-old daughter, Jae-jin, learn to read. What can you tell Jin-pyo about pre-reading skills that are related to more skilled reading in first grade?

6.  You are having a discussion with a friend about the differences in math achievement in children in the United States and children in Asian countries. During your discussion, your friend states, "It must be genetic. Or maybe Asian kids are just smarter than American kids." What can you tell your friend about the reasons for cultural differences in math achievement that refute his statement?

7.  Your friend's first-grade son, Hasani, has been writing a story every Monday in school. Your friend is concerned about Hasani's writing because she thinks that his stories aren't very good. They often have no organization and seem very incomplete. What can you tell your friend about the changes in writing ability that might make her feel better?

8.  Your friends are moving to a new community, and they are concerned about finding a good, effective school for their daughter in their new city. What can you tell your friends about the characteristics of schools where students typically succeed rather than fail?

9.  At a recent parent council meeting at your child's elementary school, a group of parents raised objections to the use of computers in the classroom. They felt that teachers used computers solely to entertain the children and that computers were a waste of instructional time. What can you tell this group of parents about the benefits of using computers in the classroom?

10. Your spouse is going to coach your 8-year-old daughter's soccer team. You want this to be a positive experience for your daughter and the other girls. What can you tell your spouse about good and bad coaches that might help the experience be as positive as possible.

# SOLUTIONS

## 6.1 KNOW THE TERMS

1. mental operations (220)
2. deductive reasoning (222)
3. Working memory (223)
4. Long-term memory (223)
5. Organization (223)
6. elaboration (223)
7. Metamemory (224)
8. metacognitive knowledge (224)
9. cognitive self-regulation (224)

## 6.1 KNOW THE DETAILS OF COGNITIVE DEVELOPMENT

1. T, (220)
2. F, (220)
3. T, (220)
4. T, (221)
5. F, (221)
6. F, (221)
7. T, (221)
8. F, (222)
9. T, (222)
10. F, (223)
11. T, (223)
12. T, (223)
13. T, (224)
14. T, (224)
15. T, (224)

## 6.2 KNOW THE TERMS

1. psychometricians (226)
2. Savants (228)
3. emotional intelligence (228)
4. Analytic ability (229)
5. Creative ability (229)
6. Practical ability (229)
7. mental age (230)
8. intelligence quotient (231)
9. Dynamic testing (232)
10. culture-fair (236)
11. Stereotype threat (236)

## 6.2 KNOW THE DETAILS OF INTELLIGENCE TESTING

1. T, (226)
2. T, (227)
3. T, (227)
4. F, (229)
5. F, (229)
6. T, (229)
7. T, (230)
8. F, (230)
9. F, (231)
10. T, (231)
11. F, (231)
12. F, (231)
13. T, (231)
14. T, (232)
15. T, (233)
16. T, (234)
17. F, (235)
18. F, (236)

## 6.3 KNOW THE TERMS

1. convergent thinking (238)
2. divergent thinking (238)
3. Mental retardation (239)
4. organic (239)
5. familial (239)
6. learning disability (240)

## 6.3 KNOW THE DETAILS OF CHILDREN'S SPECIAL NEEDS

1. T, (238)
2. T, (238)
3. F, (238)
4. F, (238)
5. F, (238)
6. F, (239)
7. T, (239)
8. F, (240)
9. T, (240)
10. F, (240)
11. T, (242)
12. F, (242)
13. F, (243)
14. F, (243)

## 6.4 KNOW THE TERMS

1. word recognition (245)
2. comprehension (245)
3. phonological awareness (245)
4. propositions (246)
5. knowledge-telling (248)
6. knowledge-transforming (248)

## 6.4 KNOW THE DETAILS OF ACADEMIC SKILLS

1. T, (245)
2. T, (245)
3. F, (245)
4. T, (246)
5. T, (246)
6. F, (248)
7. T, (249)
8. F, (250)
9. T, (251)
10. T, (252)
11. F, (252)
12. F, (253)
13. T, (254)
14. F, (254)
15. F, (254)

## 6.5 KNOW THE DETAILS OF PHYSICAL DEVELOPMENT

1. F, (256)
2. T, (256)
3. T, (257)
4. T, (257)
5. F, (257)
6. T, (258)
7. T, (259)

## SUMMARY

### 6.1 COGNITIVE DEVELOPMENT

1. egocentric (220); reverse (220); conservation (220); concrete (221); abstractly (221); logic (222); less (222); qualitatively (222)

2.  working (223); goals (224);
    monitoring (224)

## 6.2 APTITUDES FOR SCHOOL

1.  linguistic (227); musical (227);
    analytic ability (229); practical
    ability (229)
2.  intelligence quotient (231)
3.  potential (232)
4.  like (233); well-organized (234)
5.  lower (235); middle-class (236)

## 6.3 SPECIAL CHILDREN, SPECIAL NEEDS

1.  IQ (238); Creativity (238);
    flexibly (239)
2.  70 (239); less (239); lower (239)
3.  normal (240); reading (240)
4.  inattentive (242); conduct (242);
    stimulants (243)

## 6.4 ACADEMIC SKILLS

1.  sounds (245); Word recognition
    (245); Comprehension (245);
    increases (247)
2.  organizing (248); revising (248)
3.  directly (249); attitudes (251)
4.  academic excellence (252);
    monitors (252); parents (252);
    responsibility (254); mastery
    (254); monitor (254)

## 6.5 PHYSICAL DEVELOPMENT

1.  legs (256); same (256); 2,400
    (256);   one-fourth (257)
2.  in fine-motor (257); strength
    (257); cultural expectations
    (258)
3.  often enough (258);   lifetime
    (258)
4.  competition (258); performance
    (258)

# TEST YOURSELF

## MULTIPLE-CHOICE QUESTIONS

1.  D, (220)
2.  C, (220)
3.  A, (221)
4.  B, (222)
5.  A, (222)
6.  A, (222)
7.  B, (223)
8.  C, (223)
9.  A, (223)
10. A, (225)
11. C, (228)
12. A, (229)
13. B, (230)
14. A, (231)
15. C, (231)
16. D, (231)
17. D, (232)
18. B, (235)
19. B, (236)
20. C, (238)
21. D, (238)
22. B, (238)
23. D, (239)
24. A, (240)
25. A, (240)
26. B, (242)
27. D, (243)
28. A, (245)
29. D, (247)
30. B, (248)
31. C, (250)
32. A, (251)
33. D, (252)
34. A, (254)
35. B, (256)
36. B, (256)
37. A, (257)
38. A, (258)
39. B, (258)
40. D, (259)

## ESSAY QUESTIONS

1.  The behavior of Sam's sons fits Piaget's description of formal operational and concrete operational thought very
    well. According to Piaget, children who are 12 years old would be in the period of formal operations. Formal

operational children use more sophisticated, logical, deductive reasoning to solve problems like the safe problem. However, concrete operational children (such as the 8-year-old) use haphazard trial-and-error and often do not solve problems like the safe problem. Concrete operational children are more likely to try to solve problems in concrete ways such as pushing buttons, but formal operational children can think abstractly about the possible, logical combinations before attempting the button pushing. (220-222)

2. There does seem to be a hereditary component to intelligence. Studies of twins show that identical twins, who have identical genes, have more similar scores on intelligence tests than do fraternal twins or other non-twin siblings. This pattern of correlations supports the role of heredity in intelligence. Heredity also influences developmental change in IQ scores. Patterns of developmental change in IQ are more alike for identical twins than for fraternal twins. Similarly, adopted children's IQ scores become more similar to their biological parents' scores as they get older. The environment also is important in shaping one's intelligence. Children with high intelligence test scores tend to live in homes that are well-organized and have plenty of appropriate play materials. Mike will probably receive genes for above average intelligence from Mia and Mick, and they will probably provide a stimulating environment that nurtures Mike's intellectual development. (232-234)

3. First, children who develop exceptional talent in an area love the subject and have a very strong desire to master the subject. Second, children who develop exceptional talent begin instruction in the given area at an early age and they receive instruction from inspiring and talented teachers. Third, these children also receive help and support from their parents who are committed to promoting their children's talents. Lola sounds as if she is committed to supporting Lisa's piano playing and that she is willing to find inspiring and talented piano teachers for her. The critical question is whether Lisa loves to play the piano and has a strong desire to master piano playing. (238)

4. The first symptom that Antonio should be looking for in Claudio is overactivity. Can Claudio sit still in school? Children with ADHD are energetic and unable to keep still, especially in situations like school classrooms. The second sign is inattention. Children with ADHD do not pay attention in class and find it hard to concentrate on schoolwork. The final sign is that ADHD children are impulsive; they act before they think. Not all children show these symptoms to the same degree. For example, some children suffer from more inattention and others show more hyperactivity. Because of these problems, children with ADHD often are aggressive and often have problems with academic performance. (242)

5. Young children who know most of their letters and who can easily distinguish the sounds that the different letters make (phonological awareness) learn to read more readily and are more skilled readers. Jin-pyo can help Jae-jin master these skills by playing games with her that involve identifying the letters of the alphabet. Jin-pyo also can read books, such as Dr. Seuss or nursery rhymes, that contain rhymes that will increase her phonological awareness. Also, identifying letters and their sounds while reading books to Jae-jin will increase her phonological awareness. Even in older children, phonological awareness continues to be an excellent predictor of reading ability. (239)

6. Students in the United States do fare poorly on tests of math skills when compared to students in many other countries, but you can tell your friend that, in fact, there are no systematic differences in general intelligence nor in general cognitive skills between children in the United States and those in Japan or Taiwan. Experiences at home and school seem to account for the differences in math achievement. In general, children in Japan and Taiwan spend more hours in school and spend a greater percentage of those hours engaged in academic pursuits. Children in Japan and Taiwan also spend more time per week doing homework, and they rate homework as being more valuable than do children in the United States. Parents in Japan and Taiwan tend to have higher expectations for achievement in their children, and they believe that effort and experience are critical in determining achievement. In other words, differences in achievement stem from differences in cultural attitudes and school practices. (249-252)

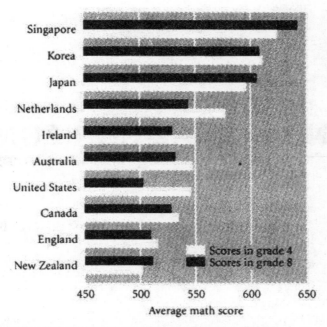

SOURCE: Based on data from the Third International Math and Science Study, 1997

7. You can tell your friend that most first-graders are not very good writers. First, their stories often are very limited because their knowledge of the world is limited. As children learn more about the world, they have more interesting information to incorporate into their stories. Second, young writers, like Hasani, use a knowledge-telling strategy in which they write down information on a topic as they retrieve it from memory. This often means that the writing is disorganized and disjointed. Third, as children become more proficient at the mechanical requirements of writing (e.g., spelling, punctuation, handwriting) they can devote more of their attention to the other aspects of writing that make a story more interesting. Finally, as children develop, they become better editors of their own writing. Older children are more likely to find problems and revise them. So, as Hasani matures during the elementary-school years his writing should improve, and his mother shouldn't be worried about his simple-minded, unorganized stories. (247-249)

8. Schools where the students typically succeed rather than fail have a number of characteristics in common. First, both the staff and students understand that academic excellence is the primary goal of the school and of every student in the school. Second, the school environment is safe and nurturing so that students can devote their energy to learning. Third, successful schools have a high level of formal and informal parental involvement. Finally, the progress of students, teachers, and programs is monitored to determine if academic goals are being met. (252)

9. First, computers allow individual instruction that occurs at the student's pace. This may be particularly helpful for students who are slower or faster than the average students in class. Second, simulation programs on computers allow for experiential learning. These simulations allow students to experience things like space travel without ever leaving the classroom. Third, graphics and word-processing programs are important tools that make many assignments easier to accomplish. Fourth, computers may free some of the teachers' time so that they can devote more attention to other aspects of instruction. (253)

10. Good coaches praise children rather than criticize them and they have realistic expectations. They also nurture children's respect for opponents, other coaches, and officials. They are good role models. Finally, they make sure that the kids have fun. Bad coaches emphasize winning over skill development and criticize or punish players for bad plays. Children who have bad coaches are more likely to lose interest and stop playing a sport. If your spouse keeps the characteristics of good coaches in mind, the season will be better for the girls. (259)

# CHAPTER 7

# EXPANDING SOCIAL HORIZONS

This chapter focuses on how the child is influenced by family members, peers, television, and their understanding of others.

# 7.1 FAMILY RELATIONSHIPS

## TO MASTER THE LEARNING OBJECTIVES:

**What are the primary dimensions of parenting? How do they affect children's development?**

- Describe the view of families as systems.

- Describe how the degree of parental warmth is related to outcomes for children.

- Explain why moderate levels of parental control are best for children.

- Describe positive aspects of control.

- Describe the authoritarian, authoritative, indulgent-permissive, and indifferent-uninvolved parental styles.

- Describe how the various parental styles are related to children's developmental outcomes.

- Compare cultural and socioeconomic differences in parental warmth and control.

- Describe the parental behaviors and other factors that influence children's behavior.

- Describe how parents' marital systems influence development.

- Explain the reciprocal influence between children and their parents.

**What determines how siblings get along?  How do first-born, later-born, and only children differ?**

- Describe how older children may react when a younger sibling is born.

- Describe how the sibling relationship changes over the first few years of life.

- Explain how gender, temperament, age, perceptions of parental treatment, and quality of the relationship between the parents are related to the quality of sibling relationships.

- Compare adopted and non-adopted children.

- Explain the differences in parental behavior with first-born and later-born children.

**How do divorce and remarriage affect children?**

- Describe how divorce affects children's lives.

- Describe how divorce influences development and which children are the most affected by parental divorce.

- Describe how blended families with stepmothers differ from blended families with stepfathers.

**What factors contribute to child abuse?**

- Define physical abuse, sexual abuse, psychological abuse, and neglect.

- Describe cultural, parental, and child factors that are related to an increased likelihood of abuse.

- Describe the effects of child abuse on the children.

- Describe some things that can be done to reduce the risk of child abuse.

## 7.1 KNOW THE TERMS

| | |
|---|---|
| **Authoritarian** | **Negative reinforcement trap** |
| **Authoritative** | **Permissive** |
| **Blended** | **Punishment** |
| **Counterimitation** | **Reinforcement** |
| **Direct instruction** | **Socialization** |
| **Disinhibition** | **Time-out** |
| **Inhibition** | **Uninvolved** |
| **Joint custody** | |

1. The process of teaching children the values, roles, and behaviors of their cultures is called

   _____ .

2. _____ parents show high levels of control and low levels of warmth toward their children.

3.  Parents who use a moderate amount of control and who are warm and responsive to their children are _____ parents.

4.  _____ parents are warm and caring, but they exert little control over their children.

5.  Parents who are neither warm nor controlling and who try to minimize the amount of time spent with their children are _____ parents.

6.  Telling a child what to do, when, and why is called _____ .

7.  Observing another's behavior and learning what should not be done is known as _____ .

8.  An increase in all behaviors like those observed is called _____ .

9.  _____ occurs when observation leads to a decreased likelihood of an entire class of behaviors.

10. _____ is an action that increases the likelihood of the response that it follows.

11. _____ is any action that discourages the reoccurrence of the response that it follows.

12. Parents may unwittingly reinforce the very behaviors that they want to discourage in a situation called a _____ .

13. _____ involves removing children who are misbehaving from a situation to a quiet, unstimulating environment.

14. In _____ both parents retain legal custody of their children after divorce.

15. _____ families consist of a biological parent, a stepparent, and children.

# 7.1 KNOW THE DETAILS OF FAMILY RELATIONSHIPS

1.  According to the systems view, parents and children influence each other.
    TRUE or FALSE

2.  Children benefit from warm and responsive parenting.
    TRUE or FALSE

3.  Children do best when parents exert a high level of control.
    TRUE or FALSE

4.  Authoritarian parenting combines high control with warmth and responsiveness to the children.
    TRUE or FALSE

5. Permissive parents are warm and caring but exert little control over their children.
TRUE or FALSE

6. Children with authoritarian parents tend to be responsible, self-reliant, and friendly.
TRUE or FALSE

7. Children with uninvolved parents more often do poorly in school and are aggressive.
TRUE or FALSE

8. Although authoritative parenting is generally considered the most beneficial, authoritarian parenting can protect children growing up in dangerous areas.
TRUE or FALSE

9. Direct instruction involves telling a child what to do, when, and why.
TRUE or FALSE

10. Counterimitation involves watching the parental model and imitating what they do.
TRUE or FALSE

11. Reinforcement is any action that increases the likelihood of the response that it follows.
TRUE or FALSE

12. A negative reinforcement trap occurs when parents unwittingly reinforce the very behaviors they want to discourage.
TRUE or FALSE

13. Punishment works best when it is used only occasionally after an undesired behavior.
TRUE or FALSE

14. Time-out involves having a child who misbehaved briefly sit alone in a quiet, unstimulating location.
TRUE or FALSE

15. Parental conflict is not harmful to children.
TRUE or FALSE

16. Children's behavior can influence the parenting style used.
TRUE or FALSE

17. The basic pattern of sibling relationship is usually established early in life and remains stable.
TRUE or FALSE

18. Sibling relations are more likely to be warm and harmonious between siblings of the opposite sex than between siblings of the same sex.
TRUE or FALSE

19. Adopted children are more prone to problems when they were adopted at an older age and when their care before adoption was poor.
TRUE or FALSE

20. Parents are usually more affectionate and more punitive with first-borns than with later-borns.
    TRUE or FALSE

21. Compared to first-born children, later-born children tend to be more intelligent and more willing to conform to parents' requests.
    TRUE or FALSE

22. Only children are worse off than children with siblings in terms of intelligence, leadership, autonomy, and maturity.
    TRUE or FALSE

23. Children of divorce are more likely than children from intact homes to experience conflict in their own marriages.
    TRUE or FALSE

24. As divorce became more common in the 1970s and 1980s, the effects on children diminished.
    TRUE or FALSE

25. Children adjust to divorce more readily if their divorced parents cooperate with each other.
    TRUE or FALSE

26. Children often adjust better to parental divorce when they live with the same-sex parent.
    TRUE or FALSE

27. Parental divorce is more harmful for school-age children and adolescents than for preschoolers or college-age adults.
    TRUE or FALSE

28. Children whose parents are married but fight often show many of the same effects associated with parental divorce.
    TRUE or FALSE

29. Children adjust better to divorce when they keep good relationships with both parents.
    TRUE or FALSE

30. Preadolescent girls tend to adjust better than preadolescent boys to having a stepfather when their mothers remarry.
    TRUE or FALSE

31. Countries that do not approve of physical punishment tend to have lower rates of child maltreatment than the U.S.
    TRUE or FALSE

32. Older children are more likely than younger children to be the targets of abuse.
    TRUE or FALSE

33. Children who are abused tend to have poor relationships with peers.
    TRUE or FALSE

# 7.2 PEERS

## TO MASTER THE LEARNING OBJECTIVES:

**What are the benefits of friendship?**

- Describe how friendship changes throughout childhood.

- Describe why intimacy and loyalty are important in friendships among adolescents.

- Explain how the source of social support changes from childhood to adolescence.

- Describe the characteristics that friends usually have in common.

- Explain the positive consequences associated with having friends.

- Describe how sexual activity is related to friends' sexual activity.

**What are important features of groups of children and adolescents? How do these groups influence individuals?**

- Describe how the status of one's crowd is related to self-esteem.

- Explain how parents influence their adolescent children's membership in crowds.

- Describe factors that determine which children and adolescents will become leaders of their groups.

- Explain the circumstances under which peer pressure is likely to be most influential.

**Why are some children more popular than others? What are the causes and consequences of being rejected?**

- Describe popular, rejected, controversial, average, and neglected children.

- Describe the characteristics that are related to popularity and rejection.

**Why are some children so aggressive? Why are others frequent targets of aggression?**

- Describe the consequences of being a rejected child.

- Explain how parental behavior and disciplinary practices are related to a child's rejection by peers.

- Explain why some children are victims of aggression.

## 7.2 KNOW THE TERMS

| | |
|---|---|
| Average | Hostile aggression |
| Clique | Instrumental aggression |
| Controversial | Neglected |
| Crowd | Popular |

**Dominance hierarchy**                    **Rejected**

**Friendship**

1.  _____ is a voluntary relationship between two people involving mutual liking.

2.  A small group of friends who are similar in age, sex, and race is called a _____ .

3.  Many cliques that have similar attitudes and values may become part of a larger group known as a _____ .

4.  Groups often have a _____ where group members with lower status defer to the group leader.

5.  Children who are _____ are liked by many classmates.

6.  Children who are _____ are disliked by many classmates.

7.  _____ children are both liked and disliked by many classmates.

8.  Children who are _____ are liked and disliked by many classmates, but without the intensity found for popular, rejected, or controversial children.

9.  Children who are _____ are ignored by classmates.

10. In _____ , a child uses aggression to achieve an explicit goal.

11. _____ is unprovoked and seems to have as its sole goal to intimidate, harass, or humiliate another child.

# 7.2 KNOW THE DETAILS OF PEERS

1.  Children begin to have friendships characterized by trust and assistance in the older elementary school years.
    TRUE or FALSE

2.  Older children and adolescents emphasize a friend's role as a playmate.
    TRUE or FALSE

3.  Intimacy is more common in girls' friendships than in boys' friendships.
    TRUE or FALSE

4.  Adolescents depend less on friends and more on family for social support than they did earlier in childhood.
    TRUE or FALSE

5. Most friends are similar in age, sex, and race.

   TRUE or FALSE

6. Researchers generally find that friends are enjoyable but do not give children any tangible benefits.

   TRUE or FALSE

7. Adolescents are more likely to e sexually active when their best friends are sexually active.

   TRUE or FALSE

8. Self-esteem in older children and adolescents is unrelated to the status of their crowd.

   TRUE or FALSE

9. When parents monitor their children's out-of-school behavior, their children are less likely to be in the druggie crowd.

   TRUE or FALSE

10. In groups of young boys, physical power is often the basis for leadership.

    TRUE or FALSE

11. Peer pressure is strongest when the standards for appropriate behavior are not clear-cut.

    TRUE or FALSE

12. Most popular children are not skilled academically.

    TRUE or FALSE

13. Many rejected children are aggressive and hostile.

    TRUE or FALSE

14. Children who are rejected by their peers are more likely to drop out of school and commit juvenile offenses.

    TRUE or FALSE

15. Inconsistent discipline is associated with antisocial, aggressive behavior in children.

    TRUE or FALSE

16. Rejected children can learn social skills that make it more likely that they will be accepted by other children.

    TRUE or FALSE

17. Instrumental aggression is unprovoked and seems to have a goal of intimidation, harassment, or humiliation of another child.

    TRUE or FALSE

18. Children's tendencies to behave aggressively are stable over time.

    TRUE or FALSE

# 7.3 TELEVISION: BOOB TUBE OR WINDOW ON THE WORLD?

## TO MASTER THE LEARNING OBJECTIVES:

**What is the impact of watching television on children's attitudes and behavior?**

- Describe how watching TV violence affects children.

- Describe how television portrays women, minorities, and the elderly.

- Explain how television influences children's sex-role stereotypes.

- Describe the view that younger and older children have of television commercials.

- Explain how TV viewing may influence prosocial behavior in children.

**How does TV viewing influence children's cognitive development?**

- Describe the impact of educational TV programs on children's cognitive development.

- Describe the criticisms of TV that are supported by research.

## 7.3 KNOW THE DETAILS OF TELEVISION

1. For most children, the amount of TV watched decreases gradually during the preschool and elementary school years.

   TRUE or FALSE

2. Boys watch more TV than girls.

   TRUE or FALSE

3. Children with higher IQs watch more TV than those with lower IQs.

   TRUE or FALSE

4. Family income is unrelated to the amount of TV watched.

   TRUE or FALSE

5. Exposure to TV violence has no effect on aggression in children.

   TRUE or FALSE

6. The view of minorities, women, and the elderly on TV accurately represents their roles in real life.

   TRUE or FALSE

7. Children who watch TV frequently tend to have more stereotyped views of males and females than children who watch TV less often (see figure below).

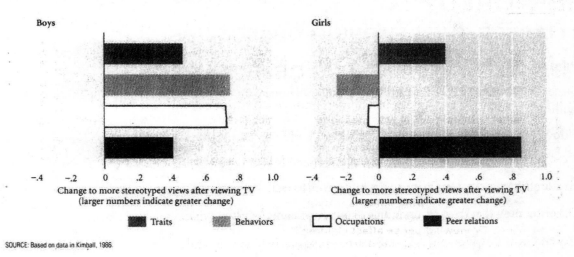

SOURCE: Based on data in Kimball, 1986.

   TRUE or FALSE

8. Children realize the persuasive intent of commercials as early as 3 years of age.

   TRUE or FALSE

9. Commercials are not usually effective sales tools with children.

   TRUE or FALSE

10. Children who watch TV shows that emphasize prosocial behavior are more likely to behave prosocially.

    TRUE or FALSE

11. Prosocial behaviors are shown on TV programs far more frequently than aggressive behaviors.

    TRUE or FALSE

12. Children who watched Sesame Street frequently tend to be better prepared for school than those who watched infrequently.

    TRUE or FALSE

13. TV watching reduces children's attention spans.

    TRUE or FALSE

# 7.4 UNDERSTANDING OTHERS

## TO MASTER THE LEARNING OBJECTIVES:

**As children develop, how do they describe others differently?**

- Describe how children's descriptions of others begin with the concrete and become more conceptual with age.

**How does understanding of others' thinking change as children develop?**

- Explain how children's perspective-taking changes with age.

**When do children develop prejudice toward others?**

- Describe how the level of prejudice typically changes during childhood.

## 7.4 KNOW THE DETAILS OF UNDERSTANDING OTHERS

1. As children get older, their descriptions of other people change from being in terms of concrete features to being in terms of abstract traits.
   TRUE or FALSE

2. Preschoolers are usually in Selman's self-reflective stage of perspective-taking.
   TRUE or FALSE

3. Children who are in Selman's undifferentiated stage of perspective-taking know that self and others can have different thoughts and feelings, but often confuse the two.
   TRUE or FALSE

4. Adolescents are typically in Selman's social-informational stage of perspective-taking.
   TRUE or FALSE

5. Individuals who realize that a third person's perspective is influenced by broader personal, social, and cultural contexts would be in Selman's societal stage of perspective-taking.
   TRUE or FALSE

6. The third-person stage is the most advanced level of Selman's perspective taking theory.
   TRUE or FALSE

7. Children with better perspective-taking skills tend to have more positive social interactions.
   TRUE or FALSE

8. Prejudice tends to increase as children move from preschool into the elementary school years.
   TRUE or FALSE

9. Young children tend to be biased positively toward their own group.
TRUE or FALSE

10. Prejudice can be reduced by having children from different groups work together toward common goals.
TRUE or FALSE

# SUMMARY

## 7.1 FAMILY RELATIONSHIPS

1. **The Family as a System**

   According to the systems approach, the family consists of _____ elements--parents and children influence each other. The family itself is influenced by other social systems, such as neighborhoods and religious organizations.

2. **Dimensions and Styles of Parenting**

   One key factor in parent-child relationships is the degree of warmth that parents express. Children clearly benefit from warm, caring parents. A second factor is control, which is complicated because neither too much nor too little control is desirable. Effective parental control involves setting appropriate standards, _____ them, and trying to anticipate conflicts. Taking into account both warmth and control, four prototypic parental styles emerge: (a) Authoritarian parents are _____ but uninvolved. (b) Authoritative parents are fairly controlling but are also _____ to their children. (c) Permissive parents are loving but exert little control. (d) Uninvolved parents are neither warm nor controlling. _____ parenting seems best for children, in terms of both cognitive and social development. But there are important exceptions associated with culture and socioeconomic status.

3. **Parental Behavior**

   Parents influence development by direct instruction and coaching. In addition, parents serve as models for their children, who sometimes imitate parents' behavior directly; sometimes children behave in ways that are similar to what they have seen (disinhibition), and sometimes in ways that are _____ of what they've seen (counterimitation). Parents also use feedback to influence children's behavior. Sometimes parents fall into the _____ , inadvertently reinforcing behaviors that they want to discourage. Punishment is effective when it is prompt, _____ , accompanied by an explanation, and delivered by a person with whom the child has a warm relationship. Punishment has limited value because it suppresses behaviors but does not _____ them, and it often has side effects. _____ is one useful form of punishment. Chronic conflict is harmful to children, but children can benefit when their parents solve problems constructively. Parenting is a team sport, but not all parents play well together because they may disagree in _____ or parenting methods. Parenting is influenced by characteristics of the children themselves. A child's age and temperament will influence how a parent tries to exert control over the child.

4. **Siblings**

The birth of a sibling can be stressful for children, particularly when the children are still young and when parents ignore their needs. Siblings get along better when they are of the _____ , believe that parents treat them _____ , enter adolescence, and have parents who get along well. As adoption became more common in the US, a myth grew that adopted children are more prone to problems. Research shows that adopted children are similar to children living with biological parents in many respects, but they are more prone to some problems such as adjusting in school and to conduct disorders. However, these results depend strongly on the child's _____ when adopted and the quality of care prior to adoption, which suggests that adoption *per se* is not a problem for children's development. Parents have higher _____ for first-born children, which explains why these children are more intelligent and more likely to go to college. Later-born children are more _____ and more innovative. Contradicting the folklore, only children are almost never worse off than children with siblings, and on some dimensions (such as intelligence, achievement, autonomy), they are often better off.

5. **Divorce and Remarriage**

Divorce can harm children in a number of domains ranging from school achievement to adjustment. The impact of divorce stems from less _____ of children following divorce, economic hardship, and _____ between parents. Children often benefit when parents have joint custody following divorce, or when they live with the _____ parent. When a mother remarries, _____ sometimes have difficulty adjusting because the new stepfather encroaches on an intimate relationship with the mother. A father's remarriage can cause problems because children fear that the stepmother will disturb intimate father-child relationships and because of tension between the stepmother and the noncustodial mother.

6. **Parent-Child Relationships Gone Awry: Child Abuse**

Cultural factors contributing to child abuse include a culture's views on violence, poverty, and _____ . Parents who abuse their children were often neglected or abused themselves and tend to be _____ and socially unskilled individuals. Younger or _____ children are more likely to be targets of abuse. Children who are abused often lag behind in cognitive and _____ development.

## 7.2 PEERS

1. **Friendships**

   Friendships among younger children are based on _____ and getting along well. As children grow, loyalty, trust, and _____ become more important features in their friendships. Friends are usually similar in age, sex, _____ , and race. Children with friends are _____ and better adjusted.

2. **Groups**

   Older children and adolescents often form _____ --groups of like-minded individuals--that become part of a crowd. Some crowds have higher status than others, and members of higher-status crowds often have higher _____ than members of lower-status crowds. Common to most groups is a dominance hierarchy, a well-defined structure with a leader at the top. _____ often determines the dominance hierarchy, particularly among boys. However, with older children and adolescents, dominance hierarchies are more often based on _____ that are important to the group. Peer pressure is neither totally powerful nor totally evil. In fact, groups influence individuals primarily in areas where standards of behavior are unclear, such as tastes in _____ or clothing, or concerning drinking, _____ , and sex.

3. **Popularity and Rejection**

   Most popular children are socially skilled. They often share, cooperate, and _____ others. A far smaller number of popular children use aggression to achieve their social goals. Some children are rejected by their peers, often because they are too _____ or withdrawn. These children are often unsuccessful in school and have behavioral problems.

4. **Aggressive Children and Their Victims**

   Many highly aggressive children end up being violent and poorly adjusted adults. Children who are chronic victims of aggression either overreact or _____ themselves.

## 7.3 TELEVISION: BOOB TUBE OR WINDOW ON THE WORLD?

1. **Influence on Attitudes and Social Behavior**

   Children's social behaviors and attitudes are influenced by what they see on TV. Youngsters who frequently watch televised violence become more _____ , whereas those who watch prosocial TV become more socially skilled. Children who watch TV frequently may adopt TV's distorted view of women, minorities, and older people.

2. **Influences on Cognition**

   TV programs designed to foster children's cognitive skills, such as *Sesame Street* are effective. Children frequently improve their _____ skills and often adjust more readily to school.

3. **Criticisms of TV**

   Many popular criticisms about TV as a medium are not consistently supported by research. TV-watching per se does not shorten children's _____ and does not consistently lead to reduced creativity.

## 7.4 UNDERSTANDING OTHERS

1. **Describing Others**

   Children's descriptions of others change in much the same way that children's descriptions of themselves change. During the early elementary school years, descriptions emphasize _____ characteristics. In the late elementary school years, they emphasize _____ . In adolescence, they emphasize providing an integral picture of others.

2. **Understanding What Others Think**

   According to Selman's theory, children's understanding of how others think progresses through five stages. In the first, the undifferentiated stage, children often confuse _____ and another's view. In the last, the societal stage, adolescents can take a _____ perspective and know that this perspective is influenced by context.

3. **Prejudice**

   Prejudice emerges in the preschool years, soon after children recognize different _____ . Prejudice _____ during childhood, as children's cognitive growth helps them to understand that social groups are heterogeneous not homogeneous. However, older children and adolescents still show prejudice, which is best reduced by additional _____ to individuals from other social groups.

# TEST YOURSELF

## MULTIPLE-CHOICE QUESTIONS

1. Children benefit most when parents exhibit _____ control over their children.
   a. no
   b. very little
   c. moderate
   d. very strong

2. Chinese parents have been found to _____ than American parents.
   a. be less controlling
   b. be more emotionally restrained
   c. be more affectionate
   d. stress individualism more

3. Jessica's parents usually explain why they set specific rules, and encourage Jessica to talk with them about their rules. While they do set expectations for Jessica's behavior, they are quite affectionate, loving, and interested in what is going on in Jessica's life. Jessica's parents most closely fit the _____ parenting style.
   a. authoritarian
   b. authoritative
   c. permissive
   d. uninvolved

4. Victoria's parents dote on her. They want her to have the best of everything and do what they can to cater to her sometimes frivolous whims. They are usually quite satisfied with Victoria's behavior and have rarely disciplined her. Their parenting style most closely resembles the _____ pattern.
   a. authoritarian
   b. authoritative
   c. permissive
   d. uninvolved

5. Children with _____ parents often have lower self-esteem and are unhappy.
   a. Authoritarian
   b. authoritative
   c. permissive
   d. uninvolved

6. Children with _____ parents usually do poorly in school and are aggressive.
   a. authoritarian
   b. authoritative
   c. permissive
   d. uninvolved

7. Jasmine's mother told her to wash her hands before she eats, explaining that she needs to wash away the germs before she eats. Jasmine's mother was using
   a. time-out.
   b. positive reinforcement.
   c. punishment.
   d. direct instruction.

8. Jordan often saw his father kick and throw things when they didn't work properly, and Jordan became less likely to kick and throw things himself. Jordan's observation resulted in
   a. counterimitation.
   b. disinhibition.
   c. reinforcement.
   d. a negative reinforcement trap.

9. Punishment is most effective when
   a. it is administered with a delay after the behavior occurs.
   b. it is administered only occasionally when the misbehavior occurs.
   c. there is no explanation of why the child was punished.
   d. the child has a warm, affectionate relationship with the punisher.

10. When parents punish children by making them sit alone in a quiet, unstimulating location for a few minutes, they are using a method of discipline called
    a. time-out.
    b. disinhibition.
    c. direct instruction.
    d. inhibition.

11. Sibling relations are less likely to be harmonious when
    a. the younger sibling approaches adolescence.
    b. siblings are of the same sex.
    c. both siblings are very emotional.
    d. parents have a warm, harmonious relationship.

12. Which of the following statements concerning birth order effects or family constellation is true?
    a. First-born children typically have higher scores on intelligence tests and are more likely than later-borns to go to college.
    b. First-born children are more innovative and popular with their peers than later-born children.
    c. Later-born children are more willing than first-borns to conform to parents' and adults' requests.
    d. Only children tend to be worse off in many ways than children with siblings.

13. The effect of divorce on children
    a. is about the same for girls and boys.
    b. is greater for preschool children than for school-age children and adolescents.
    c. became less harmful during the 1990s than it had been prior to that time.
    d. is less negative when children live with their opposite-sex parent.

14. _____ is occurring when children do not receive adequate food, clothing, or medical care.
    a. Sexual abuse
    b. Psychological abuse
    c. Physical abuse
    d. Neglect

15. Child abuse occurs more often
    a. in countries like Sweden, where physical punishment is not socially accepted, than in countries like the United States, where physical punishment is accepted.
    b. when children are older rather than younger.
    c. when parents have low expectations for their children.
    d. when families are socially isolated from other relatives or neighbors.

16. When describing her friends, 6-year-old Samantha is likely to emphasize
    a. their role as a playmate.
    b. their loyalty.
    c. mutual give and take.
    d. intimacy.

17. A new aspect of friendship during adolescence is
    a. shared activities.
    b. trust.
    c. assistance.
    d. intimacy.

18. Interracial friendships
    a. are more likely to occur when classes are large.
    b. are more likely to occur when classes are small.
    c. made in school usually extend to out-of-school settings when neighborhoods are segregated.
    d. are as likely to occur as same-race friendships.

19. Children with friends _____ than children without friends.
    a. show less prosocial behavior
    b. adapt less readily to new schools
    c. have higher self-esteem
    d. are more likely to be victimized by their peers

20. When parents have _____ parenting styles, their children are likely to become involved with crowds that _____.
    a. uninvolved or indulgent; endorse adult standards of behavior
    b. authoritative; reject adult standards of behavior
    c. authoritarian; do not use drugs
    d. authoritative; endorse adult standards of behavior

21. Nate is the leader of a group of boys that call themselves the "Arrows." The boys in the group all go along with the decisions that Nate makes about what the "Arrows" are going to do. The "Arrows" have a group structure known as
    a. power assertion.
    b. a dominance hierarchy.
    c. a blended family.
    d. authoritative.

22. Bobby, a(n) _____ child, is admired and even idolized by many of his classmates, but at the same time is detested and avoided by many of his other classmates.
    a. popular
    b. rejected
    c. controversial
    d. average

23. Popular children _____ while unpopular children _____ .
    a. are more likely to share, cooperate, and help; typically do not
    b. tend to make groups adjust to them; try to fit in with groups
    c. typically have average intelligence; are quite often gifted
    d. are more likely to break rules; are less likely to do so

24. Deirdre is very aggressive with other children, often verbally attacking them for no apparent reason. Whenever someone disagrees with her, she becomes very angry and tries to get back at them in some way. Other children tend to reject her. Compared to more popular children, Deirdre is more likely to
    a. do well in school.
    b. have parents who discipline her consistently.
    c. drop out of school.
    d. have fewer behavioral problems.

25. A child who uses aggression to achieve an explicit goal is demonstrating
    a. a dominance hierarchy.
    b. hostile aggression.
    c. instrumental aggression.
    d. relational aggression.

26. An effective strategy to for victimized children to use for dealing with aggression is to
    a. respond to aggression with aggression.
    b. show fear when threatened.
    c. increase their self-esteem so they are less tolerant of personal abuse.
    d. encourage them to avoid friendships with peers.

27. Which of the following statements concerning children's TV habits is true?
    a.  TV viewing time increases gradually during the preschool and elementary school years, reaching a peak at about 11 or 12 years of age.
    b.  Girls watch more TV than boys.
    c.  Children with higher IQs watch more TV than those with lower IQs.
    d.  Children from higher-income families watch more TV than children from lower-income families.

28. Michael frequently watches TV shows with high levels of violence. If Michael responds typically,
    a.  his behavior is not likely to be affected by the exposure to TV violence.
    b.  he is likely to become less tolerant of aggression in others.
    c.  he is likely to become less aggressive.
    d.  he is likely to become more aggressive.

29. Which of the following was NOT a recommendation in the text for parents regarding children's television-viewing?
    a.  Encourage children to know what they want to watch before they turn on the TV.
    b.  Allow children to determine how much TV per week they can watch.
    c.  Parents should watch TV with their children and discuss the programs.
    d.  Parents need to be good TV viewers themselves. That is, they shouldn't watch violent programs or others that are inappropriate for children.

30. Prosocial TV shows
    a.  have no influence on children's prosocial behavior.
    b.  have less influence on children's prosocial behavior than violent TV shows have on children's aggressive behavior.
    c.  are more common than violent TV shows.
    d.  can increase prosocial behavior.

31. Four-year-old Austin watches Sesame Street regularly. She is likely to
    a.  have better academic skills than children who watch Sesame Street less often.
    b.  find school boring by comparison and adjust poorly when she begins kindergarten.
    c.  have a smaller vocabulary than children who watch Sesame Street less often.
    d.  be more aggressive than children who watch Sesame Street less often.

32. Compared to older children's descriptions, younger children's descriptions of other people are more likely to focus on _____ traits.
    a.  psychological
    b.  abstract
    c.  personality
    d.  concrete

33. Which of Selman's stages of perspective taking is the least advanced?
    a.  social-informational
    b.  third-person
    c.  undifferentiated
    d.  societal

34. Who has the most advanced form of perspective-taking?
    a. Janda, who can step in another's shoes and view himself as others do.
    b. Michael, who knows that he and others can have different thoughts and feelings but often confuses the two.
    c. Brian, who can step out of the immediate situation to see how he and another person are viewed by a third person.
    d. Maria, who realizes that a third person's perspective is influenced by broader personal, social, and cultural contexts.

35. Prejudice
    a. is rare in preschoolers.
    b. decreases as children learn that they are part of a specific group.
    c. increases when children have more contact with children from other groups.
    d. decreases when children use role-playing to imagine what it would be like to be from a different ethnic group and experience discrimination.

## ESSAY QUESTIONS

1. Your friend Shabrisha is concerned because her 7-year-old daughter and her 5-year-old son seem to fight constantly. Shabrisha's daughter has always been temperamental, and Shabrisha thinks that the fighting may be her fault. Shabrisha remembers being very close to and fighting very little with her sister when they were children, and she thinks that her children must be unusual because they fight so much. What can you tell Shabrisha about the factors that are related to harmonious relationships between siblings?

2. Your friends Mark and Bianca are getting an amicable divorce and they are trying to decide what custody arrangement would be best for their 11-year-old daughter, Kelly. What can you tell them about the effects of various custody arrangements and the effects of remarriage on children, in general, and daughters, in particular?

3. Your friend Lars has noticed that his 15-year-old daughter, Ingrid, seems very concerned with how loyal her friends are to her. Lars doesn't remember being so concerned about his friends' loyalty to him when he was an adolescent. What can you tell Lars about loyalty and intimacy in the friendships of adolescent girls?

4. Your spouse is concerned that your 2-year-old son grow up to be popular rather than rejected and is wondering what the two of you can do to help your son achieve this goal. What can you tell your spouse about the relation between parents' behavior and disciplinary practices and their child's popularity or rejection?

5. Your friend Chuck does not have a TV in his house because he feels that TV will only have negative effects on his children--they will become more violent, they'll ask for junky toys that they see advertised, etc. Chuck feels that nothing good can come of TV viewing. What can you tell Chuck about the research on the effects of television on children?

6. Your friend is an elementary school teacher at a multi-cultural school, and he is concerned that the children in his class show a lot of prejudice toward the other students who are members of other racial

or ethnic groups in class. He is wondering what he can do to reduce the prejudice in his students. What can you tell him?

# SOLUTIONS

## 7.1 KNOW THE TERMS

1. socialization (265)
2. Authoritarian (268)
3. authoritative (268)
4. Permissive (268)
5. uninvolved (268)
6. direct instruction (239)
7. counterimitation (270)
8. disinhibition (270)
9. Inhibition (270)
10. Reinforcement (263)
11. Punishment (270)
12. negative reinforcement trap (270)
13. Time-out (271)
14. joint custody (277)
15. Blended (278)

## 7.1 KNOW THE DETAILS OF FAMILY RELATIONSHIPS

1. T, (266)
2. T, (267)
3. F, (267)
4. F, (268)
5. T, (268)
6. F, (268)
7. T, (268)
8. T, (269)
9. T, (269)
10. F, (270)
11. T, (270)
12. T, (270)
13. F, (270)
14. T, (271)
15. F, (271)
16. T, (273)
17. T, (274)
18. F, (275)
19. T, (276)
20. T, (276)
21. F, (276)
22. F, (276)
23. T, (277)
24. T, (277)
25. T, (277)
26. T, (277)
27. T, (278)
28. T, (278)
29. T, (278)
30. F, (279)
31. T, (280)
32. F, (281)
33. T, (281)

## 7.2 KNOW THE TERMS

1. Friendship (283)
2. clique (287)
3. crowd (287)
4. dominance hierarchy (287)
5. popular (289)
6. rejected (289)
7. Controversial (289)
8. average (289)
9. neglected (289)
10. instrumental aggression (290)
11. Hostile aggression (290)

## 7.2 KNOW THE DETAILS OF PEERS

1. T, (284)
2. F, (284)
3. T, (284)
4. F, (284)
5. T, (284)
6. F, (285)
7. T, (286)
8. F, (287)
9. T, (287)
10. T, (287)
11. T, (288)
12. F, (289)
13. T, (289)
14. T, (289)
15. T, (290)
16. T, (290)
17. F, (290)
18. T, (290)

# 7.3 KNOW THE DETAILS OF TELEVISION

1. F, (292)
2. T, (292)
3. F, (292)
4. F, (292)
5. F, (292)
6. F, (293)
7. T, (293)
8. F, (294)
9. F, (294)
10. T, (295)
11. F, (295)
12. T, (295)
13. F, (296)

# 7.4 KNOW THE DETAILS OF UNDERSTANDING OTHERS

1. T, (297)
2. F, (299)
3. T, (299)
4. F, (299)
5. T, (299)
6. F, (299)
7. T, (300)
8. F, (300)
9. T, (300)
10. T, (301)

# SUMMARY

## 7.1 FAMILY RELATIONSHIPS

1. interacting (266)
2. enforcing (267); controlling (268); responsive (268); Authoritative (268)
3. opposite (270); negative reinforcement trap (270); consistent (270); eliminate (271); Time-out (271); child-rearing goals (272)
4. same sex (275); similarly (275); age (276); expectations (276); popular (276)
5. supervision (277); conflict (277); same-sex (277); daughters (279)
6. social isolation (280); unhappy (281); unhealthy (281); social (281)

## 7.2 PEERS

1. liking each other (284); intimacy (284); attitudes (284); more skilled socially (285)
2. cliques (287); self-esteem (287); Physical power (287); skills (287); music (288); drug use (288)
3. help (289); aggressive (290)
4. refuse to defend (291)

## 7.3 TELEVISION: BOOB TUBE OR WINDOW ON THE WORLD?

1. aggressive (292)
2. academic (295)
3. attention span (296)

## 7.4 UNDERSTANDING OTHERS

1. concrete (298); personality traits (298)
2. their own (298); third-person's (299)
3. social groups (300); declines (300); exposure (301)

# TEST YOURSELF

## MULTIPLE-CHOICE QUESTIONS

| | | |
|---|---|---|
| 1. C, (267) | 13. A, (278) | 25. C, (290) |
| 2. B, (268) | 14. D, (280) | 26. C, (291) |
| 3. B, (268) | 15. D, (280) | 27. A, (292) |
| 4. C, (268) | 16. A, (284) | 28. D, (292) |
| 5. A, (268) | 17. D, (284) | 29. B, (294) |
| 6. D, (268) | 18. B, (284) | 30. D, (295) |
| 7. D, (269) | 19. C, (285) | 31. A, (295) |
| 8. A, (270) | 20. D, (287) | 32. D, (297) |
| 9. D, (271) | 21. B, (287) | 33. C, (299) |
| 10. A, (271) | 22. C, (289) | 34. D, (299) |
| 11. C, (275) | 23. A, (289) | 35. D, (301) |
| 12. A, (276) | 24. C, (289) | |

## ESSAY QUESTIONS

1.  The first factor that is related to the quality of sibling relationships is gender. Same-sex sibling pairs tend to have more harmonious relationships than mixed-sex pairs. The second factor is temperament. Siblings tend to have better relationships when neither one of them is emotionally temperamental. Third, siblings' perceptions that their parents are treating them equally are more likely to lead to a compatible relationship. Fourth, relationships generally improve as the younger sibling approaches adolescence. Fifth, a better relationship between parents is related to a better relationship between siblings. Based on these factors, Shabrisha's children already have 2 factors working against a harmonious relationship: they are a mixed-sex pair and one of them is emotionally temperamental. Shabrisha should also look at her treatment of the children and the quality of her relationship with her husband to see if she can change the relationships. Even if there is nothing that she can do, the sibling relationship should improve as her son approaches adolescence. (274-275)

2.  Fortunately, Mark and Bianca get along and are concerned about their daughter. This one factor alone will help ease their daughter's adjustment to their divorce. Because they get along, they might want to consider joint custody where they will both maintain legal custody of Kelly. If they don't want to pursue joint custody, research has shown that children usually fare better when their same-sex parent has custody, so it might be better if Bianca has custody. However, if Bianca remarries, her preadolescent daughter may feel her new stepfather is intruding on her relationship with her mother. By adolescence, though, Kelly should adjust and benefit from the presence of a warm and caring stepfather and the involvement of 2 caring parents. (277-279)

3.  Lars probably wasn't as concerned as his daughter is about the loyalty of friends. Adolescent girls are more concerned than adolescent boys about loyalty because they tend to have more intimate relationships with their friends. This intimacy means that they tell private information to their friends and they are concerned that their friends remain loyal so that this information isn't spread to other people. Lars should realize that Ingrid isn't paranoid but is reacting like many other adolescent girls. (276)

4.  You and your spouse can help your son be popular by modeling effective social skills for him. Children who have social skills are more likely to be popular while children who are rejected are more likely to use aggression and intimidation with peers. These rejected children usually have parents who have modeled aggression and intimidation as solutions to problems. Parents' disciplinary practices also are related to children's behavior with peers. Inconsistent discipline is related to antisocial, aggressive behavior that leads to rejection, and consistent discipline is related to social skills that may lead to popularity. (289-290)

5.  Chuck is mostly, but not entirely, correct. A number of negative effects are associated with large amounts of television viewing: children who watch violent TV programs are more likely to behave violently and be

desensitized to violence; children who watch a lot of TV are more likely to have stereotyped views of women, minorities, and the elderly. However, children are more likely to engage in prosocial behavior if they see it modeled on TV, and children who watch educational programs, like Sesame Street, are more proficient in the skills that have been taught on the programs and adjust to school more readily. Unfortunately, there are many more violent, stereotyped programs than prosocial, educational programs on television. However, if Chuck monitors what his children watch and limits their viewing, they could learn some good things from television. (292-295)

6. You can tell your friend that he can take two different approaches to reducing prejudice. First, your friend can create group projects in which children from different groups work together toward a common goal. For example, the groups might create a mural to decorate the room or they might do a group science project. Another activity that your friend should try is role playing. In role playing, the children would be asked to imagine that they were insulted or not allowed to participate in a particular activity because of their race, ethnic background, or gender. For example, the children would be asked to imagine that they weren't invited to a birthday party because they are Hispanic. After the role playing, the children are asked to reflect upon their feelings when they were the target of prejudice and discrimination. The children also are asked to think of behavior that would be fair in the situation. (301-302)

# RITES OF PASSAGE

This chapter focuses on the physical changes that are associated with puberty, threats to health that occur during adolescence, cognitive changes in adolescence, and changes in moral reasoning during adolescence.

# 8.1 PUBERTAL CHANGES

## TO MASTER THE LEARNING OBJECTIVES:

**What physical changes occur in adolescence that mark the transition to a mature young adult?**

- Describe when the adolescent growth spurts begin and end for both boys and girls.

- Describe the physical events and their timing that occur during puberty in both boys and girls.

**What factors cause the physical changes associated with puberty?**

- Explain the causes of puberty.

- Describe how the onset of puberty is influenced by both one's genes and nutrition and health.

- Know the environmental contributions to the onset of puberty, including paternal investment theory.

**How do physical changes affect adolescents' psychological development?**

- Describe teenagers' body images and their reactions to spermarche and menarche.

- Explain the causes of teenage moodiness.

- Describe the costs and benefits of early maturation for both boys and girls.

## 8.1 KNOW THE TERMS

**Menarche**                                          **Secondary sex characteristics**

**Primary sex characteristics**                **Spermarche**

**Puberty**

1.  The growth of breasts or testes and the growth spurt of early adolescence are all physical events that occur during _____ .

2.  Organs that are directly involved in reproduction are called _____ .

3.  Physical signs of maturity that are not linked directly to the reproductive organs are _____ .

4.  The onset of menstruation in girls is called _____ .

5.  _____ is the first spontaneous ejaculation of sperm-laden fluid.

## 8.1 KNOW THE DETAILS OF PUBERTY

1.  Girls usually start the growth spurt at about 11, boys at about 13.
    TRUE or FALSE

2.  The appearance of facial hair and changes in the voice are examples of changes in primary sex characteristics.
    TRUE or FALSE

3.  Menarche typically occurs at about age 13.
    TRUE or FALSE

4.  Spermarche refers to the first spontaneous ejaculation of sperm-laden fluid.
    TRUE or FALSE

5.  The pituitary gland has a key role in regulating pubertal changes.
    TRUE or FALSE

6.  The timing of puberty is determined by genetic factors, with the environment having very little influence on it.
    TRUE or FALSE

7.  Puberty has been reached at about the same age for many generations.
    TRUE or FALSE

8. Menarche occurs later in girls who experience chronic stress.
   TRUE or FALSE

9. Adolescent boys and girls are equally likely to be dissatisfied with their appearance.
   TRUE or FALSE

10. The primary reason that adolescents are moodier than adults is fluctuating hormone levels.
    TRUE or FALSE

11. Early maturation has more harmful effects for girls than for boys.
    TRUE or FALSE

# 8.2 HEALTH

## TO MASTER THE LEARNING OBJECTIVES:

**What are the elements of a healthy diet for adolescents? Why do some adolescents suffer from eating disorders?**

- Describe a healthy diet for teenagers and the typical teenager's diet.

- Describe the causes, effects, and treatments of being overweight.

- Describe the causes of anorexia and bulimia.

**Do adolescents get enough exercise? What are the pros and cons of participating in sports in high school?**

- Describe the amount of exercise that the typical American teen gets.

- Describe the benefits and problems associated with sports participation.

**What are common obstacles to healthy growth in adolescence?**

- Describe how the causes of death in teens differ by gender and ethnicity.

- Explain the decision-making process that teens use.

## 8.2 KNOW THE TERMS

**Anorexia nervosa**                    **Basal metabolic rate**

**Body mass index (BMI)**               **Bulimia nervosa**

1. The _____ is an adjusted ratio of weight to height.

2. The _____ is the speed at which the body consumes calories.

3. The eating disorder that is marked by a persistent refusal to eat and an irrational fear of being overweight is called _____ .

4. Individuals with _____ alternate between periods of binge eating and purging through self-induced vomiting or the use of laxatives.

## 8.2 KNOW THE DETAILS OF HEALTH

1. Children and adolescents who are in the upper 5% of body mass index are defined as being overweight.
   TRUE or FALSE

2. Overweight children and adolescents are frequently less popular and have lower self-esteem than children of normal weight.
   TRUE or FALSE

3. Adolescents with a lower basal metabolic rate burn off calories more quickly.
   TRUE or FALSE

4. Relying on internal rather than external cues to stop eating encourages obesity.
   TRUE or FALSE

5. Anorexic teenagers usually have an accurate body image, understanding that they are extremely underweight.
   TRUE or FALSE

6. Males and females are equally likely to suffer from anorexia or bulimia.
   TRUE or FALSE

7. Eating disorders are more likely when parents give daughters a great deal of freedom.
   TRUE or FALSE

8. Most adolescents do not get enough regular exercise.
   TRUE or FALSE

9. Anabolic steroids increase muscle size and strength but can cause both physical and mental health problems.
   TRUE or FALSE

10. Among male and female adolescents, most deaths are due to natural causes.
    TRUE or FALSE

11. Adolescents tend to put more emphasis on health risks than on social consequences in their decision-making.
    TRUE or FALSE

# 8.3 INFORMATION PROCESSING DURING ADOLESCENCE

## TO MASTER THE LEARNING OBJECTIVES:

**How does information processing become more efficient during adolescence?**

- Describe the changes in working memory, processing speed, content knowledge, strategies, and metacognitive skill.

**Why is adolescent thinking sometimes not as sophisticated as it could be?**

- Explain how adolescents' beliefs interfere with effective thinking.

## 8.3 KNOW THE DETAILS OF INFORMATION PROCESSING

1. Information-processing theorists believe that major qualitative changes in cognition occur during adolescence.

   TRUE or FALSE

2. Adolescents' working memory has about the same capacity as adults' working memory.

   TRUE or FALSE

3. Adolescents usually process information more slowly than adults.

   TRUE or FALSE

4. Adolescents become better at selecting appropriate strategies and monitoring their progress when trying to complete a task.

   TRUE or FALSE

5. Adolescents' pre-existing beliefs can interfere with their scientific reasoning.

   TRUE or FALSE

# 8.4 REASONING ABOUT MORAL ISSUES

## TO MASTER THE LEARNING OBJECTIVES:

**How do adolescents reason about moral issues?**

- Define moral reasoning.

- Describe how moral reasoning differs at Kohlberg's 3 levels.

- Describe the research on Kohlberg's theory regarding progression through the stages, skipping stages, and regression through the stages.

- Describe the research that supports link between moral reasoning and moral action.

**Is moral reasoning similar in all cultures?**

- Describe research on cultural differences in moral reasoning.

**How does concern for justice and caring for other people contribute to moral reasoning?**

- Explain the difference between Gilligan's view and Kohlberg's view of moral reasoning.

**What factors help promote more sophisticated reasoning about moral issues?**

- Describe Eisenberg's levels of prosocial reasoning.

- Describe the effects of exposure to more advanced moral reasoning and exposure to Just Communities on moral reasoning.

# 8.4 KNOW THE TERMS

| | |
|---|---|
| **Approval-focused** | **Obedience** |
| **Conventional** | **Postconventional** |
| **Empathic** | **Preconventional** |
| **Hedonistic** | **Social contract** |
| **Interpersonal norms** | **Social system** |
| **Instrumental** | **Universal ethical** |
| **Needs-oriented** | |

1. At Kohlberg's _____ level, moral reasoning is based on external forces.

2. People using Kohlberg's Stage 1 of moral reasoning have an _____ orientation where they believe that authority figures know what is right and what is wrong.

3. People in Kohlberg's Stage 2 of moral reasoning have an _____ orientation where they look out for their own needs.

4. Adolescents and adults in Kohlberg's _____ level of moral reasoning look to society's norms for moral guidance.

5. Individuals in Kohlberg's Stage 3 base their moral reasoning on _____ and winning the approval of others.

6.  Kohlberg's Stage 4 morality is based on maintenance of order in society, or _____ morality.

7.  Moral reasoning at Kohlberg's _____ level is based on a personal moral code.

8.  Kohlberg's Stage 5 morality is based on a _____ , or the belief that laws and expectations are for the good of all members of society.

9.  Kohlberg's Stage 6 moral reasoning is based on _____ principles.

10. Most preschool and elementary-school children have a _____ orientation in which they pursue their own pleasure.

11. Some preschool and many elementary-school children have a _____ orientation in which they are concerned about others' needs and want to help.

12. Many elementary-school children and adolescents have a stereotyped, _____ orientation in which they behave as they think society expects "good people" to behave.

13. Some children and many adolescents develop an _____ orientation in which they consider the injured child's perspective and how their own actions will make them feel.

# 8.4 KNOW THE DETAILS OF MORAL REASONING

1.  In the earliest stages of Kohlberg's theory, moral reasoning is based on external forces such as reward and punishment.
    TRUE or FALSE

2.  When people look out for their own needs when reasoning about a moral dilemma, they are at the preconventional level.
    TRUE or FALSE

3.  At the conventional level of Kohlberg's theory, moral reasoning is based on a personal moral code.
    TRUE or FALSE

4.  The postconventional level focuses on society's norms for moral guidance.
    TRUE or FALSE

5.  At the highest stage of Kohlberg's theory, moral reasoning is determined by universal ethical principles.
    TRUE or FALSE

6.  Kohlberg stated that individuals often skip stages of moral reasoning and move back and forth between stages.
    TRUE or FALSE

7. Kohlberg suggested that moral reasoning is related to the level of cognitive development

   TRUE or FALSE

8. Moral reasoning is not related to moral action.

   TRUE or FALSE

9. Moral reasoning is influenced by cultural standards.

   TRUE or FALSE

10. Gilligan criticized Kohlberg's theory for emphasizing justice over caring and responsibility.

    TRUE or FALSE

11. Eisenberg proposed that most of children's moral dilemmas involve choosing between self-interest and helping others.

    TRUE or FALSE

12. In Eisenberg's theory, children at a low level of moral development reasoning have an empathic orientation whereas those at a high level have a hedonistic orientation.

    TRUE or FALSE

13. Moral reasoning can be advanced by observing others who have more advanced moral reasoning.

    TRUE or FALSE

# SUMMARY

## 8.1 PUBERTAL CHANGES

1. **Signs of Physical Maturation**

   Puberty includes bodily changes in _____ and weight as well as sexual maturation. Girls typically begin the growth spurt earlier than boys, who acquire more muscle, _____ , and greater heart and lung capacity. Sexual maturation, which includes primary and secondary sex characteristics, occurs in _____ sequences for boys and girls.

2. **Mechanisms of Maturation**

   Pubertal changes take place when the pituitary gland signals the adrenal gland, ovaries, and _____ to secrete hormones that initiate physical changes. The timing of puberty is influenced strongly by health and _____ . In addition, the timing of puberty is influenced by the social environment, coming earlier when girls experience family conflict or _____ .

3. **Psychological Impact of Puberty**

Pubertal changes affect adolescents' psychological functioning. Teens, particularly girls, become concerned about their _____ . When forewarned, adolescents respond positively to menarche and spermarche. Adolescents are _____ than children and adults, primarily because their mood shifts in response to frequent changes in activities and social setting. Early maturation tends to be harmful to _____

## 8.2 HEALTH

1. **Nutrition**

   For proper growth, teenagers need to consume adequate calories, calcium, and iron. Unfortunately, many teenagers do not eat properly and do not receive adequate nutrition. Anorexia nervosa and bulimia nervosa are eating disorders that typically affects adolescent girls. They are characterized by an irrational fear of being _____ . Several factors contribute to these disorders, including heredity, a childhood history of _____ , and during adolescence, _____ and a preoccupation with one's body and weight. Treatment and prevention programs emphasize changing adolescents' views toward thinness and their eating-related behaviors.

2. **Physical Fitness**

   Individuals who work out at least 3 times weekly often have improved physical and _____ health. Unfortunately, many high school students do not get enough exercise. Millions of American boys and girls participate in sports. Football and _____ are the most popular sports for boys and girls, respectively. The benefits of participating in sports include improved physical fitness, enhanced _____ , and understanding teamwork. The potential costs include _____ or abuse of performance-enhancing drugs.

3. **Threats to Adolescent Well-Being**

   Accidents involving automobiles or _____ are the most common cause of death in American teenagers. Many of these deaths could be prevented if, for example, adolescents did not drive recklessly (e.g., too fast and without wearing seat belts). Adolescents and adults often make decisions similarly, considering the _____ , the consequences of each alternative, and the desirability and _____ of these consequences. The outcomes of decision making sometimes differ because adolescents are more likely to emphasize the _____ consequences of actions.

## 8.3 INFORMATION PROCESSING DURING ADOLESCENCE

1. **How Does Information Processing Improve in Adolescence?**

   According to information-processing theorists, adolescence is a time of gradual cognitive change. Working memory and _____ achieve adult-like levels; content knowledge increases, to expert-like levels in some domains; and strategies and _____ skills become more sophisticated.

2. **Limits on Information Processing**

   Adolescents do not always think as effectively as they can. Sometimes they resort to simpler, less mature levels of thinking, and sometimes their _____ blind them to more sophisticated forms of thought.

## 8.4 REASONING ABOUT MORAL ISSUES

1. **Kohlberg's Theory**

   Kohlberg proposed that moral reasoning includes preconventional, conventional, and postconventional levels. Each level has two stages, creating a 6-stage developmental sequence. In the early stages, moral reasoning is based on _____ , in the latter stages on _____ moral codes. As predicted by the theory, people progress through the stages in sequence, _____ regress, and morally advanced reasoning is associated with more frequent moral behavior. However, few people attain the most advanced levels of reasoning, and _____ differ in the bases for moral reasoning.

2. **Cultural Differences in Moral Reasoning**

   Not all cultures emphasize justice in moral reasoning. The Hindu religion emphasizes duty and _____ to others, and consistent with these beliefs, Hindu children emphasize _____ other people in their moral reasoning.

3. **Beyond Kohlberg's Theory**

   Gilligan proposed that females' moral reasoning is often based on caring and _____ , not justice. Research does not support consistent sex differences in moral reasoning but has found that males and females both consider caring as well as _____ in their moral judgments, depending upon the situation. According to Eisenberg, reasoning about prosocial dilemmas shifts gradually from a self-interested, _____ orientation to concern for others based on empathy.

4. **Promoting Moral Reasoning**

Many factors can promote more sophisticated moral reasoning, including (a) noticing that one's current thinking is _____ (is contradictory or does not lead to clear actions), (b) observing that others reason at more _____ levels, and (c) _____ moral issues with peers, teachers, and parents.

# TEST YOURSELF

## MULTIPLE-CHOICE QUESTIONS

1. The collection of physical changes that occur during early adolescence is called
   a. puberty.
   b. menarche.
   c. spermarche.
   d. physical growth.

2. Changes in primary sex characteristics include changes in
   a. breasts.
   b. ovaries.
   c. the voice
   d. body hair.

3. The beginning of puberty is marked by _____ in girls and by _____ in boys.
   a. the onset of menstruation; the growth of the testes and scrotum
   b. the appearance of pubic hair; the first spontaneous ejaculation
   c. the onset of menstruation; the first spontaneous ejaculation
   d. the growth of the breasts; the growth of the testes and scrotum

4. Puberty occurs
   a. earlier in adolescents who are well-nourished and healthy.
   b. earlier in girls who are lighter and shorter.
   c. later in girls who experience much family conflict.
   d. later in Western European and North American countries than in African countries.

5. What are the psychological consequences of early maturation?
   a. Both boys and girls who mature early are likely to be more self-confident.
   b. Girls who mature early are likely to be more popular with peers.
   c. Girls who mature early are likely to associate with older adolescents.
   d. Early studies suggested that early maturation is harmful to boys.

6. If Seiko's basal metabolic rate is significantly higher than Yoko's, you would expect to find that
   a. Seiko gains weight more easily than Yoko.
   b. Yoko gains weight more easily than Seiko.
   c. Yoko exercises more than Seiko.
   d. Yoko consumes more calories than Seiko.

7. According to what we know from research about obesity,
   a. obesity is almost entirely due to environmental factors.
   b. obesity is a result of both genetic and environmental factors.
   c. if obese youths lose weight, they will always regain it.
   d. obese youth will not be able to lose weight.

8. You watch an infomercial about a weight loss program for adolescents. Which of these components would you NOT expect the program to have if it is indeed an effective program?
   a. having adolescents monitor their own eating, exercise, and sedentary behavior
   b. training parents to help children set realistic goals
   c. having parents monitor their own lifestyles to be sure they aren't encouraging the child's obesity
   d. emphasizing external eating signals rather than internal ones

9. Heather sometimes eats uncontrollably and then vomits or takes laxatives. Heather appears to have
   a. bulimia nervosa.
   b. anorexia nervosa.
   c. a basal metabolic rate.
   d. obesity.

10. Anorexia is most likely to occur in
    a. early childhood.
    b. males.
    c. adolescents with a history of eating problems as children.
    d. adolescents with uninvolved parents.

11. Which of the following statements about causes of death during adolescence in the U.S. is true?

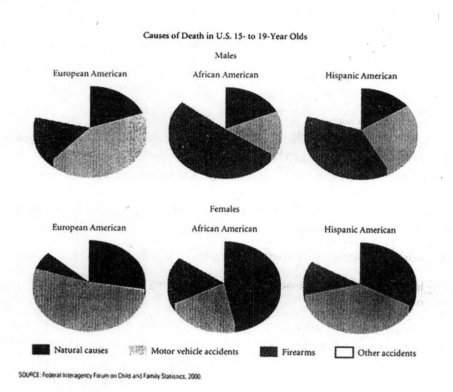

**Causes of Death in U.S. 15- to 19-Year Olds**

Males

European American      African American      Hispanic American

Females

European American      African American      Hispanic American

■ Natural causes    ▨ Motor vehicle accidents    ■ Firearms    □ Other accidents

SOURCE: Federal Interagency Forum on Child and Family Statistics, 2000.

    a. Most adolescent deaths are due to disease.
    b. Causes of death do not differ by ethnicity during adolescence.
    c. Among boys, most deaths are due to natural causes or firearms.
    d. Among girls, most deaths are due to natural causes or accidents involving motor vehicles.

12. During adolescence,
    a. working memory capacity is less than it will be during adulthood.
    b. information processing speed is faster than it was during childhood.
    c. increased knowledge interferes with information processing ability.
    d. there is unlikely to be any monitoring of the effectiveness of strategies used for a task.

13. When adolescents were asked to rate the quality of scientific studies, some of which were favorable to their religious affiliation and some of which were unfavorable,
    a. they tended to rate the quality of the study objectively, not being influenced by it's consistency with their beliefs.
    b. they were more critical of studies that were unfavorable to their beliefs than of those that were favorable.
    c. they were more critical of studies that were favorable to their beliefs than of those that were unfavorable.
    d. they became more biased in their ratings the older they were.

14. In Kohlberg's theory, moral reasoning is based on external forces at the _____ level.
    a. care-based
    b. preconventional
    c. conventional
    d. postconventional

15. An adolescent who makes a decision about a moral dilemma based on what is best for her own needs is in Kohlberg's _____ stage of moral reasoning.
    a. obedience orientation
    b. interpersonal norms
    c. instrumental orientation
    d. social system morality

16. Someone in Kohlberg's _____ stage of moral reasoning might respond to the Heinz dilemma by saying the man should steal the drug for his wife because that is what a "good" husband would do.
    a. obedience orientation
    b. interpersonal norms
    c. universal ethical principles
    d. social contract

17. A person who is in Kohlberg's conventional level of moral reasoning might decide to help someone because
    a. they would be punished if they didn't.
    b. helping is part of their personal moral code.
    c. the other person might help them in return.
    d. helping is part of society's norms for morality.

18. The highest level of moral reasoning in Kohlberg's theory is the stage of
    a. obedience orientation.
    b. social system morality.
    c. universal ethical principles.
    d. instrumental orientation.

19. Which of the following is not one of the tenets of Kohlberg's theory?
    a. The stages of moral reasoning follow an invariant sequence.
    b. The level of moral reasoning is associated with cognitive development.
    c. Moral reasoning changes qualitatively over the life span.
    d. Cultural factors determine the sequence of stages.

20. The Real People feature concerning the movie Schindler's List described how Oskar Schindler's moral reasoning underwent a shift from the _____ level to the _____ level over the course of the movie.
    a. preconventional; postconventional
    b. conventional; postconventional
    c. postconventional; preconventional
    d. preconventional; conventional

21. When asked to respond to a moral dilemma, people living in the U.S. were more likely to choose a _____ solution whereas people living in India more often chose a _____ solution.
    a. reward-based; punishment-based
    b. punishment-based; reward-based
    c. justice-based; care-based
    d. care-based; justice-based

22. Carol Gilligan criticized Kohlberg's theory for
    a. claiming that moral development proceeds through stages.
    b. emphasizing the association between cognitive development and moral reasoning.
    c. ignoring the importance of justice in moral reasoning.
    d. downplaying the importance of care and responsibility in interpersonal relationships to moral reasoning.

23. The highest stage of Gilligan's developmental progression of moral reasoning emphasizes
    a. personal moral principles.
    b. caring for others and oneself in all personal relationships by denouncing exploitation and violence between people.
    c. being preoccupied with one's own needs.
    d. caring for others.

24. Children who pursue their own pleasure are in Eisenberg's _____ stage of prosocial reasoning.
    a. needs-oriented
    b. approval-focused
    c. hedonistic orientation
    d. empathic orientation

25. Kohlberg suggested that people develop more advanced forms of moral reasoning
    a. through biological maturation.
    b. as a result of rewards and punishments.
    c. through discussion about moral issues with people who are at a higher level of moral reasoning.
    d. when they are exposed to people with lower levels of moral reasoning than their own.

## ESSAY QUESTIONS

1. You have an 11-year-old daughter and your best friend has an 11-year-old son. Your friend thinks that your daughter has entered puberty and is wondering when his son will begin puberty and what physical events will occur during puberty. What can you tell your friend about puberty in general and the differences in onset of puberty in boys and girls?

2. Your friend Wanda is upset because her adopted 13-year-old daughter is overweight. No one else in the family has a problem with obesity. What can you tell Wanda about the influence of heredity and environment on one's weight? What advice can you give Wanda about weight loss in children?

3. Your friend, Felicia, is the mother of a 13-year-old daughter, Yvonne. Felicia is concerned that Yvonne is anorexic because she "eats like a bird." What can you tell Felicia about the causes and symptoms of anorexia that will help her identify if Yvonne is anorexic?

4. Recently you and a friend were at a ski resort. You both noticed a group of teenagers who were engaged in very reckless behavior on the slopes. Your friend said to you, "Teenagers are so stupid and they make so many irrational decisions. Obviously, their decision-making processes are completely different from adults' processes." What can you tell your friend about similarities and differences in the decision-making processes of adolescents and adults?

5. You and 3 of your friends were talking about Kohlberg's Heinz Dilemma. One of your friends said that Heinz should not steal the drug for his wife because it is illegal and laws are in place to protect people and property. Your other friend, who is a Hindu, said that Heinz should steal the drug because it is a husband's responsibility to care for his wife. After these 2 friends left, your third friend commented on the differences between the 2 answers. What can you tell your friend about cultural differences in moral reasoning?

# SOLUTIONS

## 8.1 KNOW THE TERMS

1. puberty (308)
2. primary sex characteristics (309)
3. secondary sex characteristics (309)
4. menarche (310)
5. Spermarche (310)

## 8.1 KNOW THE DETAILS OF PUBERTY

1. T, (309)
2. F, (309)
3. T, (310)
4. T, (310)
5. T, (310)
6. F, (310)
7. F, (311)
8. F, (311)
9. F, (312)
10. F, (313)
11. T, (313)

## 8.2 KNOW THE TERMS

1. body mass index (316)
2. basal metabolic rate (316)
3. anorexia nervosa (317)
4. bulimia nervosa (317)

## 8.2 KNOW THE DETAILS OF HEALTH

1. T, (316)
2. T, (316)
3. F, (317)
4. F, (317)
5. F, (317)
6. F, (317)
7. F, (318)
8. T, (318)
9. T, (319)
10. F, (320)
11. F, (321)

## 8.3 KNOW THE DETAILS OF INFORMATION PROCESSING

1. F, (322)
2. T, (322)
3. F, (322)
4. T, (323)
5. T, (325)

## 8.4 KNOW THE TERMS

1. preconventional (327)
2. obedience (327)
3. instrumental (327)
4. conventional (327)
5. interpersonal norms (327)
6. social system (327)
7. postconventional (327)
8. social contract (327)
9. universal ethical (328)

10. hedonistic (332)
11. needs-oriented (332)
12. approval-focused (332)
13. empathic (332)

## 8.4 KNOW THE DETAILS OF MORAL REASONING

1. T, (327)
2. T, (327)
3. F, (327)
4. F, (327)
5. T, (328)

6. F, (329)
7. T, (329)
8. F, (330)
9. T, (330)
10. T, (331)

11. T, (332)
12. F, (332)
13. T, (333)

# SUMMARY

## 8.1 PUBERTAL CHANGES

1. height (308); less fat (309); predictable (310)

2. testes (310); nutrition (311); depression (311)

3. appearance (312); moodier (313); girls (313).

## 8.2 HEALTH

1. overweight (317); eating problems (318); negative self-esteem (318)

2. mental (318); basketball (319); self-esteem (319); injury (319)

3. firearms (320); alternatives (321); likelihood (321); social (321)

## 8.3 INFORMATION PROCESSING DURING ADOLESCENCE

1. processing speed (322); metacognitive (323)

2. beliefs (324)

## 8.4 REASONING ABOUT MORAL ISSUES

1. rewards and punishments (327); personal (327); do not (329); cultures (330)

2. responsibility (330); caring for (331)

3. responsibility for others (331); justice (332); hedonistic (332)

4. inadequate (333); advanced (333); discussing (333)

# TEST YOURSELF

## MULTIPLE-CHOICE QUESTIONS

1. A, (308)
2. B, (309)
3. D, (310)
4. A, (311)
5. C, (314)
6. B, (317)
7. B, (317)
8. D, (317)

9. A, (317)
10. C, (318)
11. D, (320)
12. B, (324)
13. B, (325)
14. B, (327)
15. C, (327)
16. B, (327)

17. D, (327)
18. C, (328)
19. D, (329)
20. A, (329)
21. C, (331)
22. D, (331)
23. B, (331)
24. C, (332)

25. C, (333)

## ESSAY QUESTIONS

1.  Puberty is characterized by many physical changes, which usually begin at age 11 in girls and at about age 13 in boys. The adolescent growth spurt is a period of very rapid growth when adolescents put on both height and weight. This growth spurt usually lasts about 4 years. In girls puberty begins with the growth of the breasts, the start of the adolescent growth spurt, the emergence of pubic hair, and finally the onset of menstruation, or menarche, which usually occurs around age 13. For boys, puberty usually begins with the growth of the testes and scrotum, followed by the appearance of pubic hair, the start of the growth spurt, and growth of the penis. At about age 13, boys experience spermarche, the first spontaneous ejaculation of sperm-laden fluid. Because girls tend to begin puberty at earlier ages than do boys, it is quite likely that your daughter has entered puberty and that your friend's son has not. Tell your friend not to worry because his son has not yet reached the average age at which boys enter puberty. (308-310)

2.  Tell Wanda that heredity plays an important role in juvenile obesity. Adopted children's weight is related to the weight of their biological parents and not to the weight of their adoptive parents. Genetic influence may contribute to obesity by determining a person's activity level and one's basal metabolic rate (the speed with which the body consumes calories). A less active person with a slower basal metabolic rate will be more likely to be overweight than someone who is active and has a faster basal metabolic rate. Wanda may also be providing an environment that encourages her daughter to eat even when she is not hungry. For example, many parents encourage their children to clean their plates at the dinner table even though the child may be full. Parents may also allow too much snacking or snacking on the wrong kinds of food. Wanda's daughter can lose weight but she should remember that weight loss in obese children and adolescents is most successful if the whole family is involved in decreasing the number of calories consumed and increasing the amount of exercise. The most effective weight-loss programs involve monitoring eating, exercise, and sedentary behavior. Parents should help children set realistic goals and use behavioral principles to help children meet these goals. Parents should also evaluate their own lifestyles to be sure they are not inadvertently fostering their child's obesity. (316-317)

3.  Tell Felicia that the typical anorexic is an adolescent female like Yvonne. Anorexics often have a childhood history of eating problems such as being a picky eater or eating non-food objects. During adolescence, anorexics often have negative self-esteem, a mood or anxiety disorder, and are overly concerned about body size and weight. Anorexics' homes often have overprotective parents. Even if Yvonne and her family match this description, she may not be anorexic. An anorexic will limit food intake to such a great extent that she will become painfully thin but will perceive herself as being overweight. If Yvonne shows any of these signs, she should seek medical treatment right away. If left untreated, anorexia can lead to death. (317-318)

4.  You can tell your friend that, in fact, adolescents and adults follow very similar processes when making decisions. Typically, both adolescents and adults determine 1) the alternative courses of action available to them, 2) the consequences of each action, and 3) the desirability and likelihood of these consequences. The main difference between adolescents and adults is that adolescents are more likely to consider the social consequences (e.g., I'll make my friends mad or my friends will think I'm a wimp if I don't participate) and less likely to consider the health consequences (e.g., I might be hurt or hurt someone else with my reckless behavior) when making decisions. (321)

5.  Cross-cultural research has shown that children and adolescents in North America reason at Stages 2 and 3, which is similar to findings in other cultures. However, adults in many non-Western cultures do not emphasize justice in moral reasoning. The emphasis on justice is apparent in cultures where the rights of the individual are emphasized. In cultures where the primary religion emphasizes different values, principles other than justice are used in moral reasoning. For example, the Hindu religion emphasizes duties and responsibilities toward others. In fact, research has shown that those reared with traditional Hindu beliefs do emphasize care and responsibility to others in moral reasoning. So, what you and your friend observed was a cultural difference in moral reasoning. (330-331)

# MOVING INTO THE ADULT SOCIAL WORLD

9.1 Identity and Self-Esteem

9.2 Romantic Relationships and Sexuality

9.3 The World of Work

9.4 The Dark Side

This chapter focuses on the challenging issues that face adolescents: the search for identity, romantic and sexual relationships, work, and problems of adolescence.

# 9.1 IDENTITY AND SELF-ESTEEM

## TO MASTER THE LEARNING OBJECTIVES:

**How do adolescents achieve an identity?**

- Describe the developmental crisis during adolescence of identity vs. role confusion as proposed by Erik Erikson.

- Describe Marcia's 4 identity statuses--achievement, moratorium, foreclosure, and diffusion--and describe how the likelihood of occurrence for each status changes throughout adolescence.

- Define adolescent egocentrism, imaginary audience, the personal fable, and the illusion of invulnerability.

- Describe how adolescents' identity formation is related to their parents' styles of parenting.

**What is an ethnic identity?  What are the stages in acquiring an ethnic identity?**

- Describe the 3 phases of achieving ethnic identity.

- Describe the development of ethnic identity in immigrant adolescents.

- Describe the benefits of having a strong ethnic identity.

**How does self-esteem change in adolescence?**

- Describe changes in self-esteem for boys and girls in different domains.

- Describe the things that influence self-esteem in adolescence.

- Explain how most adolescents feel about their parents.

# 9.1 KNOW THE TERMS

| | |
|---|---|
| **Achievement** | **Illusion of invulnerability** |
| **Adolescent egocentrism** | **Imaginary audience** |
| **Diffusion** | **Moratorium** |
| **Ethnic identity** | **Personal fable** |
| **Foreclosure** | |

1. Individuals in Marcia's identity status of _____ , which occurs during early adolescence, do not have an identity and are doing nothing to achieve one.

2. Individuals in Marcia's identity status of _____ may have an identity that was chosen based on advice from adults, rather than an identity that was a result of personal exploration of alternatives.

3. Individuals in Marcia's identity status of _____ are still examining different alternatives and have yet to find a satisfactory identity.

4. Individuals in Marcia's identity status of _____ have explored alternative identities and are now secure in their chosen identities.

5. The self-absorption that is characteristic of teenagers as they search for identity is called _____ .

6. Many adolescents feel that their behavior is constantly being watched by their peers. This phenomenon is called the _____ .

7. The _____ is the feeling that many adolescents have that their feelings and experiences are unique and have never been experienced by anyone else before.

8. The belief that misfortune only happens to others is called an _____ .

9. Feeling a part of ones ethnic group and learning the special customs and traditions of their group's culture and heritage is known as _____ .

# 9.1 KNOW THE DETAILS OF THE SEARCH FOR IDENTITY

1. According to Erik Erikson, persons who are confused about their identity will never experience intimate human relationships.

   TRUE or FALSE

2. While in the moratorium identity status, individuals have an identity that is based on advice from adults rather than from personal exploration of alternatives.

   TRUE or FALSE

3. Individuals in the achievement identity status have no identity and are doing nothing to achieve one.

   TRUE or FALSE

4. The feeling adolescents have that their peers are watching their behavior is called adolescent egocentrism.

   TRUE or FALSE

5. The tendency of adolescents to believe that their experiences and feelings are unique and that no one else has ever felt or thought as they do is called the personal fable.

   TRUE or FALSE

6. Achievement and moratorium identity statuses become more common during later adolescence and young adulthood (see graphs).

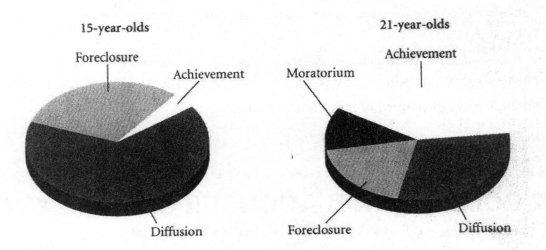

   TRUE or FALSE

7. Parents who encourage discussion and adolescent autonomy have adolescents more likely to reach achievement identity status.

   TRUE or FALSE

8.  When parents set rules with little explanation, adolescents are more likely to stay in the foreclosure identity status.
    TRUE or FALSE

9.  Adolescents in the first phase of achieving ethnic identity have spent a lot of time exploring their ethnic roots.
    TRUE or FALSE

10. Adolescents in the second phase of achieving ethnic identity have begun to explore the personal impact of their ethnic heritage.
    TRUE or FALSE

11. Adolescents who have attained an ethnic identity tend to have lower levels of self-esteem than those who have not.
    TRUE or FALSE

12. Adolescents with a strong ethnic identity tend to do better in school than adolescents whose ethnic identities are weaker.
    TRUE or FALSE

13. Self-esteem becomes more differentiated as children enter adolescence.
    TRUE or FALSE

14. Self-esteem remains stable with age and across settings.
    TRUE or FALSE

15. Parents who don't set rules tend to have adolescents with higher self-esteem.
    TRUE or FALSE

16. Over the course of adolescence, parent-teen relationships become more egalitarian.
    TRUE or FALSE

17. Most teenagers adopt many of their parents' values.
    TRUE or FALSE

# 9.2 ROMANTIC RELATIONSHIPS AND SEXUALITY

## TO MASTER THE LEARNING OBJECTIVES:

**Why are some adolescents sexually active? Why do so few use contraceptives?**

*   Describe the changing functions of dating.
*   Explain the ethnic differences in dating patterns.

- Describe how peers' and parents' attitudes influence sexual activity in teens.

- Explain why adolescents are susceptible to contracting sexually-transmitted diseases such as AIDS.

- Describe how teenage pregnancy is related to poor outcomes for both the teenage mother and her child.

- Describe the frequency with which most teens use contraception and the common reasons for not using contraception.

- Describe the sex education programs that seem to be the most effective in getting teens to either abstain from sex or to use contraception when they are sexually active.

**What determines an adolescents' sexual orientation?**

- Describe how biology might influence one's sexual orientation.

**What circumstances can make date rape especially likely?**

- Explain the factors that are related to date rape.

# 9.2 KNOW THE DETAILS OF ROMANTIC RELATIONSHIPS

1. Latino American and Asian American adolescents often begin dating at an earlier age than European American adolescents.
   TRUE or FALSE

2. Adolescents are more likely to have sex when they believe that their friends are also sexually active.
   TRUE or FALSE

3. Teenagers living in rural areas and inner cities are more likely to be sexually active than teens living in the suburbs.
   TRUE or FALSE

4. Chlamydia, syphilis, and gonorrhea are sexually transmitted diseases that cannot be cured.
   TRUE or FALSE

5. Adolescents are especially susceptible to AIDS because they are more likely than adults to engage in unprotected sex and to use intravenous drugs.
   TRUE or FALSE

6. Most sexually active adolescents use contraceptives.
   TRUE or FALSE

7. Common reasons why adolescents do not use birth control include ignorance, an illusion of invulnerability, and a desire to become pregnant.
   TRUE or FALSE

8. Most adolescents who are emotionally or sexually attracted to a person of their own sex eventually identify themselves as gay.
   TRUE or FALSE

9. Children raised by gay and lesbian parents usually end up adopting their parents' sexual orientation.
   TRUE or FALSE

10. Biology plays an important role in determining a person's sexual orientation.
    TRUE or FALSE

11. Homosexuality is currently considered to be a psychological disorder by the American Psychological Association.
    TRUE or FALSE

12. Drinking alcohol increases the risk of date rape.
    TRUE or FALSE

# 9.3 THE WORLD OF WORK

## TO MASTER THE LEARNING OBJECTIVES:

**How do adolescents select an occupation?**

- List and describe Super's 3 phases of vocational choice.

- List and describe Holland's 6 personality prototypes and how they are related to vocational choice.

**What is the impact of part-time employment on adolescents?**

- Describe the extent of part-time employment in teens and how part-time employment differs for teens in the United States versus those in other industrialized countries.

- Describe the 3 problems associated with part-time employment of teens during the school year.

## 9.3 KNOW THE TERMS

| | |
|---|---|
| **Crystallization** | **Personality-type theory** |
| **Implementation** | **Specification** |

1. A 13-year-old in Super's _____ phase has decided that he likes to play the piano and that he might like to be a concert pianist.

2. When the budding concert pianist is 18 years old, he learns that being a concert pianist requires many hours of practicing each day and that very few jobs in this area exist, so he decides that being a music teacher might be a better job for him. He is in Super's _____ phase.

3.  A 23-year-old who has just graduated from college with a degree in music education and has begun a job as a high school music teacher would be in Super's _____ phase.

4.  According to Holland's _____ , people find their work fulfilling when the important features of a job or profession fit the workers' personalities.

## 9.3 KNOW THE DETAILS OF THE WORLD OF WORK

1.  According to Super, identity is a key factor in determining an adolescent's career choice.
    TRUE or FALSE

2.  During Super's crystallization phase, adolescents enter the work force and learn firsthand about jobs.
    TRUE or FALSE

3.  During Super's specification phase, adolescents limit their career possibilities by learning more about specific types of work and starting to obtain the training that is required for a job.
    TRUE or FALSE

4.  According to Holland, personality-type is related to how fulfilling people find a profession to be.
    TRUE or FALSE

5.  A person with an investigative personality type is skilled verbally and interpersonally and enjoys solving problems using these skills.
    TRUE or FALSE

6.  An individual with a conventional personality type is well-suited for professions such as poet, musician, and actor.
    TRUE or FALSE

7.  Less than half of all high school seniors have a part-time job.
    TRUE or FALSE

8.  High school students in the U.S. are more likely than students in Western Europe and Asia to hold a part-time job.
    TRUE or FALSE

9.  Part-time work does not affect high school performance.
    TRUE or FALSE

10. Adolescents who work more than 15 or 20 hours a week are more likely to experience anxiety and depression.
    TRUE or FALSE

11. Extensive part-time work is associated with increased substance abuse.
    TRUE or FALSE

12. Working part-time helps adolescents develop more realistic expectations about how income can be allocated.

    TRUE or FALSE

# 9.4 THE DARK SIDE

## TO MASTER THE LEARNING OBJECTIVES:

**Why do teenagers drink?**

- Describe the trends in illicit drug use among teenagers in the United States.

- Describe how the attitudes and behavior of family and peers concerning drinking are related to teenage drinking.

- Describe changes in the incidence of teenage smoking and the factors that are related to teenage smoking.

- Describe the programs that are most effective in reducing teenage smoking.

**What leads some adolescents to become depressed? How can depression be treated?**

- Describe the possible causes and treatments of depression.

- Describe the warning signs of suicide.

**What are the causes of juvenile delinquency?**

- Explain the differences between status offenses and index offenses and the differences between life-course persistent antisocial behavior and adolescent-limited antisocial behavior.

- Describe how poverty, family processes, cognitive processes, and biology are related to juvenile delinquency.

- Describe the factors that are most likely to lead to successful treatment and prevention of juvenile delinquency.

## 9.4 KNOW THE TERMS

| | |
|---|---|
| **Adolescent-limited** | **Life-course persistent** |
| **Depression** | **Norepinephrine** |
| **Index offenses** | **Serotonin** |
| **Juvenile delinquency** | **Status offenses** |
| **Learned helplessness** | |

1. Pervasive feelings of sadness, irritability, and low self-esteem are characteristic of _____ .

2. The feeling that one is always at the mercy of external events and that one does not have any control over one's own destiny is called _____ .

3. _____ is a neurotransmitter that helps control brain centers that allow people to experience pleasure, and are related to depression.

4. _____ is a neurotransmitter that helps control brain centers that allow people to experience pleasure, and are related to depression.

5. _____ consists of adolescents committing illegal acts that are destructive toward themselves or others.

6. _____ are acts that are not crimes if they are committed by an adult. This would include truancy and running away from home.

7. Acts that are illegal regardless of the age of the perpetrator are called _____ .

8. Antisocial behavior that emerges at an early age and continues throughout life is known as _____ antisocial behavior.

9. _____ antisocial behavior refers to youth who engage in relatively minor criminal acts yet aren't consistently antisocial.

# 9.4 KNOW THE DETAILS OF THE PROBLEMS OF ADOLESCENCE

1. Many teenagers drink because their peers pressure them to.
   TRUE or FALSE

2. When drinking is an important part of their parents' social lives, adolescents are more likely to drink.
   TRUE or FALSE

3. In the U.S., teen-age smoking typically begins between 6th and 9th grades.
   TRUE or FALSE

4. Teens are less likely to smoke when their parents have an authoritative parenting style.
   TRUE or FALSE

5. Adolescent boys are depressed more often than girls.
   TRUE or FALSE

6. Depressed adolescents yearn for the company of others more than adolescents who are not depressed.
   TRUE or FALSE

7. In learned helplessness, adolescents believe that they control what happens in their lives.
   TRUE or FALSE

8. Heredity appears to play a part in depression.
   TRUE or FALSE

9. Both antidepressant drugs and psychotherapy are often used to treat depression.
   TRUE or FALSE

10. Teen suicide is more common among boys than girls.
    TRUE or FALSE

11. In of teen suicide, there are warning signals before it occurs.
    TRUE or FALSE

12. When a teenager threatens suicide, it is typically just to get attention, so the threats should be treated lightly or ignored.
    TRUE or FALSE

13. Index offenses are not crimes if committed by an adult.
    TRUE or FALSE

14. Adolescent-limited antisocial behavior refers to antisocial behavior that emerges at an early age and continues throughout life.
    TRUE or FALSE

15. The incidence of adolescent crime is the same in all socioeconomic levels.
    TRUE or FALSE

16. Adolescents with low supervision are more likely to become delinquent.
    TRUE or FALSE

17. Delinquent youth tend to be impulsive and have difficulty delaying gratification.
    TRUE or FALSE

# SUMMARY

## 9.1 IDENTITY AND SELF-ESTEEM

1. **The Search for Identity**

   The task for adolescents is to find an identity. This search for identity typically involves four statuses.

   Diffusion and _____ are more common in early adolescence; _____ and achievement are more common in late adolescence and young adulthood. As they seek identity, adolescents often believe that others are always watching them and that no one else has felt as they do. Adolescents are more likely to achieve identity when parents encourage _____ and recognize their autonomy; they are least likely to achieve identity when parents set rules and enforce them without explanation.

2. **Ethnic Identity**

Adolescents from ethnic groups often progress through three phases in acquiring an ethnic identity: initial disinterest, _____ and identity _____ Achieving an ethnic identity usually results in higher _____ but is not consistently related to the strength of one's identification with mainstream culture.

3. **Self-Esteem in Adolescence**

Social comparisons begin anew when children move from elementary school to junior high school, and, consequently, self-esteem usually declines somewhat during this transition. However, self-esteem begins to rise in middle and late adolescence as teenagers see themselves acquiring more adult-like skills and _____ . Self-esteem is linked to adolescents' actual competence in domains that matter and to how parents and peers view them.

4. **The Myth of Storm and Stress**

The parent-child relationship becomes more egalitarian during the adolescent years, reflecting adolescents' growing independence. Contrary to myth, adolescence is not usually a period of storm and stress. Most adolescents love their parents, rely upon them for _____ , and adopt their _____ .

## 9.2 ROMANTIC RELATIONSHIPS AND SEXUALITY

1. **Romantic Relationships**

Romantic relationships emerge in mid-adolescence. For younger adolescents, dating is for both companionship and sexual exploration; for older adolescents, it is a source of trust and _____ .

2. **Sexual Behavior**

By the end of adolescence, most American boys and girls have had sexual intercourse, which boys view as _____ but girls see as romantic. Adolescents are more likely to be sexually active if they believe that their parents and peers approve of sex. Sexually transmitted diseases and pregnancy are two common consequences of adolescent sexual behavior, because sexually active adolescents use contraceptives _____ .

3. **Sexual Orientation**

   A small percentage of adolescents are attracted to members of their own sex. Sexual orientation probably has roots in _____ . Gay and lesbian youth face many special challenges and consequently often suffer from _____ problems.

4. **Sexual Coercion**

   Adolescent and young adult females are sometimes forced into sex against their will. Girls are more likely to be victims of sexual violence when they've been _____ and they hold traditional views of gender. Boys are more likely to perpetrate violence when they've experienced violence at _____ , when they drink, and when their _____ perpetrate sexual violence. Date-rape workshops work to improve communication between males and females.

## 9.3 THE WORLD OF WORK

1. **Career Development**

   Super's theory of vocational choice proposes three phases of vocational development during adolescence and young adulthood: _____ , in which basic interests are identified; specification, in which jobs associated with interests are identified; and _____ , which marks entry into the work force. Holland proposed six different work-related _____ types: realistic, investigative, social, conventional, enterprising, and artistic. Each is uniquely suited to certain jobs. People are _____ when their personality fits their job and less happy when it does not.

2. **Part-Time Employment**

   Most adolescents in the United States have part-time jobs. This phenomenon, which gathered steam in the 1980s, is unique to the United States. Adolescents who are employed more than _____ hours per week during the school year typically do poorly in school, often have lowered _____ and increased anxiety, and have problems interacting with others. Employed adolescents save relatively _____ of their income and, instead, spend most of it on clothing, food, and entertainment for themselves, which can give misleading expectations about how to allocate income. Part-time employment can be beneficial if adolescents work relatively few hours, if the work allows them to use existing _____ or to acquire new ones, and if teens _____ some of their earnings. Summer employment, because it does not conflict with the demands of school, can also be beneficial.

## 9.4 THE DARK SIDE

1. **Drug Use**

   Today, many adolescents drink alcohol regularly. Adolescents are attracted to alcohol and other drugs by their need for experimentation, for _____ , and for feelings of exhilaration. The primary factors that influence whether adolescents drink are encouragement from others (parents and peers) and stress. Similarly, teenage smoking is influenced by parents and peers.

2. **Depression**

   Depressed adolescents have little enthusiasm for life, believe that others are _____ , and wish to be left alone. Depression can be triggered by an event that deprives them of rewarding experiences, by an event in which they felt unable to _____ their own destiny, or by an imbalance in neurotransmitters such as norepinephrine and serotonin. Treating depression relies upon medications that correct the levels of _____ and therapy designed to improve social skills and restructure adolescents' _____ of events.

3. **Delinquency**

   Many young people engage in antisocial behavior briefly during adolescence. In contrast, the small percentage of adolescents who engage in life-course persistent anti-social behavior are involved in one-fourth to one-half of the serious crimes committed in the United States. Life-course persistent anti-social behavior has been linked to poverty, _____ , cognitive processes, and _____ Efforts to reduce adolescent criminal activity must address all of these variables.

# TEST YOURSELF

## MULTIPLE-CHOICE QUESTIONS

1. According to Erikson, the developmental task of adolescence is to
   a. establish intimacy with another person.
   b. establish a sense of trust.
   c. achieve an identity.
   d. achieve generativity.

2. Teens in the _____ and _____ identity statuses have not explored alternative identities.
   a. achievement; moratorium
   b. diffusion; foreclosure
   c. diffusion; achievement
   d. moratorium; foreclosure

3. Individuals who are examining different alternatives, but have yet to find a satisfactory identity, are in the _____ identity status.
   a. diffusion
   b. foreclosure
   c. moratorium
   d. achievement

4. Which of the following is true of attaining identity?
   a. Once the achievement status is attained, an individual's identity remains constant throughout the lifespan.
   b. After an identity is attained an individual may return to the moratorium status and emerge with a modified identity.
   c. Most people attain an identity during early adolescence.
   d. Parents do not influence teens' identity status.

5. Tori is a 15-year-old who feels that everyone at school is watching her and will notice the stain on the front of her skirt. Tori is experiencing
   a. the imaginary audience.
   b. the personal fable.
   c. identity foreclosure.
   d. identity achievement.

6. Natalie thought that there was no way anyone else could understand how upset she was when her boyfriend broke up with her. This kind of thinking is most strongly associated with which feature of adolescent thinking?
   a. imaginary audience
   b. personal fable
   c. illusion of invulnerability
   d. adolescent egocentrism

7. Achievement status is associated with parents who
   a. encourage discussion and recognize children's autonomy.
   b. set rules with little justification or explanation.
   c. provide children with explicit direction for their identities.
   d. discourage their children from experimenting with different identities.

8.  Maria is interested in learning more about her culture. She has not yet achieved a distinct ethnic self-concept, but she has begun reading books, attending festivals, and talking to her grandmother about her Mexican American heritage. Maria is in the _____ phase of achieving ethnic identity.
    a.  first
    b.  second
    c.  third
    d.  fourth

9.  Compared to adolescents who do not have a strong ethnic identity, those adolescents with a strong ethnic identity tend to
    a.  have higher self-esteem.
    b.  find their interactions with family and friends less satisfying.
    c.  do worse in school.
    d.  have a more negative view of their own ethnic group.

10. Children are more likely to have higher self-esteem when
    a.  parents do not set rules.
    b.  they do well in something important to them and are valued by people important to them.
    c.  they do not participate in extracurricular activities.
    d.  teachers do not seem to care about them or listen to them.

11. Most adolescents
    a.  admire and love their parents.
    b.  do not rely on their parents for advice.
    c.  do not accept many of their parents' values.
    d.  feel unloved by their parents.

12. Teens
    a.  spend less time with their parents than they did when they were younger.
    b.  are more affectionate with their parents than they were when they were younger.
    c.  have a less egalitarian relationship with their parents as they get older.
    d.  argue less often with their parents than they did when they were younger.

13. Darrell is less likely to be sexually active as an adolescent if
    a.  his parents don't monitor his activities closely.
    b.  he believes that his friends are sexually active.
    c.  his peers do not approve of having sex.
    d.  his parents' values encourage sex.

14. Which of the following is most likely to keep Shannon, a teenage girl, from becoming a teenage mother?
    a.  having an illusion of invulnerability
    b.  lack of access to contraceptives
    c.  participating in a comprehensive sex education program
    d.  not knowing the facts of conception

15. Gay adolescents
    a. usually identify themselves as gay during mid-adolescence and publicly declare their sexual orientation at that time.
    b. usually identify themselves as gay during mid-adolescence but wait until early adulthood to publicly reveal their sexual orientation.
    c. are generally not sexually active and remain unaware of their sexual orientation until early adulthood.
    d. who openly acknowledge their homosexuality are generally supported and accepted by their peers.

16. Which of the following statements about determinants of sexual orientation is true?
    a. Sons become gay when raised by a domineering mother and a weak father.
    b. Children raised by gay and lesbian parents usually end up adopting their parents' sexual orientation.
    c. Gay and lesbian adults were, as children, seduced by an older person of their sex.
    d. Biology plays an important role in determining a person's sexual orientation.

17. Date rape is least likely to occur when
    a. the woman has a clear and consistent sexual policy.
    b. the individuals involved have traditional sex-role orientations.
    c. the couple has previously had sex.
    d. the woman reasons with the man but does not struggle or scream.

18. In Super's theory of vocational choice, individuals go through the phases of choosing a career in which of the following sequences?
    a. specification, implementation, crystallization
    b. specification, crystallization, implementation
    c. crystallization, specification, implementation
    d. crystallization, implementation, specification

19. Jane enjoys taking care of her little sister's scraped knees and is fascinated by her high school biology class. She doesn't know much about the kind of training involved, but thinks she might want to go into a health care profession. Jane is in Super's _____ phase of vocational choice.
    a. specification
    b. crystallization
    c. establishment
    d. implementation

20. Steve has always enjoyed sports, is going to college on a basketball scholarship, and now thinks he might want to have a career in coaching. He has talked with his high school and college coaches about the opportunities available at different levels. Steve liked working with high school students at summer basketball camps, and he decided to major in education in order to be prepared to teach and coach at the high school level. Steve is in Super's _____ phase of career development.
    a. specification
    b. crystallization
    c. establishment
    d. implementation

21. Individuals enter the work force and learn first-hand about jobs during Super's _____ phase of career development.
    a. specification
    b. crystallization
    c. establishment
    d. implementation

22. According to Holland, people find work most fulfilling when
    a. they are highly compensated financially.
    b. the job requirements fit the worker's personality.
    c. they are in the specification phase of career development.
    d. they have a realistic personality type.

23. Nick has an enterprising personality type. Which career is he likely to find most fulfilling?
    a. scientist
    b. counselor
    c. real estate agent
    d. bank teller

24. Sarah is task-oriented and enjoys thinking about abstract relations. She would best be described as having a(n) _____ personality type.
    a. realistic
    b. enterprising
    c. conventional
    d. investigative

25. Teenagers in the United States
    a. are more likely to work now than they were in the 1970s.
    b. are less likely than Western European and Asian teenagers to have a part-time job while in high school.
    c. rarely hold a part-time job while in high school.
    d. who work are likely to be paid more if they are a girl rather than a boy.

26. When students work over 15 hours a week during the school year,
    a. they learn good work habits and usually get better grades than students who do not work.
    b. they spend less time studying and tend to get lower grades than students who do not work.
    c. their grades are not usually affected, either positively or negatively.
    d. boys' grades tend to suffer but girls' grades tend to improve.

27. Compared to adolescents who do not have a part-time job, adolescents who work long hours
    a. are likely to have higher self-esteem.
    b. are more likely to be anxious and depressed.
    c. have a more realistic understanding of how to manage money.
    d. tend to argue with their parents more.

28. Chad, a high school junior, is eager to work. His parents are not so sure he should work. Which of the following contingencies should Chad's parents set on his employment situation to make it less likely that working would be harmful for Chad?
    a. Have him work at a simple, repetitive job rather than a more demanding, skill-oriented job.
    b. Make sure he takes the summer off and works only during the school year.
    c. Allow him to work no more than 5 to 10 hours a week.
    d. Working is harmful for high school students under all circumstances, so Chad should not work at all.

29. Which of the following substances is most likely to be used by adolescents?
    a. marijuana
    b. cocaine
    c. amphetamines
    d. alcohol

30. Which of the following statements concerning the decisions made by adolescents about whether to drink or not is true?
    a. Peers are influential in the decision to drink, but parents are not.
    b. Parents are influential in the decision to drink, but peers are not.
    c. Both parents and peers play a part in a teenager's decision to drink or not.
    d. Most teenagers make the decision about whether to drink or not solely on the basis of how alcohol makes them feel.

31. Pervasive feelings of sadness, irritability, and low self-esteem characterize an individual
    a. with depression.
    b. who has a drinking problem.
    c. with an addiction to drugs.
    d. who is a juvenile delinquent.

32. Depression
    a. is associated with increased levels of norepinephrine and serotonin.
    b. is more common in males than in females.
    c. can be triggered by feelings of learned helplessness.
    d. cannot be treated successfully.

33. Suicide
    a. is more common among boys than girls.
    b. is equally common in boys and girls.
    c. is more common among African American adolescents than among European American adolescents.
    d. is more common in European American adolescents than in Native American adolescents.

34. Recently Maxie has lost interest in shopping, which used to be one of her favorite activities; has changed from being a very happy-go-lucky girl to being very quiet and serious; and has given her favorite CD's to her best friend. Maxie
    a. appears to be making a typical transition from adolescence to adulthood.
    b. is showing signs that she may be considering suicide.
    c. appears to have fallen in love.
    d. probably has a drug addiction.

35. An adolescent who _____ has committed an index offense.
    a. robs a convenience store
    b. runs away from home
    c. is sexually promiscuous
    d. skips school

36. _____ are acts that are not crimes if committed by an adult, such as truancy, sexual promiscuity, and running away from home.
    a. Status offenses
    b. Index offenses
    c. Diffusion statuses
    d. Foreclosure statuses

37. Which of the teenagers described below is most at risk for becoming a juvenile delinquent?
    a. Jared, who is from a middle-class environment and wants the best electronic equipment he can find.
    b. Lyle, whose mother is always home after school because she doesn't trust Lyle to stay home alone.
    c. Wayne, whose parents consistently discipline him whenever he breaks a house rule, which is at least once a week.
    d. Jake, who is very impulsive and tends to act before he thinks.

## ESSAY QUESTIONS

1. Your friend thinks that there is something wrong with her 16-year-old son. One week he says that he wants to be a famous rock-and-roll drummer and the next he says that he wants to be a pediatrician. Your friend doesn't believe that a normal adolescent can change identities so rapidly. Based on what you know about achieving an identity in adolescence, what can you tell your friend to make her feel better?

2. Another friend is having trouble with her teenage daughter. She thinks that her daughter must feel unloved and has rejected all of her parents' values because they argue all the time about her daughter's choice of music and clothes. What can you tell your friend about adolescents to make her feel better?

3. At a recent parent council meeting at your son's high school, another parent suggested that condoms should be sold at school at a low price to slow down the increasing number of teenage pregnancies at school. This parent stated that many teens don't use contraceptives because they don't know how to obtain them or can't afford them. This other parent also said that teens will have sex no matter what so they might as well have contraceptives readily available to them. What can you tell the parent council about programs that seem to be effective in delaying sexual intercourse and increasing the use of contraceptives by teens?

4.  Your friend Enrique has a co-worker that he thinks is gay. Enrique said that he thought that his co-worker was gay because the co-worker's mother must have been domineering, and his co-worker could become heterosexual if he really wanted. What can you tell Enrique about the myths surrounding the causes of homosexuality and the role of biology in determining sexual orientation?

5.  Your artistic, unconventional teenage daughter has told you that she would like to be a research scientist and discover the cure for heart disease when she grows up. You are not so sure that this is a good idea. What can you tell her about Holland's personality-type theory of occupational choice that might change her mind?

6.  Your 16-year-old son wants to get a part-time job at the local fast food restaurant. This job would involve working about 20 hours per week during the school year. Your spouse thinks that this is a great idea and that a part-time job will make your son more responsible and will teach him the value of money. You, however, have read this textbook and don't think that the part-time job during the school year is a good idea. What can you tell your spouse about part-time employment during the school year for teens and the negative effects associated with it?

7.  Your friend Jevan is concerned that his teenage daughter, Antigone, might be drinking. What can you tell Jevan about the factors associated with teenage alcohol abuse that might help him and his daughter?

8.  Your brother is worried that his daughter Yolanda might be depressed and suicidal. What can you tell your brother about the signs of suicide and the course of action if these signs are present that could help him and your niece?

# SOLUTIONS

## 9.1 KNOW THE TERMS

1. diffusion (341)
2. foreclosure (341)
3. moratorium (341)
4. achievement (341)
5. adolescent egocentrism (342)
6. imaginary audience (342)
7. personal fable (342)
8. illusion of invulnerability (342)
9. ethnic identity (343)

## 9.1 KNOW THE DETAILS OF THE SEARCH FOR IDENTITY

1. T, (340)
2. F, (341)
3. F, (341)
4. F, (342)
5. T, (342)
6. T, (342)
7. T, (342)
8. T, (343)
9. T, (343)
10. T, (343)
11. F, (344)
12. T, (344)
13. T, (345)
14. F, (345)
15. F, (346)
16. T, (346)
17. T, (346)

## 9.2 KNOW THE DETAILS OF ROMANTIC RELATIONSHIPS

1. F, (348)
2. T, (349)
3. T, (349)
4. F, (349)
5. T, (349)
6. F, (349)
7. T, (349)
8. F, (351)
9. F, (351)
10. T, (351)
11. F, (352)
12. T, (352)

## 9.3 KNOW THE TERMS

1. crystallization (355)
2. specification (355)
3. implementation (356)
4. personality-type theory (356)

## 9.3 KNOW THE DETAILS OF THE WORLD OF WORK

1. T, (355)
2. F, (355)
3. T, (355)
4. T, (356)
5. F, (357)
6. F, (357)
7. F, (358)
8. T, (358)
9. F, (358)
10. T, (358)
11. T, (358)
12. F, (359)

## 9.4 KNOW THE TERMS

1. depression (363)
2. learned helplessness (363)
3. Norepinephrine or Serotonin (363)
4. Serotonin or Norepinephrine (363)
5. Juvenile delinquency (365)
6. Status offenses (365)
7. index offenses (365)
8. life-course persistent (365)
9. Adolescent-limited (365)

## 9.4 KNOW THE DETAILS OF THE PROBLEMS OF ADOLESCENCE

1. T, (361)
2. T, (361)
3. T, (362)
4. T, (362)
5. F, (363)
6. F, (363)
7. F, (363)
8. T, (363)
9. T, (363)
10. T, (364)
11. T, (364)
12. F, (364)
13. F, (365)
14. F, (365)
15. F, (366)
16. T, (366)
17. T, (366)

## SUMMARY

### 9.1 IDENTITY AND SELF-ESTEEM

1. foreclosure (340); moratorium (340); discussion (342)
2. exploration (343); achievement (343); self-esteem (344)
3. responsibilities (345)
4. advice (346); values (346)

### 9.2 ROMANTIC RELATIONSHIPS AND SEXUALITY

1. support (348)
2. recreational (349); infrequently (349)
3. biology (351); mental-health (352)
4. drinking (352); home (352); friends (353)

### 9.3 THE WORLD OF WORK

1. crystallization (355); implementation (356); personality (356); happier (357)
2. 15 (358); self-esteem (358); little (359); skills (359); save (359)

### 9.4 THE DARK SIDE

1. relaxation (361)
2. unfriendly (363); control (363); neurotransmitters (363); interpretation (364)
3. family processes (366); biology (365).

# TEST YOURSELF

## MULTIPLE-CHOICE QUESTIONS

1.  C, (340)
2.  B, (340)
3.  C, (341)
4.  B, (342)
5.  A, (342)
6.  B, (342)
7.  A, (342)
8.  B, (343)
9.  A, (344)
10. B, (346)
11. A, (346)
12. A, (346)
13. C, (349)

14. C, (350)
15. B, (351)
16. D, (351)
17. A, (353)
18. C, (355)
19. B, (355)
20. A, (355)
21. D, (356)
22. B, (356)
23. C, (357)
24. D, (357)
25. A, (358)

26. B, (358)
27. D, (359)
28. C, (359)
29. D, (360)
30. C, (361)
31. A, (363)
32. C, (363)
33. A, (364)
34. B, (364)
35. A, (365)
36. A, (365)
37. D, (365)

## ESSAY QUESTIONS

1.  During early adolescence, most teens either have no identity (diffusion status) or have chosen an identity that is based on advice from adults (foreclosure status). As teens progress through adolescence they begin to "try-on" different identities to see how each one fits (moratorium status). These different identities may be as diverse as rock-and-roll drummer and pediatrician. Eventually, during late adolescence or early adulthood, after trying many different identities one finds an identity that "fits" and one in which the person feels secure (achievement status). In other words, your friend's son is acting like other teens, and he probably won't settle on an identity for a few years yet. (340-342)

2.  Research findings do not support the view that adolescence is a time of storm and stress. In fact, most adolescents love their parents, turn to their parents for advice, accept many of their parents' values, feel loved by their parents, and report that they are happy most of the time. However, as teens become more independent they may seem as if they do not love their parents as much, because they spend less time with them and are less affectionate with them. Teens also are more likely to argue with their parents over more trivial topics such as music, clothes, and curfews. (346-347)

3.  You can tell the parent council that while it is true that some teens do not use contraceptives because they are not readily available and are too expensive, there are many other factors that are related to teenage sexual activity and contraceptive use. For example, teens may become sexually active because they think that "all of their friends" are, and they might not use contraceptives because they are ignorant of many of the true facts about conception and the transmission of sexually transmitted diseases. Programs that seem to be most effective in preventing teenage pregnancy and sexually transmitted diseases are ones that teach the biological facts and also focus on responsible sexual behavior or abstaining from premarital sex altogether. These also include discussing the pressures to become sexually active and role playing strategies for responding to these pressures. Students who participate in these programs are less likely to have intercourse; when they do have intercourse, they are more likely to use contraceptives. (34-351)

4.  Enrique should know that research has shown that a number of the myths that people have about sexual orientation are wrong. The myths include the belief that sons become gay when they are reared by a domineering mother and a weak father, that girls become lesbians because their fathers are their primary role models, that children who are reared by homosexual parents usually become homosexual themselves, and that homosexual adults were seduced by an older, same-sex person when they were children. In fact, many scientists now believe that heredity and hormones influence sexual orientation. Another explanation is that a pregnant woman's immune system responds

to some biochemical feature of a male fetus that increases the likelihood that her later-born sons will be gay. Another idea is that genes and hormones produce children who have a preference for opposite-sex activities which may lead to a different gender identity. In other words, Enrique's co-worker probably won't be able to change his sexual orientation by simply "wanting to" any more than he could change the color of his eyes. (351-352)

5. According to Holland's personality-type theory of vocational choice, one's personality should be a major factor in choosing a vocation. Holland suggested that people will feel more satisfied with their jobs and more productive if they choose jobs that fit their personality characteristics. Holland suggested 6 personality types. The first type is the realistic person who likes physical labor and likes to solve concrete problems. The second type is the investigative person who is task-oriented and enjoys thinking abstractly. The artistic person likes to express himself through unstructured tasks. The enterprising person likes to use verbal skill in positions of power or leadership. The conventional person likes to apply verbal and quantitative skill to well-defined tasks that are assigned by others. Finally, the social person is skilled verbally and socially and likes to use those skills to solve problems. Your daughter fits the artistic personality but the job of scientist fits the investigative personality. According to Holland, if your daughter would become a scientist she may not enjoy the job. (356-357)

6. Tell your spouse that part-time employment of over 15 hours during the school year for teens is associated with a number of negative outcomes. First, school performance drops because teens who are employed part-time don't seem to use their free time efficiently to do their homework. Second, teens who work over 15 hours per week during the school year are more likely to be depressed and suffer from anxiety. Even though many part-time jobs are boring and repetitive they may be very stressful during busy times which may lead to anxiety. This anxiety may also be related to increased substance abuse and problem behavior that is seen in teens who work many hours per week. Third, these part-time jobs rarely teach teens the value of money. Teens rarely save their money for college or help their parents pay for necessary items. Instead teens tend to spend most of their money on entertainment and personal items such as cosmetics or CDs. Because such a large percentage of their pay checks goes toward "fun" items, teens develop very unrealistic expectations about finances and budgeting. However, there is one long-term benefit. People who have stressful part-time jobs as adolescents are better able to cope with stressful jobs as adults. (358-359)

7. You can tell Jevan that adolescents often drink because their peers do and they pressure them to join them. However, the family atmosphere and the example that parents set for drinking behavior are also important. If drinking is an important part of their parents' social lives, teens are more likely to drink. Teens are also more likely to drink if their parents set arbitrary or unreasonable standards for them. Many teens drink to reduce stress such as problems with parents, friends, or school. In particular, teens are more likely to drink to reduce stress if family problems are frequent. Jevan can help his daughter by helping her reduce stress in her life and by setting a good example of responsible drinking behavior. (360-361)

8. If Yolanda has been depressed or if she has engaged in substance abuse, your brother should be worried because these are 2 common precursors of suicide. Some other warning signs include the person threatening to commit suicide, being preoccupied with death, changing her eating or sleeping habits, losing interest in activities that used to be important, exhibiting marked changes in personality, expressing persistent feelings of gloom and helplessness, and giving away valued possessions. If Yolanda shows any of these signs, your brother should NOT ignore them but should ask Yolanda if she is planning to hurt herself. Your brother should remain calm and supportive. If Yolanda appears to have made preparations to commit suicide, she shouldn't be left alone. Your brother should also insist that Yolanda seek professional help to treat her feelings of depression and hopelessness that may be leading to the suicidal thoughts. (364-365)

# BECOMING AN ADULT

This chapter focuses on the transition to adulthood and physical, cognitive, and personality changes that occur during young adulthood.

# 10.1 WHEN DOES ADULTHOOD BEGIN?

## TO MASTER THE LEARNING OBJECTIVES:

**What role transitions mark entry into adulthood in Western societies? How do non-Western cultures mark the transition to adulthood?**

- Define role transitions and how they are related to age.

- Describe rituals and indicators of adulthood that can be found in non-Western cultures.

**How does going to college fit in the transition to adulthood?**

- Describe the changes in the age composition of college students in the United States.

- Compare returning adult students to traditional-aged college students.

- Describe ways in which the ADA has helped people with disabilities.

**What psychological criteria mark the transition to adulthood?**

- Explain how adolescents and adults differ in terms of engaging in reckless behavior.

- Describe Erikson's psychosocial conflict of intimacy versus isolation and explain how this conflict relates to achieving identity.

- Describe the pattern of behavior for forming an identity and establishing intimacy in both men and women.

**What aspects of early young adulthood make it a separate developmental stage?**

- Define the term *threshholder*.

# 10.1 KNOW THE TERMS

| | |
|---|---|
| **Intimacy versus isolation** | **Rites of passage** |
| **Returning adult** | **Role transitions** |

1. _____ involve assuming new responsibilities and duties and are often used to determine whether a person has attained adulthood.

2. Rituals that mark the initiation into adulthood are called _____ .

3. College students over the age of 25 years are often referred to as _____ students.

4. According to Erikson, the psychosocial conflict of young adulthood is one of _____ .

# 10.1 KNOW THE DETAILS OF BECOMING AN ADULT

1. The average age for completing education has increased since the early 1900s.
   TRUE or FALSE

2. The markers for entrance into adulthood are much clearer in Western societies than in non-Western societies.
   TRUE or FALSE

3. Rites of passage are rituals that mark initiation into adulthood.
   TRUE or FALSE

4. Returning adult students tend to be less motivated than younger college students.
   TRUE or FALSE

5. The ADA prohibits discrimination on the basis of disability.
   TRUE or FALSE

6. The frequency of reckless behavior decreases significantly between adolescence and adulthood.
   TRUE or FALSE

7. According to Erikson, the major task for young adults is dealing with the psychosocial conflict of trust versus mistrust.

   TRUE or FALSE

8. Most men resolve intimacy issues before identity issues.

   TRUE or FALSE

# 10.2 PHYSICAL DEVELOPMENT AND HEALTH

## TO MASTER THE LEARNING OBJECTIVES:

**In what respects are young adults at their physical peak?**

- Describe physical functioning in young adults.

- Describe sensory acuity during young adulthood.

**How healthy are young adults in general?**

- Explain the general, overall health found in young adults in the United States.

- Describe the frequency of death from disease and death from accidents during young adulthood.

- Explain the gender and ethnic differences in causes of death in young adults.

**How do smoking, drinking alcohol, and nutrition affect young adults' health?**

- Describe the negative health effects of smoking and second-hand smoke and the health benefits of quitting smoking.

- Describe the factors related to, negative effects of, and prevention of binge drinking.

- Describe the consequences associated with alcohol addiction.

- Describe the nutritional requirements and eating habits of young adults.

- Explain how dietary fat intake and cholesterol levels are related to cardiovascular disease.

- Define BMI and describe how it is related to health.

**How does young adults' health differ as a function of socioeconomic status, gender, and ethnicity?**

- Describe how income and level of education are linked to health in the United States.

- Describe how men and women differ in health and health behaviors.

- Explain ethnic differences in health.

## 10.2 KNOW THE TERMS

| | |
|---|---|
| **Addiction** | **High-density** |
| **Binge drinking** | **Low-density** |
| **Body mass index (BMI)** | **Metabolism** |

1. Consuming four or more drinks in a row within a two-week period is _____ .

2. People who have an _____ are physically dependent on a particular substance, such as alcohol, and suffer from withdrawal symptoms when they do not use the substance.

3. How much energy one's body needs is known as _____ .

4. _____ lipoproteins cause fatty acids to accumulate in arteries which impedes the flow of blood.

5. _____ lipoproteins help clear arteries and break down LDLs.

6. The ratio of body weight and height, which is related to total body fat, is known as _____ .

## 10.2 KNOW THE DETAILS OF PHYSICAL DEVELOPMENT AND HEALTH

1. Physical functioning peaks during middle adulthood.
   TRUE or FALSE

2. Sensory acuity is at its peak in the early 20s.
   TRUE or FALSE

3. Accidents are the leading cause of death between the ages of 25 and 44.
   TRUE or FALSE

4. Young adult men are twice as likely to die as women of the same age.
   TRUE or FALSE

5. Alcohol is the single biggest contributor to health problems.
   TRUE or FALSE

6. Over half of all cancers are related to smoking.
   TRUE or FALSE

7. Exposure to second hand smoke increases the risk of smoking-related diseases.
   TRUE or FALSE

8. Total consumption of alcohol in industrialized countries has increased for the past few decades.
   TRUE or FALSE

9. Binge drinking increases the likelihood of engaging in unwanted sexual behavior.
   TRUE or FALSE

10. More men than women are alcohol dependent.
    TRUE or FALSE

11. Nutrition directly affects one's mental, emotional, and physical functioning.
    TRUE or FALSE

12. Body metabolism speeds up with age.
    TRUE or FALSE

13. Socioeconomic status and education are the two most important social influences on health.
    TRUE or FALSE

14. Women use health care services more often than men do.
    TRUE or FALSE

# 10.3 COGNITIVE DEVELOPMENT

## TO MASTER THE LEARNING OBJECTIVES:

### What is intelligence in adulthood?

- Explain what is meant by multidimensional and multidirectional intelligence.
- Explain what is meant by interindividual variability and plasticity in intelligence.

### What types of abilities have been identified? How do they change?

- Define primary mental abilities.
- Describe age differences and cohort differences in primary mental abilities.
- List and describe the variables that are related to reduced cognitive decline in old age.
- Explain the difference between fluid intelligence and crystallized intelligence and explain how each changes with age.

### What is postformal thought? How does it differ from formal operations?

- Explain how adults' thinking differs from the formal operational thought that is seen in adolescence.
- Describe how thought changes during the college years.
- Define postformal thought and reflective judgment.
- Describe the development of absolutist, relativistic, and dialectical thinking.
- Describe the importance of emotion and logic throughout adolescence and adulthood.

**How do stereotypes influence thinking?**

• Describe how people are influenced by stereotypes.

• Describe age differences in social beliefs.

# 10.3 KNOW THE TERMS

| | |
|---|---|
| **Crystallized** | **Postformal** |
| **Fluid** | **Primary mental** |
| **Implicit stereotyping** | **Reflective judgment** |
| **Interindividual variability** | **Secondary mental** |
| **Multidimensional** | **Skill acquisition** |
| **Multidirectionality** | **Stereotypes** |
| **Optimal level of development** | **Stereotype threat** |
| **Plasticity** | |

1. Most theories of intelligence are _____ because they identify many different areas of intellectual abilities.

2. Intellectual abilities show _____ because some aspects of intelligence improve and other aspects decline across adulthood.

3. _____ means that the patterns of change in intelligence are different for different people.

4. _____ in intellectual ability also occurs when certain conditions modify one's ability at any point during adulthood.

5. Groups of related intellectual skills (e.g., spatial skill, mathematical skill, etc.) are called _____ abilities.

6. Broader categories of intellectual skills that subsume and organize the primary abilities are called _____ abilities.

7. _____ intelligence includes abilities such as thinking in a flexible, adaptive manner, drawing inferences, and understanding relations between concepts.

8. _____ intelligence reflects knowledge that has been acquired through experience and education in a particular culture.

9. Thought that is characterized by the realization that the correct answer may vary from situation to situation, that problem solutions must be realistic, that most situations are ambiguous, and that emotion and other subjective factors are an important part of thought is called _____ thought.

10. _____ is a way in which adults reason about dilemmas involving current affairs, religion, science, and personal relationships.

11. The _____ is the highest level of information-processing capacity that a person is capable of doing.

12. _____ is the gradual, somewhat haphazard process by which people learn new abilities.

13. _____ are a special type of social knowledge that represent organized prior knowledge about a group of people that affects how we interpret new information.

14. The activation of strong stereotypes that is automatic and nonconscious is called _____ .

15. An evoked fear of being judged with a negative stereotype about a group to which you belong is called _____ .

# 10.3 KNOW THE DETAILS OF COGNITIVE DEVELOPMENT

1. Interindividual variability refers to some aspects of intelligence improving and others declining during adulthood.
   TRUE or FALSE

2. Plasticity refers to the modifiability of people's abilities.
   TRUE or FALSE

3. Fluid and crystallized intelligence are called primary mental abilities.
   TRUE or FALSE

4. Schaie's Seattle Longitudinal Study found that older cohorts outperformed younger cohorts on all primary mental abilities.
   TRUE or FALSE

5. Adults who remain cognitively active through reading and lifelong learning have a lower risk of cognitive decline in old age.
   TRUE or FALSE

6. Patterns of intellectual change over the course of adulthood vary a great deal from person to person.
   TRUE or FALSE

7. Factual knowledge is a form of fluid intelligence.
   TRUE or FALSE

8. Fluid intelligence increases throughout adulthood.
   TRUE or FALSE

9. Crystallized intelligence increases throughout adulthood.
   TRUE or FALSE

10. Adults are more likely than adolescents to consider situational constraints and circumstances when solving problems.
    TRUE or FALSE

11. As they go through the college years, students increasingly rely on the expertise of authority figures to determine which ways of thinking are right and which are wrong.
    TRUE or FALSE

12. Postformal thought is characterized by logical, deductive reasoning that is not influenced by emotion or subjective factors.
    TRUE or FALSE

13. Individuals in the stages of prereflective thought do not acknowledge that knowledge is uncertain.
    TRUE or FALSE

14. Absolutist thinking becomes progressively more common over the course of adulthood.
    TRUE or FALSE

15. Mature adult thinking is marked by the tendency to separate emotion and logic.
    TRUE or FALSE

16. Implicit stereotyping is an evoked fear of being judged in accordance with a negative stereotype about a group to which you belong.
    TRUE or FALSE

# 10.4 WHO DO YOU WANT TO BE? PERSONALITY IN YOUNG ADULTHOOD

## TO MASTER THE LEARNING OBJECTIVES:

**What is the life-span construct? How do adults create scenarios and life stories?**

- Define life-span construct and list the factors that lead to the development of one.

- Define scenario and explain how it is related to a social clock.

- Define life story and explain why distortions may occur in one's memory for autobiographical events.

**What are possible selves?  Do they show differences during adulthood?**

- Describe possible selves and explain how they motivate behavior.

- Explain how concerns about and the number of possible selves change with age.

**What are personal control beliefs?**

- Define personal control beliefs and explain how they may vary across different domains of one's life.

- Know the difference between primary and secondary control and how they change with age.

# 10.4 KNOW THE TERMS

| | |
|---|---|
| **Life-span construct** | **Possible selves** |
| **Life story** | **Scenario** |
| **Personal control** | **Social clock** |

1.  A _____ is a unified sense of the past, present, and future that is based on one's experiences and input from others.

2.  The first manifestation of the life-span construct that consists of expectations about the future is called a _____ .

3.  Associating future events with a time or age by which one expects to complete them creates a _____ .

4.  The second manifestation of the life-span construct, the _____ , is a personal narrative that organizes past events into a coherent sequence.

5.  _____ represents what one could become, what one would like to become, and what one is afraid of becoming.

6.  _____ beliefs are beliefs about the degree to which one's performance in a situation is within one's control.

# 10.4 KNOW THE DETAILS OF PERSONALITY IN YOUNG ADULTHOOD

1. A life-span construct is created from personal experience and input from other people and represents a unified sense of the past, present, and future.
   TRUE or FALSE

2. Tagging future events with a particular time or age by which they are to be completed creates a life story.
   TRUE or FALSE

3. Possible selves represent what we could become, what we would like to become, and what we are afraid of becoming.
   TRUE or FALSE

4. Health tends to become a less important aspect of feared self as people get older.
   TRUE or FALSE

5. Personal control beliefs are generally similar across different domains.
   TRUE or FALSE

# SUMMARY

## 10.1 WHEN DOES ADULTHOOD BEGIN?

1. **Role Transitions Marking Adulthood**

   The most widely used criteria for deciding whether a person has reached adulthood are role transitions, which involve assuming new _____ and duties. Some societies use rituals, called _____ , to mark this transition clearly. These rituals tend to focus mainly on men. However, such rituals are largely absent in Western culture.

2. **Going to College**

   Over half of all college students are _____ . These returning adult students tend to be more _____ and have many other positive characteristics. College also serves as a catalyst for cognitive development.

3. **Psychological View**

   Adolescents and adults _____ in different ways. A second major difference is a drop in the rate of participation in _____ .

4. **So When Do People Become Adults?**

In cultures without clearly defined rites of passage, people become adults when they fully
_____ like adults.

## 10.2 PHYSICAL DEVELOPMENT AND HEALTH

1. **Growth, Strength, and Physical Functioning**

   Young adulthood is the time when height and several physical abilities peak: strength, _____ ,
   coordination, dexterity, and _____ Most of these abilities begin to decline in middle age.

2. **Health Status**

   Young adults are also at the peak of health. Death from disease is relatively _____ especially
   during the 20s. Accidents are the leading cause of death. However, homicide and _____ are
   major factors in some groups, and _____ is also a major barrier to good health.

3. **Lifestyle Factors**

   Smoking is the single biggest contributor to health problems. It is related to half of all cancers and is a
   primary cause of respiratory and _____ disease. Although it is difficult, quitting smoking has
   many health benefits. For most people, drinking alcohol poses few health risks. Several treatment
   approaches have been used for alcoholics. Nutritional needs change somewhat across adulthood,
   mostly due to changes in _____ . Some nutrient needs, such as carbohydrates, change. The
   ratio of LDLs to HDLs in serum cholesterol, which can be controlled through diet in most people, is an
   important risk factor in _____ disease

4. **Social, Gender, and Ethnic Issues in Health**

   The two most important social factors in health are socioeconomic status and _____ The
   poorest health conditions exist for _____ living in poor, inner-city neighborhoods. Other
   ethnic groups who have limited access to health care also suffer. Whether women or men are healthier
   is difficult to answer because women have been _____ from much health research. Higher
   education is associated with better health due to better access to health care and more _____
   about proper diet and life style.

## 10.3 COGNITIVE DEVELOPMENT

1. **How Should We View Intelligence in Adults?**

Most modern theories of intelligence are _____ For instance, Baltes' research shows that development varies among individuals and across different categories of abilities.

2. **What Happens to Intelligence in Adulthood?**

Intellectual abilities can be studied as groups of related skills called primary mental abilities. These abilities show different developmental trends which change in succeeding _____ More recent cohorts perform better on some skills, such as _____ reasoning, but older cohorts perform better on number skills. Fluid intelligence consists of abilities that make people flexible and adaptive thinkers. Fluid abilities generally _____ across adulthood. Crystallized intelligence reflects knowledge that people acquire through life _____ and education in a particular culture. Crystallized abilities _____ until late life.

3. **Going Beyond Formal Operations:  Thinking in Adulthood**

Postformal thought is characterized by a recognition that _____ may vary from one situation to another, that solutions must be realistic, that ambiguity and _____ are the rule, and that _____ and subjectivity play a role in thinking. One example of postformal thought is reflective judgment. Stereotypes are a special type of social knowledge structure or social belief that represent organized _____ knowledge about a group of people that affects how we _____ new information. Activating stereotypes can have a powerful effect on cognitive processing.

## 10.4 WHO DO YOU WANT TO BE? PERSONALITY IN YOUNG ADULTHOOD

1. **Creating Scenarios and Life Stories**

Young adults create a _____ that represents a unified sense of the past, present, and future. This is manifested in two ways: through a scenario that maps out the _____ based on a social clock and in the life story, which creates an autobiography.

2. **Possible Selves**

People create possible selves by projecting themselves into the future and thinking about what they would like to become, what they could become, and what they are _____ of becoming. Age differences in these projections depend on the dimension examined. In hoped-for selves, 18- to 24-year-olds and 40- to 59-year-olds report _____ issues as most important, whereas 25- to 39-year-olds and older adults report personal issues to be most important. All groups report _____ aspects as their most feared selves.

3. **Personal Control Beliefs**

   Personal control is an important concept with broad applicability. However, the developmental trends are complex, because personal control beliefs _____ considerably from one domain to another.

# TEST YOURSELF

## MULTIPLE-CHOICE QUESTIONS

1. _____ involve assuming new responsibilities, such as beginning full-time employment or getting married, which indicate that an individual has reached adulthood.
   a. Role transitions
   b. Possible selves
   c. Rites of passage
   d. Personal control beliefs

2. In non-Western cultures, _____ is the most important marker of adult status.
   a. beginning a full-time job
   b. completing one's education
   c. getting married
   d. becoming a parent

3. Ron is a returning adult student. He is likely to
   a. be a full-time student.
   b. have life experiences that relate to course work.
   c. need a high level of direction from others.
   d. have difficulty with problem solving.

4. Compared to the way he behaved at age 16, at age 25 Rafael
   a. probably has less self-control.
   b. is less likely to engage in reckless behavior.
   c. is less likely to adhere to social conventions.
   d. is more likely to drive at a high speed.

5. According to Erikson, the major issue during young adulthood involves
   a. trust versus mistrust.
   b. identity versus role confusion.
   c. intimacy versus isolation.
   d. integrity versus despair.

6. Research on Erikson's theory suggests that
    a. most men and career-oriented women resolve identity issues before intimacy issues.
    b. most men resolve intimacy issues before identity issues.
    c. most women, including those who are and who are not career-oriented, tend to resolve intimacy issues before identity issues.
    d. only career-oriented women tend to resolve intimacy issues before identity issues.

7. Who is most likely to be at the peak of physical strength for his lifetime?
    a. 18-year-old Cassius
    b. 28-year-old Joe
    c. 38-year-old Rocky
    d. 48-year-old George

8. _____ often starts to decline in the late 20s.
    a. Vision
    b. Taste
    c. Smell
    d. Hearing

9. The leading cause of death for young adults is
    a. AIDS.
    b. accidents.
    c. cancer.
    d. cardiovascular disease.

10. Which of the following lifestyle factors is the greatest contributor to health problems in our society today?
    a. lack of exercise
    b. drinking
    c. smoking
    d. poor nutrition

11. Binge drinking is more common
    a. among 17- to 23-year-olds than among older students.
    b. in students who are not in a fraternity.
    c. in students who work in part-time jobs.
    d. in students who study more than four hours per day.

12. Body metabolism _____ with age.
    a. decreases
    b. increases
    c. decreases in females and increases in males
    d. does not change

13. High levels of _____ is a protective health factor.
    a. high density lipoproteins
    b. low density lipoproteins
    c. sodium
    d. fat

14. Which of the following statements about factors related to health is true?
    a. Men are healthier than women.
    b. African Americans are healthier than European Americans.
    c. Higher income is positively related to health.
    d. Education level is negatively related to health.

15. Theories of intelligence that identify different domains of intellectual abilities are
    a. addressing interindividual variability.
    b. multidirectional.
    c. multidimensional.
    d. addressing plasticity.

16. Number, word fluency, verbal meaning, inductive reasoning, and spatial orientation are all
    a. primary mental abilities.
    b. secondary mental abilities.
    c. forms of fluid intelligence.
    d. forms of crystallized intelligence.

17. Schaie's longitudinal study of adult intelligence found that older cohorts outperformed younger cohorts on tasks that involved
    a. inductive reasoning.
    b. number skills.
    c. verbal meaning.
    d. word fluency.

18. Adults' scores on tests of primary mental abilities tend to improve until the
    a. late 20s or early 30s.
    b. late 30s or early 40s.
    c. late 50s or early 60s.
    d. late 60s or early 70s.

19. Who of the following 60-year-olds has the lowest risk of cognitive decline in old age?
    a. Ruth, who is not yet satisfied with her life achievements
    b. Mary, who recently went back to school
    c. Louise, who has a rigid personality style
    d. Betty, who suffers from cardiovascular disease

20. Which of the following tasks requires the use of fluid intelligence?
    a. defining the word "intelligence"
    b. naming the 2006 NCAA Division I women's basketball champion
    c. describing the main features of the three periods of prenatal development
    d. finding the shortest way from Point A to Point B in a maze

21. Fluid intelligence _____ throughout adulthood while crystallized intelligence _____.
    a. declines; improves
    b. improves; declines
    c. declines; also declines
    d. improves; also improves

22. _____ thought is marked by an understanding that truth may vary from situation to situation, that solutions must be realistic, and that emotion and subjective factors usually play a role in thinking.
    a. Formal operational
    b. Absolutist
    c. Postformal
    d. Concrete operational

23. According to Kramer, adult thinking develops in which of the following sequences?
    a. absolutist, dialectical, relativistic
    b. relativistic, dialectical, absolutist
    c. dialectical, relativistic, absolutist
    d. absolutist, relativistic, dialectical

24. Who is most likely to say, "There is only one solution to this problem and I know what it is."
    a. Rafe, a reflective thinker
    b. Diane, a dialectical thinker
    c. Abby, an absolutist thinker
    d. Riley, a relativistic thinker

25. A _____ represents a unified sense of the past, present, and future.
    a. life-span construct
    b. social clock
    c. scenario
    d. life story

26. Jasmine plans to get her engineering degree when she is 22, get married by the time she is 25, have two children by the time she is 30, and retire at age 55. Jennifer's personal timetable for important events in her future is called a
    a. life-span construct.
    b. social clock.
    c. scenario.
    d. life story.

27. At age 22, Jerry envisions himself as an entrepreneur who will use his talents to start and successfully run his own business in the future. Jerry's view of himself in the future is called a
    a. social clock.
    b. life story.
    c. scenario.
    d. life-span construct.

28. At age 42, Jerry is successfully running his own business and has two failed marriages behind him. Although he was very upset about his marital breakups at the time they occurred, he now looks at them as inevitable due to the hours he was spending at work and has decided they were good learning experiences. Jerry's organization of his past life events is called a
    a. life-span construct.
    b. scenario.
    c. possible self.
    d. life story.

29. Young adults, 18- to 24-year-olds, most commonly mention _____ issues when asked about their hoped-for selves.
    a. family
    b. career
    c. personal
    d. physical

30. Enrique believes that the degree of success he has in college will be highly related to how much he goes to class and how hard he studies. Enrique has a strong sense of
    a. self-concept.
    b. perceived competence.
    c. possible self.
    d. personal control.

## ESSAY QUESTIONS

1. Your 2 younger sisters seem to be very different. Ashlee is 25 and she has started a career in an area that she loves, and she is engaged to be married. The other sister, Jessica, is 27, she has changed jobs frequently since college, and she doesn't seem to really have an established identity. Everyone in the family is worried that until Jessica establishes an identity she will never get married. What can you tell your family about the research on identity and intimacy in women that might relieve some of their anxieties?

2. Your friend Frank, a smoker, is upset about the decreasing number of places where he is allowed to smoke. He thinks smokers are singled out and picked on unfairly. Frank feels that if someone wants to smoke, they should be able to when and where they want. What can you tell Frank about the effects of second-hand smoke?

3. Your friend, Julian, is thin and he never watches what he eats. He thinks that all of the recommendations about dietary fat are to help people lose weight and because he doesn't need to lose weight he doesn't

need to worry about dietary fat. What can you tell Julian about problems other than obesity that are related to dietary fat intake?

4. The other day a friend of yours said, "We had better enjoy being smart now because when we get older intelligence really goes down hill." After reading this section of the text on intelligence, what can you tell your friend that contradicts this statement?

5. You and your 2 brothers are talking about your sister and her husband who are having marital problems. Your 17-year-old brother said, "She should leave him because he is a jerk." Your 35-year-old brother said, "Well, he may be a jerk but how will she support herself and the 2 kids? And she does love him even if he is a jerk." Your 17-year-old brother then told your 35-year-old brother to stop being so wishy-washy. What can you tell your 17-year-old brother about postformal thought?

6. You and 2 friends are talking one day about your lives. Your friend Erik said that he was glad that he had spent a lot of time with his kids when he was in graduate school even if it meant that it took him 10 years to get his degree. When Erik left, your friend Sandy said that she remembers that when Erik started graduate school he was very enthusiastic and planned to get his degree in 4 years and make a name for himself in his field within 10 years. What can you tell Sandy about distortions in autobiographical events as one constructs a life story?

# SOLUTIONS

## 10.1 KNOW THE TERMS

1. Role transitions (379)
2. rites of passage (379)
3. returning adult (380)
4. intimacy vs isolation (382)

## 10.1 KNOW THE DETAILS OF BECOMING AN ADULT

1. T, (379)
2. F, (379)
3. T, (379)
4. F, (381)
5. T, (381)
6. T, (382)
7. F, (382)
8. F, (382)

## 10.2 KNOW THE TERMS

1. binge drinking (386)
2. addiction (388)
3. metabolism (388)
4. Low-density (389)
5. High-density (389)
6. body mass index (389)

## 10.2 KNOW THE DETAILS OF PHYSICAL DEVELOPMENT AND HEALTH

1. F, (384)
2. T, (384)
3. T, (385)
4. T, (385)
5. F, (385)
6. T, (385)
7. T, (385)
8. F, (386)
9. T, (387)
10. T, (388)
11. T, (388)
12. F, (388)
13. T, (390)
14. T, (390)

## 10.3 KNOW THE TERMS

1. multidimensional (392)
2. multidirectionality (392)
3. Interindividual variability (392)
4. Plasticity (392)
5. primary mental (392)
6. secondary mental (394)
7. Fluid (395)
8. Crystallized (395)
9. postformal (397)
10. Reflective judgment (397)
11. optimal level of development (399)
12. Skill acquisition (399)
13. Stereotypes (401)
14. implicit stereotyping (401)
15. stereotype threat (402)

## 10.3 KNOW THE DETAILS OF COGNITIVE DEVELOPMENT

| | | |
|---|---|---|
| 1. F, (392) | 7. F, (395) | 13. T, (397) |
| 2. T, (392) | 8. F, (395) | 14. F, (399) |
| 3. F, (392) | 9. T, (395) | 15. F, (399) |
| 4. F, (393) | 10. T, (397) | 16. F, (401) |
| 5. T, (394) | 11. F, (397) | |
| 6. T, (394) | 12. F, (397) | |

## 10.4 KNOW THE TERMS

| | | |
|---|---|---|
| 1. life-span construct (405) | 3. social clock (405) | 5. Possible selves (406) |
| 2. scenario (405) | 4. life story (405) | 6. Personal control (408) |

## 10.4 KNOW THE DETAILS OF PERSONALITY IN YOUNG ADULTHOOD

| | | |
|---|---|---|
| 1. T, (405) | 3. T, (406) | 5. F, (409) |
| 2. F, (405) | 4. F, (407) | |

## SUMMARY

### 10.1 WHEN DOES ADULTHOOD BEGIN?

1. responsibilities (379); rites of passage (379)
2. over age 25 (380); motivated (380)
3. think (381); reckless behavior (382)
4. feel (383)

### 10.2 PHYSICAL DEVELOPMENT AND HEALTH

1. muscle development (380); sensory acuity (384).
2. rare (385); violence (385); poverty (385)
3. cardiovascular (385); metabolism (388); cardiovascular (389)
4. education (390).; African Americans (390); excluded (390); knowledge (390)

### 10.3 COGNITIVE DEVELOPMENT

1. multidimensional (392).
2. cohorts (393); inductive (393); decline (395); experiences (395); improve (395)
3. truth (397); contradiction (397); emotion (397); prior (401); interpret (401)

## 10.4 WHO DO YOU WANT TO BE? PERSONALITY IN YOUNG ADULTHOOD

1. life-span construct (405); future (405)
2. afraid (407); family (407); physical (408)
3. vary (408)

# TEST YOURSELF

## MULTIPLE-CHOICE QUESTIONS

| | | |
|---|---|---|
| 1. A, (379) | 11. A, (387) | 21. A, (395) |
| 2. C, (379) | 12. A, (388) | 22. C, (397) |
| 3. B, (380) | 13. A, (389) | 23. D, (399) |
| 4. B, (382) | 14. C, (390) | 24. C, (399) |
| 5. C, (382) | 15. C, (392) | 25. A, (405) |
| 6. A, (382) | 16. A, (392) | 26. B, (405) |
| 7. B, (384) | 17. B, (393) | 27. C, (405) |
| 8. D, (384) | 18. B, (393) | 28. D, (405) |
| 9. B, (385) | 19. B, (394) | 29. A, (407) |
| 10. C, (385) | 20. D, (395) | 30. D, (408) |

## ESSAY QUESTIONS

1. Erik Erikson said that young adults must establish an identity before they can create a shared identity with another person, which is an essential ingredient for true intimacy. Some research has supported Erikson's theory. Young adults who have achieved an identity status are more likely to be in committed relationships. However, this seems to be true for men and career-oriented women but not for all women. Some women attain intimacy before attaining identity while other women resolve intimacy and identity issues simultaneously, and they do not conform to the pattern suggested by Erikson. As far as your sisters, Ashlee seems to conform to the pattern suggested by Erikson but Jessica does not. This does not mean, though, that Jessica will not develop an intimate relationship until she establishes an identity. Jessica may be one of the women who will establish intimacy before, or simultaneously with, establishing her identity. (382)

2. Research points to the fact that the negative health effects associated with smoking are NOT limited to smokers, but people who breathe second-hand smoke are at risk, too. Nonsmokers who are exposed to second-hand smoke have a greater risk for developing lung cancer, other lung problems, and cardiovascular disease. So, smoking in public places such as a workplace does have negative effects on the health of those who breathe smokers' second-hand smoke, and the increasing number of bans on smoking is not just an unfair attack on smokers. (385-386)

3. Dietary fat, particularly saturated fat, is related not only to being overweight but also to incidence of cardiovascular disease. By replacing foods high in saturated fat with low-fat foods, one can reduce the level of cholesterol in the blood. There are two types of cholesterol: low-density lipoproteins (LDLs) and high-density lipoproteins (HDLs). LDLs cause fatty deposits to accumulate in arteries and impede blood flow, but HDLs keep arteries clear and break down LDLs. High levels of HDLs are considered a protective factor in cardiovascular disease. HDL levels can be raised through exercise and high-fiber diet. So, while Julian may not be concerned about his weight, he could be increasing his risk for cardiovascular disease by eating large amounts of fat in his diet. (389)

4. The first fact to tell your friend is that intelligence is multidimensional. In other words, there are many different aspects of intelligence. Second, intellectual development is also multidirectional, which means that these different aspects of intelligence are not affected in the same way by aging. In fact, fluid intelligence seems to decline with age but crystallized intelligence, which includes knowledge acquired from education and experience, seems to increase with age until late old age. Third, intellectual aging also shows interindividual variability. In other

words, some people show the general age-related trends in intellectual functioning and others don't. Fourth, people's abilities show plasticity which means that their abilities are not fixed and can be modified at any point. So, your friend's statement isn't accurate on many dimensions. (392)

5.  You can tell your 17-year-old brother that your other brother is not being wishy washy but is displaying postformal thought, which is typical of middle-aged adults. Your 17-year-old brother is using formal operational thought, and he thinks that he is right because he used logical thinking to formulate his solution: if one is married to a jerk, then one should dump him. Your 35-year-old brother is using postformal thought. He is considering the pragmatic and emotional aspects of the situation. He realizes that all of these things are important and do not lead to an easy, logical answer, and he is not being wishy-washy. (397-399)

6.  People use life-span constructs to link their identities with a view of themselves. Initially, a person may develop a scenario of what they would like to become. The completion of the goal in this scenario is usually linked to an age or time which creates a social clock. When Erik began graduate school, he created a scenario about graduate school and a career including a social clock for completion of graduate school and "making it" in his field. However, it took Erik much longer than he had planned to finish graduate school and now Erik's memories of life events have been distorted so he can see himself in a more favorable light, or so he can soothe his ego for not attaining his goals. In any case, he has taken the past events of his life and has constructed a life story that fits the events. (405-406)

# BEING WITH OTHERS

11.1 Relationships

11.2 Lifestyles

11.3 The Family Life Cycle

11.4 Divorce and Remarriage

This chapter focuses on adults' relationships, life-style choices, the family life cycle, and divorce and remarriage.

# 11.1 RELATIONSHIPS

## TO MASTER THE LEARNING OBJECTIVES:

**What types of friendships do adults have?  How do adult friendships develop?**

- Describe the ABCDE stages of adult friendships.

- Describe the 3 themes that underlie adult friendships.

- Know the characteristics and development of online friendships.

- Describe the differences in men's and women's friendships.

**What is love?  How does it begin?  How does it develop through adulthood?**

- Describe Sternberg's 3 components of love:  passion, intimacy, and commitment.

- Describe how different forms of love become dominant at different points during the course of a relationship.

- Describe the aspects of love relationships that remain constant across different ages.

- Describe the stages that occur to form a couple.

- Explain the cross-cultural research on the effects of culture and gender on mate selection.

- Describe how developmental forces influence relationships.

**What is the nature of violence in some relationships?**

- Describe the continuum of aggressive behaviors that occur in abusive relationships.

- Explain how the causes of aggressive behavior change as the level of aggression changes.

- Explain the difference between common couple violence and patriarchal terrorism.

- Explain how gender and culture influence aggressive behavior.

# 11.1 KNOW THE TERMS

**Abusive**                                          **Common couple violence**

**Assortative mating**                    **Patriarchal terrorism**

**Battered woman syndrome**

1. The theory of _____ states that people find partners based on their similarity to each other.

2. An _____ relationship is one in which one partner becomes aggressive toward the other partner.

3. The _____ occurs when a woman believes that she cannot leave an abusive situation.

4. Violence that occurs occasionally and that can be instigated by either partner is known as

   _____ .

5. _____ refers to women who are victims of systematic violence from men.

# 11.1 KNOW THE DETAILS OF ADULT RELATIONSHIPS

1. Acquaintanceship, buildup, continuation, deterioration, and ending are the stages of adult friendship.
   TRUE or FALSE

2. People tend to have more friends during the period of late adulthood than at any other time in life.
   TRUE or FALSE

3. Life satisfaction is strongly related to the quantity and quality of contacts with friends.
   TRUE or FALSE

4. Online environments are less conducive to developing friendships for people who are lonely.
   TRUE or FALSE

5. Intimacy and emotional sharing are a bigger part of men's friendships than women's friendships.
   TRUE or FALSE

6. Competition is often a part of men's friendships.
   TRUE or FALSE

7. Passion, intimacy, and commitment are the three basic components of love.
   TRUE or FALSE

8. Early in a relationship, intimacy tends to be high, but passion and commitment tend to be low.
   TRUE or FALSE

9. The theory of assortative mating states that people find partners based on their similarity to each other.
   TRUE or FALSE

10. The kind of attachment relationships an individual has as a child influences the kind of partner relationships formed as an adult.
    TRUE or FALSE

11. Around the world, men value chastity in women, and women look for physically attractive men.
    TRUE or FALSE

12. Characteristics that are valued in a mate in one culture may not be valued in another culture.
    TRUE or FALSE

13. The battered woman syndrome occurs when a woman believes that she cannot leave the abusive situation and may even go so far as to kill her abuser.
    TRUE or FALSE

14. Patriarchal terrorism refers to women who are victims of systematic violence from men.
    TRUE or FALSE

15. The most pertinent causes of aggressive behavior toward a male partner by women are the need to control, misuse of power, and jealousy.
    TRUE or FALSE

16. The incidence of abuse is higher in cultures where female purity, male status, and honor are valued.
    TRUE or FALSE

# 11.2 LIFESTYLES

## TO MASTER THE LEARNING OBJECTIVES:

**Why do some people decide not to marry, and what are these people like?**

- Describe the gender differences in singlehood.

- Describe ethnic differences in singlehood.

- Describe the pluses and minuses associated with being single.

**What are the characteristics of cohabiting people?**

- Explain how age is related to cohabitation.

- List the three main reasons for cohabiting.

- Describe cultural differences in cohabiting.

- Describe the effects that cohabiting may have on a later marriage.

**What are gay and lesbian relationships like?**

- Compare sexual expression and interpersonal relations in heterosexual couples with that in gay and lesbian couples.

- Describe gender differences in relationships.

**What is marriage like through the course of adulthood?**

- Describe how age at the time of first marriage is related to marital success.

- Define homogamy and exchange theory and explain how they are related to marital success.

- Describe the course of marital satisfaction.

- Describe some of the adjustments that newly-married couples must make.

- Describe how level of education and pooling resources are related to marital satisfaction.

- Explain how children affect marital satisfaction.

- Describe husbands' and wives' marital satisfaction during mid-life.

- Describe the factors that are related to marital satisfaction in couples during the retirement years.

- Describe the factors that are related to marital satisfaction.


# 11.2 KNOW THE TERMS

| | |
|---|---|
| **Cohabitation** | **Homogamy** |
| **Exchange** | |


1. Living with someone with whom one has a committed, intimate, sexual relationship is called

   _____ .

2. Similarity of values and interests is called _____ .

3. According to _____ theory, marriage is based on each partner contributing something to the relationship that the other would be hard-pressed to provide.

## 11.2 KNOW THE DETAILS OF ADULT LIFESTYLES

1. In early adulthood, increasing numbers of adults are choosing to stay single.
   TRUE or FALSE

2. Fewer women than men remain unmarried throughout adulthood.
   TRUE or FALSE

3. Women with lower levels of education are over-represented among unmarried adults.
   TRUE or FALSE

4. More African Americans than European Americans are single during young adulthood.
   TRUE or FALSE

5. Single men have higher mortality rates and higher incidence of alcoholism, suicide, and mental health problems.
   TRUE or FALSE

6. Most singles who choose to stay that way are content with their lives.
   TRUE or FALSE

7. In the U.S., cohabitation has become less common in recent years.
   TRUE or FALSE

8. In the U.S., cohabitation before marriage results in happier marriages.
   TRUE or FALSE

9. Lesbians are likely to have fewer, longer lasting relationships than gay men.
   TRUE or FALSE

10. Gay and lesbian couples tend to get less support from family members than do married couples.
    TRUE or FALSE

11. The median age at first marriage in the U.S. has been rising for several decades.
    TRUE or FALSE

12. The similarity of partners' values and interests is an important predictor of a successful marriage.
    TRUE or FALSE

13. Marriages are more successful when one partner contributes more to the relationship than the other.
    TRUE or FALSE

14. Marital satisfaction tends to be lowest early in a marriage.
    TRUE or FALSE

15. Marital satisfaction usually increases in later life.

    TRUE or FALSE

16. Married couples who do not pool their financial resources tend to experience greater satisfaction with their marriage.

    TRUE or FALSE

17. For most couples, marital satisfaction increases during the empty nest after the children leave.

    TRUE or FALSE

18. Marital satisfaction increases shortly after retirement.

    TRUE or FALSE

19. The level of marital satisfaction in older couples is related to the degree of social engagement they have.

    TRUE or FALSE

# 11.3 THE FAMILY LIFE CYCLE

## TO MASTER THE LEARNING OBJECTIVES:

**Why do people have children?**

- Describe the factors that are related to the decision to have children.

- Describe the advantages and disadvantages for couples who decide to remain child-free.

**What is it like to be a parent? What differences are there in different types of parenting?**

- Describe the advantages of being an older parent.

- Describe how ethnic background influences parenting.

- Explain the feelings that are typical of most divorced single parents and describe the problems that single parents face.

- Describe the obstacles that may interfere with foster, adoptive, or stepchildren forming bonds with his or her new parents.

- Describe the problems associated with forming attachments in foster parent-child relationships.

- Describe the effects associated with being raised by gay or lesbian parents.

## 11.3 KNOW THE TERMS

**Extended**                                        **Nuclear**

**Familism**

1. The most common family form in Western societies is the _____ family which consists of parents and children.

2. The most common family form around the world is the _____ family which consists of parents, children, grandparents, and other relatives living together.

3. The idea that the well-being of the family takes precedence over the concerns of individual family members is called _____ .

## 11.3 KNOW THE DETAILS OF THE FAMILY LIFE CYCLE

1. Although the most common form of family in Western societies is the extended family, the most common form around the world is the nuclear family.
   TRUE or FALSE

2. In an extended family, grandparents and other relatives live with parents and children.
   TRUE or FALSE

3. Child-free couples tend to have happier marriages than couples with children.
   TRUE or FALSE

4. Compared to older mothers, younger mothers are more at ease with being parents, spend more time with their babies, and are more affectionate and sensitive to them.
   TRUE or FALSE

5. Men who become fathers in their 30s are more invested in their paternal role than men who become fathers in their 20s.
   TRUE or FALSE

6. Fathers are usually as involved in direct child care as mothers.
   TRUE or FALSE

7. African American husbands are more likely than European American men to help with household chores and help with child care.
   TRUE or FALSE

8. Two key values among European American families are familism and the extended family.
   TRUE or FALSE

9. The number of single parents is increasing.
   TRUE or FALSE

10. Single parents are usually as well-off financially as married parents.
    TRUE or FALSE

11. Many stepparents and stepchildren develop good relationships with each other.
    TRUE or FALSE

12. Children raised by gay or lesbian parents develop sexual identity problems.
    TRUE or FALSE

# 11.4 DIVORCE AND REMARRIAGE

## TO MASTER THE LEARNING OBJECTIVES:

**Who gets divorced? How does divorce affect parental relationships with children?**

• Compare the divorce rate in the United States to those found in other industrialized countries.

• Explain how the divorce rate differs for various ethnic groups in the United States.

• List the common reasons that men and women give for getting a divorce.

• Know the predictors of early and later divorce.

• Discuss the reasons for and against covenant marriages.

• Describe the psychological effects of divorce on the divorced couple.

• Describe the different effects of divorce for men and women.

• Describe the effects of divorce for middle-aged and elderly adults.

• Describe the typical situation for a divorced mother with young children.

• Describe the contact that most divorced fathers have with their children.

• Describe how divorce affects adult children.

**What are remarriages like? How are they similar to and different from first marriages?**

• Describe the ethnic and gender differences in the likelihood of remarriage.

## 11.4 KNOW THE DETAILS OF DIVORCE AND REMARRIAGE

1. Today, about 50% of marriages in the U.S. end in divorce.
   TRUE or FALSE

2. Ethnically mixed marriages are at greater risk of divorce than ethnically homogenous ones.
   TRUE or FALSE

3. Infidelity is the most commonly reported cause of divorce.
   TRUE or FALSE

4. Negative emotions displayed during conflict between a couple predicts early divorce, but not later divorce.
   TRUE or FALSE

5. The absence of positive emotions is related to later divorce more than early divorce.
   TRUE or FALSE

6. Under a covenant marriage, divorces are easier to obtain.
   TRUE or FALSE

7. Divorced people are more likely than married, never-married, and widowed people to say that they are "very happy" with their lives.
   TRUE or FALSE

8. Low preoccupation with thoughts of a former partner is the key to healthy post-divorce relationships.
   TRUE or FALSE

9. Men are more likely than women to be blamed for the problems that led to the divorce.
   TRUE or FALSE

10. Women who initiated divorce in middle age report self-focused growth and optimism.
    TRUE or FALSE

11. Fathers are given custody of their children about 50% of the time.
    TRUE or FALSE

12. After a divorce, most fathers remain active and involved in their children's lives.
    TRUE or FALSE

13. Adults whose parents divorce are unlikely to be emotionally affected by the divorce.
    TRUE or FALSE

14. The divorce rate for remarriages is higher than the divorce rate for first marriages.
    TRUE or FALSE

# SUMMARY

## 11.1 RELATIONSHIPS

1. **Friendships**

People tend to have more friendships during _____ than during any other period. Friendships are especially important for maintaining life satisfaction throughout adulthood. Men tend to have fewer close friends and base them on _____ such as sports. Women tend to have more close friendships, and base them on _____ and emotional sharing. Differences in same-gender friendship patterns may explain the difficulties men and women have forming cross-gender friendships.

2.  **Love Relationships**

    _____ intimacy, and commitment are the key components of love. Although styles of love change with age, the priorities within relationships do not. Selecting a mate works best when there are shared values, _____ and interests. There are _____ in which specific aspects of these are considered most important.

3.  **The Dark Side of Relationships:  Violence**

    Levels of aggressive behavior range from _____ aggression, to physical aggression, to _____ one's partner. The causes of aggressive behaviors become more _____ as the level of aggression increases. People remain in abusive relationships for many reasons, including _____ and the belief that they cannot leave.

## 11.2 LIFESTYLES

1.  **Singlehood**

    Most adults decide by age 30 whether they plan on getting married. Never-married adults often develop a strong network of close friends. Dealing with other people's expectations that they should _____ is often difficult for single people.

2.  **Cohabitation**

    Young adults usually cohabit as a _____ toward marriage, and adults of all ages may also cohabit for financial reasons. In the United States, cohabitation is only rarely seen as an _____ to marriage. Overall, more similarities than differences exist between cohabiting and married couples.

3.  **Gay and Lesbian Couples**

    Gay and lesbian relationships are _____ to marriages in terms of relationship issues. _____ couples tend to be more egalitarian, and are _____ likely to remain together than gay couples. Frequency of sexual expression varies with gay, heterosexual, and lesbian couples.

4.  **Marriage**

The most important factors in creating stable marriages are _____ , _____ of values and interests, effective communication, and the contribution of unique skills by each partner. For couples with children, marital satisfaction tends to _____ until the children leave home, although individual differences are apparent, especially in long-term marriages. Most long-term marriages are happy.

## 11.3 THE FAMILY LIFE CYCLE

1. **Family Life-Cycle Stages**

   Although the _____ family is the most common form of family in Western societies, the most common form around the world is the _____ family.

2. **Deciding Whether to Have Children**

   Although having children is stressful and very _____ most people do it anyway. However, the number of child-free couples is increasing.

3. **The Parental Role**

   The timing of parenthood is important in how involved parents are in their families as opposed to their _____ Single parents are faced with many problems, especially if they are women and are divorced. The main problem is significantly reduced _____ resources. A major issue for adoptive, foster, and stepparents is how strongly the child will _____ with them. Each of these relationships has some special characteristics. Gay and lesbian parents also face numerous obstacles, but usually prove to be good parents.

## 11.4 DIVORCE AND REMARRIAGE

1. **Divorce**

   Currently, odds are about _____ that a new marriage will end in divorce. Recovery from divorce is different for men and women. Men tend to have a tougher time in the short run. Women clearly have a harder time in the long run, often because of _____ reasons. Difficulties between divorced partners usually involve _____ and child support. Disruptions also occur in divorced parents' relationships with their children, whether the children are young or are adults themselves.

2. **Remarriage**

Most divorced couples remarry. Second marriages are especially vulnerable to stress if spouses must adjust to having _____ Remarriage in middle age and beyond tends to be happy.

# TEST YOURSELF

## MULTIPLE-CHOICE QUESTIONS

1.  Three broad themes that underlie adult friendships are:
    a.  passion, intimacy, and commitment.
    b.  affective basis, shared or communal aspects, and sociability and compatibility.
    c.  stimulus, values, and role.
    d.  traditional vs. Western-industrial values, importance of education and intelligence, and chastity.

2.  Women tend to base friendships on _____ while men are more likely to base friendships on _____.
    a.  shared activities; competition
    b.  intimacy and emotional sharing; shared activities
    c.  shared interests; emotional sharing
    d.  competition; discussing personal matters

3.  Which of the following is not one of Sternberg's components of love?
    a.  passion
    b.  intimacy
    c.  commitment
    d.  sociability

4.  Early in a relationship
    a.  passion and intimacy are high but commitment is usually low.
    b.  passion and commitment are high but intimacy is usually low.
    c.  intimacy is high but passion and commitment tend to be low.
    d.  passion is high but intimacy and commitment tend to be low.

5.  According to the theory of assortative mating, who is most likely to become partners?
    a.  Ted, who is Jewish, and Sarah, who is Catholic
    b.  John, who is 42, and Jennifer, who is 22
    c.  Dave, who is intelligent, and Denise, who is also intelligent
    d.  Bill, who is a Democrat, and Elizabeth, who is a Republican

6.  In Murstein's classic theory, the three filters that people apply when they meet a potential mate are:
    a.  stimulus, values, and role.
    b.  passion, commitment, and intimacy.
    c.  acquaintanceship, buildup, and continuation.
    d.  affective basis, shared or communal aspects, and sociability and compatibility.

7. Cross-cultural research has found that in cultures around the world men look for _____ in a mate and women look for _____.
   a. physical attractiveness; men who will be good providers
   b. physical attractiveness; physical attractiveness, too
   c. chastity; love
   d. intelligence; a pleasing disposition

8. Lana's husband, Luther, severely abused her verbally and physically and told her that he would never let her leave him. One day, as Luther approached her with his belt in his hand, Lana shot him, killing him instantly. Lana's behavior was most likely caused by
   a. a need to control.
   b. jealousy.
   c. misuse of power.
   d. battered woman syndrome.

9. Violence that occurs occasionally and that can be instigated by either partner is referred to as
   a. patriarchal terrorism.
   b. common couple violence.
   c. battered woman syndrome.
   d. familism.

10. Singlehood
    a. has more negative health and longevity effects on women than on men.
    b. has become less common among young adults in recent years.
    c. is more common among African Americans than among European Americans during young adulthood.
    d. is more common among men than among women throughout adulthood.

11. Cohabitation prior to marriage
    a. is associated with happier marriages.
    b. is associated with less happy marriages and a higher risk of divorce.
    c. does not appear to be related to marital satisfaction or divorce rate.
    d. is a more common alternative to marriage in the U.S. than in the Netherlands, Norway, and Sweden.

12. Lesbian couples
    a. argue more over personal values, social and political issues, and relationships with in-laws than do heterosexual couples.
    b. tend to have more distrust, particularly in regard to former lovers, than do heterosexual couples.
    c. have less egalitarian relationships than heterosexual couples.
    d. are less likely to be in dual-worker relationships than are heterosexual couples.

13. Which of the following is associated with greater marital satisfaction?
    a. being over 20 rather than under 20 at the time of marriage
    b. having dissimilar values and interests
    c. having one partner contribute more to the relationship
    d. cohabiting prior to marriage

14. Similarity of values and interests is referred to as
    a. exchange theory.
    b. homogamy.
    c. assortative mating.
    d. nuclear family.

15. Mike and Yolanda are preparing for the birth of their first child. If they are like most couples, what will happen to their marital satisfaction after the birth of their child?
    a. Their marital satisfaction will increase.
    b. They will experience no change in marital satisfaction.
    c. Their marital satisfaction will decrease.
    d. Yolanda's marital satisfaction will increase while Mike's will decrease.

16. When Mike and Yolanda's children leave home,
    a. their marital satisfaction is likely to increase.
    b. they are not likely to experience any changes in marital satisfaction.
    c. their marital satisfaction is likely to decrease.
    d. Mike's marital satisfaction is likely to increase, but Yolanda's marital satisfaction is likely to decrease.

17. The most common form of family in Western societies is the
    a. nuclear family.
    b. extended family.
    c. life cycle family.
    d. empty nest family.

18. Couples who choose not to have children
    a. have less happy marriages.
    b. have less freedom.
    c. have lower standards of living.
    d. face social criticism.

19. Today, couples have fewer children and
    a. have their first child later than in the past.
    b. have their first child earlier than in the past.
    c. have their first child at about the same time as in the past.
    d. space them further apart.

20. Frank first became a father at age 36. His brother, Ben, had his first child at age 22. Which of the following statements about Frank and Ben is most likely to be true?
    a. Ben is more likely than Frank to resent time lost to his career.
    b. Frank is likely to spend more time than Ben caring for his child.
    c. Ben is likely to be more invested in his paternal role than Frank is.
    d. Frank and Ben probably do not differ in their paternal roles.

21. The idea that the well-being of the family takes precedence over the concerns of individual family members is known as
    a. the nuclear family.
    b. the extended family.
    c. familism.
    d. homogamy.

22. _____ must be willing to tolerate considerable ambiguity in their relationships with their children and have few expectations about the future.
    a. Stepparents
    b. Adoptive parents
    c. Foster parents
    d. Gay male and lesbian parents

23. Compared to children reared by heterosexual couples, children reared by lesbian couples
    a. are more likely to develop problems of sexual identity.
    b. show deficits in cognitive development.
    c. have more problems in school.
    d. do not have any more problems.

24. Which of the following statements about divorce is false?
    a. Divorce is more common in the U.S. than in Canada, Great Britain, and Germany.
    b. African Americans are more likely than European Americans to divorce.
    c. Divorced people sometimes find the transition very difficult.
    d. Men and women are affected by divorce in the same ways.

25. Doug and Marsha are divorcing after 20 years of marriage. Which of the following statements is true?
    a. Doug and Marsha are equally likely to get remarried.
    b. Doug is more likely to get custody of the children.
    c. Marsha's financial resources are likely to decrease.
    d. Marsha is more likely to be blamed for the problems that led to the divorce.

26. Which of the following statements about remarriage is true?
    a. Men and women typically wait about four years before they remarry.
    b. African Americans remarry more quickly than European Americans.
    c. Women remarry more quickly than men.
    d. For most ethnic groups, the divorce rate for remarriages is lower than for first marriages.

## ESSAY QUESTIONS

1. Your brother and sister were talking, and your brother told your sister that he thought that she and her friends were boring because the only thing that she does with her friends is sit around and talk. What can you tell your brother about gender differences in friendships?

2. Recently, you and your friends, Ishan and Lola, were talking. Ishan mentioned that he had just broken up with his girlfriend, Hedda. Lola said, "But, Ishan, just 3 months ago you told us that Hedda was

the one and only one for you, that this was true love, and that she was definitely Ms. Right." Ishan replied that he had broken up with Hedda because things weren't as good as they had been before. Lola was amazed that anyone could change his mind so drastically about a relationship in such a short time. How would you explain Ishan's behavior in terms of Sternberg's three elements of passion, intimacy, and commitment?

3. Your friend Fritz has decided to marry Marie. Fritz has told you that he likes Marie because "she is so different." For example, Fritz and Marie come from different ethnic backgrounds, Fritz is very goal-oriented and Marie is very laid back, and Fritz is very conservative and Marie is very liberal. What can you tell Fritz about the importance of homogamy to marital success?

4. Your friends Nick and Nora are trying to decide if they want to become parents. They have a very companionable marriage, both are invested in their careers, and they like to travel. What can you tell them about the factors they should consider and some of the benefits of remaining child-free?

5. Your friend Lisa recently got a divorce and she is feeling depressed. She was the one who wanted to end the marriage, and she thinks that it is abnormal that she is feeling depressed. What can you tell Lisa about the psychological effects of divorce on the divorced couple?

# SOLUTIONS

## 11.1 KNOW THE TERMS

1. assortative mating (419)
2. abusive (422)
3. battered woman syndrome (422)
4. common couple violence (424)
5. Patriarchal terrorism (424)

## 11.1 KNOW THE DETAILS OF ADULT RELATIONSHIPS

1. T, (416)
2. F, (416)
3. T, (416)
4. F, (417)
5. F, (417)
6. T, (418)
7. T, (418)
8. F, (418)
9. T, (419)
10. T, (419)
11. F, (420)
12. T, (420)
13. T, (422)
14. T, (424)
15. F, (424)
16. T, (425)

## 11.2 KNOW THE TERMS

1. cohabitation (427)
2. homogamy (431)
3. exchange (432)

## 11.2 KNOW THE DETAILS OF ADULT LIFESTYLES

1. T, (426)
2. F, (426)
3. F, (426)
4. T, (426)
5. T, (427)
6. T, (427)
7. F, (427)
8. F, (428)
9. T, (430)
10. T, (430)
11. T, (430)
12. T, (431)
13. F, (432)
14. F, (432)
15. T, (432)
16. F, (433)
17. T, (434)
18. T, (434)
19. T, (434)

## 11.3 KNOW THE TERMS

1. nuclear (435)
2. extended (435)
3. familism (437)

## 11.3 KNOW THE DETAILS OF THE FAMILY LIFE CYCLE

1. F, (435)

| | | |
|---|---|---|
| 2. T, (435) | 6. F, (437) | 10. F, (438) |
| 3. T, (436) | 7. T, (437) | 11. T, (439) |
| 4. F, (436) | 8. F, (437) | 12. F, (439) |
| 5. T, (436) | 9. T, (438) | |

# 11.4 KNOW THE DETAILS OF DIVORCE AND REMARRIAGE

| | | |
|---|---|---|
| 1. T, (441) | 7. F, (443) | 13. F, (445) |
| 2. T, (441) | 8. T, (443) | 14. T, (446) |
| 3. T, (441) | 9. T, (444) | |
| 4. T, (442) | 10. T, (444) | |
| 5. T, (442) | 11. F, (444) | |
| 6. F, (443) | 12. F, (444) | |

# SUMMARY

## 11.1 RELATIONSHIPS

1. young adulthood (416); shared activities (417); intimacy (417)
2. Passion (418); goals (419); cross-cultural differences (420)
3. verbal (423); murdering (423); complex (423); low self-esteem (424)

## 11.2 LIFESTYLES

1. marry (426)
2. step (428); alternative (428)
3. similar (429); Lesbian (430); more (430)
4. maturity of the partners (431); similarity (431); decline (433)

## 11.3 THE FAMILY LIFE CYCLE

1. nuclear (435); extended (435)
2. expensive (436),
3. careers (436); fin ancial (438); bond (438)

## 11.4 DIVORCE AND REMARRIAGE

1. 50-50 (441); financial (444); visitation (444)
2. stepchildren (446).

# TEST YOURSELF

## MULTIPLE-CHOICE QUESTIONS

| | | |
|---|---|---|
| 1. B, (417) | 8. D, (422) | 15. C, (433) |
| 2. B, (417) | 9. B, (424) | 16. A, (434) |
| 3. D, (418) | 10. C, (426) | 17. A, (435) |
| 4. D, (418) | 11. B, (428) | 18. D, (436) |
| 5. C, (419) | 12. B, (429) | 19. A, (436) |
| 6. A, (419) | 13. A, (430) | 20. B, (436) |
| 7. A, (420) | 14. B, (431) | 21. C, (437) |

22. C, (439)  24. D, (444)  26. A, (446)
23. D, (439)  25. C, (444)

## ESSAY QUESTIONS

1.  In young adulthood, women tend to base friendships on intimacy and emotional sharing. When women get together with friends they confide in each other and discuss personal matters. So, it is not unusual for women to spend time together "just sitting around and talking." Men, however, tend to base friendships on shared activities and interests, and when they get together they participate in those shared activities that are often competitive. In general, men's friendships do not involve intimacy. So, both your brother and sister seem to have friendships that are gender-typical. (417-418)

2.  According to Sternberg, love has three components: 1) passion, an intense physical desire for someone, 2) intimacy, the feeling that one can share all of one's thoughts and actions with another, and 3) commitment, the willingness to stay with a person through good times and bad times. At the beginning of a relationship, passion is usually very high but intimacy and commitment are low. This combination of passion, intimacy, and commitment is known as infatuation. Infatuation usually doesn't last long, and as passion fades, the relationship needs to acquire emotional intimacy or it will probably end. So, Ishan showed lots of passion in his relationship with Hedda, but as the passion faded and intimacy did not occur, the relationship ended. (418)

3.  An important factor related to marital success is homogamy which means that the partners share similar goals, values, attitudes, and ethnic backgrounds. The fact that Fritz and Marie are so different may be a problem later in their marriage. The lack of homogamy in the relationship may be a source of marital problems. Perhaps they should rethink, or postpone, the decision to marry. (431-432)

4.  Some of the benefits of having children are personal satisfaction, fulfilling personal needs, continuing the family line, and companionship. Having children also has negative effects such as creating a financial drain, drastically changing the couple's lifestyle, decreasing marital satisfaction, and interfering with one's career. Couples who decide to remain child-free tend to have happier marriages, more freedom, and higher standards of living. Given that Nick and Nora are both highly invested in their careers, that they enjoy the freedom to travel, and that they have a very close marriage, they may be better candidates for a child-free lifestyle. (435-436)

5.  Divorce can have negative psychological effects for years after the divorce. In fact, feeling unhappy is a common feeling of divorced people. Divorced people of all ages are less likely than other groups to report that they are "very happy" with their lives. In addition to feeling unhappy, divorced people feel deeply disappointed, misunderstood, and rejected. Also, people who are not preoccupied with their former spouses and who have feelings of friendship toward them tend to adjust better to the divorce. So, Lisa's feelings are not abnormal, nor atypical, even though she had wanted the divorce. (443-444)

# WORK AND LEISURE

12.1 Occupational Selection and Development

12.2 Gender, Ethnicity, and Discrimination Issues

12.3 Occupational Transitions

12.4 Work and Family

12.5 Time to Relax: Leisure Activities

This chapter focuses on occupational selection and development, discrimination in the work place, occupational transitions, managing the demands of work and family, and relaxing away from the work place.

# 12.1 OCCUPATIONAL SELECTION AND DEVELOPMENT

## TO MASTER THE LEARNING OBJECTIVES:

**How do people view work? How do occupational priorities vary with age?**

- Explain the meanings associated with work.

**How do people choose their occupations?**

- Describe the problems with Holland's theory in the way it addresses gender differences, ethnic differences, and economic factors.

**What factors influence occupational development?**

- Describe Super's implementation, establishment, maintenance, deceleration, and retirement phases of occupational development.

- Describe how occupational expectations are related to forming and modifying a dream.

- Describe how mentors are related to occupational success and the relation between generativity and mentoring.

- Describe the problems that women have in establishing good mentor relationships.

**What is the relation between job satisfaction and age?**

- Describe the factors that are related to increasing job satisfaction with age.

- Describe the cyclical nature of job satisfaction.

- Describe the factors that are related to feelings of alienation on the job.

- Describe the things that employers can do to avoid feelings of alienation in their workers.

- Define burnout and describe the factors that are related to it.

- Describe the 3 factors that may help avoid burnout.


# 12.1 KNOW THE TERMS

| | |
|---|---|
| **Alienation** | **Job satisfaction** |
| **Burnout** | **Vocational maturity** |
| **Dream** | |


1. The match between vocational behaviors and what is expected of a worker at different ages is a measure of _____ .

2. A young adult's hopes and expectations about his future, particularly her career, is called a

   _____ .

3. _____ is the positive feeling that results from an appraisal of one's work.

4. A feeling of _____ results when one feels that what one does on the job is meaningless, not valued, or unrelated to the final product.

5. Depletion of energy and motivation, loss of occupational idealism, and feeling one is being exploited on the job is called _____ .

## 12.1 KNOW THE DETAILS OF OCCUPATIONAL SELECTION AND DEVELOPMENT

1. Four common meanings of work are developing and becoming self, union with others, expressing self, and serving others.

   TRUE or FALSE

2. Occupation is often an important part of identity.

   TRUE or FALSE

3. Men and women are equally distributed among Holland's personality types.

   TRUE or FALSE

4. Holland's theory stresses the effect of cultural context on occupational selection.

   TRUE or FALSE

5. In Super's theory of occupational development, people go through stages related to changing self-concepts throughout adulthood.

   TRUE or FALSE

6. Super's establishment stage is a transition time during middle age, as workers begin to reduce the amount of time they spend fulfilling work roles.

   TRUE or FALSE

7. According to Levinson, forming a dream in regard to one's career is essentially a waste of time.

   TRUE or FALSE

8. Occupational success often depends on the quality of the mentor-protégé relationship.

   TRUE or FALSE

9. The majority of professional women have a mentor during early adulthood.

   TRUE or FALSE

10. Job satisfaction tends to decrease with age.

    TRUE or FALSE

11. Work typically becomes more of a focus in people's lives over the course of adulthood.

    TRUE or FALSE

12. Burnout is least common among people in the helping professions, such as health care and teaching.

    TRUE or FALSE

13. Burnout can be minimized by reducing stress, getting workers to lower their expectations of themselves, and improving communication within organizations.

    TRUE or FALSE

# 12.2 GENDER, ETHNICITY, AND DISCRIMINATION ISSUES

## TO MASTER THE LEARNING OBJECTIVES:

**How do women's and men's occupational expectations differ? How are people viewed if they enter occupations that are not traditional for their gender?**

- Describe how the socialization of boys and girls is related to their later occupational behavior.

- Describe the personal experiences that are related to women choosing nontraditional occupations.

- Describe the personal feelings that women have about their performance in male-dominated occupations.

**What factors are related to women's occupational development?**

- Describe the important family and work issues of women who are working full time.

**What factors affect ethnic minority workers' occupational experiences and occupational development?**

- Explain how African American women prepare for nontraditional occupations.

- Describe how vocational identity is related to ethnicity and gender.

- Describe how occupational aspirations are related to ethnicity.

**What types of bias and discrimination hinder occupational development of women and ethnic minority workers?**

- Describe how sex discrimination and the glass ceiling influence women's occupational advancement.

- Define comparable worth.

- Describe sexual harassment and explain the effects on both men and women.

- Explain the gender differences in perceptions of sexual harassment and how it is related to the reasonable woman standard.

- Define age discrimination and describe many ways in which it occurs in the workplace.

## 12.2 KNOW THE TERMS

Age discrimination

Comparable worth

Glass ceiling

Gender discrimination

Reasonable woman standard

1. Denying a job to someone solely on the basis of whether the person is a man or woman is known as

   _____ .

2. The highest level to which women rise and then stop in a company is known as the _____ .

3. Equating pay in equivalent occupations that differ in terms of the gender distribution of the people in them is known as _____ .

4. The _____ says that if a reasonable woman finds some behavior offensive, even if a man did not intend it to be, then sexual harassment has occurred.

5. Denying a job or promotion to someone solely on the basis of age is known as _____ .

## 12.2 KNOW THE DETAILS OF DISCRIMINATION

1. Traditionally, occupational training and achievement has been a larger part of socialization experiences for males than for females.
   TRUE or FALSE

2. Women who choose nontraditional occupations are more likely to be viewed negatively.
   TRUE or FALSE

3. People are less likely to perceive incidents of sexual coercion as harassing when a woman is in a nontraditional occupation.
   TRUE or FALSE

4. Women in the 1950s had fewer occupational choices than women today.
   TRUE or FALSE

5. The most important workplace issues for women who work full-time are unsupportive work environments, organizational politics, and lack of occupational development opportunities.
   TRUE or FALSE

6. European American women are more likely than African American women to enter nontraditional occupations.
   TRUE or FALSE

7. Latino American men are more likely than European American and African American men to define their identity primarily in terms of work.
   TRUE or FALSE

8. The responsiveness of an organization to the needs of ethnic minorities makes little difference to employees.
   TRUE or FALSE

9. Same-ethnicity mentors provide more psychosocial support than cross-ethnicity mentors.

TRUE or FALSE

10. Gender discrimination in the workplace is no longer common.

TRUE or FALSE

11. In many occupations men are paid substantially more than women in the same positions.

TRUE or FALSE

12. Comparable worth refers to equalizing pay across occupations that are determined to be equivalent in importance but differ in the gender distribution of the people doing the job.

TRUE or FALSE

13. In the U.S., women are more likely than men to view specific interactions as harassment.

TRUE or FALSE

14. In the U.S., it is legal for employers to refuse to hire or discharge a worker solely on the basis of age.

TRUE or FALSE

# 12.3 OCCUPATIONAL TRANSITIONS

## TO MASTER THE LEARNING OBJECTIVES:

**Why do people change occupations?**

- Describe the benefits associated with occupational changes.

- Describe the situations that make retraining necessary.

- Define career plateauing.

**Is worrying about potential job loss a major source of stress?**

- Describe the effects of worrying about one's job.

**How does the timing of job loss affect the amount of stress experienced?**

- Describe the effects of losing one's job, particularly for middle-aged men.

- Describe how the effects of losing one's job differ depending on when during the adult life cycle the loss occurs.

## 12.3 KNOW THE DETAILS OF OCCUPATIONAL TRANSITIONS

1.  Changing jobs several times during adulthood is more common today than it was in the past.
    TRUE or FALSE

2.  Retraining is often a successful way of dealing with career plateauing or job loss.
    TRUE or FALSE

3.  Feelings of job insecurity can negatively impact mental health.
    TRUE or FALSE

4.  Unemployment is related to declines in physical health and self-esteem.
    TRUE or FALSE

5.  Women usually experience less decline in health following the loss of a job than do men.
    TRUE or FALSE

6.  Middle-aged men are less vulnerable to negative effects of job loss than are older or younger men.
    TRUE or FALSE

7.  Unemployment rates for many ethnic minority groups are substantially higher than they are for European Americans.
    TRUE or FALSE

# 12.4 WORK AND FAMILY

## TO MASTER THE LEARNING OBJECTIVES:

**What are the issues faced by employed people who care for dependents?**

*   Describe how attachment to one's job influences why women return to work after having children.

*   Describe the negative effects of providing dependent care on work and workers.

*   Describe the things that employers can do to reduce work-family conflicts.

**How do partners view the division of household chores?  What is work-family conflict?  How does it affect couples' lives?**

*   Explain how dual-worker couples divide household and childcare responsibilities.

*   Describe the division of household tasks that men find fair and that women find fair.

*   Describe ethnic and cross cultural differences in the division of household tasks in dual-worker couples.

*   Describe how occupational and family roles are related to each other.

- Describe the factors that are related to the successful combination of family and occupational responsibilities in dual-worker couples.

- Explain the cross cultural and gender differences in burnout from work and parenting.

## 12.4 KNOW THE DETAILS OF WORK AND FAMILY

1.  The number of families in which both parents are employed has decreased over the past few decades.
    TRUE or FALSE

2.  The degree to which women are attached to their work influences whether they decide to return to work after having children.
    TRUE or FALSE

3.  Women who are responsible for dependent care do not usually miss work any more often than women who are not responsible for dependent care.
    TRUE or FALSE

4.  When supervisors are sympathetic and supportive regarding family issues and day care, parents have higher absenteeism.
    TRUE or FALSE

5.  In dual-earner couples today, most men and women share household and child care tasks equally (see graph below).

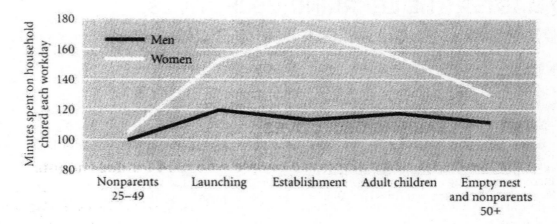

N=829 men, 887 women.
Gender and life stage differences are significant at $p<.01$.
Gender $\times$ life stage at $p<.01$.

SOURCE: Cornell Couples and Careers Study, 1998.

TRUE or FALSE

6. Women have decreased the amount of time they spend on housework since the 1970s, and men have increased the amount of time they spend on such tasks.

   TRUE or FALSE

7. Women are most satisfied with the division of labor regarding household tasks when men are willing to perform women's traditional chores.

   TRUE or FALSE

8. European American men tend to spend more time doing household tasks than do African American and Hispanic American men.

   TRUE or FALSE

9. The number of children a woman has is related to the amount of stress she experiences related to work-family conflict.

   TRUE or FALSE

10. Burnout from work and parenting is equally likely to affect men and women.

    TRUE or FALSE

# 12.5 TIME TO RELAX: LEISURE ACTIVITIES

## TO MASTER THE LEARNING OBJECTIVES:

**What activities are leisure activities? How do people choose among them?**

- Describe how preoccupations, interests, and activities are related.

- Describe the many factors that influence leisure repertoires.

**What changes in leisure activities occur with age?**

- Explain what cross-sectional and longitudinal studies tell us about age differences in leisure activities.

**What do people derive from leisure activities?**

- Describe how leisure activities are related to a sense of positive well-being.

## 12.5 KNOW THE DETAILS OF LEISURE

1. Work is defined as discretionary activity which includes simple relaxation, activities for enjoyment, and creative pursuits.

   TRUE or FALSE

2. People tend to select leisure activities based on perceived competence and psychological comfort with the activity.
   TRUE or FALSE

3. Middle-aged adults participate in a greater range of leisure activities than do young adults.
   TRUE or FALSE

4. Young adults tend to prefer more physically intense leisure activities than do middle-aged adults.
   TRUE or FALSE

5. Preferences for certain types of leisure activities are established early in life.
   TRUE or FALSE

6. Involvement in leisure activities is related to well-being.
   TRUE or FALSE

# SUMMARY

## 12.1 OCCUPATIONAL SELECTION AND DEVELOPMENT

1. **The Meaning of Work**

   Although most people work for money, other reasons are highly variable. There are four common meanings: developing self, _____ expressing self, and serving others. Occupation is a key element in a person's sense of _____ and self-efficacy.

2. **Holland's Theory of Occupational Choice Revisited**

   Holland's theory is based on the idea that people choose occupations to optimize the fit between their individual traits and their occupational _____ Six personality types that represent different combinations of these have been identified. Support for these types have been found in several studies.

3. **Occupational Development**

   Super's developmental view of occupations is based on _____ and adaptation to an occupational role. Super describes five stages: implementation, _____ maintenance, deceleration, and _____ . _____ is the realization that one's expectations about an occupation are different from the reality one experiences, and is common among young workers. A mentor is a co-worker who teaches a new employee the _____ rules and fosters occupational development. Mentor-protégé relationships develop over time, through stages, like other relationships.

4. **Job Satisfaction**

Older workers report _____ job satisfaction than younger workers, but this may be partly due to _____ unhappy workers may quit. Other reasons for this difference include intrinsic satisfaction, good fit, _____ importance of work, finding nonwork diversions, and life-cycle factors. _____ and burnout are important considerations in understanding job satisfaction. Both involve significant stress for workers.

## 12.2 GENDER, ETHNICITY, AND DISCRIMINATION ISSUES

1. **Gender Differences in Occupational Selection**

   Boys and girls are socialized differently for work, and their occupational choices are affected as a result. Women choose nontraditional occupations for many reasons, including expectations and personal feelings. Women in such occupations are still viewed more _____ than men in the same occupations.

2. **Women and Occupational Development**

   Women leave well-paid occupations for many reasons, including _____ obligations and the workplace environment. Women who continue to work full-time have _____ and look for ways to further their occupational development.

3. **Ethnicity and Occupational Development**

   Vocational identity and vocational goals vary in different ethnic groups. Whether an organization is sensitive to ethnicity issues is a strong predictor of _____ among ethnic minorities.

4. **Bias and Discrimination**

   Sex discrimination remains the chief barrier to women's occupational development. In many cases, this operates as a glass ceiling which _____ women's occupational advancement. _____ inequity is also a problem. Sexual harassment is a problem in the workplace. Current criteria for judging harassment are based on the _____ woman standard. Denying employment to anyone over the age of 40 because of age is age discrimination.

## 12.3 OCCUPATIONAL TRANSITIONS

1. **Retraining Workers**

To adapt to the effects of a _____ economy and an _____ work force, many corporations are providing retraining opportunities for workers. Retraining is especially important in cases of outdated skills and _____ .

2. **Occupational Insecurity**

Important reasons why people change occupations include personality, _____ of one's job, and economic trends. Occupational insecurity is a growing problem. Fear that one may lose one's job is a better predictor of _____ than actual likelihood of losing one's job.

3. **Coping With Unemployment**

Losing one's job is a traumatic event that can affect _____ aspect of a person's life. The effects of job loss vary with _____ and gender.

## 12.4 WORK AND FAMILY

1. **The Dependent Care Dilemma**

Whether a woman returns to work after having a child depends largely on how _____ she is to her work. Simply providing child care on-site does not always result in higher job satisfaction. The more important factor is the degree to which supervisors are _____ regarding child care issues.

2. **Juggling Multiple Roles**

Although women have _____ the amount of time they spend on household tasks over the past two decades, they still do most of the work. European American men are _____ likely than either African American or Latino American men to help with traditionally _____ household tasks. _____ work schedules and number of _____ are important factors in role conflict. Recent evidence shows that work stress has a much _____ impact on family life than family stress has on work performance. Some women pay a high personal price for having careers.

## 12.5 TIME TO RELAX: LEISURE ACTIVITIES

1. **Types of Leisure Activities**

_____ is discretionary activity that includes simple relaxation, activities for enjoyment, and creative pursuits. Preoccupations can become more focused as interests, which can lead to the selection of particular leisure activities. People develop a repertoire of _____ leisure activities.

2. **Developmental Changes in Leisure**

As people grow older, they tend to engage in leisure activities that are less _____ and more _____ oriented. Leisure preferences in adulthood are a reflection of those established _____ in life.

3. **Consequences of Leisure Activities**

   Leisure activities _____ and can benefit all aspects of people's lives.

# TEST YOURSELF

## MULTIPLE-CHOICE QUESTIONS

1. Holland's theory of occupational choice
   a. focuses on the context in which occupational decisions are made.
   b. proposes stages of occupational interests that occur throughout adulthood.
   c. considers the fit between individuals' traits and their occupational interests.
   d. accounts for ethnic differences in occupational interests.

2. Women are more likely than men to be in Holland's _____ personality types.
   a. social, artistic, and conventional
   b. investigative, social, and enterprising
   c. realistic, conventional, and investigative
   d. artistic, enterprising, and investigative

3. Twenty-two-year-old Darrell is considering a career in physical therapy and has taken a summer job as an aide in a physical therapy clinic. Darrell is in Super's _____ stage of occupational development.
   a. deceleration
   b. establishment
   c. maintenance
   d. implementation

4. Thirty-four-year-old Peter is an accountant in a large accounting firm. He often works 90 hours a week, has advanced rapidly, and hopes to eventually become a partner in the firm. Peter is in Super's _____ stage of occupational development.
   a. maintenance
   b. establishment
   c. implementation
   d. deceleration

5. Forty-eight-year-old Sebastian is a tenured college professor. He has recently cut back on the number of hours he works and has even found time to coach his son's soccer and baseball teams. Sebastian is in Super's _____ stage of occupational development.
   a. maintenance
   b. retirement
   c. establishment
   d. implementation

6. Sixty-two-year-old Dorothy is a pediatrician. She has given her on-call responsibilities to her younger partners and has cut back the number of hours she works per week from 60 to 40. She wants to live near water when she retires in two years and has been investigating oceanfront property in order to find just the right place. Dorothy is in Super's _____ stage of occupational development.
   a. maintenance
   b. deceleration
   c. retirement
   d. implementation

7. Rhett began serving as Tom's mentor when Tom was new to the company. Now that Tom has learned the ropes, they spend less time together. Rhett and Tom's mentorship relationship is in the _____ phase.
   a. redefinition
   b. initiation
   c. separation
   d. cultivation

8. Which of the following statements about mentors is true?
   a. Mentors usually take credit for all the work their protégée did.
   b. Men have a greater need for a mentor than do women.
   c. Women have more difficulty finding a mentor than do men.
   d. Women who have female mentors are less productive than women who have male mentors.

9. Job satisfaction
   a. tends to increase with age.
   b. tends to decrease with age.
   c. tends to increase with age for women and decrease with age for men.
   d. tends to increase with age for men and decrease with age for women.

10. Ike works in a box factory, assembling boxes. He feels that his job is very unimportant, that no one appreciates the work he does, and is frustrated because he never sees the boxes used for anything. Ike is likely to
    a. have high job satisfaction.
    b. develop a sense of alienation.
    c. develop burnout.
    d. have a low absenteeism rate.

11. Women in nontraditional occupations for females tend to be viewed
    a. positively.
    b. as having negative interpersonal characteristics.
    c. as more respectable than men in the same occupations.
    d. as giving, honest, and collaborative.

12. Which of the following statements concerning women and occupational development is true?
    a. The characteristics and aspirations of women who entered the workforce in the 1950s and those from Generation X are very similar.
    b. Working mothers are usually viewed as being a team player in the work environment.
    c. Women tend to value working interdependently with others more than men do.
    d. Women feel very connected to the workplace.

13. Which of the following statements concerning ethnicity and occupational development is true?
    a. More African American than European American women choose nontraditional occupations.
    b. When they graduate from college, African American and European American men have higher vocational identities than do Latino men.
    c. Latino Americans and European Americans have the same occupational aspirations and expectations.
    d. African American women who choose nontraditional occupations tend to plan for less formal education than necessary to achieve their goals.

14. The level to which women may rise in a company but beyond which they may not go is referred to as
    a. vocational maturity.
    b. a career plateau.
    c. comparable worth.
    d. a glass ceiling.

15. Verbal or nonverbal sexual conduct in the workplace or school that is not wanted by the victim and creates an intimidating, hostile, or offensive environment is called
    a. sexual coercion.
    b. unwanted sexual attention.
    c. gender harassment.
    d. the reasonable woman standard.

16. When asked whether certain behaviors constitute sexual harassment,
    a. women are more likely than men to view the behaviors as offensive.
    b. men are more likely than women to view the behaviors as offensive.
    c. men and women have similar views as to whether the behaviors are offensive.
    d. the average of men's and women's standards was determined to be the appropriate legal criterion for deciding whether sexual harassment had occurred.

17. The U.S. Age Discrimination in Employment Act of 1986 protects workers over the age of
    a. 40.
    b. 50.
    c. 60.
    d. 70.

18. Career _____ occurs when there is either a lack of promotional opportunity in the organization or when a person decides not to seek advancement.
    a. burnout
    b. alienation
    c. plateauing
    d. retraining

19. Forty-six-year-old Allan, a European American mid-level manager, lost his job in a recent downsizing in the corporation where he had worked for twenty years. He is likely to experience
    a. decreased physical health and self-esteem.
    b. less distress than a female in a similar position.
    c. less distress than a young adult in a similar position.
    d. more distress than an African American male in a similar position.

20. Who is most likely to experience negative effects as a result of losing a job?
    a. young men
    b. middle-aged men
    c. older men
    d. young, middle-aged, and older men are equally vulnerable to negative effects

21. In dual-career households,
    a. most couples share household and child care tasks equally.
    b. men assume the greatest responsibility for household and child care tasks.
    c. women spend about 50% more hours per week than men in family work.
    d. European American men spend more time doing household tasks than Hispanic or African American men.

22. Men are most satisfied when the division of labor for household tasks is based on _____, whereas women are most satisfied when _____.
    a. traditional gender-typing of chores; it's divided by hours spent performing tasks
    b. women performing men's traditional chores; men perform men's traditional chores
    c. the number of hours spent; men perform women's traditional chores
    d. the amount of income each spouse brings in; it's divided by the number of hours spent

23. Sherry has a meeting with her regional boss scheduled for the same time that her daughter is competing in the high school state swimming finals. These competing demands cause
    a. work-family conflict.
    b. burnout.
    c. plateauing.
    d. alienation.

24. _____ is a key factor related to stress levels in working women.
    a. Age of the woman
    b. Age of children
    c. Guilt
    d. Number of children

25. Jack's favorite leisure activities include going to college football games, the symphony, and luncheon meetings for community organizations. Jack's leisure activities tend to be in the _____ classification.
    a. physical
    b. social
    c. cultural
    d. solitary

26. Joelin enjoys spending her free time visiting friends and going to parties. These kinds of activities would be classified in the _____ category.
    a. physical
    b. social
    c. cultural
    d. solitary

27. During later middle age, less leisure time is spent in _____ activities.
    a. expensive
    b. intellectually demanding
    c. strenuous physical
    d. social

28. The leisure activities engaged in by an individual tend to
    a. change greatly over the years.
    b. be stable over long periods of time.
    c. become more physically intense with age.
    d. become less family-oriented upon entering middle-age.

## ESSAY QUESTIONS

1. Your friend Pam recently started a job as a social worker. Pam has noticed that many of her coworkers who have been on the job a few years seem to have no energy or motivation. They also seem to depersonalize their clients by referring to them as case numbers. Pam doesn't understand why these people chose a helping profession if they aren't interested in helping people. What can you tell Pam about burnout that might explain her coworkers' behavior and what she can do to avoid her own burnout?

2. Your friend Hilka has been with the same company for a number of years. She thinks that she works very hard. In fact, she feels that she has not received promotions that have gone to men who don't work as hard as she does. The other day she found out that a man in a comparable position made quite a bit more money than she did last year. Hilka is beginning to wonder if there is something wrong with her and her job performance. What can you tell Hilka about the glass ceiling and pay discrimination?

3.  Your friend Jelisa has told you that her boss compliments her appearance everyday, calls her "honey" or "sweetie," and sometimes when they talk he will put his hand on her shoulder. Jelisa isn't sure if she is a victim of sexual harassment or if her boss is just being friendly. What can you tell Jelisa about the factors that are considered when determining if sexual harassment has occurred?

4.  Your 49-year-old neighbor, Ira, just lost his job of 25 years when his company merged with another company. His wife, Marina, is worried about him. He feels ill much of the time and just sits around the house. What can you tell Marina about the effects of losing one's job especially for people in Ira's position?

5.  Your friends Fran and Jack are expecting their first baby soon. Both Fran and Jack intend to continue working after the baby is born but they are worried about the conflict between work, parenting, and running a household. What advice can you give Fran and Jack?

6.  Your friend Jermaine went hang gliding a few weeks ago, and he thought that it was a fantastic activity. Ever since, he has been bothering you to go with him the next time he goes. You don't really want to and don't think that you will enjoy hang gliding. What can you tell Jermaine about the factors that influence which leisure activities one chooses to participate in and about the importance of satisfaction with leisure activities?

# SOLUTIONS

## 12.1 KNOW THE TERMS

1. vocational maturity (454)
2. dream (456)
3. Job satisfaction (457)
4. alienation (459)
5. burnout (460)

## 12.1 KNOW THE DETAILS OF OCCUPATIONAL SELECTION AND DEVELOPMENT

1. T, (453)
2. T, (453)
3. F, (453)
4. F, (454)
5. T, (454)
6. F, (455)
7. F, (456)
8. T, (457)
9. F, (457)
10. F, (457)
11. F, (459)
12. F, (460)
13. T, (461)

## 12.2 KNOW THE TERMS

1. gender discrimination (466)
2. glass ceiling (466)
3. comparable worth (467)
4. reasonable woman standard (469)
5. age discrimination (469)

## 12.2 KNOW THE DETAILS OF DISCRIMINATION

1. T, (462)
2. T, (463)
3. T, (463)
4. T, (463)
5. T, (464)
6. F, (465)
7. F, (465)
8. F, (465)
9. T, (465)
10. F, (466)
11. T, (467)
12. T, (467)
13. T, (468)
14. F, (469)

## 12.3 KNOW THE DETAILS OF OCCUPATIONAL TRANSITIONS

1. T, (471)
2. T, (472)
3. T, (473)
4. T, (474)
5. F, (474)
6. F, (474)
7. T, (475)

## 12.4 KNOW THE DETAILS OF WORK AND FAMILY

1. F, (475)
2. T, (476)
3. F, (477)
4. F, (477)
5. F, (478)
6. T, (487)
7. T, (479)
8. F, (479)
9. T, (480)
10. F, (480)

## 12.5 KNOW THE DETAILS OF LEISURE

1. F, (482)
2. T, (482)
3. F, (482)
4. T, (482)
5. T, (483)
6. T, (483)

## SUMMARY

### 12.1 OCCUPATIONAL SELECTION AND DEVELOPMENT

1. union with others (453); identity (453)
2. interests (453).
3. self-concept (454); establishment (455); retirem ent (455); Reality shock (456); unwritten (456)
4. higher (457); self-selection (458); lower (459); Alienation (459)

### 12.2 GENDER, ETHNICITY, AND DISCRIMINATION ISSUES

1. negatively (463)
2. family (464); adequate child care (464)
3. satisfaction (465)
4. stops (466); Pay (467); reasonable (469)

### 12.3 OCCUPATIONAL TRANSITIONS

1. global (473); aging (473); career plateauing (472)
2. obsolescence (473); anxiety (473)
3. every (474); age (474)

### 12.4 WORK AND FAMILY

1. attached (476); sympathetic (477)
2. reduced (478); less (479); female (479); Flexible (480); children (480); bigger (481)

### 12.5 TIME TO RELAX: LEISURE ACTIVITIES

1. Leisure (482); preferred (482)
2. strenuous (483); family (483); earlier (483)
3. enhance well-being (483)

## TEST YOURSELF

### MULTIPLE-CHOICE QUESTIONS

1. C, (453)

| | | |
|---|---|---|
| 2. A, (453) | 11. B, (463) | 20. B, (474) |
| 3. D, (454) | 12. C, (464) | 21. C, (478) |
| 4. B, (455) | 13. B, (465) | 22. C, (479) |
| 5. A, (455) | 14. D, (466) | 23. A, (479) |
| 6. B, (455) | 15. B, (469) | 24. D, (480) |
| 7. C, (457) | 16. A, (469) | 25. C, (482) |
| 8. C, (457) | 17. A, (469) | 26. B, (482) |
| 9. A, (457) | 18. C, (472) | 27. C, (483) |
| 10. B, (459) | 19. A, (474) | 28. B, (483) |

## ESSAY QUESTIONS

1. People experience job burnout when the pressures of the job become too great to handle. Signs of burnout include emotional exhaustion, depletion of energy and motivation, and feelings that one is being exploited. People in the helping professions are particularly prone to burnout. Pam is probably wrong about her coworkers--they entered social work because they wanted to help others. Unfortunately, people in helping professions are constantly confronted with people who have no easy solutions to their problems and who need help dealing with an unfriendly and inflexible bureaucracy. Soon people in the helping professions become so frustrated, disillusioned, and exhausted that they suffer from burnout. Three things can help decrease the likelihood that Pam will experience burnout. First, Pam should have realistic expectations. She needs to know that she cannot change the world all by herself and that she needs to appreciate small changes. Second, good communication across different aspects of organizations can help workers follow the progress of someone they have helped and can give the workers a feeling of accomplishment. Third, workers need to feel that they are important to the organization. (460-461)

2. The glass ceiling refers to the level to which women rise in a company and then go no further. Studies have shown that many women rise to the upper levels of lower-tier jobs but rarely enter the upper-tier of jobs. This glass ceiling keeps women in lower level jobs in spite of their personal attributes and qualifications. Women in the workplace also are victims of pay discrimination. In the United States, women earn 80% of the salary that men receive in comparable jobs. If Hilka thinks that she has been working hard but has not been rewarded for her work, she's probably right. Hilka should not view this as a personal insult but as a problem in the workplace that affects many women. (466-467)

3. According to the reasonable woman standard, Jelisa's boss could be found guilty of sexual harassment. According to this standard, if a reasonable woman finds the behavior offensive, then it is harassment regardless of the man's intentions. Sexual harassment is difficult to define but can be broken down into 3 categories: sexual coercion (forcing sexual compliance in return for benefits or to avoid a punishment), unwanted sexual attention (unwanted verbal or nonverbal attention such as repeated requests for dates), and gender harassment (sexist remarks or behavior based on gender stereotypes). Jelisa should let her boss know that she finds his behavior offensive. If the behavior persists, she should pursue a complaint against him. (468-469)

4. Poor physical and mental health and decreased satisfaction with life, marriage, and family are common effects associated with the loss of one's job. Men Ira's age are particularly vulnerable to these effects because they have greater financial responsibilities than younger men. Ira's poor health and signs of depression are fairly typical of men in his position. If Ira does not improve, Marina should seek outside help for him. (474-475)

5. Yes, dual-worker couples do experience a lot of role conflict between their multiple roles, but these roles can be juggled successfully. First, women who have juggled these roles successfully report that they limit their stress by limiting the number of children that they have. Second, men limit their stress by doing more child-care tasks. Third, men report less stress if they have flexible work schedules that allow them to care for sick children. Fourth, women tend to be happier if their husbands not only do more around the house, but also do traditionally female work like cooking, the dishes, etc. In other words, Fran and Jack will probably be happier if

they only have 1 or 2 children, Jack helps with the children, Jack has a flexible work schedule, and Jack does traditionally female chores around the house. (480)

6.  Our choice of leisure activities is influenced by a number of factors. First, how well we think that we will perform at the activity, or perceived competence, is important. Hang gliding may be an activity that many people would perceive that they wouldn't do well. Second, how well our performance matches our goals for performance, or psychological comfort, is important. You may be afraid that your goal of not making a fool of yourself or not hurting yourself may not be met if you go with Jermaine. Other factors include income (do you have the money for hang gliding?), interest (you've already told Jermaine you aren't interested), physical health and ability (are you healthy enough and coordinated enough to hang glide?), transportation, education, and social characteristics. Involvement in leisure activities also is important in promoting feelings of well-being. If one is forced to participate in a leisure activity, then little, or no, well-being will result from participation. In other words, leisure activities and satisfaction from them varies from person-to-person. One person's fantastic experience may be another person's nightmare. (482)

# MAKING IT IN MIDLIFE

This chapter focuses on the changes that occur during middle age such as changes in physical well-being, cognition, personality, and family dynamics.

# 13.1 PHYSICAL CHANGES AND HEALTH

## TO MASTER THE LEARNING OBJECTIVES:

**How does appearance change in middle age?**

- Explain the physical changes that cause wrinkles, gray hair, baldness, and middle-aged bulge.

- Describe the causes and possible prevention of osteoporosis and explain why it is more common in women than in men.

- Describe changes in the joints and problems such as osteoarthritis and rheumatoid arthritis.

**What reproductive changes occur in men and women in middle age?**

- Describe the physical changes that occur in women during the climacteric.

- Explain how ethnicity and culture are related to menopause.

- Describe how reproductive technology has changed the age of childbearing.

- Describe the risks and benefits associated with hormone replacement therapy.

- Describe changes in men's fertility with age.

- Describe the changes that occur in men's sexual functioning with age.

**What is stress?  How does it affect physical and psychological health?**

- Describe how control over one's job is related to stress.

- Describe how reported stress differs by age and gender.

- Describe the stress and coping paradigm.

- Describe how stress is related to one's physical health.

- Define Type A and Type B behavior patterns and explain how both are related to cardiovascular disease.

- Describe how stress and psychological health are related.

**What benefits are there to exercise?**

- Describe the physiological effects of exercise.

- Describe changes across adulthood in the reasons why people exercise.


# 13.1 KNOW THE TERMS

| | |
|---|---|
| Aerobic exercise | Osteoarthritis |
| Appraise | Osteoporosis |
| Climacteric | Rheumatoid arthritis |
| Coping | Stress and coping |
| Hassles | Type A |
| Hormone replacement | Type B |
| Menopause | |


1. The physical condition in which bones become porous like honeycombs and are extremely easy to break is called _____ .

2. A disease marked by gradual onset and disability with minor signs of inflammation of the joints is called _____ .

3. A destructive disease of the joints that develops slowly and typically affects the joints in fingers, wrists, and ankles is called _____

4. The physical and hormonal changes that are associated with the loss of the ability to bear children is called the _____ .

5. The eventual end of menstruation is called _____ .

6. _____ therapy involves women taking low doses of estrogen and progestin to alleviate symptoms associated with the climacteric.

7. The _____ paradigm is concerned with whether or not someone interprets a situation as stressful and how that person deals with the stress.

8. How people _____ a situation determines whether or not they will experience an event as taxing or stressful.

9. The day-to-day _____ or things that annoy us, are the most stressful, in general.

10. One's attempt to deal with stress is called _____ .

11. People with the _____ behavior pattern tend to be intensely competitive, angry, hostile, impatient, aggressive, and restless.

12. People with the _____ behavior pattern tend to be patient, relaxed, and laid back.

13. _____ places a moderate stress on the heart and provides adults with many physiological benefits.

# 13.1 KNOW THE DETAILS OF PHYSICAL CHANGES AND HEALTH

1. Exposure to sunlight and smoking cigarettes can cause wrinkles.
   TRUE or FALSE

2. During middle adulthood, metabolism speeds up.
   TRUE or FALSE

3. Osteoporosis causes bones to become porous and to break more easily.
   TRUE or FALSE

4. Osteoporosis is more common in men than women.
   TRUE or FALSE

5. Estrogen replacement therapy reduces bone loss in women.
   TRUE or FALSE

6. Osteoarthritis usually first becomes apparent in late middle age or early old age.
   TRUE or FALSE

7. Rheumatoid arthritis is not as destructive as osteoarthritis.
   TRUE or FALSE

8. In women, the climacteric usually begins in the 50s and is complete by age 60 or 65.
   TRUE or FALSE

9. During the climacteric, estrogen production increases.
   TRUE or FALSE

10. Symptoms of perimenopause and menopause include hot flashes, night sweats, headaches, mood changes, difficulty concentrating, and vaginal dryness.
    TRUE or FALSE

11. Reproductive technology has made it possible for postmenopausal women to have children.
    TRUE or FALSE

12. The decline in estrogen during the climacteric is related to an increased risk of osteoporosis, cardiovascular disease, and memory loss.
    TRUE or FALSE

13. Hormone replacement therapy is associated with a decreased risk of endometrial cancer and breast cancer.
    TRUE or FALSE

14. Men are still capable of fathering a child when they are in their 80s.
    TRUE or FALSE

15. Workers in jobs where they have little control over their jobs tend to have higher levels of stress than do workers who have more direct control over their jobs.
    TRUE or FALSE

16. Men are more likely than women to rate their stressful experiences as more negative and uncontrollable.
    TRUE or FALSE

17. Stress tends to be highest in early adulthood.
    TRUE or FALSE

18. Stress results when you appraise a situation or event as taxing or exceeding your personal, social, or other resources and endangering your well-being.
    TRUE or FALSE

19. Experiencing stressful events results in lower immune system functioning.
    TRUE or FALSE

20. People with the Type B behavior pattern tend to be intensely competitive, angry, hostile, restless, aggressive, and impatient.
    TRUE or FALSE

21. Physical exercise slows the physiological aging process.
    TRUE or FALSE

22. People who exercise aerobically report lower levels of stress, better moods, and better cognitive functioning.

    TRUE or FALSE

# 13.2 COGNITIVE DEVELOPMENT

## TO MASTER THE LEARNING OBJECTIVES:

**How does practical intelligence develop in adulthood? What are the developmental trends of exercised and unexercised abilities?**

- Define practical intelligence and explain how it differs from traditional measures of intelligence.

- Explain the difference between optimally exercised and unexercised abilities and describe the developmental course of both.

- Describe the applications of practical intelligence.

- Explain the differences between the mechanics and pragmatics of intelligence.

**How does a person become an expert?**

- Describe the differences in the thinking of experts and novices and describe the developmental course of expert performance.

- Define encapsulation and explain how it is related to the ability to explain how one arrives at a particular answer.

**What is meant by life-long learning? What differences are there between adults and young people in how they learn?**

- Explain why lifelong learning is becoming the norm.

- Describe the 4 ways in which adult learners differ from younger learners.

## 13.2 KNOW THE TERMS

| | |
|---|---|
| Encapsulated | Processes |
| Optimally exercised | Products |
| Practical intelligence | Unexercised |

1. _____ involves the skills and knowledge that people use to adapt to their physical and social environments.

2. _____ abilities are ones that are not used very often, and they represent the level of performance a person exhibits without practice or training.

3. _____ abilities are those that one uses the most, and they reflect the level of performance that a normal, healthy adult demonstrates under the best conditions of training or practice.

4. Fluid intelligence, memory, and information processing are the _____ of thinking.

5. In expertise, the process of thinking becomes connected, or _____ to the products of thinking.

6. The _____ of thinking are the results of thinking that are apparent in expertise.

# 13.2 KNOW THE DETAILS OF COGNITIVE DEVELOPMENT

1. Cognitive development goes through many rapid changes during middle adulthood.
   TRUE or FALSE

2. Traditional intelligence tests provide a good measure of practical intelligence.
   TRUE or FALSE

3. The level of performance a person exhibits without practice or training is referred to as unexercised ability.
   TRUE or FALSE

4. Performance is usually higher for unexercised abilities than for optimally exercised abilities.
   TRUE or FALSE

5. Both unexercised and optimally exercised abilities increase until young adulthood, plateau through middle age, and decline thereafter.
   TRUE or FALSE

6. The difference between performance on practical problems and optimally exercised ability is hypothesized to increase greatly during middle age.
   TRUE or FALSE

7. Late middle-aged adults most often take a passive-dependent or avoidant-denial approach to dealing with highly emotional problems.

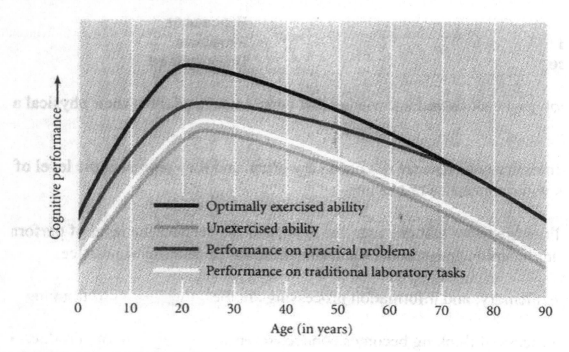

SOURCE: From "Aging and Cognitive Changes," by N. W. Denney. In B. B. Wolman (Ed.), *Handbook of Developmental Psychology.* p. 821. Copyright © 1982. Reprinted by permission of Prentice-Hall, Inc., Upper Saddle River: NJ.

TRUE or FALSE

8. Middle-aged adults are less likely than adolescents or young adults to use problem-focused strategies in dealing with instrumental issues such as home management.

TRUE or FALSE

9. The pragmatics of intelligence is more closely associated with neurophysiology than with sociocultural forces.

TRUE or FALSE

10. Individuals who are expert in one area tend to be experts in most areas.

TRUE or FALSE

11. Experts are more likely than beginners to skip steps when solving a problem.

TRUE or FALSE

12. Encapsulation can hinder the ability to explain to others how to solve a problem.

TRUE or FALSE

13. The need for lifelong learning is increasing.

TRUE or FALSE

# 13.3 PERSONALITY

## TO MASTER THE LEARNING OBJECTIVES:

**What is the five-factor model? What evidence is there for stability in personality traits?**

- Describe Costa and McCrae's 5 dimensions of personality: neuroticism, agreeableness, openness to experience, conscientiousness, and extraversion.

- Describe the evidence that personality traits remain stable across adulthood.

- Describe the evidence for personality change during adulthood.

**What changes occur in people's priorities and personal concerns? How does a person achieve generativity? How is midlife best described?**

- Describe how priorities change over the course of one's lifetime.

- Explain generativity and stagnation and ethnic differences in generativity.

- Explain how changes in self-descriptions of gender-role are related to changes in behavior across adulthood.

- Define mid-life crisis and explain whether or not the mid-life crisis is universal.

## 13.3 KNOW THE TERMS

| | |
|---|---|
| **Agreeableness** | **Mid-life crisis** |
| **Conscientiousness** | **Neuroticism** |
| **Ego resilience** | **Openness to experience** |
| **Extraversion** | **Stagnation** |
| **Generativity** | |

1. A crisis that occurs during middle age is called the _____ .

2. People who are high on the personality dimension of _____ tend to be anxious, hostile, self-conscious, depressed, vulnerable, and impulsive.

3. People who are high on the personality dimension of _____ love social interaction, like to talk, take charge easily, are very energetic, and prefer challenging and stimulating environments.

4. People who are high on the dimension of _____ tend to have a vivid imagination and dream life, appreciate art, and will try anything once.

5. People who are high on _____ are caring, accepting of others, and willing to work with others.

6. Those with high levels of _____ are hard working, ambitious, energetic, scrupulous, and persevering.

7. According to Erikson, _____ occurs when middle-aged adults try to help younger generations to ensure the continuation of society.

8. According to Erikson, _____ occurs when middle-aged adults cannot meet the needs of their children or cannot mentor younger adults.

9. A powerful personality resource that enables people to handle midlife is called _____ .

## 13.3 KNOW THE DETAILS OF PERSONALITY

1. People who are high on the neuroticism dimension of personality thrive on social interaction, like to talk, take charge easily, like to keep busy, and have boundless energy.
   TRUE or FALSE

2. Individuals who are high on the openness to experience dimension of personality tend to have a vivid imagination and dream life, an appreciation of art, and a strong desire to try anything once.
   TRUE or FALSE

3. People's personality traits tend to be stable over long periods of time.
   TRUE or FALSE

4. According to Erikson, helping others in order to ensure the continuation of society by guiding the next generation becomes more important during middle adulthood.
   TRUE or FALSE

5. Jung proposed a "crossover effect" of gender identity during middle age.
   TRUE or FALSE

6. Self-descriptions data suggests that men and women are most different in their gender role identities in middle adulthood.
   TRUE or FALSE

7. Convergence in gender roles seems to occur more behaviorally than internally.
   TRUE or FALSE

8. The majority of research evidence does not support the view of a universal stage, such as a midlife crisis, that everyone experiences at the same point in life.
   TRUE or FALSE

9. Normative midlife events, such as menopause, are more likely than nonnormative unexpected events, such as job change, to create stress.
   TRUE or FALSE

10. Individuals low in ego resilience are more likely to handle midlife successfully.
    TRUE or FALSE

# 13.4 FAMILY DYNAMICS AND MIDDLE AGE

## TO MASTER THE LEARNING OBJECTIVES:

**How does the relationship between middle-aged parents and their young adult children change?**

- Describe the role of kinkeeper that many middle-aged mothers assume.

- Define what is meant by the sandwich generation.

- Describe how the relationship between parents and children changes as the children move from adolescence to young adulthood.

- Explain how most parents feel when they have an empty nest.

- Explain the reasons why adult children return home.

**How do middle-aged adults deal with their aging parents?**

- Describe the gender difference in caring for aging parents.

- Define filial obligation.

- Describe the 2 factors that contribute to negative feelings about caring for one's aging parents.

- Explain some of the psychological costs of caregiving.

- Describe ethnic differences in adult caregivers' stress.

**What styles of grandparenthood do middle-aged adults experience? How do grandchildren and grandparents interact?**

- Explain how personal and social dimensions of grandparenting influence grandparenting.

- Describe the different meanings of grandparenthood.

- Describe ethnic differences in grandparenthood.
- Describe how the role of grandparent has changed in recent years.

# 13.4 KNOW THE TERMS

| | |
|---|---|
| **Centrality** | **Indulgence** |
| **Cultural conservator** | **Kinkeepers** |
| **Fictive** | **Reinvolvement with personal past** |
| **Filial obligation** | **Sandwich generation** |
| **Immortality through clan** | **Valued elder** |

1. Middle-aged mothers often take on the role of _____ because they gather the family together for celebrations and keep family members in touch with each other.

2. Middle-aged adults are sometimes called the _____ because they must juggle the demands of their children and their aging parents.

3. The feeling of responsibility for caring for one's aging parents is called _____ .

4. For some grandparents, grandparenting is the most important thing in their lives, which is called _____ .

5. For some grandparents, the meaning of grandparenthood comes from being seen as wise or as a _____ .

6. For some grandparents, the meaning of grandparenthood comes from spoiling their grandchildren or _____ .

7. For some grandparents, the meaning of grandparenthood involves recalling the relationship that they had with their own grandparents, or _____ .

8. For some grandparents, the meaning of grandparenthood comes from taking pride in the fact that they will be followed by two generations, or _____ .

9. _____ grandparenting allows adults to fill in for missing or deceased biological grandparents.

10. The _____ style occurs in Native American grandparents whose grandchildren live with them so they can learn the native customs.

## 13.4 KNOW THE DETAILS OF FAMILY DYNAMICS AND MIDDLE AGE

1. Fathers are more likely than mothers to take on the role of kinkeeper.
   TRUE or FALSE

2. Parent-child relationships usually improve when children become adults.
   TRUE or FALSE

3. Female adult children are more likely than male adult children to move back in with their parents.
   TRUE or FALSE

4. Daughters and sons are equally likely to provide care for their aging parents.
   TRUE or FALSE

5. Becoming a caregiver to aging parents usually has no impact on a woman's employment situation.
   TRUE or FALSE

6. Being securely attached to one's parent may reduce the stress of caregiving.
   TRUE or FALSE

7. The valued elder dimension of parenting refers to grandparenting being the most important thing in their lives.
   TRUE or FALSE

8. Grandparenting style varies with ethnicity.
   TRUE or FALSE

9. Fictive grandparenting is when grandparents request that their grandchildren be allowed to live with them to ensure that the grandchildren learn the native ways.
   TRUE or FALSE

10. Fewer grandparents today are serving as surrogate parents for their grandchildren than they did in years past.
    TRUE or FALSE

## SUMMARY

### 13.1 PHYSICAL CHANGES AND HEALTH

1. **Changes in Appearance**

   Some of the signs of aging that appear in middle age include _____ gray hair, and

   _____

2. **Changes in Bones and Joints**

An important change, especially in women, is loss of bone mass, which in severe form may result in the disease _____ Women are more vulnerable to this disease because they have less bone mass, they don't consume enough _____ and the drop in estrogen after menopause _____ bone loss. Osteoarthritis generally becomes noticeable in late middle or early old age. Rheumatoid arthritis is a more common form affecting fingers, wrists, and ankles.

3. **Reproductive Changes**

The _____ (loss of the ability to bear children by natural means), and _____ (cessation of menstruation) occur in the 40s and 50s. Most women do not have severe physical symptoms associated with the hormonal changes. Hormone replacement therapy is a _____ approach to treatment of menopausal symptoms. Reproductive changes in men are much less dramatic; even older men are typically still fertile. Physical changes do affect sexual response.

4. **Stress and Health**

In the stress and coping paradigm, stress is viewed as an _____ of an event as taxing one's resources. Daily hassles are viewed as the primary source of stress. The types of situations people find stressful change across adulthood. Family and _____ issues are more important for young- and middle-aged adults; _____ issues are more important for older adults. Type A behavior pattern is characterized by intense _____ anger, hostility, restlessness, aggression, and _____ and is linked with first heart attack and _____ disease. Type B behavior pattern is the opposite of Type A, and is associated with lower risk of first heart attack, but poorer prognosis afterward should one occur. Following an initial heart attack, Type A behavior pattern individuals have a _____ recovery rate. Whereas stress is unrelated to serious psychopathology, it is related to social isolation and distrust.

5. **Exercise**

Aerobic exercise has numerous benefits, especially to cardiovascular health and fitness. Other physical benefits include lower _____ better strength, endurance, flexibility, and _____ Possible psychological benefits include lower levels of _____ better moods, and better _____ functioning. The best results are obtained through a _____ exercise program maintained throughout adulthood.

## 13.2 COGNITIVE DEVELOPMENT

1. **Practical Intelligence**

   Research on practical intelligence reveals differences between optimally exercised ability and unexercised ability. This gap closes during _____ adulthood. Practical intelligence does not appear to _____ appreciably until late life.

2. **Becoming an Expert**

   People tend to become experts in some areas and not in others. Experts tend to think in more _____ ways than novices and are able to _____ steps in solving problems which may make it difficult for them to explain solutions to novices. In experts, the _____ of thinking are encapsulated to the products of thinking. Expert performance tends to peak in middle age.

3. **Lifelong Learning**

   Adults learn differently than children and youth. Older students need practical _____ and rationale for learning, and are more motivated to learn by _____ factors.

## 13.3 PERSONALITY

1. **Stability Is the Rule: The Five-Factor Model**

   The five-factor model postulates five dimensions of personality: neuroticism, _____ openness to experience, _____ and conscientiousness. Several longitudinal studies indicate that personality traits show long-term _____ but increasing evidence shows that traits change across adulthood.

2. **Change Is the Rule: Changing Priorities at Midlife**

   Erikson believed that middle-aged adults become more concerned with doing for others and passing social values and skills to the _____ a set of behaviors and beliefs he labeled generativity. Those who do not achieve generativity are thought to experience _____ For the most part, there is little support for the theories based on the premise that all adults go through predictable life stages at specific points in time. Individuals may face similar stresses, but transitions may occur at any time in adulthood. Research evidence indicates that not everyone experiences a _____ at midlife. There is some evidence that gender-role identity _____ in middle age, to the extent that men and women are more likely to endorse similar self-descriptions. However, these similar descriptions do not necessarily translate into more similar behavior.

## 13.4 FAMILY DYNAMICS AND MIDDLE AGE

1. **Letting Go: Middle-Aged Adults and Their Children**

   Middle-aged mothers tend to adopt the role of kinkeeping in order to keep family traditions alive and as a way to _____ generations. Middle age is sometimes referred to as the sandwich generation due to its position between one's children and _____ Parent-child relations _____ dramatically when children emerge from adolescence. Most parents _____ having an empty nest. Difficulties emerge to the extent that raising children has been a primary source of personal identity for parents. However, once children have left home, parents still provide considerable support. Children are more likely to move back home if they are men, _____ a low sense of autonomy, and an expectation that parents would provide a large portion of their income.

2. **Giving Back: Middle-Aged Adults and Their Aging Parents**

   Middle-aged children contact their parents _____ and use the visits to strengthen the relationship. Caring for aging parents usually falls to a daughter or daughter-in-law. Caregiving creates a stressful situation due to conflicting feelings and roles; the potential for conflict is high as is _____ pressure. Caregiving stress is usually greater in women, who must deal with multiple roles. Older parents are often dissatisfied with the situation as well.

3. **Grandparenting**

   Becoming a grandparent means assuming new roles. Styles of interaction vary across grandchildren and with the _____ of the grandchild. Also relevant are the personal and social dimensions of grandparenting. Grandparents derive several different types of meaning regardless of style: centrality, _____ indulgence, reinvolvement with personal past, and immortality through clan. Ethnic differences exist in the degree to which grandparents take an active role in their grandchildren's lives. In an increasingly mobile society, grandparents are more frequently assuming a _____ relationship with their grandchildren. An increasing number of grandparents serve as the _____ parent. These arrangements are typically stressful.

# TEST YOURSELF

## MULTIPLE-CHOICE QUESTIONS

1. Which of the following is associated with an increased risk of osteoporosis?
   a. eating foods high in calcium
   b. reducing alcohol intake
   c. exercising
   d. being postmenopausal

2. For women, the most significant change during the climacteric is a
   a. dramatic increase in testosterone levels.
   b. gradual decrease in testosterone levels.
   c. dramatic decrease in estrogen production.
   d. gradual increase in estrogen production.

3. A decline in estrogen is related to
   a. a decreased risk of osteoporosis.
   b. a decreased risk of memory loss.
   c. an increased risk of extreme weight loss.
   d. an increased risk of cardiovascular disease.

4. Hormone-replacement therapy for women during the climacteric increases the risk of
   a. osteoporosis.
   b. colorectal cancer.
   c. breast cancer.
   d. hot flashes.

5. Men
   a. continue to produce sperm at a constant rate throughout adulthood.
   b. experience a gradual decline in sperm production, but remain fertile throughout adulthood.
   c. experience a dramatic decline in sperm production in middle adulthood, comparable to the changes women go through during menopause, and lose fertility at that time.
   d. normally experience a complete loss of fertility during late adulthood.

6. The _____ paradigm emphasizes the interaction between a person and the environment and is the dominant framework used to study stress.
   a. five-factor
   b. encapsulation
   c. exercised-unexercised abilities
   d. stress and coping

7. Who is likely to have the highest level of stress?
   a. Dan, a 50-year-old male business executive
   b. Stella, a 45-year-old waitress
   c. Martha, a 70-year-old female community volunteer
   d. Raymond, a 75-year-old male retiree

8. _____ results when you appraise a situation or event as exceeding your personal, social, or other resources.
   a. Type A behavior
   b. Type B behavior
   c. Coping
   d. Stress

9. Harry hates to wait in lines, is very competitive, has a quick temper, and is often hostile towards others. Harry shows many symptoms of a _____ behavior pattern.
   a. Type A
   b. Type B
   c. Type C
   d. Type D

10. Rick has a Type B behavior pattern, whereas John has a Type A behavior pattern. John is
    a. more likely to have a heart attack and less likely to recover from one.
    b. less likely to have a heart attack and less likely to recover from one.
    c. more likely to have a heart attack and more likely to recover from one.
    d. less likely to have a heart attack but more likely to recover from one.

11. _____ exercise has the best impact on health.
    a. No
    b. Mild
    c. Moderate
    d. Strenuous

12. The broad range of skills related to how individuals shape, select, or adapt to their physical and social environments is called is referred to as
    a. fluid intelligence.
    b. crystallized intelligence.
    c. practical intelligence.
    d. unexercised ability.

13. Which of the following tasks would be most appropriate to use as a measure of practical intelligence?
    a. reconciling a sample bank statement with a checkbook register
    b. memorizing a list of fifty unrelated words
    c. naming as many words as one can think of that begin with the letter "t"
    d. using blocks to reconstruct a pattern shown in a picture

14. Which of the following is NOT a way that practical intelligence problems differ from traditional intelligence test problems?
    a. People are more motivated to solve them.
    b. They rely more heavily on personal experience.
    c. They are less realistic.
    d. They usually have more than one correct answer.

15. Fifty-five-year-old Beth has been solving crossword puzzles in the daily newspaper nearly every day of her adult life. Her ability to solve crossword puzzles would best be considered
    a. an optimally exercised ability.
    b. an unexercised ability.
    c. practical intelligence.
    d. fluid intelligence.

16. When Margaret is faced with a practical problem, she tackles the problem head on and does something about it. What kind of approach does Margaret use to solve problems?
    a. passive-dependent behavior
    b. avoidant thinking and denial
    c. cognitive-analysis
    d. problem-focused action

17. When solving a problem in their areas of expertise, experts are more likely than novices to
    a. follow the rules.
    b. skip steps.
    c. be faster in terms of raw processing speed.
    d. be less flexible.

18. Encapsulation occurs when
    a. fluid intelligence increases and crystallized intelligence decreases.
    b. experts instruct novices in how to solve a problem.
    c. one withdraws from a situation in order to solve a problem.
    d. the processes of thinking become connected to the products of thinking.

19. Which of the following statements comparing learning during adulthood to learning during youth is true?
    a. Adults are more willing to learn to deal with abstract, hypothetical situations than with real-world problems.
    b. Most adults are more motivated to learn by external factors (e.g., job promotion) than by internal factors (e.g., self-esteem).
    c. Adults enter a learning situation with less varied experience on which to build.
    d. Adults have a higher need to know why they should learn something before undertaking it.

20. _____ and _____ are part of the five-factor model of personality.
    a. The Type A behavior pattern; the Type B behavior pattern
    b. Extraversion; conscientiousness
    c. Unexercised abilities; optimally exercised abilities
    d. Generativity; stagnation

21. Raymond is highly anxious, hostile, self-conscious, and impulsive. Raymond appears to be high on the _____ personality dimension.
    a. extraversion
    b. neuroticism
    c. openness to new experience
    d. conscientiousness

22. Costa and McCrae's research examining personality traits has found evidence suggesting that
    a. personality traits are generally stable across adulthood.
    b. personality traits change greatly across adulthood.
    c. personality is primarily due to environmental factors.
    d. personality is primarily due to age factors.

23. According to Erikson, _____ becomes of increased importance during middle adulthood.
    a. identity
    b. integrity
    c. intimacy
    d. generativity

24. In McAdams' multidimensional model of generativity, individuals derive personal meaning from being generative through
    a. generative action.
    b. generative concern.
    c. cultural demands.
    d. constructing a life story or narration.

25. Men and women
    a. both behave more similarly and have more similar internal gender role identities as they get older.
    b. behave more similarly but have less similar internal gender role identities as they get older.
    c. have increasingly similar internal gender role identities but do not necessarily behave more similarly as they get older.
    d. have increasingly dissimilar internal gender role identities and behavior as they get older.

26. Research evidence suggests that
    a. midlife is no more or less traumatic than other periods of life.
    b. midlife is slightly more likely to be a time of crisis than are other periods of life.
    c. midlife crisis is a universal stage.
    d. no fundamental changes of any kind occur during adulthood.

27. _____ appears to be a key factor in how well people negotiate the challenges and issues of midlife.
    a. Type A versus Type B personality
    b. Stress
    c. Ego resilience
    d. Encapsulation

28. _____ are most likely to take on the role of kinkeeper.
    a. Sons
    b. Young daughters
    c. Fathers
    d. Mothers

29. Who is a member of the sandwich generation?
    a. 64-year-old Mary, who has a husband, three daughters, and two sons
    b. 48-year-old Jan, who has two daughters in college and parents who live with her
    c. 28-year-old Shauna, who lives with her parents
    d. 54-year-old Sandy, who has an older brother and a younger sister

30. Adult children are more likely to move back in with their parents,
    a. when the parents are in poor health.
    b. when adult children had high college GPAs.
    c. when adult children have a low sense of autonomy.
    d. when parents were verbally or physically abusive.

31. Who is most likely to provide care for aging parents?
    a. sons and daughters
    b. sons and daughters-in-law
    c. daughters and sons-in-law
    d. daughters and daughters-in-law

32. The sense of responsibility that adult children feel to care for their parent if necessary is called
    a. filial obligation.
    b. immortality through clan.
    c. cultural conservator.
    d. kinkeeper.

33. Who is least likely to experience stress due to caring for aging parents?
    a. Claudine, whose children moved out ten years ago
    b. Jeannine, whose mother has Alzheimer's Disease
    c. Francine, whose job entails working long hours
    d. Geraldine, whose mother is experiencing cognitive decline

34. Compared to European Americans, Latino American and African American caregivers are
    a. likely to report higher levels of caregiver stress.
    b. likely to believe more strongly in filial obligation.
    c. less likely to use prayer, faith, or religion as a coping strategy.
    d. less likely to be caring for people who are at higher risk of chronic disease and more disabled.

35. Grandparents who derive meaning from their relationship with their grandchildren because of being seen as wise are focusing on the _____ dimension of meaning.
    a. centrality
    b. reinvolvement with personal past
    c. valued elder
    d. immortality through clan

36. Compared to European American grandparents, African American grandparents
    a. tend to be more involved in teaching their grandchildren.
    b. are less willing to take a grandparent education course.
    c. perceive grandparenthood as a central role to a lesser degree.
    d. over 60 are less likely to feel that they are fulfilling an important role.

37. Grandparents who request that their grandchildren be allowed to live with them in order to ensure that the grandchildren learn the native ways have a _____ grandparenting style.
    a. fictive
    b. cultural conservator
    c. valued elder
    d. centrality

## ESSAY QUESTIONS

1. In the past few months, your mother has had headaches frequently and often feels very hot when no one else in the room does. In fact, sometimes she wakes in the middle of the night drenched with perspiration. Your mother has heard about the use of hormone replacement therapy to relieve the symptoms during the climacteric, but she also has heard that this therapy causes cancer. What can you tell your mother about the benefits and risks of hormone replacement therapy?

2. Your 40-year-old friend Inga recently commented on the fact that many of her same-age friends have begun to exercise regularly. Inga has never been overweight so she has never felt the need to exercise but now she is wondering if her friends know something that she doesn't. What can you tell Inga about the physical and psychological benefits associated with a program of regular exercise?

3. Your friend Lynn does not know how to cook so you sent her to learn from your friend Bill who is an expert cook. After a few lessons, Lynn became frustrated and told you that she could never learn to cook from Bill because he adds ingredients that aren't in the recipes, he doesn't measure things carefully, and doesn't do a very good job of explaining what he is doing. What can you tell Lynn about the differences between thinking in experts and novices that might explain her frustration?

4. Recently your friend Josh commented on the fact that his parents seem to be very different from the way they used to be. For example, when Josh was a child his father seemed to have a lot of power and his mother seemed to go along with his father. His mother also used to be more affectionate and involved than his father was. Now, Josh thinks that his mother exercises much more power than she used to and his father is much more affectionate and involved with his grandchildren than he was with his own children. Josh was wondering if this kind of change is typical. What can you tell Josh about the convergence of gender-role identities with age?

5. Your 55-year-old friend Hattie was wondering when she was going to experience her mid-life crisis. She told you that she has been happy with being a teacher, has been happy with her children, and has been satisfied with her marriage, but she keeps hearing about the mid-life crisis. What can you tell Hattie about the evidence for a universal mid-life crisis?

6. Your friends Miriam and Jake had been living in an empty nest since their last child left home a year ago, but 3 months ago their son Stan moved back home. Both Miriam and Jake think that Stan is very unusual. What can you tell Miriam and Jake about the frequency of young adults returning home and the factors related to it?

7. Your friend Mona's mother recently moved in with her. Mona told you that she feels pulled in many directions because she needs to do things for her children, her mother, and her husband. She also wonders if they can afford to support her mother. Sometimes Mona feels angry and frustrated and wishes that her mother didn't live with her, and she feels guilty about those feelings. What can you tell Mona about the common effects of caregiving that might help alleviate some of her guilt?

# SOLUTIONS

## 13.1 KNOW THE TERMS

1. osteoporosis (492)
2. osteoarthritis (494)
3. rheumatoid arthritis (494)
4. climacteric (494)
5. menopause (494)
6. Hormone replacement (496)
7. stress and coping (498)
8. appraise (499)
9. hassles (499)
10. coping (499)
11. Type A (500)
12. Type B (500)
13. Aerobic exercise (501)

## 13.1 KNOW THE DETAILS OF PHYSICAL CHANGES AND HEALTH

1. T, (491)
2. F, (491)
3. T, (492)
4. F, (493)
5. T, (493)
6. T, (494)
7. F, (494)
8. F, (495)
9. F, (495)
10. T, (495)
11. T, (495)
12. T, (496)
13. F, (497)
14. T, (497)
15. T, (498)
16. F, (498)
17. F, (498)
18. T, (499)
19. T, (500)
20. F, (500)
21. T, (501)
22. T, (502)

## 13.2 KNOW THE TERMS

1. Practical intelligence (503)
2. Unexercised (504)
3. Optimally exercised (504)
4. processes (507)
5. encapsulated (507)
6. products (507)

## 13.2 KNOW THE DETAILS OF COGNITIVE DEVELOPMENT

1. F, (503)
2. F, (503)
3. T, (504)
4. F, (504)
5. T, (505)
6. F, (505)
7. T, (505)
8. F, (505)
9. F, (506)
10. F, (507)
11. T, (507)
12. T, (508)
13. T, (509)

## 13.3 KNOW THE TERMS

1. mid-life crisis (510)
2. neuroticism (510)
3. extraversion (510)

4. openness to experience (511)  6. conscientiousness (511)  8. stagnation (514)
5. agreeableness (511)  7. generativity (513)  9. ego resilience (516)

## 13.3 KNOW THE DETAILS OF PERSONALITY

1. F, (510)  5. T, (515)  9. F, (516)
2. T, (511)  6. F, (515)  10. F, (517)
3. T, (511)  7. F, (515)
4. T, (513)  8. T, (516)

## 13.4 KNOW THE TERMS

1. kinkeepers (517)  5. valued elder (524)  8. immortality through clan (524)
2. sandwich generation (518)  6. indulgence (524)  9. Fictive (525)
3. filial obligation (520)  7. reinvolvement with personal  10. cultural conservator (525)
4. centrality (524)  past (524)

## 13.4 KNOW THE DETAILS OF FAMILY DYNAMICS AND MIDDLE AGE

1. F, (517)  5. F, (522)  9. F, (525)
2. T, (519)  6. T, (522)  10. F, (525)
3. F, (519)  7. F, (524)
4. F, (520)  8. T, (524)

## SUMMARY

### 13.1 PHYSICAL CHANGES AND HEALTH

1. wrinkles (491),; weight gain (491).
2. osteoporosis (492).; calcium (493); accelerates (493)
3. climacteric (494); menopause (494); controversial (496)
4. appraisal (499); career (500); health (500); competitiveness (500); impatience (500); cardiovascular (500); higher (500)
5. blood pressure (502); coordination (502); stress (502); cognitive (502); moderate (502)

### 13.2 COGNITIVE DEVELOPMENT

1. middle (505); decline (505)

2. flexible (507); skip (507) ;
   processes (507)
3. connections (509); internal (509)

## 13.3 PERSONALITY

1. extraversion (510);
   agreeableness (511); stability
   (511),

2. next generation (513); stagnation
   (514).; crisis (516); converges
   (515)

## 13.4 FAMILY DYNAMICS AND MIDDLE AGE

1. link (518); aging parents (518).;
   improve (519); look forward to
   (519); had low college GPAs
   (519),

2. frequently (520); financial (522)
3. age (523); valued elder (524);
   distant (525); custodial (525)

# TEST YOURSELF

## MULTIPLE-CHOICE QUESTIONS

1. D, (493)
2. C, (495)
3. D, (496)
4. C, (497)
5. B, (497)
6. D, (498)
7. B, (498)
8. D, (498)
9. A, (500)
10. C, (500)
11. C, (501)
12. C, (503)
13. A, (503)

14. C, (503)
15. A, (504)
16. D, (505)
17. B, (507)
18. D, (507)
19. D, (508)
20. B, (510)
21. B, (510)
22. A, (511)
23. D, (513)
24. D, (514)
25. C, (515)

26. A, (516)
27. C, (516)
28. D, (517)
29. B, (518)
30. C, (519)
31. D, (520)
32. A, (520)
33. A, (521)
34. B, (522)
35. C, (524)
36. A, (524)
37. B, (525)

## ESSAY QUESTIONS

1. During the climacteric, there is a dramatic drop in the production of the female hormone estrogen. This drop in estrogen leads to many physical symptoms such as hot flashes, night sweats, vaginal dryness, urine leakage, and the eventual end of menstruation. For most women these symptoms are not severe, but your mother sounds like an exception to this rule. Hormone replacement therapy involves giving women low doses of estrogen and progestin to alleviate the symptoms associated with the climacteric. Research has shown that women who are on HRT do show an increased risk of breast cancer, heart attack, stroke, and blood clots. However, women on HRT did have fewer hip fractures and a lowered risk of colorectal cancer. Your mother should discuss the various risks and benefits of HRT with her physician. (494-497)

2. Adults who engage in moderate, aerobic exercise on a regular basis show better cardiovascular functioning, lower blood pressure, greater strength, greater endurance, better coordination, and better flexibility. People who exercise regularly report lower levels of stress, better moods, and better cognitive functioning. Many middle-aged people do not exercise for appearance reasons but exercise for health reasons, so Inga's reasons for exercising would not be that different from those of other people her age. (501-502)

3.  Bill is not trying to frustrate Lynn; he is merely acting like an expert. Experts often skip steps that novices need to follow. Experts often don't follow the rules (or the recipes) like novices do. As experts' thinking becomes more encapsulated (the process of thinking becomes more connected to the products of thinking), experts become more efficient thinkers. Bill is merely using his expert cooking knowledge to be creative, skip unnecessary steps, etc. Bill's expertise also means that he doesn't need to think about each step, so he may not be very good at explaining what he is doing. Perhaps Lynn should take cooking lessons from someone who is not an expert or who is an experienced teacher. (507-508)

4.  Josh's parents may not be unusual. Some theorists suggest that there is a "crossover effect" of gender identity during middle age as women place more emphasis on achievement and accomplishment and men place more emphasis on familial and nurturant concerns. The data on changes in gender-role identity are mixed. In general, data support the view that gender-role identities in men and women are the most different in late adolescence and early adulthood but become more similar in middle and old age. However, Josh's parents may differ from other people their ages in that people's actual behavior may not change even though their self-descriptions do. For example, women who have never exercised power may find it difficult to do so even though they feel more powerful. (515)

5.  Most of the evidence for a mid-life crisis comes from a few theories that are based on very small samples of select populations. Most research evidence does not support age-related, major changes. Instead, unexpected life events (such as divorce or job loss) are more likely to create stress and upheaval than normative life events (such as menopause or becoming a grandparent). Even when a mid-life crisis occurs, the classic profile is only seen in a handful of cases. So, Hattie should not feel unusual about not having had a mid-life crisis because many people do not have them and they do not occur at a specific age when they do occur. (516-517)

6.  You can tell Miriam and Jake that Stan is not that unusual. In fact, approximately half of all young adults in the United States return to their parents' home to live at least once after leaving. This situation is more likely if the parents are in good health and they continue to do most of the housework. Also, children who are most likely to move back are male, have low college GPAs, have a low sense of autonomy, and expect that their parents would provide a large portion of their income following graduation. So, Miriam and Jake should realize that Stan is not unusual by moving back home. (519)

7.  Mona's feelings are typical of many middle-aged adults who are caring for their children and their aging parents. Most aging adults and their children report that they would prefer not living together. In fact, when they do live together there may be conflicts over daily routines and life styles. Feelings of depression, resentment, anger, and guilt are all common in caregivers. The feeling of financial burden also is typical. Mona may feel less stress if she can make arrangements so that caring for her mother is less confining and infringes less on the other aspects of her life. (520-522)

# THE PERSONAL CONTEXT OF LATER LIFE

This chapter focuses on the physical changes, cognitive changes, and mental health issues that are important to aging individuals.

## 14.1 WHAT ARE OLDER ADULTS LIKE?

### TO MASTER THE LEARNING OBJECTIVES:

**What are the characteristics of older adults in the population?**

- Describe how the shape of the population pyramid has changed since 1900.

- Describe how the population of developing countries is changing.

- Describe the composition of the future older adult population in terms of gender, ethnicity, and education.

- Describe how prepared the United States is for the financial strain of increased numbers of elderly.

**How long will most people live? What factors influence this?**

- Define the average life expectancy and describe the factors that have led to its increase.

- Define average life expectancy, useful life expectancy, and maximum life expectancy.

- Describe the genetic factors that are linked to life expectancy.

- Describe the environmental factors that are related to life expectancy.

- Describe ethnic differences in life expectancy.

- Describe the gender differences in life expectancy.

- Describe international differences in life expectancy.

- Define the Third Age and explain how it differs from the Fourth Age.

## 14.1 KNOW THE TERMS

| | |
|---|---|
| **Average** | **Maximum** |
| **Demographers** | **Population pyramid** |
| **Longevity** | **Useful** |

1.  People who study population trends are called _____ .

2.  A _____ is a graphic technique that shows the distribution of people of various ages in a population.

3.  The number of years that a person will live that is influenced by both genetic and environmental factors is called _____ .

4.  The age at which half of the people born in a particular year will have died is called _____ life expectancy.

5.  The number of years that a person lives that is free from debilitating chronic disease and impairment is called _____ life expectancy.

6.  The oldest age to which any person lives is _____ life expectancy.

## 14.1 KNOW THE DETAILS OF THE DEMOGRAPHICS OF AGING

1.  There have never been as many older adults alive as there are now.
    TRUE or FALSE

2.  Projections suggest that by 2030 the number of people over 65 will outnumber those in any other age group.
    TRUE or FALSE

3.  Older women outnumber older men in the U.S.
    TRUE or FALSE

4. The number of older adults is growing more rapidly among European Americans than among ethnic minority groups.

   TRUE or FALSE

5. In the future, older adults are expected to be better educated than older adults are today.

   TRUE or FALSE

6. The number of older adults is increasing more rapidly in industrialized countries than in developing countries.

   TRUE or FALSE

7. Longevity is determined solely by genetic factors.

   TRUE or FALSE

8. Average life expectancy is the number of years that a person is free from debilitating chronic disease and impairment.

   TRUE or FALSE

9. The current maximum life expectancy is around 75 years of age.

   TRUE or FALSE

10. Social class is related to longevity.

    TRUE or FALSE

11. The average life expectancy is the same for all ethnic groups.

    TRUE or FALSE

12. African Americans who survive to age 85 tend to be healthier than their European American counterparts.

    TRUE or FALSE

13. Women's average longevity is about 7 years more, on average, than men's at birth.

    TRUE or FALSE

14. Longevity is very similar in different countries around the world.

    TRUE or FALSE

15. The term "The Third Age" is used to refer to the young-old population.

    TRUE or FALSE

# 14.2 PHYSICAL CHANGES AND HEALTH

## TO MASTER THE LEARNING OBJECTIVES:

**What are the major biological theories of aging?**

- Describe the wear-and-tear, cellular, metabolic, and programmed cell death theories of aging.

**What physiological changes normally occur in later life?**

- Define neurofibrillary tangles and describe why they are a problem.

- Describe the changes in the dendrites that occur with aging.

- Define neuritic plaques and explain why they are a problem.

- Describe age changes in levels of neurotransmitters.

- Explain what imaging of the brain tells us about age-related declines in cognitive functioning.

- Describe the changes in the cardiovascular system with age.

- Explain the causes and effects of cerebral vascular accidents.

- Describe the cause and progression of vascular dementia.

- Describe how cerebral vascular accidents and vascular dementia are diagnosed.

- Describe how the respiratory system changes with age and define chronic obstructive pulmonary disease.

- Describe the causes, symptoms, and treatments for Parkinson's disease.

- Describe the changes that occur in the eye with age.

- Define presbycusis and its causes.

- Describe age-related changes in the sense of smell.

- Describe the consequences of age-related changes in balance.

- Describe the changes that one can make to one's home so that falls are less likely to occur.

**What are the principal health issues for older adults?**

- Describe the sleep disturbances that are common in older adults and describe their possible causes.

- Describe the nutritional needs of older adults.

- Describe how the risk of getting cancer changes with age and explain the importance of early detection and screening.

- Explain how immigrant status affects health.

# 14.2 KNOW THE TERMS

Cellular

Cerebral vascular accidents

Chronic obstructive pulmonary

Circadian rhythm

Cross-linking

Free radicals

Hemorrhage

Metabolic

Neurofibrillary tangles

Neuritic plaques

Neurotransmitters

Parkinson's

Presbycusis

Presbyopia

Programmed cell death

Stroke

Telomeres

Transient ischemic attacks (TIAs)

Vascular dementia

Wear-and-tear

1.  The _____ theory of aging suggests that aging is a result of the body deteriorating and wearing out over time.

2.  _____ theories of aging focus on processes that occur in individual cells that cause deterioration or the build-up of harmful substances over one's lifetime.

3.  The tips of the chromosomes are called _____ .

4.  _____ are chemicals that are produced during normal cell metabolism that bind with other substances in cells, which causes cellular damage and impaired functioning.

5.  _____ theories of aging assume that certain proteins interact randomly with body tissue such as muscles and arteries, causing them to be less flexible.

6.  _____ theories of aging focus on aspects of the body's metabolism to explain aging.

7.  _____ theories of aging suggest that aging is genetically programmed.

8.  When fibers of the axon become twisted, the resulting spiral-shaped masses that are formed are called _____ .

9.  Damaged and dying neurons that collect around a core of protein produce _____ .

10. Chemicals that allow communication between neurons are called _____ .

11. _____ is another name for cerebral vascular accident.

12. _____ are caused by interruptions of blood flow to the brain due to a blockage or bleeding in a cerebral artery.

13. _____ occurs when a cerebral blood artery ruptures.

14. _____ involve interruption in blood flow to the brain and are often an early warning sign of stroke.

15. Numerous small cerebral vascular accidents can lead to _____ .

16. The most common form of chronic respiratory disease in older adults is _____ disease.

17. _____ disease is caused by deterioration of the neurons in the midbrain, and it is characterized by very slow walking and hand tremors.

18. The difficulty in seeing close objects clearly is called _____ .

19. A substantial loss in the ability to hear high-pitched tones is called _____ .

20. The disruption of one's sleep-wake cycle, or _____ can lead to sleep disturbances.

# 14.2 KNOW THE DETAILS OF PHYSICAL CHANGES AND HEALTH

1. Cellular theories explain aging by focusing on processes that occur within individual cells, leading to the buildup of harmful substances over a lifetime.
   TRUE or FALSE

2. Free radicals and cross-linking are part of wear-and-tear theories of aging.
   TRUE or FALSE

3. Metabolic theories of aging state that aging is genetically programmed.
   TRUE or FALSE

4. Large numbers of neurofibrillary tangles are associated with Alzheimer's disease.
   TRUE or FALSE

5. With age, some dendrites shrivel up and die whereas others continue to grow.
   TRUE or FALSE

6. With age, the levels of neurotransmitters increase.
   TRUE or FALSE

7. The incidence of cardiovascular diseases increases significantly with age.
   TRUE or FALSE

8. Transient ischemic attacks (TIAs) are a form of incapacitating respiratory disease.
   TRUE or FALSE

9. Vascular dementia always has a gradual onset and progresses gradually.
   TRUE or FALSE

10. Chronic obstructive pulmonary disease is the most common incapacitating respiratory disease among older adults.
    TRUE or FALSE

11. Very slow walking, difficulty getting into and out of chairs, and a slow hand tremor are symptoms of Parkinson's disease.
    TRUE or FALSE

12. Presbycusis causes older adults' vision to become more susceptible to glare.
    TRUE or FALSE

13. Smell declines more than taste in late adulthood.
    TRUE or FALSE

14. Sensory changes may lead to accidents around the home.
    TRUE or FALSE

15. Older adults have more trouble sleeping than do younger adults.
    TRUE or FALSE

16. The incidence of cancer decreases with age.
    TRUE or FALSE

# 14.3 COGNITIVE PROCESSES

## TO MASTER THE LEARNING OBJECTIVES:

**What changes occur in attention and reaction time as people age? How do these changes relate to everyday life?**

- Define selective attention, vigilance, and attentional control and describe the age differences in each.

- Describe how reaction time and its components change with age.

- Describe how practice and experience influence psychomotor speed.

- Describe the physical changes that affect driving.

**What changes occur in memory with age? What can be done to remediate these changes?**

- Describe what happens to working memory with age and how this affects cognitive performance.

- Define explicit, implicit, episodic, and semantic memory and describe the typical age differences in each.

- Describe which autobiographical memories are most likely to be recalled.

- Describe how one's beliefs about one's memory affect memory ability.

- Describe the 2 steps that someone should take when trying to determine if one is suffering from abnormal memory problems.

- Explain the difference between internal and external memory aids and describe how the E-I-E-I-O framework combines these types of memory and memory aids.

**What is wisdom, and how is it related to age?**

- Explain how creative output varies across disciplines and across adulthood.

- Describe the 4 characteristics of wisdom that Baltes and his colleagues have described.

- Explain how life experiences and empathy are related to wisdom.

- Describe the 3 factors that seem to foster wisdom.


# 14.3 KNOW THE TERMS

| | |
|---|---|
| **Attentional control** | **Psychomotor speed** |
| **Episodic** | **Selective** |
| **Explicit** | **Semantic** |
| **External** | **Vigilance** |
| **Implicit** | **Working memory** |
| **Internal** | |


1. _____ attention involves the ability to pick out important from irrelevant information in the environment.

2. _____ also called sustained attention, involves the maintenance of attention over time.

3. The ability to focus, switch, and divide attention is called _____ .

4. The speed with which one can make a particular response is called _____ .

5. The processes and structures involved in holding information in mind while simultaneously using it is called _____ .

6. _____ memory involves the conscious and intentional recall of information.

7. _____ memory involves the unconscious and effortless recall of information.

8. The type of explicit memory that has to do with the conscious recollection of information from a specific time or event is called _____ .

9. The type of explicit memory that involves remembering words or concepts not tied to a specific time or event is called _____ .

10. _____ memory aids rely on environmental resources such as calendars or notebooks.

11. _____ memory aids rely on mental processes such as mental imagery.

## 14.3 KNOW THE DETAILS OF COGNITIVE PROCESSES

1. Research suggests that older adults perform more poorly than younger adults on tasks requiring selective attention.
   TRUE or FALSE

2. Older adults perform more poorly than younger adults on attentional control tasks when attention must be shifted fast or if the task is complex.
   TRUE or FALSE

3. Psychomotor speed increases with age.
   TRUE or FALSE

4. Reaction times slow down with age primarily because it takes older adults longer to decide that they need to respond.
   TRUE or FALSE

5. Working memory has an unlimited capacity.
   TRUE or FALSE

6. Working memory does not decline with age.
   TRUE or FALSE

7. Older adults perform equally to younger adults on episodic memory recall tasks.
   TRUE or FALSE

8. Age differences are greater on recognition memory tests than on recall memory tests.
   TRUE or FALSE

9. Beliefs about what happens to memory with aging can influence memory performance.
   TRUE or FALSE

10. Rote rehearsal is an example of an implicit-internal memory aid.
    TRUE or FALSE

11. The most frequently used memory interventions are classified as explicit-external according to the E-I-E-I-O framework.

    TRUE or FALSE

12. Creative output increases steadily throughout adulthood.

    TRUE or FALSE

13. Wisdom is more dependent on having extensive life experience in a particular area than on age.

    TRUE or FALSE

# 14.4 MENTAL HEALTH AND INTERVENTION

## TO MASTER THE LEARNING OBJECTIVES:

**How does depression in older adults differ from depression in younger adults? How is it diagnosed and treated?**

- Describe how depression is diagnosed, particularly in older adults.

- Describe the biological and psychosocial factors that may cause depression and how the influence of these factors may change with age.

- Describe the effects and possible side effects of HCAs, MAO inhibitors, and SSRIs when treating depression.

- Describe how behavior therapy and cognitive therapy can be used to treat depression.

**How are anxiety disorders treated in older adults?**

- Describe the symptoms associated with anxiety disorders.

- Describe how anxiety disorders are treated, particularly in older adults.

**What is Alzheimer's disease? How is it diagnosed and managed? What causes it?**

- Describe the symptoms and progression of Alzheimer's disease.

- Describe how Alzheimer's disease is diagnosed.

- Describe the possible causes of Alzheimer's disease.

- Describe what can be done to help Alzheimer's patients.

- Describe how spaced retrieval can be used to improve memory performance in Alzheimer's patients.

# 14.4 KNOW THE TERMS

| | |
|---|---|
| Alzheimer's disease | Heterocyclic |
| Amyloid | Incontinence |
| Anxiety disorders | Internal belief system |
| Behavior | MAO inhibitors |
| Cognitive | Selective serotonin reuptake inhibitors |
| Dementia | Spaced retrieval |
| Dysphoria | |

1. Feeling sad or down, which is the most prominent symptom of depression, is called _____ .

2. What one tells oneself about why certain events happen, or _____ may be a cause of depression.

3. _____ antidepressants are drugs that are used to treat depression, but they cannot be used by people who take medication to control hypertension or who have certain metabolic disorders.

4. _____ are drugs that are used to treat depression, but they cause dangerous interactions with certain foods such as cheddar cheese, wine, and chicken liver.

5. Antidepressants that work by boosting the level of serotonin are called _____ .

6. The basic assumption of _____ therapy is that depressed people experience too few rewards from their environments.

7. _____ therapy is based on the assumption that beliefs about oneself are responsible for depression.

8. _____ are characterized by severe anxiety for no apparent reason, phobias, and obsessive-compulsive disorders.

9. _____ is a family of diseases involving serious impairment of behavioral and cognitive functioning.

10. _____ is characterized by gradual decline in memory, confusion, difficulties in communicating, and changes in personality.

11. The loss of bladder control is called _____ .

12. _____ is a protein that is produced in abnormally high levels in Alzheimer's patients.

13. _____ involves teaching people with Alzheimer's to remember new information by gradually increasing the time between retrieval attempts.

# 14.4 KNOW THE DETAILS OF MENTAL HEALTH AND INTERVENTION

1.  The rate of severe depression increases from young adulthood to old age.
    TRUE or FALSE

2.  The most prominent symptom of depression is dysphoria.
    TRUE or FALSE

3.  Depression in later adulthood is likely to be a biochemical problem.
    TRUE or FALSE

4.  Depression in late adulthood does not respond well to treatment.
    TRUE or FALSE

5.  Anxiety disorders in late adulthood can be effectively treated with medication and psychotherapy.
    TRUE or FALSE

6.  The incidence of Alzheimer's disease increases with age.
    TRUE or FALSE

7.  The earlier the onset of Alzheimer's disease, the slower the disease usually progresses.
    TRUE or FALSE

8.  Definitive diagnosis of Alzheimer's disease is possible only by an autopsy of the brain after death.
    TRUE or FALSE

9.  Some forms of Alzheimer's disease appear to be inherited.
    TRUE or FALSE

10. Alzheimer's disease can be permanently reversed with medication.
    TRUE or FALSE

# SUMMARY

## 14.1 WHAT ARE OLDER ADULTS LIKE?

1.  **The Demographics of Aging**

The number of older adults is growing rapidly, especially the number of people over age _____ . In the future, older adults will be more _____ diverse and _____ educated than they are now.

2. **How Long Will You Live?**

Average life expectancy has _____ dramatically since 1900 century due mainly to improvements in health care. Useful life expectancy refers to the number of years one has that is free from debilitating disease. _____ life expectancy is the longest time any human can live. Genetic factors that can influence longevity include familial longevity and family history of certain diseases. Environmental factors that can influence longevity include acquired diseases, toxins, _____ and life style. Women have a longer average life expectancy at birth than men. Ethnic group differences are complex; depending on how old people are, the patterns of differences change.

3. **The Third-Fourth Distinction**

The Third Age refers to changes in research that led to cultural, medical, and economic advances for older adults (e.g., longer average longevity, increased quality of life). In contrast, the Fourth Age reflects the fact that the oldest-old are at the limits of their _____ , the rates of diseases such as cancer and dementia increase dramatically, and other aspects of psychological functioning (e.g., memory) also undergo significant and fairly _____ decline.

## 14.2 PHYSICAL CHANGES AND HEALTH

1. **Biological Theories of Aging**

There are four main biological theories of aging. _____ theory postulates that aging is caused by body systems simply wearing out. Cellular theories focus on reactions within cells involving _____ , telomeres, and cross-linking. Metabolic theories focus on changes in cell _____ . Programmed cell death theories propose that aging is genetically _____ . No single theory is sufficient to explain aging.

2. **Physiological Changes**

Three important structural changes in the neuron are: _____ , dendritic changes, and neuritic plaques. Each of these has important consequences for functioning because they reduce the effectiveness with which neurons transmit information. The risk of cardiovascular disease increases with age. Normal changes in the cardiovascular system include a build-up of _____ deposits

in the heart and arteries, decrease in the amount of blood the heart can pump, decline in heart
_____ tissue, and stiffening of the arteries. Most of these changes are affected by life style.
Stroke and vascular dementia cause significant cognitive impairment that depends on the area of the
brain damage. Strictly age-related changes in the respiratory system are hard to identify due to the
lifetime effects of pollution. However, older adults suffer _____ and the risk of chronic
obstructive pulmonary disorder increases. Parkinson's disease is caused by insufficient levels of
_____ and can be effectively managed with the drug L-dopa. In a minority of cases, dementia
develops. Age-related declines in vision and hearing are well documented. The main changes in vision
concern the structure of the eye and the retina. Changes in hearing mainly involve presbycusis; loss of
hearing, especially for _____ -pitched tones. However, similar declines with age, in taste,
smell, touch, pain, and temperature are not as clear.

3. **Health Issues**

Older adults have more _____ disturbances than do younger adults. Some of these
disturbances may be due to disrupted _____ rhythms. Nutritionally, most older adults do
not need vitamin or mineral supplements. Cancer risk _____ sharply with age. Being an
immigrant is related to having poorer health status due to _____ and barriers to care.

## 14.3 COGNITIVE PROCESSES

1. **Information Processing**

Older adults are much slower than younger adults at the _____ unless there is an advance
signal. Age differences in attention tasks are complex and depend on the level of difficulty; on easy
tasks, there are _____ differences, but on hard tasks younger adults do _____ . Older
adults' psychomotor speed is slower than younger adults'. However, the amount of slowing is lessened
if older adults have _____ or expertise on the task. Sensory and information processing
changes create problems for older drivers. _____ is another powerful explanatory concept
for changes in information processing with age.

2. **Memory**

Older adults typically do worse on tests of _____ ; age differences are less on recognition
tasks. Semantic memory is largely unaffected by aging, as is implicit memory. People tend to remember
best those events that occurred to them between the ages of _____ . What people believe to be

true about their memories is related to their memory _____ . Beliefs about whether cognitive abilities are supposed to change may be most important. Differentiating memory changes associated with aging from memory changes due to disease should be done through comprehensive evaluations. Memory training can be achieved in many ways. A useful framework is to combine _____ memory distinctions with external-internal types of memory aids.

3. **Creativity and Wisdom**

Research indicates that creative output peaks in late _____ or early middle age and declines thereafter, but that the point of peak activity _____ across disciplines and occupations. Wisdom has more to do with being an _____ in living than with age per se. Three factors that help people become wise are general personal conditions, specific _____ conditions, and facilitative life contexts.

## 14.4 MENTAL HEALTH AND INTERVENTION

1. **Depression**

The key symptom of depression is persistent sadness. Other psychological and physical symptoms also occur, but the importance of these depends on the _____ of the person reporting them. Major causes of depression include imbalances in _____ and psychosocial issues such as loss and internal belief systems. Depression can be treated with medications such as heterocyclic antidepressants, MAO inhibitors, and selective serotonin reuptake inhibitors, and through psychotherapy such as behavioral or _____ therapy.

2. **Anxiety Disorders**

A variety of anxiety disorders afflict many older adults. All of these disorders can be effectively treated with either medications or _____ .

3. **Dementia: Alzheimer's Disease**

Dementia is a family of diseases that causes severe _____ impairment. Alzheimer's disease is the most common form of irreversible dementia. Symptoms of Alzheimer's disease include memory impairment, _____ changes, and behavioral changes. These symptoms usually worsen gradually, with rates varying considerably among individuals. Definitive diagnosis of Alzheimer's disease can only be made following a _____ . Diagnosis of probable Alzheimer's disease can be made only after a thorough process through which other potential causes are eliminated. Most researchers are focusing on a probable genetic cause of Alzheimer's disease. Although Alzheimer's disease is incurable, various therapeutic interventions, such as _____ , can be made to improve the quality of the patient's life.

# TEST YOURSELF

## MULTIPLE-CHOICE QUESTIONS

1. The fastest growing age group in the United States is
   a.  20 to 40 years.
   b.  40 to 60 years.
   c.  60 to 85 years.
   d.  over 85 years.

2. According to the graph below, which of the following ethnic groups has had the smallest increase in the relative number of older adults?

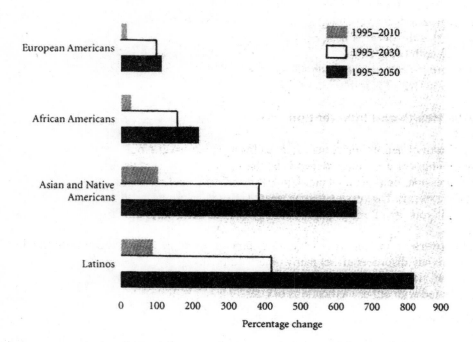

a. Native Americans
b. Asian Americans
c. Hispanic Americans
d. European Americans

3. The age at which half of the people born in a particular year will have died is referred to as
   a. longevity.
   b. useful life expectancy.
   c. average life expectancy.
   d. maximum life expectancy.

4. The maximum life expectancy for humans is about
   a. 80 years.
   b. 100 years.
   c. 120 years.
   d. 150 years.

5. Which of the following statements about life expectancy is true?
   a. At birth, the life expectancy of African Americans is longer than that of European Americans.
   b. At 85 years of age, the life expectancy of African Americans is longer than that of European Americans.
   c. At birth, the life expectancy for males is longer than for females.
   d. At 85 years of age, the life expectancy for males is longer than for females.

6. Which of the following descriptions accurately characterizes the Fourth Age?
   a. substantial potential for physical and mental fitness, with improvement in each generation
   b. high levels of emotional and personal well-being
   c. effective strategies to master the gains and losses of later life
   d. high prevalence of dementia

7. _____ adequately explains most aspects of aging.
   a. Wear-and-tear theory
   b. Cellular theory
   c. Programmed cell death theory
   d. No single theory

8. The _____ theory of aging compares the aging human body to an old, deteriorating machine.
   a. cellular
   b. metabolic
   c. wear-and-tear
   d. programmed cell death

9. Theories of aging that focus on free radicals or cross-linking are categorized as _____ theories of aging.
   a. cellular
   b. metabolic
   c. wear-and-tear
   d. programmed cell death

10. When a neuron's axon fibers become twisted together they form spiral-shaped masses called
    a. neuritic plaques.
    b. dendritic changes.
    c. neurofibrillary tangles.
    d. neurotransmitters.

11. Damaged and dying neurons sometimes collect around a core of protein, producing
    a. neurofibrillary tangles.
    b. neuritic plaques.
    c. neurotransmitters.
    d. transient ischemic attacks.

12. _____ is caused by interruptions in the blood flow in the brain.
    a. Cardiac arrest
    b. A stroke
    c. Hypertension
    d. Chronic obstructive pulmonary disease

13. Fred walks very slowly, has difficulty getting in and out of chairs, and has a hand tremor. Fred exhibits many of the symptoms of
    a. cardiovascular disease.
    b. Alzheimer's disease.
    c. Parkinson's disease.
    d. vascular dementia.

14. Older adults _____ than younger adults.
    a. are less bothered by glare
    b. take less time to adapt to changes in illumination
    c. have more difficulty seeing details
    d. require less light to see

15. Henry is 75 years of age. He is most likely to have experienced a decline in
    a. smell.
    b. taste.
    c. temperature sensitivity.
    d. pain sensitivity.

16. The ability to distinguish important from irrelevant information in the environment is referred to as
    a. selective attention.
    b. attentional control.
    c. vigilance.
    d. free recall.

17. On tasks requiring attentional control,
    a. older adults perform significantly better than younger adults on all tasks.
    b. younger adults perform significantly better than older adults on all tasks.
    c. younger adults perform significantly better when tasks are simple, but there is no difference when tasks are complex.
    d. younger adults perform significantly better when tasks are complex, but there is no difference when tasks are simple.

18. Researchers agree that _____ is a universal behavioral change in aging.
    a. an increase in wisdom
    b. psychomotor slowing
    c. recognition memory decline
    d. intellectual decline

19. On episodic memory recall tasks,
    a. older adults tend to perform more poorly than younger adults.
    b. younger adults usually perform more poorly than older adults.
    c. younger and older adults usually perform similarly.
    d. age differences are eliminated when cues or reminders are given during recall.

20. Seventy-year-old Marvella believes her memory is much worse than it used to be. Which of the following statements about Marvella is most likely to be true?
    a. Marvella will probably work harder at trying to remember something than individuals who believe their memories are good.
    b. Marvella's beliefs about her memory getting worse may actually cause her to perform more poorly on memory tasks.
    c. Marvella's beliefs about how memory changes with age are not likely to affect her estimates of her own memory.
    d. Marvella probably has Alzheimer's Disease.

21. In the E-I-E-I-O framework, memory aids that rely on mental processes such as imagery are referred to as
    a. internal.
    b. external.
    c. implicit.
    d. explicit.

22. Margaret always prepares a list before going shopping. Her shopping list is an example of an _____ memory aid.
    a. implicit-internal
    b. implicit-external
    c. explicit-external
    d. explicit-internal

23. Wisdom is
    a. the same thing as creativity.
    b. found exclusively in older adults.
    c. associated with life experience.
    d. unrelated to cognitive ability.

24. Which of the following is not a factor that would help one to become wise?
    a. general personal conditions
    b. specific expertise conditions
    c. facilitative life contexts
    d. self-absorption

25. Trudy is suffering from dysphoria. In other words, Trudy
    a. has an anxiety disorder.
    b. has Alzheimer's disease.
    c. is unable to speak.
    d. is feeling sad and depressed.

26. Internal belief systems are of particular relevance for views of depression that focus on _____ factors.
    a. psychosocial
    b. biochemical
    c. neurological
    d. physiological

27. Lauren was diagnosed as depressed. To treat her depression, she was advised to increase the number of activities in which she was involved, so she joined a community service organization and started going out with friends at least once a week. This kind of treatment is associated with
    a. cognitive therapy.
    b. behavior therapy.
    c. psychoanalysis.
    d. a biochemical approach.

28. Anxiety disorders
    a. are more common in younger adults than in older adults.
    b. can be effectively treated with relaxation therapy.
    c. cannot be successfully treated with psychotherapy.
    d. require larger doses of medication to treat the disorder in late adulthood than in early adulthood.

29. Eighty-year-old Alfred is becoming very forgetful, is frequently confused about where he is, often can't think of words he wants to use, and sometimes fails to recognize members of his family. Alfred is displaying many of the symptoms of
    a. depression.
    b. an anxiety disorder.
    c. Alzheimer's disease.
    d. normal aging.

30. Definitive diagnosis of Alzheimer's disease can only be made based on
    a. blood tests.
    b. neurological tests.
    c. psychological tests.
    d. autopsy of the brain after the person has died.

31. _____ is a protein that is produced in abnormally high levels in Alzheimer's patients, perhaps causing the neurofibrillary tangles and neuritic plaques associated with the disease.
    a. Amyloid
    b. Monoamine oxidase inhibitor
    c. Serotonin
    d. Thioridazine

32. Spaced retrieval is a behavioral intervention that has been used to treat individuals with
    a. depression.
    b. anxiety disorders.
    c. Alzheimer's disease.
    d. presbycusis.

## ESSAY QUESTIONS

1.  Recently your friend Mitchell visited an old cemetery while on vacation, and he was shocked at the number of young children, adolescents, and young adult children who died one-hundred years ago. One family had 5 children and only one lived to old age. Mitchell knows that people live longer now but had no idea that things had changed that much. What can you tell Mitchell about the reasons for increased average life expectancy?

2.  Recently you and a friend were talking about growing old and aging. Your friend said, "Well, I think that you grow old because everything just wears out. The average television lasts 15 years, the average VCR lasts 10 years, and the average person lasts about 75 years." What can you tell your friend about the adequacy of wear-and-tear theories of aging in explaining aging in general?

3.  Another friend, who lives with his grandmother, commented on the fact that every time his grandmother walks into a room she turns on some lights even if the room isn't dark. Your friend thinks that this is strange behavior particularly when his grandmother complains about the glare on bright, sunny days. What can you tell your friend about the age-related changes in the eye and their effects on vision that will explain his grandmother's behavior?

4.  In the last few weeks, your grandmother forgot an item at the grocery store, she misplaced her keys, and forgot about a dentist appointment. She is worried that these memory failures are a symptom of a more serious problem such as Alzheimer's disease. What can you tell your grandmother about age differences in memory and the incidence of abnormal memory problems that might relieve some of her worries?

5.  Recently, a friend asked you for advice and then told you that you were "wise beyond your years." What can you tell your friend about the relation between age and wisdom, characteristics of wise people, and Baltes' 3 factors that facilitate becoming wise?

6.  Lately your grandfather has been staying in bed most of the day, he seems to be apathetic and expressionless, and he has lost his appetite. Your parents are worried about him because they think that there may be something physically wrong with him. What can you tell your parents about the signs of depression in older adults?

# SOLUTIONS

## 14.1 KNOW THE TERMS

1. demographers (536)
2. population pyramid (536)
3. longevity (539)
4. average (540)
5. useful (540)
6. maximum (540)

## 14.1 KNOW THE DETAILS OF THE DEMOGRAPHICS OF AGING

1. T, (536)
2. T, (536)
3. T, (538)
4. F, (538)
5. T, (538)
6. F, (539)
7. F, (539)
8. F, (540)
9. F, (540)
10. T, (540)
11. F, (542)
12. T, (541)
13. T, (541)
14. F, (542)
15. T, (543)

## 14.2 KNOW THE TERMS

1. wear-and-tear (544)
2. Cellular (544)
3. telomeres (545)
4. Free radicals (545)
5. Cross-linking (545)
6. Metabolic (545)
7. Programmed cell death (545)
8. neurofibrillary tangles (546)
9. neuritic plaques (547)
10. neurotransmitters (547)
11. Stroke (547)
12. Cerebral vascular accidents (547)
13. Hemorrhage (548)
14. Transient ischemic attacks (548)
15. vascular dementia (548)
16. chronic obstructive pulmonary (549)
17. Parkinson's (549)
18. presbyopia (550)
19. presbycusis (551)
20. circadian rhythm (553)

## 14.2 KNOW THE DETAILS OF PHYSICAL CHANGES AND HEALTH

1. T, (544)
2. F, (545)
3. F, (545)
4. T, (546)
5. T, (546)
6. F, (547)
7. T, (547)
8. F, (548)
9. F, (548)
10. T, (549)
11. T, (549)
12. F, (551)
13. T, (552)
14. T, (552)
15. T, (553)
16. F, (554)

## 14.3 KNOW THE TERMS

1. Selective (555)

2. Vigilance (555)
3. attentional control (555)
4. psychomotor speed (556)
5. working memory (558)

6. Explicit (558)
7. Implicit (558)
8. episodic (558)
9. semantic (558)

10. External (561)
11. Internal (561)

## 14.3 KNOW THE DETAILS OF COGNITIVE PROCESSES

1. T, (555)
2. T, (556)
3. F, (556)
4. T, (556)
5. F, (558)

6. F, (558)
7. F, (559)
8. F, (559)
9. T, (560)
10. F, (561)

11. T, (561)
12. F, (562)
13. T, (563)

## 14.4 KNOW THE TERMS

1. dysphoria (565)
2. internal belief systems (566)
3. Heterocyclic (566)
4. MAO inhibitors (566)

5. selective serotonin reuptake inhibitors (566)
6. behavior (566)
7. Cognitive (567)
8. Anxiety disorders (567)

9. Dementia (567)
10. Alzheimer's disease (568)
11. incontinence (568)
12. Amyloid (569)
13. Spaced retrieval (571)

## 14.4 KNOW THE DETAILS OF MENTAL HEALTH AND INTERVENTION

1. F, (565)
2. T, (565)
3. T, (566)
4. F, (567)

5. T, (567)
6. T, (568)
7. F, (568)
8. T, (569)

9. T, (569)
10. F, (571)

## SUMMARY

### 14.1 WHAT ARE OLDER ADULTS LIKE?

1. 85 (538); ethnically (538); more (538)

2. increased (540); Maximum (540); pollutants (540)

3. functional capacity (543); rapid (543)

### 14.2 PHYSICAL CHANGES AND HEALTH

1. Wear-and-tear (544); free radicals (544); metabolism (545); programmed (545)

2. neurofibrillary tangles (546); fat (547); muscle (547); shortness of breath (549); dopamine (549); high (551)

3. sleep (553); circadian (553); increases (554); communication problems (554)

## 14.3 COGNITIVE PROCESSES

1. visual search (555); few (555); better (555); practice (556); Working memory (558)

2. episodic recall (559); 10 and 30 (559); performance (560); implicit-explicit (561)

3. young adulthood (563); varies (563); expert (563); expertise (563)

## 14.4 MENTAL HEALTH AND INTERVENTION

1. age (565); neurotransmitters (566); cognitive (567)

2. psychotherapy (567)

3. cognitive (568); personality (568); brain autopsy (569); spaced retrieval (571)

# TEST YOURSELF

## MULTIPLE-CHOICE QUESTIONS

1. D, (538)
2. D, (538)
3. C, (540)
4. C, (540)
5. B, (541)
6. D, (543)
7. D, (544)
8. C, (544)
9. A, (545)
10. C, (546)
11. B, (547)

12. B, (547)
13. C, (549)
14. C, (550)
15. A, (552)
16. A, (551)
17. D, (555)
18. B, (556)
19. A, (559)
20. B, (559)
21. A, (561)
22. C, (561)

23. C, (563)
24. D, (563)
25. D, (565)
26. A, (566)
27. B, (566)
28. B, (567)
29. C, (568)
30. D, (569)
31. A, (569)
32. C, (571)

## ESSAY QUESTIONS

1. The average life expectancy is the age at which half of the people born in a particular year will have died. Average life expectancy has increased dramatically since the early 1900s. Many people used to die during childhood from diseases or died as young adults from infections or complications of pregnancy and childbirth. Life expectancy increased when diseases such as polio and small pox were eliminated and drugs such as antibiotics were developed. One's life expectancy is determined by genetic factors and environmental factors. Even though many aspects of the environment have improved since the turn of the century, diseases, pollution, and lifestyle factors continue to influence life expectancy. Genes also may influence one's risk for certain disease as well as how well older people cope with disease. In other words, average life expectancy is much greater for people now, but there are still many factors that work to decrease one's life expectancy. (539-541)

2. Your friend has just explained the wear-and-tear theory of aging. This theory suggests that people are like machines, and with age their bodies don't work as well and eventually wear out. This wear-and-tear view is good at explaining osteoarthritis where the cartilage in joints wears out after years of use. While this theory of aging may explain some aspects of aging, it does not adequately explain aging in general. (544)

3. With age, less light passes through the eye which means that older adults need more illumination to see. Older adults also are more sensitive to glare and take longer to adapt to changes in illumination. So, a young person

like your friend may find that there is adequate illumination in a room, but an older adult may need to turn on a few lights to see. Even though older adults need more light, the increased sensitivity to glare means that they are more likely to be uncomfortable in the bright sunlight. In other words, the behavior of your friend's grandmother is not unusual for someone her age. (549)

4. It is true that older adults don't do as well as younger adults on tests of episodic recall, but their memory performance improves when the memory task is easier (e.g, they are given cues or are only asked to recognize information). Unfortunately, though, older adults often believe that they have poor memories. These negative beliefs may lead older adults to put less effort into remembering information and, as a result, they will remember less. People may even convince themselves that their memory problems are much worse than they really are. Your grandmother should realize that Alzheimer's is not a normal part of aging and most older adults are not affected by it. Your grandmother also should realize that younger adults frequently have similar memory failures, and until her memory failures interfere with her daily living, she should not assume she is becoming senile. In fact, she may have better memory functioning if she changes her beliefs about her memory and finds ways to compensate for the areas in which she shows some decline. (559-561)

5. Contrary to popular opinion, research does not find an association between age and wisdom. Being wise seems to be associated more with extensive life experiences with the type of problem given. Wise people also are more likely to integrate thinking and feeling to come up with a solution to a problem. So, empathy and compassion seem to be important characteristics of wise people. Baltes identified 3 factors that facilitate the development of wisdom: 1) general personal condition such as mental ability, 2) specific expertise conditions such as mentoring or practice, and 3) facilitative life contexts such as education or life experiences. So, you can tell your friend that you are wise because you are an empathic and compassionate person and you have many life experiences in the area in which he needed advice. (563)

6. Your grandfather may have a physical problem, but he may also be suffering from depression. In older adults, depression is characterized not only by feelings of dysphoria but also by apathy, expressionless behavior, confining oneself to bed, neglecting oneself, and making derogatory comments about oneself. Loss of appetite, insomnia, and trouble breathing can also be signs of depression. Your grandfather should be evaluated to rule out any physical problems and to consider the possibility of depression. (565-566)

# SOCIAL ASPECTS OF LATER LIFE

This chapter focuses on the social aspects of later life such as theories of psychosocial aging, personality, retirement, social relationships with family and friends, and the social issues of aging.

# 15.1 THEORIES OF PSYCHOSOCIAL AGING

## TO MASTER THE LEARNING OBJECTIVES:

**What is continuity theory?**

- Define continuity theory and describe the difference between internal and external continuity.

**What is the competence and environmental press model, and how do docility and proactivity relate to the model?**

- Define competence and environmental press and explain how they are related.

- Define adaptation level, zone of maximum performance potential, and zone of maximum comfort.

- Define proactivity and docility and describe how they are related to competence and environmental press.

# 15.1 KNOW THE TERMS

**Adaptation level**     **Environmental press**

**Competence**      **Proactivity**

**Continuity**       **Maximum performance potential**

**Docility**        **Zone of maximum comfort**

1. According to _____ theory, people tend to cope with daily life in later adulthood in the same ways that they coped during earlier periods of life.

2. _____ is the upper limit of a person's functioning in the domains of physical health, sensory-perceptual skills, motor skills, cognitive skills, and ego strength.

3. _____ is the number and types of physical, interpersonal, or social demands that the environment puts on people.

4. _____ is the area where the press level is average for a particular level of competence, and behavior and affect are normal.

5. Press levels that are slightly higher than average tend to improve performance so that it is in the zone of _____ .

6. Press levels that are slightly below average create the _____ where people are able to live happily without having to worry about environmental demands.

7. When people exert control over their lives and choose new behaviors to meet new needs, they are exhibiting _____ .

8. When people have little control over their lives and they allow situations to dictate their options, they are exhibiting _____ .

# 15.1 KNOW THE DETAILS OF THEORIES OF PSYCHOSOCIAL AGING

1. According to continuity theory, people cope best with aging if there is as much change as possible in their lives.
   TRUE or FALSE

2. Maintaining internal, but not external, continuity is important for adaptation in later life.

   TRUE or FALSE

3. According to the competence and environmental press model (see figure on next page), people tend to cope with daily life in later adulthood by applying familiar strategies based on past experience.

   TRUE or FALSE

4. Competence is defined as the upper limit of a person's ability to function in five domains.

   TRUE or FALSE

5. The zone of maximum comfort occurs when the environmental press is slightly higher than average for a particular level of competence.

   TRUE or FALSE

6. Few demands on a person with high competence tends to result in maladaptive behavior and negative affect.

   TRUE or FALSE

7. Proactivity occurs when people allow the situation to dictate the options they have.

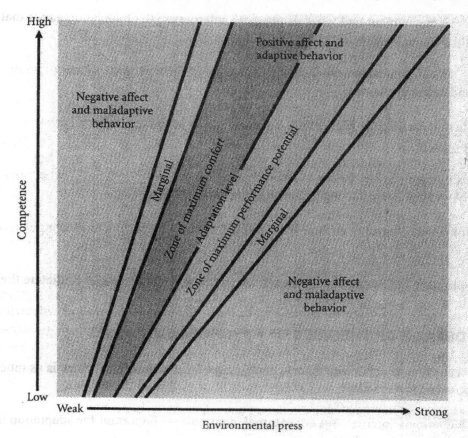

SOURCE: From "Ecology of the Aging Process," by M. P. Lawton and L. Nahemow. In C. Eisdorfer and M. P. Lawton (Eds.), *The Psychology of Adult Development and Aging*, pp. 619–674. Copyright © 1973 American Psychological Association. Reprinted with permission of the authors.

TRUE or FALSE

# 15.2 PERSONALITY, SOCIAL COGNITION, AND SPIRITUALITY

## TO MASTER THE LEARNING OBJECTIVES:

**What is integrity in late life? How do people achieve it?**

- Describe Erikson's crisis of integrity vs despair, and explain how the life review process is related to this crisis.

- Describe the results of research on the relations between the life review process and achieving integrity.

**How is well-being defined in adulthood? How do people view themselves differently as they age?**

- Define subjective well-being and the factors related to it.

- Describe the 3 processes that are related to control beliefs in later life.

- Explain how and why control beliefs vary across different domains.

- Define assimilative and accommodative activities and explain how they are related to age.

**What role does religion play in late life?**

- Describe how religion is used to cope with stress.

- Describe the effects of spiritual support on personal well-being and self-worth.

- Explain the 3 steps involved in using spirituality to cope with problems.

- Describe the importance of religion and the church in the lives of African Americans.

- Describe the importance of religion to Mexican Americans and Native Americans.

## 15.2 KNOW THE TERMS

| | |
|---|---|
| **Integrity vs despair** | **Spiritual support** |
| **Life review** | **Subjective well-being** |

1. According to Erikson, the crisis of later life _____ involves the process by which people try to make sense of their lives.

2. The process by which people reflect over the events and experiences they have had over their lives is called _____ .

3. The positive evaluation of one's life associated with positive feelings is called _____ .

4. _____ includes seeking pastoral care, participation in organized and non-organized religious activities, and expressing faith in a God who cares for people.

## 15.2 KNOW THE DETAILS OF PERSONALITY, SOCIAL COGNITION, AND SPIRITUALITY

1. According to Erikson, people begin struggling with the issue of intimacy versus isolation during late adulthood.
   TRUE or FALSE

2. To achieve integrity, a person must come to terms with the choices and events that made his or her life unique.

   TRUE or FALSE

3. Engaging in a life review is associated with achieving integrity.

   TRUE or FALSE

4. Subjective well-being refers to a positive evaluation of one's life associated with positive feelings.

   TRUE or FALSE

5. Subjective well-being is related to hardiness, chronic illness, marital status, social network, and stress.

   TRUE or FALSE

6. Compared to middle-aged adults, older adults report lower stress regarding health and higher stress regarding finances and housing conditions.

   TRUE or FALSE

7. Accommodative activities tend to increase during childhood then plateau across adulthood whereas assimilative activities increase with age across adulthood.

   TRUE or FALSE

8. Older adults use religion more than they use family or friends to help themselves cope.

   TRUE or FALSE

9. When under high levels of stress, individuals who rely on spiritual support report better personal well-being than do people who do not rely on spiritual support.

   TRUE or FALSE

10. Regular church attendance is a predictor of life satisfaction among African Americans.

    TRUE or FALSE

# 15.3 I USED TO WORK AT....: LIVING IN RETIREMENT

## TO MASTER THE LEARNING OBJECTIVES:

**What does being retired mean?**

- Describe how retirement is related to one's occupational identity.

- Explain the differences between "crisp" and "blurred" retirement processes.

- Define *bridge job*.

- Describe ethnic differences in the retirement process.

**Why do people retire?**

- Describe how health is related to the decision to retire.

- Describe the main factors that influence a woman's decision to retire.

- Describe ethnic differences in the decision to retire.

**How satisfied are retired people?**

- Describe the factors that are related to a successful adjustment to retirement.

- Describe the 3 stereotypes about retirement and explain the research results that refute the stereotypes.

**How do retirees keep busy?**

- Give examples of the activities that cater to retired adults.

- Explain the reasons why retirees volunteer in the community.

- Explain the reasons for an increased rate of volunteerism by retirees.

# 15.3 KNOW THE DETAILS OF RETIREMENT

1. Retirement is best defined as a complete withdrawal from the work force.
   TRUE or FALSE

2. A "blurred" retirement involves making a clean break from employment by stopping work entirely.
   TRUE or FALSE

3. The meaning of retirement varies by culture.
   TRUE or FALSE

4. Feeling that retirement is a choice rather than a requirement is related to adjustment to retirement.
   TRUE or FALSE

5. Men and women base their decisions to retire on the same factors.
   TRUE or FALSE

6. Retirement is an important life transition.
   TRUE or FALSE

7. Men who place more importance on family roles are more satisfied with retirement.
   TRUE or FALSE

8. Health begins to decline as soon as people stop working.
   TRUE or FALSE

9. Retirement dramatically reduces the number and quality of personal friendships.
   TRUE or FALSE

10. Retired people become much less active overall.

    TRUE or FALSE

11. The rate of volunteerism among older adults is expected to decline in the future.

    TRUE or FALSE

# 15.4 FRIENDS AND FAMILY IN LATE LIFE

## TO MASTER THE LEARNING OBJECTIVES:

**What role do friends and family play in late life?**

- Define social convoy and describe how the size and amount of support from it are related to different generations.

- Describe the importance of friendships to older women, particularly widows.

- Describe the 5 types of sibling relationships that are found among older adults: intimate, congenial, loyal, apathetic, and hostile.

- Explain how sibling relationships with sisters differ from those with brothers.

**What are older adults' marriages like?**

- Describe marital satisfaction in older couples.

- Describe the characteristics of older married couples.

- Describe long-term gay and lesbian partnerships and the possible effects of aging.

**What is it like to provide basic care for one's partner?**

- Explain how spousal caregiving is related to marital satisfaction and the caregivers' emotional state.

- Describe how feelings of competence affect spousal caregivers.

**How do people cope with widowhood? How do men and women differ?**

- Describe who is most likely to be widowed and describe the typical length of widowhood.

- Describe how widowhood affects other social relationships.

- Describe the similarities and differences in how men and women react to widowhood.

**What special issues are involved in being a great-grandparent?**

- Describe the typical characteristics of great-grandparents.

- Describe the 3 important aspects of great-grandparenthood.

## 15.4 KNOW THE TERMS

**Social convoy**                    **Socioemotional selectivity**

1.  The group of people who provides support during good and bad times throughout one's life is called a

    _____ .

2.  _____ implies that social contact is motivated by many goals, including information seeking, self-concept, and emotional regulation.

## 15.4 KNOW THE DETAILS OF FRIENDS AND FAMILY IN LATE LIFE

1.  The size of the social convoy gets larger with age.
    TRUE or FALSE

2.  Older adults' life satisfaction is more strongly related to the quality of relationships with younger family members than with the quality of relationships with friends.
    TRUE or FALSE

3.  Older adults develop fewer new relationships than do younger or middle-aged adults.
    TRUE or FALSE

4.  The majority of older adults have hostile and apathetic relationships with their siblings.
    TRUE or FALSE

5.  Marital satisfaction is usually high in older couples.
    TRUE or FALSE

6.  Spousal caregivers who perceive themselves as competent to provide care report fewer and less intense caregiving problems than spousal caregivers who see themselves as less competent.
    TRUE or FALSE

7.  Men are more likely than women to experience the death of a spouse.
    TRUE or FALSE

8.  Men have a higher risk than women of dying, themselves, after the death of their spouses.
    TRUE or FALSE

9.  Men are usually older than women when they are widowed.
    TRUE or FALSE

10. Remarriage after being widowed is more likely than after divorce.
    TRUE or FALSE

11. Great-grandparents are usually less involved with the children than are grandparents.
    TRUE or FALSE

# 15.5 SOCIAL ISSUES AND AGING

## TO MASTER THE LEARNING OBJECTIVES:

**Who are frail older adults? How common is frailty?**

- Define frail older adults and describe how the proportion of these older adults changes with increasing age.

- Define activities of daily living and instrumental activities of daily living.

- Describe the prevalence of frailty.

**Where do older adults live in the community?**

- Describe the percentage of people who live in nursing homes from various age groups.

- Explain how the increase in the number of assisted-living facilities has influenced the rate of nursing home residence.

- Define intermediate care and skilled nursing care.

**Who are the most likely people to live in nursing homes? What are the characteristics of good nursing homes?**

- Describe the typical nursing home resident and explain why these people are more likely to be in nursing homes.

- Describe the factors that are important in determining if a nursing home is good or not.

- Describe important things one should do when visiting someone in a nursing home.

**How do you know if an older adult is abused or neglected? Which people are most likely to be abused and to be abusers?**

- Describe the problems associated with defining elder abuse and neglect.

- Describe the prevalence of elder abuse and neglect.

- Describe the victims of elder abuse.

- Explain the causes of elder abuse.

**What are key social policy issues affecting older adults?**

- Describe political activity in older adults.

- Describe how the aging of baby boomers will affect Social Security.

- Describe how the aging of baby boomers will affect Medicare.

## 15.5 KNOW THE TERMS

| | |
|---|---|
| **Activities of daily living** | **Instrumental activities of daily living** |
| **Assisted living** | **Intermediate** |
| **Frail older adults** | **Patronizing** |
| **Infantilization** | **Skilled nursing** |

1. People over the age of 65 who have physical disabilities, are very ill, and may have some cognitive or psychological disorders are considered _____ .

2. Basic self-care tasks that include bathing, eating, toileting, walking, and dressing are called _____ .

3. Activities that require intellectual competence and planning such as paying bills, shopping, and taking medications properly are called _____ .

4. _____ facilities provide a supportive living arrangement for people who need assistance with ADLs or IADLs, but who are not so impaired that they need 24-hour care.

5. _____ care in nursing homes involves 24-hour supervision but not at an intense level.

6. _____ care in nursing homes involves 24-hour care with constant monitoring and provision of medical services.

7. Speech that is slower, has exaggerated intonation, higher pitch, increased volume, more repetitions, closed-ended questions, and simplified vocabulary and grammar is called _____ speech.

8. The inappropriate use of a person's first name, terms of endearment, simplified expressions, short imperatives, and assumptions that a person has no memory is called _____ .

## 15.5 KNOW THE DETAILS OF SOCIAL ISSUES AND AGING

1. Frail older adults constitute a majority of the population over 65.
   TRUE or FALSE

2. Bathing and dressing are examples of activities of daily living.
   TRUE or FALSE

3. Instrumental activities of daily living are actions that require some intellectual competence and planning.
   TRUE or FALSE

4. The number of people needing help with activities of daily living decreases with age.
   TRUE or FALSE

5. The majority of older adults live in nursing homes.
   TRUE or FALSE

6. Men are more likely than women to be in a nursing home.
   TRUE or FALSE

7. Nursing homes with a "person-centered planning" approach try to increase residents perceived level of personal control.
   TRUE or FALSE

8. Using a person's first name when it is not appropriate is a form of infantilization.
   TRUE or FALSE

9. The most common form of elder abuse is neglect.
   TRUE or FALSE

10. Adults over age 80 are abused more often than people under age 80.
    TRUE or FALSE

11. Abuse is associated with intrapersonal problems of the caregiver, such as substance abuse and behavior problems.
    TRUE or FALSE

12. The economic well-being of the majority of older adults is much worse now than it used to be.
    TRUE or FALSE

13. Adults over age 65 are the least politically active of all age groups.
    TRUE or FALSE

14. Social Security was originally designed to provide complete financial support for older adults.
    TRUE or FALSE

15. U.S. citizens over 65 are eligible to receive Medicare for their medical insurance.
    TRUE or FALSE

# SUMMARY

## 15.1 THEORIES OF PSYCHOSOCIAL AGING

1. **Continuity Theory**

Continuity theory is based on the view that people respond to daily life in later adulthood by applying _____ strategies based on past experience to maintain and preserve both internal and external structures.

2. **Competence and Environmental Press**

According to competence-environmental press theory, people's optimal adaptation occurs when there is a balance between their ability to cope and the level of environmental _____ placed on them. When balance is not achieved, behavior becomes maladaptive. When people choose _____ behaviors they exert proactive control over their lives. When people allow the situation to dictate their options they demonstrate _____ . Several studies support the applicability of competence-environmental press theory to a variety of real world situations.

## 15.2 PERSONALITY DEVELOPMENT IN LATER LIFE

1. **Integrity Versus Despair**

Older adults face the Eriksonian struggle of _____ versus despair, primarily through a life review. Integrity involves _____ one's life for what it is; despair involves _____ about one's past. People who reach integrity become self-affirming and self-accepting, and judge their lives to have been worthwhile and good.

2. **Well-Being and Social Cognition**

Subjective well-being is a positive evaluation of _____ associated with positive feelings. Personal control beliefs also play a major role in behavior and _____ . The development of personal control across adulthood _____ across domains.

3. **Religiosity and Spiritual Support**

Older adults use religion and spiritual support more often than any other strategy to help them _____ with problems of life. This is especially true for _____ who are more active in their church groups and attend services more frequently.

## 15.3 I USED TO WORK AT...: LIVING IN RETIREMENT

1. **What Does Being Retired Mean?**

Retirement is a complex _____ by which people withdraw from _____ employment. No single definition is adequate for all ethnic groups; self-definition involves several factors, including _____ for certain social programs.

2. **Why Do People Retire?**

People generally retire because they _____ although some people are forced to retire or retire because of serious _____ problems such as cardiovascular disease or cancer. However, there are important gender and ethnic differences in reasons people retire and how they label themselves after retirement. Most of the research is based on European American men from traditional marriages.

3. **Adjustment to Retirement**

Retirement is an important life transition. Most people are _____ with retirement. Most retired people typically maintain their _____ , friendship networks, and _____ levels, at least in the years immediately following retirement. For men, _____ are all-important; little is known about predictors of women's retirement satisfaction. Most retired people stay busy in activities such as volunteer work and helping others.

4. **Keeping Busy in Retirement**

From a life course perspective, it is important to maintain social integration in retirement. Participation in community organizations and _____ are primary ways of achieving this.

## 15.4 FRIENDS AND FAMILY IN LATER LIFE

1. **Friends and Siblings**

A person's _____ is an important source of satisfaction in late life. Patterns of friendships among older adults are very similar to those of young adults, but older adults are more _____ Sibling relationships are especially important in old age. Five types of sibling relationships have been identified: intimate, congenial, loyal, apathetic, and hostile. Loyal and congenial types are the most common. Ties between _____ are the strongest.

2. **Marriage and Gay and Lesbian Partnerships**

Long-term marriages tend to be happy until one partner develops serious _____ problems. Older married couples show a lower potential for _____ and greater potential for pleasure. Long-term gay and lesbian relationships tend to be very _____ in characteristics to long-term heterosexual marriages.

3.  **Caring for a Spouse**

    Caring for a spouse puts considerable strain on the relationship. The degree of marital _____ strongly affects how spousal caregivers perceive stress. Although caught off guard initially, most spousal caregivers are able to provide _____ care. Perceptions of _____ among spousal caregivers at the outset of caregiving may be especially important.

4.  **Widowhood**

    Widowhood is a difficult transition for most people. Feelings of _____ are hard to cope with, especially during the first few months following bereavement. Widows and widowers often have _____ social contact than when they were married. Men generally have problems in social relationships and in _____ tasks; women tend to have more severe _____ problems.

5.  **Great-Grandparenthood**

    Becoming a great-grandparent is an important source of personal _____ for many older adults. Great-grandparents as a group are more _____ to each other than grandparents are. Three aspects of great-grandparenthood are most important: sense of personal and family renewal; new _____ in life; and a major life milestone.

## 15.5 SOCIAL ISSUES AND AGING

1.  **Frail Older Adults**

    The number of frail older adults is growing. Frailty is defined in terms of impairment in activities of daily living (basic _____ skills) and instrumental activities of daily living (actions that require _____ or planning). As many as half of the women over age 85 may need assistance with ADLs or IADLs. Supportive environments are useful in optimizing competence and environmental press.

2.  **Living in Nursing Homes**

    Two levels of care are provided in nursing homes: intermediate care and skilled nursing care. Most residents of nursing homes are European American _____ who are in poor health. Ethnic minority older adults have a _____ rate of placement in nursing homes than European Americans. Maintaining a resident's sense of _____ is an important component of good nursing homes. Communication with residents must not involve patronizing speech or _____ .

3.  **Elder Abuse and Neglect**

Abuse and neglect of older adults is an increasing problem, both in the community and in nursing homes. However, abuse and neglect are difficult to define precisely; several categories are used, including _____ psychological or emotional, sexual, _____ abandonment, neglect, and _____ . Most perpetrators of elder abuse and neglect are _____ of the victims. Research indicates that abuse results from a complex interaction of characteristics of the caregiver and care recipient.

4. **Politics, Social Security, and Medicare**

Treating all generations fairly in terms of government programs is a difficult public policy challenge. The U.S. Congress has enacted several changes in social program benefits to older adults to address the changing demographics of the U.S. population. Older adults are the most _____ active age group. Numerous organizations are dedicated to furthering issues and positions pertaining to older adults. Although designed as an income supplement, _____ has become the primary source of retirement income for U.S. citizens. The aging of the Baby Boom generation will place considerable stress on the financing of the system. _____ is the principle health insurance program for adults over age 65 in the United States. Cost containment is a major concern, resulting in emphases on health maintenance organizations and home health care.

# TEST YOURSELF

## MULTIPLE-CHOICE QUESTIONS

1. _____ states that people tend to cope with daily life in later adulthood by applying familiar strategies based on past experience to maintain and preserve both internal and external structures.
   a. The competence and environmental press model
   b. Continuity theory
   c. The zone of maximum comfort
   d. The zone of maximum performance potential

2. Internal continuity concerns one's
   a. physical and social environments.
   b. role relationships.
   c. activities.
   d. personal identity.

3. _____ refers to the number and types of physical, interpersonal, or social demands that environments put on people.
   a. Competence
   b. Environmental press
   c. Adaptation level
   d. Zone of maximum performance

4. When the demands put on individuals by the environment are slightly lower than their competence level, they are in the
   a. adaptation level.
   b. zone of maximum performance potential.
   c. zone of maximum comfort.
   d. environmental press.

5. When people show control over their lives by choosing new behaviors to meet new needs or desires in their lives they are displaying
   a. docility.
   b. continuity.
   c. environmental press.
   d. proactivity.

6. Proactivity is more likely to occur in highly competent people, whereas _____ is more likely to occur in people with relatively low competence.
   a. docility
   b. continuity
   c. adaptation
   d. integrity

7. Erikson proposed that during late adulthood the issue of _____ is of central importance.
   a. generativity versus stagnation
   b. intimacy versus isolation
   c. identity versus role confusion
   d. integrity versus despair

8. In order to achieve integrity, older adults engage in
   a. life review.
   b. despair.
   c. a fear of death.
   d. blaming others for their troubles.

9. Which of the following factors is most strongly associated with the achievement of integrity?
   a. socioeconomic status
   b. cultural background
   c. self-acceptance
   d. self-criticism

10. Bringing oneself into line with the environment is considered an
    a.  assimilative activity.
    b.  accommodative activity.
    c.  activity of daily living.
    d.  instrumental activity.

11. Older adults rely on _____ more than anything or anyone else to help them cope with problems.
    a.  spouses
    b.  children
    c.  friends
    d.  religious faith

12. Who is most active in church groups and attends church services most frequently?
    a.  African American men
    b.  African American women
    c.  European American men
    d.  European American women

13. Using "the faith of the people" is a coping strategy most strongly associated with older adults of which ethnic background?
    a.  European
    b.  African
    c.  Native American
    d.  Mexican

14. Who would be best described as having a "crisp" retirement?
    a.  Suzanne, who retired from her engineering job when she was 65 and started her own consulting business
    b.  John, who worked full-time as a financial consultant until age 70 at which time he began working part-time
    c.  Olive, who taught high school math until she was 65 and then retired completely
    d.  Steve, who retired from nursing at age 65, didn't work for several years, then began working part-time at a hospice

15. Ken retired from his position as a research scientist but now works in a state park gift shop on weekends. Ken would be best described as having a
    a.  crisp retirement.
    b.  bridge job.
    c.  social convoy.
    d.  volunteer position.

16. The majority of workers retire
    a.  by choice.
    b.  because they turned 65.
    c.  because they lost their jobs.
    d.  because of health reasons.

17. When people retire,
    a. health soon begins to decline.
    b. the number and quality of personal friendships decline.
    c. they become less active.
    d. most feel good about being retired if finances, health, and social support are adequate.

18. Older adults' life satisfaction is strongly related to
    a. the number of relationships with younger family members.
    b. the quality of relationships with younger family members.
    c. the number and quality of their friendships.
    d. neither relationships with younger family members nor friendships.

19. Which of the following 75-year-olds would you expect to be most involved with friends?
    a. Gus, who is a widower
    b. Carol, who is married
    c. Jane, who is a widow
    d. Henrietta, who was never married

20. Which of the following sibling relationships most closely fits the congenial type of sibling relationship?
    a. Joanne and Jessica, who feel very close to each other, are highly involved in each others lives, see each other an average amount, and have very little envy or resentment towards each other
    b. Edith and Amy Lois, who are about average on closeness, involvement, and contact with each other, and are relatively low in envy and resentment of each other
    c. Lynn and Mary, who are not very close or involved with each other, don't see each other very often, and don't have much envy or resentment towards each other
    d. Susan and Shirley, who are very involved in each others' lives but have a lot of resentment towards each other, are not close, and have low levels of contact

21. The strongest sibling relationships usually occur between
    a. two brothers.
    b. two sisters.
    c. a brother and a sister.
    d. any combination of brothers and sisters -- no real differences between genders has been found.

22. Older married couples
    a. usually have fairly high marital satisfaction.
    b. usually had higher marital satisfaction when their children were at home.
    c. have increased potential for marital conflict.
    d. show more gender differences in sources of pleasure.

23. Which of the following statements about widowhood is true?
    a. Widowers are at higher risk than widows of dying, themselves, soon after their spouses.
    b. Widows usually suffer less financial loss than widowers after the death of their spouses.
    c. Widowers are more likely than widows to form new, close friendships.
    d. Widows are less likely than widowers to join support groups.

24. Which of the following is NOT true about great-grandparenthood?
    a. It provides a sense of personal and family renewal.
    b. Great-grandchildren provide new diversions in great-grandparents' lives.
    c. Great-grandparents are usually as involved with the great-grandchildren as grandparents are with grandchildren.
    d. Becoming a great-grandparent is usually perceived positively because it is a mark of longevity that most people don't reach.

25. Edna needs help with eating, bathing, and dressing. These tasks are called
    a. instrumental activities of daily living.
    b. activities of daily living.
    c. social tasks.
    d. cognitive tasks.

26. The number of adults needing assistance with tasks of daily living increases dramatically after age
    a. 55.
    b. 65.
    c. 75.
    d. 85.

27. Which of the following statements concerning nursing home residents is true?
    a. Women are more likely than men to be nursing home residents.
    b. Men are more likely than women to be nursing home residents.
    c. There are no ethnic differences in rates of nursing home placement.
    d. Ethnic minority older adults are more likely than European Americans to be nursing home residents.

28. Regina is going to visit her grandmother in a nursing home. During her visit Regina should
    a. not ask her grandmother for advice on problems.
    b. avoid talking about her grandmother's past.
    c. allow her grandmother to exert control over the visit.
    d. not bring her children with her.

29. _____ are most likely to abuse older adults.
    a. Nursing home caregivers
    b. Family members
    c. Attorneys
    d. Clergy

30. Who is most likely to write a letter to an elected representative?
    a. 21-year-old Mike
    b. 35-year-old John
    c. 55-year-old Stu
    d. 70-year-old Charles

## ESSAY QUESTIONS

1. Your 78-year-old grandmother is relatively healthy and competent, but recently she told the family that she wants to sell the house that she has lived in for 35 years and move into an apartment that has an emergency call system, 24-hour security, and housecleaning services. Everyone in your family is puzzled by this decision. How would you explain your grandmother's situation using the competence-environmental press framework?

2. Your sister told you that she doesn't like to visit your grandmother because she is tired of hearing your grandmother talk about the past and the decisions that she made earlier in life. What can you tell your sister about Erikson's crisis of integrity vs despair and the importance of life review in achieving integrity?

3. Recently you were talking to 2 friends, one whose grandmother is widowed and the other whose grandfather is widowed. Your friends were discussing whether or not widowhood is harder on men or women. What can you tell your friends about the gender differences in the effects of widowhood?

4. Recently your sister had a baby which made your grandmother a great-grandmother. Your sister told you that your grandmother seems to be very proud of being a great-grandmother, and your sister is surprised that being a great-grandmother doesn't make your grandmother feel very old. What can you tell your sister about the importance of great-grandparenthood to great-grandparents?

5. One of your friends is looking for a nursing home for his father. He is concerned about finding a good one but he isn't sure what to look for other than obvious things like cleanliness, qualifications of the staff, patient to worker ratios, etc. What can you tell your friend about some other factors that are important to consider when choosing a nursing home?

# SOLUTIONS

## 15.1 KNOW THE TERMS

1. continuity (578)
2. Competence (579)
3. Environmental press (579)
4. Adaptation level (579)
5. maximum performance potential (579)
6. zone of maximum comfort (579)
7. proactivity (580)
8. docility (580)

## 15.1 KNOW THE DETAILS OF THEORIES OF PSYCHOSOCIAL AGING

1. F, (578)
2. F, (579)
3. F, (579)
4. T, (579)
5. F, (579)
6. T, (580)
7. F, (580)

## 15.2 KNOW THE TERMS

1. integrity vs despair (582)
2. life review (582)
3. subjective well-being (583)
4. Spiritual support (586)

## 15.2 KNOW THE DETAILS OF PERSONALITY, SOCIAL COGNITION, AND SPIRITUALITY

1. F, (582)
2. T, (582)
3. T, (582)
4. T, (583)
5. T, (583)
6. F, (583)
7. F, (585)
8. T, (586)
9. T, (586)
10. T, (587)

## 15.3 KNOW THE DETAILS OF RETIREMENT

1. F, (589)
2. F, (589)
3. T, (590)
4. T, (590)
5. F, (591)
6. T, (591)
7. T, (591)
8. F, (592)
9. F, (592)
10. F, (592)
11. F, (593)

## 15.4 KNOW THE TERMS

1.  social convoy (593)
2.  Socioemotional selectivity (594)

## 15.4 KNOW THE DETAILS OF FRIENDS AND FAMILY IN LATE LIFE

1.  F, (593)
2.  F, (594)
3.  T, (594)
4.  F, (596)
5.  T, (596)
6.  T, (598)
7.  F, (599)
8.  T, (599)
9.  T, (599)
10. F, (599)
11. T, (600)

## 15.5 KNOW THE TERMS

1.  frail older adults (601)
2.  activities of daily living (601)
3.  instrumental activities of daily living (601)
4.  Assisted living (603)
5.  Intermediate (603)
6.  Skilled nursing (603)
7.  patronizing (605)
8.  infantilization (605)

## 15.5 KNOW THE DETAILS OF SOCIAL ISSUES AND AGING

1.  F, (601)
2.  T, (601)
3.  T, (601)
4.  F, (602)
5.  F, (603)
6.  F, (603)
7.  T, (605)
8.  T, (605)
9.  T, (607)
10. T, (607)
11. T, (607)
12. F, (608)
13. F, (609)
14. F, (609)
15. T, (611)

# SUMMARY

## 15.1 THEORIES OF PSYCHOSOCIAL AGING

1.  familiar (578)
2.  demands (579); new (580); docility (580)

## 15.2 PERSONALITY DEVELOPMENT IN LATER LIFE

1.  integrity (582); accepting (582); bitterness (582)

2. one's life (583); thought (583); varies (585)

3. cope (586); African American women (587)

## 15.3 I USED TO WORK AT...: LIVING IN RETIREMENT

1. process (589); full-time (589); eligibility (590)
2. choose to (590); health (590)

3. satisfied (591); health (591); activity (591); personal life priorities (591)

4. volunteering (592)

## 15.4 FRIENDS AND FAMILY IN LATER LIFE

1. social convoy (593); selective (594).; sisters (595)
2. health (597); marital conflict (597); similar (597)

3. satisfaction (597); adequate (598); competence (598)
4. loneliness (599); less (599); household (599); financial (599)

5. satisfaction (600); similar (600); diversions (600)

## 15.5 SOCIAL ISSUES AND AGING

1. self-care (601); intellectual competence (601)
2. women (603); lower (603); control (605); infantilization (605)

3. physical (606); material or financial (606), ; self-neglect (606); adult children (607)
4. politically (609); Social Security (609); Medicare (611)

# TEST YOURSELF

## MULTIPLE-CHOICE QUESTIONS

1. B, (578)
2. D, (578)
3. B, (579)
4. C, (579)
5. D, (580)
6. A, (580)
7. D, (582)
8. A, (582)
9. C, (582)
10. B, (585)
11. D, (586)

12. B, (587)
13. D, (587)
14. C, (589)
15. B, (590)
16. A, (590)
17. D, (591)
18. C, (594)
19. C, (594)
20. A, (595)
21. B, (595)
22. A, (596)

23. A, (599)
24. C, (600)
25. B, (601)
26. D, (602)
27. A, (603)
28. C, (605)
29. B, (607)
30. D, (609)

## ESSAY QUESTIONS

1. According to the competence-environmental press framework, competence is defined as a person's upper-limit of functioning in the domains of physical health, sensory-perceptual skills, motor skills, cognitive skills, and ego strength. Environmental press refers to the number and types of physical, social, and interpersonal demands that the environment puts on a person. Both competence and environmental press change throughout the life span. The adaptation level is the area where press is average for a particular level of competence. If press is increased slightly, performance tends to improve. This is the zone of maximum performance potential. The zone of maximum comfort occurs when press is decreased slightly and people are able to live happily without worrying about environmental demands. Even though your grandmother is relatively healthy she may find that

living in a house puts slightly higher than average demands on her so that she is living in the zone of maximum performance potential. Living in a house has increased her performance because she has cleaned it, changed storm windows, maintained the yard, dealt with security issues, etc. As she sees her physical competence decreasing she may feel that these demands from the environment are too great. A move to an apartment where she doesn't have to worry about maintenance, housecleaning, and security means that she can live in an environment with fewer demands and greater comfort (zone of maximum comfort). Your grandmother's behavior is a good example of proactive behavior. (579-581)

2. According to Erik Erikson, the crisis of later life is one of integrity vs despair. Older adults who can look back on their lives and feel a sense of satisfaction and contentment have achieved integrity. However, older adults who are bitter about their earlier choices and feel that their lives are meaningless will feel despair. Reviewing one's life, or life review, seems to be important in achieving integrity. In one study, older adults who participated in life review activities showed an increased quality of life. This positive effect was still apparent 3 months later. Also, older women who accepted the past were less likely to show signs of depression. It appears as if life review is an important step in achieving integrity. (582-583)

3. Both older widows and widowers may become more socially isolated because others may feel uncomfortable around their grief, or they may not be included anymore by friends who are still couples. Widowers are at a higher risk of dying themselves soon after their spouse. Some people believe that widowers have a more difficult time than do widows. For example, widowers are more likely to die, themselves, soon after their spouses' deaths. Also, older men are ill-equipped to do many of routine tasks such as laundry, cooking, cleaning, and shopping. By losing a wife, older men often lose their only intimate friend, and they are less likely than widows to form new friendships. Older widowers are also less likely to form new friendships than widows. Some of these effects experienced by widowers may be due to the fact that widowers are generally older than widows when they lose their spouses. Widows usually suffer more financially when they lose their spouses, but they may have more friendships to provide social support. Widows also are much less likely to remarry. Overall, widowers may have a harder time adjusting to the death of a spouse than do widows. (598-599)

4. In general great-grandparents are not as involved with children as are grandparents, but they do view the role of great-grandparent as an important role. Three aspects of great-grandparenthood seem particularly important. First, being a great-grandparent provides a sense of personal and family renewal. The many generations make it clear that the family line will continue for many years into the future. Second, great-grandchildren provide new diversions in the great-grandparents' lives. Third, becoming a great-grandparent provides a sense of achievement and longevity that most people view positively. In other words, your grandmother's attitude about being a great-grandparent is not unusual. (600)

5. First, your friend should evaluate his father's current and future needs and find a nursing home that is most able to meet those needs. For example, if your friend's father needs help going to the toilet then the nursing home must have adequate staffing so that he won't have to wait for someone to help him. If your friend's father is confused then the nursing home should provide a safe and stable environment. The nursing home should provide tasty meals. Second, nursing homes that foster family visitation and involvement in the residents' care are better. Third, the nursing home should have person-centered planning. Residents who feel that they have more control tend to fare better than those who feel that they are at the mercy of the staff. Your friend may want to talk to both residents and staff at the nursing homes that he is considering for his father. (604-605)

# THE FINAL PASSAGE

16.1 Definitions and Ethical Issues

16.2 Thinking About Death: Personal Aspects

16.3 Surviving the Loss: The Grieving Process

16.4 Dying and Bereavement Experiences Across the Life Span

This chapter focuses on defining death, ethical issues surrounding death, people's personal feelings about death, dealing with grief, and coping with different types of loss.

# 16.1 DEFINITIONS AND ETHICAL ISSUES

## TO MASTER THE LEARNING OBJECTIVES:

**How is death defined?**

- Describe the sociocultural definitions of death.

- Explain how culture influences mourning rituals and states of bereavement.

- Describe the different views of death.

**What legal and medical criteria are used to determine when death occurs?**

- Define clinical death, whole-brain death, and persistent vegetative state.

**What are the ethical dilemmas surrounding euthanasia?**

- Define bioethics, euthanasia, active euthanasia, and passive euthanasia, and explain how they are related to each other.

- Describe the laws in the Netherlands and Oregon that deal with physician-assisted suicide.

- Describe the importance of living wills, durable power of attorney, and DNR orders.

# 16.1 KNOW THE TERMS

**Active euthanasia**                    **Passive euthanasia**

**Bioethics**                            **Persistent vegetative state**

**Clinical death**                       **Whole-brain death**

**Euthanasia**

1.  The lack of respiration and heart beat is termed _____ .

2.  The lack of spontaneous movement, respiration, reflexes, and a flat EEG for a specified period of time is called _____ .

3.  The lack of cortical functioning accompanied by brain stem activity is called a _____ from which people do not recover.

4.  The area of study that examines the interface between human values and technological advances in health and life sciences is called _____ .

5.  The practice of ending life for merciful reasons is called _____ .

6.  _____ involves deliberately ending someone's life based on a statement of the person's wishes or a decision made by someone with the legal authority to make such a decision.

7.  _____ involves letting someone die by withholding an available treatment.

# 16.1 KNOW THE DETAILS OF DEFINITIONS AND ETHICAL ISSUES

1.  Mourning rituals and bereavement are very similar across cultures.
    TRUE or FALSE

2.  Clinical death is defined as a lack of heartbeat and respiration.
    TRUE or FALSE

3.  When a person is declared brain dead there is no cortical functioning, but there may be some brainstem activity.
    TRUE or FALSE

4.  Euthanasia refers to the practice of ending life for reasons of mercy.
    TRUE or FALSE

5. Allowing someone to die by withholding available treatment is a form of active euthanasia.
   TRUE or FALSE

6. A living will enables people to state their wishes about the use of life support and other treatments in the event they are unconscious and decisions need to be made.
   TRUE or FALSE

7. A durable power of attorney names an individual who has the legal authority to speak for a person if necessary.
   TRUE or FALSE

# 16.2 THINKING ABOUT DEATH: PERSONAL ASPECTS

## TO MASTER THE LEARNING OBJECTIVES:

**How do feelings about death change over adulthood?**

- Describe young adults' feelings about death.

- Explain how middle-aged people feel about death.

- Describe middle-aged adults' perceptions of time.

- Describe older adults' feelings about death.

**How do people deal with their own death?**

- Describe Kübler-Ross' 5 stages of dying: denial, anger, bargaining, depression, and acceptance.

- Describe contextual theories of dying.

**What is death anxiety and how do people show it?**

- Explain terror management theory and how it is related to death anxiety.

- Describe how the level of death anxiety changes over the life span.

- Describe the ways in which people can cope with death anxiety.

**How do people deal with end-of-life issues and create a final scenario?**

- Define end-of-life issues and creating a final scenario.

**What is hospice?**

- Define hospice and describe how it differs from the hospital model of care.

- Describe the differences between in-patient hospices and hospitals.

- Explain the 6 considerations people should use to determine if hospice care is appropriate for them.

## 16.2 KNOW THE TERMS

**End-of-life issues**                                   **Hospice**

**Final scenario**                                       **Terror management theory**

1. _____ proposes that ensuring that one's life continues is a primary motive underlying behavior.

2. Management of the final phase of life, after-death disposition of their body, memorial services, and distribution of assets are known as _____ .

3. Making choices about how one wants one's life to end is known as a _____ .

4. _____ is an approach to care for dying individuals that emphasizes pain management and death with dignity.

## 16.2 KNOW THE DETAILS OF THINKING ABOUT DEATH

1. During middle adulthood, thinking about time tends to change from thinking about how long they have lived to how long they have left to live.
   TRUE or FALSE

2. Older adults tend to be less anxious about death than any other age group.
   TRUE or FALSE

3. According to Kübler-Ross, people's first reaction to finding out that they are dying is typically depression.
   TRUE or FALSE

4. All terminally ill patients progress through Kübler-Ross' stages in the same order.
   TRUE or FALSE

5. Corr identified bodily needs, psychological security, interpersonal attachments, and spiritual energy and hope as four dimensions of the tasks of dying.
   TRUE or FALSE

6. Lower ego integrity, more physical problems, and more psychological problems are predictive of lower levels of death anxiety in older adults.
   TRUE or FALSE

7. Taking part in an experiential workshop about death can significantly lower death anxiety.
   TRUE or FALSE

8. A final scenario involves making choices known about how one does or does not want one's life to end.
TRUE or FALSE

9. The emphasis in a hospice is on quality of life.
TRUE or FALSE

10. Hospice patients are less mobile, more anxious, and more depressed than hospital patients.
TRUE or FALSE

# 16.3 SURVIVING THE LOSS: THE GRIEVING PROCESS

## TO MASTER THE LEARNING OBJECTIVES:

**How do people experience the grief process?**

- Define bereavement, grief, and mourning.

- Describe the 4 activities that need to occur during the grief process.

- Describe the 3 misconceptions that people have concerning the grief process.

- Describe the risk factors that may make bereavement more difficult.

**What feelings do grieving people have?**

- Describe the feelings that are typical of normal grief reactions.

- Define grief work and anniversary reaction.

- Describe the results of longitudinal research on older adults' grief work.

- Describe family stress before and after bereavement.

- Describe the research on the effects of religiosity on grief.

- Describe the theories of coping with grief, including the grief work as rumination view.

**What is the difference between normal and abnormal grief?**

- Describe traumatic grief reactions and how they can be differentiated from typical grief reactions.

## 16.3 KNOW THE TERMS

| | |
|---|---|
| **Anniversary reaction** | **Grief work** |
| **Bereavement** | **Grief work as rumination** |
| **Grief** | **Mourning** |

1.  The state or condition caused by loss through death is known as _____

2.  The sorrow, hurt, anger, guilt, confusion, and other feelings that arise after suffering a loss is known as _____ .

3.  The ways in which we express our grief is known as _____ .

4.  The psychological side of coming to terms with bereavement is called _____

5.  Changes in behavior and feelings of sadness that are associated with the date of death is known as an _____ .

6.  The view that rejects the necessity of grief processing and views extensive grief processing as a form of rumination that may actually increase distress is called the _____ hypothesis.

## 16.3 KNOW THE DETAILS OF THE GRIEVING PROCESS

1.  Bereavement is the sorrow, hurt, anger, guilt, confusion, and other feelings that arise after suffering a loss.
    TRUE or FALSE

2.  All people go through the process of grieving in the same way.
    TRUE or FALSE

3.  Grief is a process over which we have no control.
    TRUE or FALSE

4.  Researchers and therapists suggest that a person needs at least one year following a loss to begin recovery.
    TRUE or FALSE

5.  When death is expected, people go through a period of anticipatory grieving that helps buffer the impact of the loss when it does come.
    TRUE or FALSE

6.  Women have higher rates of depression than men following bereavement.
    TRUE or FALSE

7. The most difficult type of loss is the loss of a child.
   TRUE or FALSE

8. The psychological side of coming to terms with bereavement is referred to as grief work.
   TRUE or FALSE

9. Muller's themes of grief are mourning and bereavement.
   TRUE or FALSE

10. Holidays and the anniversary of the death of a loved one may reintroduce feelings of grief for individuals who suffered a loss years ago.
    TRUE or FALSE

11. Bereaved individuals reporting stress prior to the death show a significant increase in physical symptoms 6 months after the death.
    TRUE or FALSE

12. According to the four component model of grieving, dealing with grief is a complex process that can only be understood as a complex outcome that unfolds over time.
    TRUE or FALSE

13. In the dual process model of coping with bereavement, loss-oriented stressors are those relating to adapting to the survivor's new life situation.
    TRUE or FALSE

14. The distinguishing features between normal and traumatic grief are related to symptoms of separation distress and traumatic distress.
    TRUE or FALSE

15. Common forms of traumatic grief are excessive guilt and self-blame.
    TRUE or FALSE

# 16.4 DYING AND BEREAVEMENT EXPERIENCES ACROSS THE LIFE SPAN

## TO MASTER THE LEARNING OBJECTIVES:

**What do children understand about death? How should adults help them deal with it?**

• Explain the differences in the ways that young children and older children view death.

• Describe how developmental changes in cognitive-language ability, psychosocial development, and coping skills influence children's understanding and reactions to death.

- Describe how death should be explained to children.

**How do adolescents deal with death?**

- Describe the effects of bereavement on adolescents.

- Describe how adolescents may react to the death of a sibling, a parent, or a friend.

**How do adults deal with death? What are the special issues they face concerning the death of a child or parent?**

- Describe the reactions of young adults to death.

- Describe the effects of loss of a partner in young adulthood.

- Explain the effects of the death of a parent or a partner during mid-life.

- Describe the effects of the death of a child during young and middle adulthood.

- Describe the effects of the death of a parent during adulthood.

**How do older adults face the loss of a child, grandchild, or partner?**

- Describe the effects of the death of a child.

- Describe how older adults react to the loss of a grandchild.

- Explain the effects of the death of a partner.

- Describe the sanctification that occurs in some widows.

- Describe the reactions that occur in gay and lesbian couples when the loss of a partner occurs.

# 16.4 KNOW THE DETAILS OF DYING AND BEREAVEMENT EXPERIENCES

1. American society tends to distance itself from death.
   TRUE or FALSE

2. Preschool children usually believe that death is temporary.
   TRUE or FALSE

3. Children in Piaget's concrete operational stage understand that death is final and permanent.
   TRUE or FALSE

4. It's not unusual for children to react to the death of someone close to them by feeling guilt for causing the death.
   TRUE or FALSE

5. Using euphemisms such as "Grandma is just sleeping" to explain death to children will help them understand death better.
   TRUE or FALSE

6. When teenagers experience the death of someone close to them, they are usually able to make sense of the event.

   TRUE or FALSE

7. When adolescents lose a sibling or parent due to death, their friends are often uncomfortable talking to them about it.

   TRUE or FALSE

8. When adolescents lose a friend to death, they often feel survivor guilt.

   TRUE or FALSE

9. Young adults feel strongly that those who die at this point is their lives would be cheated out of their future.

   TRUE or FALSE

10. Young adult widows typically continue grieving for 5 to 10 years after the loss.

    TRUE or FALSE

11. The loss of a child through miscarriage or stillbirth is a type of loss that is often overlooked by society.

    TRUE or FALSE

12. There is pressure from society to mourn the loss of one's partner for a period of time and then to "move on."

    TRUE or FALSE

13. The number of friends is more important than the quality of the support system in determining how well one adjusts to the loss of a spouse.

    TRUE or FALSE

14. Some widows tend to describe their late husbands in idealized ways.

    TRUE or FALSE

# SUMMARY

## 16.1 DEFINITIONS AND ETHICAL ISSUES

1. **Sociocultural Definitions of Death**

   Death is a very difficult concept to define precisely. Different cultures have different _____ for death. Some of the meanings in Western culture include images, _____ events, state of being, analogy, mystery, boundary, thief of meaning, basis for anxiety, and _____ or punishment.

2. **Legal and Medical Definitions**

For many centuries, a _____ definition of death based on the absence of a heartbeat and _____ was used. Currently, brain death is the most widely used definition and is based on several highly specific criteria such as brain _____ and responses to specific stimuli.

3. **Ethical Issues**

Two types of euthanasia are distinguished. Active euthanasia consists of _____ ending someone's life based on the patient's wishes by taking some action, such as turning off a life support system. Physician-assisted suicide is a controversial issue and form of active euthanasia. Passive euthanasia is ending someone's life by _____ some type of intervention or treatment, such as stopping nutrition. It is essential that people make their wishes known, either through a durable power of attorney or a _____ .

## 16.2 THINKING ABOUT DEATH: PERSONAL ASPECTS

1. **A Life Course Approach to Dying**

Young adults report a sense of being _____ by death. Cognitive developmental level is important for understanding how young adults view death. Middle-aged adults begin to confront their own mortality and undergo a change in their sense of time _____ and time until death. Older adults are more _____ of death.

2. **Dealing with One's Own Death**

Kübler-Ross' theory includes five stages: denial, anger, _____ depression, and acceptance. Some people do not progress through all these stages, and some people move through them at different _____ . People may be in more than one stage of dying at a time and do not necessarily go through all of them or go through them in order. A contextual theory of dying emphasizes the _____ a dying person must face. Four dimensions of these tasks have been identified: bodily needs, psychological security, _____ and spiritual energy and hope. A contextual theory would be able to incorporate differences in reasons people die and the places people die.

3. **Death Anxiety**

Most people exhibit some degree of anxiety about death, even though it is difficult to define and measure. Individual difference variables include gender, religiosity, _____ , ethnicity, and occupation. Death anxiety may have some benefits. The main ways death anxiety is shown are by avoiding death (e.g., refusing to go to funerals) and deliberately challenging it (e.g., engaging in dangerous sports). Other ways of showing it include changing lifestyles, dreaming and fantasizing, using _____ , displacing fears, and becoming a death professional. Several ways to deal with anxiety exist: living life to the fullest, personal reflection, and education. Death education has been shown to be extremely effective.

4. **Creating a Final Scenario**

Managing the final aspects of life, after-death disposition of the body and memorial services, and _____ of assets are important end-of-life issues. Making choices about what people do and do not want done constitutes a _____

5. **The Hospice Option**

The goal of a hospice is to maintain the _____ and to manage the pain of terminally ill patients. Hospice clients typically have cancer, AIDS, or a progressive neurological disorder. Family members tend to stay involved in the care of hospice clients.

## 16.3 SURVIVING THE LOSS: THE GRIEVING PROCESS

1. **The Grief Process**

Grief is an active process of coping with loss. Four aspects of grieving must be confronted: the _____ of the loss, the emotional turmoil, adjusting to the environment, and _____ with the deceased. When death is expected, survivors may go through _____ grief; unexpected death is usually more difficult for people to handle.

2. **Normal Grief Reactions**

Dealing with grief, called grief work, usually takes at least _____ Normal grief reactions include _____ and _____ reactions. Religiosity may provide a support mechanism for people who are coping with a loss.

3. **Coping with Grief**

The four component model proposes that the context of the loss, continuation of subjective meaning associated with the loss, _____ of the lost relationship over time, and the role of coping and emotion-regulation processes describe the grief process. The grief work as rumination hypothesis suggests that grief processing is form of rumination that serves _____ distress. The dual process model of coping with bereavement focuses on loss-oriented stressors and restoration-oriented stressors.

4. **Traumatic Grief Reactions**

Traumatic grief involves symptoms of separation distress and symptoms of _____ . Excessive guilt and _____ are common manifestations of traumatic grief.

## 16.4 DYING AND BEREAVEMENT EXPERIENCES ACROSS THE LIFE SPAN

1. **Childhood**

   The cognitive and psychosocial developmental levels of children determine their understanding of and ability to cope with death. This is especially evident in the behaviors children use to display their grief. Research indicates that there are few _____ effects of bereavement in childhood.

2. **Adolescence**

   Adolescents may have difficulty making sense of death, and are often _____ affected by bereavement. Adolescents are often _____ to discuss their feelings of loss, and peers often provide little support.

3. **Adulthood**

   Young and middle-aged adults usually have _____ feelings about death. Attachment theory provides a useful framework to understand these feelings. Midlife is a time when people usually deal with the death of their parents and confront their own _____ The death of one's child is especially difficult to cope with. The death of one's parent deprives an adult of many important things, and the feelings accompanying it are often complex.

4. **Late Adulthood**

   Older adults are _____ anxious about death and deal with it better than any other age group. The death of a grandchild may be very traumatic for older adults, and the feelings of loss may never go away. The death of one's partner represents a deep personal loss, especially when the couple had a long and close relationship.

# TEST YOURSELF

## MULTIPLE-CHOICE QUESTIONS

1. A person who asks, "How many years do I have left?" is viewing death as an(n)
   a. analogy.
   b. thief of meaning.
   c. boundary.
   d. image or object.

2. _____ is now the most widely accepted criteria for determining when death has occurred.
   a. Clinical death
   b. Whole-brain death
   c. A persistent vegetative state
   d. Bioethics

3. After an automobile accident, Lynn was left with brainstem activity but no cortical functioning. Lynn would be classified as
   a. clinically dead.
   b. brain dead.
   c. in a persistent vegetative state.
   d. euthanized.

4. When Dr. Jack Kevorkian used his suicide machine to end the life of a terminally ill patient, he was committing
   a. active euthanasia.
   b. passive euthanasia.
   c. suicide.
   d. a universally accepted act.

5. _____ is defined as allowing a person to die by withholding an available treatment.
   a. A living will
   b. Durable power of attorney
   c. Active euthanasia
   d. Passive euthanasia

6. A shift from thinking about time in terms of how long one has lived to thinking about how long one has left to live usually occurs during
   a. adolescence.
   b. early adulthood.
   c. middle adulthood.
   d. late adulthood.

7. _____ tend to be more accepting and less anxious about death than any other age group.
   a. Adolescents
   b. Young adults
   c. Middle-aged adults
   d. Older adults

8. The initial sequence of Kübler-Ross' stages of dying was
   a. anger, denial, depression, acceptance, bargaining.
   b. acceptance, depression, denial, anger, bargaining.
   c. denial, anger, bargaining, depression, acceptance.
   d. denial, depression, anger, bargaining, acceptance.

9. When Helen's physician informed her that she had an incurable disease and only six months to live, Helen promptly made an appointment at a major medical center for a second opinion and expected a more favorable diagnosis. Helen appears to be in Kübler-Ross' _____ stage of dying.
   a. anger
   b. bargaining
   c. depression
   d. denial

10. Roger is terminally ill. His family is concerned because he seems to be emotionally withdrawing from them, but they are glad that he seems to be at peace with the fact of his imminent death. Ralph is most likely in Kübler-Ross' _____ stage of dying.
    a. acceptance
    b. bargaining
    c. depression
    d. denial

11. In hospices,
    a. the emphasis is on prolonging life.
    b. families are discouraged from visiting.
    c. a goal of medical care is to control pain.
    d. there is no medical care available.

12. The state or condition caused by loss through death is called _____, whereas the ways in which we express our grief are called _____.
    a. mourning; grieving
    b. bereavement; mourning
    c. grieving; mourning
    d. mourning; bereavement

13. Elaine's husband died several weeks ago. In Elaine's grief process, she should
    a. expect to be "back to normal" soon.
    b. expect to make a full recovery in about two years.
    c. expect to begin recovery in a year or two.
    d. expect that she may never "recover" from her loss, but will learn to live with her loss.

14. The psychological side of coming to terms with bereavement is called
    a. an anniversary reaction.
    b. grief work.
    c. mourning.
    d. traumatic grief.

15. The death of a _____ is generally believed to be the worst type of loss.
    a. child
    b. parent
    c. spouse
    d. sibling

16. According to the four component model, grief is based on the context of the loss, continuation of subjective meaning associated with loss, changing representations of the lost relationship over time, and
    a. the role of coping and emotion-regulation processes
    b. the rumination hypothesis
    c. loss-oriented stressors.
    d. restoration-oriented stressors.

17. The theme related to the experience of grief that refers to what people do to deal with their loss, in terms of what helps them, is called
    a. affect.
    b. narrative.
    c. change.
    d. coping.

18. Loss-oriented stressors and restoration-oriented stressors are part of
    a. the four component model of grieving.
    b. the dual process model of coping with bereavement.
    c. traumatic grief reactions.
    d. the anniversary reaction.

19. After Sarah's husband died, she was preoccupied with her late husband to the point that it interfered with her everyday functioning, she continued to feel disbelief about his death, and she became detached from others as a result of the death. Sarah appears to be experiencing
    a. an anniversary reaction.
    b. restoration-oriented stressors.
    c. a normal grief reaction.
    d. a traumatic grief reaction.

20. By about _____ years of age, most children begin to realize that death is permanent, that everyone dies eventually, and that all biological functions stop when a person dies.
    a. 2 to 3
    b. 5 to 7
    c. 9 to 12
    d. 13 to 15

21. When their child is faced with the death of someone close to them, parents should
    a. explain death as being similar to sleeping.
    b. not allow the child to attend the funeral.
    c. keep explanations simple but truthful.
    d. avoid talking about the death.

22. Which one of the following statements regarding death and adolescence is true?
    a. Only a very small minority of adolescents have experienced the loss of a family member or friend.
    b. Unresolved grief during adolescence has been linked to depression, chronic illness, and low self-esteem.
    c. Adolescents are usually very willing to discuss their grief.
    d. Adolescents tend to recover from the death of a sibling fairly quickly.

23. When older adults lose a grandchild,
    a. they may try to control and hide their grief behavior to shield their child.
    b. they are unlikely to feel survivor guilt.
    c. they usually have no regrets about their relationship with the deceased grandchild.
    d. they usually experience only slight emotional upset.

24. Which of the following statements concerning spousal bereavement and ratings of the marital relationship is true?
    a. Bereaved widows and widowers rate their marriage more positively than nonbereaved spouses.
    b. Bereaved widows and widowers rate their marriage less positively than nonbereaved spouses.
    c. There are no differences between bereaved and nonbereaved adults in the way they rate their marriages.
    d. The more depressed the bereaved spouse, the less positively the marriage is rated.

## ESSAY QUESTIONS

1. Recently a friend of yours said that if he had a terminal illness he would not like to receive life-prolonging treatments. What can you tell your friend about the legal issues that surround euthanasia?

2. You have a friend whose father was just told that he has cancer of the liver. Your friend was wondering what changes he should anticipate in his father's feelings and behavior. What can you tell your friend about Kübler-Ross' stages of dying?

3. The wife of one of your coworkers, Brandon, died 18 months ago. When you see Brandon he often says that it is his fault that his wife died. Recently, Brandon has not been coming to work. You have heard that he just spends the day lying in bed watching TV. Everyone at work is beginning to wonder if Brandon's grief is normal. What can you tell everyone about the differences between normal and abnormal grieving?

4. Last month, while you and your sister were crying over the death of a close friend, your 3-year-old son came into the room and asked why you were crying. You tried to explain that you were crying because you missed your friend who had died. Your son responded that you shouldn't cry because

your friend would come back. Your sister thought that this was an inappropriate remark. What can you tell your sister about young children's conceptions of death?

5. Recently, your teenage daughter told you that her best friend's dad died, but her friend doesn't want to talk about her feelings. Your daughter is wondering if this is normal. What can you tell your daughter about grief in adolescents?

6. Your friend Liz's first husband, Jack, died in an accident when she was 23 years old. She is now 38 years old, has remarried, and has a family with her new husband. Jack's mother continues to call Liz every year on the anniversary of Jack's death. Liz grieved greatly when Jack died, but has since moved forward in her life and can't understand why her former mother-in-law doesn't seem to be able to do the same thing. She feels guilty about this but wishes that her former mother-in-law would stop dragging up the past by calling her every year. What can you tell Liz that might help her understand her mother-in-law's feelings compared to her own?

# SOLUTIONS

## 16.1 KNOW THE TERMS

1. clinical death (620)
2. whole-brain death (620)
3. persistent vegetative state (621)
4. bioethics (621)
5. euthanasia (621)
6. Active euthanasia (621)
7. Passive euthanasia (623)

## 16.1 KNOW THE DETAILS OF DEFINITIONS AND ETHICAL ISSUES

1. F, (619)
2. T, (620)
3. F, (621)
4. T, (621)
5. F, (621)
6. T, (625)
7. T, (625)

## 16.2 KNOW THE TERMS

1. Terror management theory (630)
2. end-of-life issues (631)
3. final scenario (632)
4. Hospice (633)

## 16.2 KNOW THE DETAILS OF THINKING ABOUT DEATH

1. T, (627)
2. T, (627)
3. F, (628)
4. F, (629)
5. T, (629)
6. F, (631)
7. T, (631)
8. T, (632)
9. T, (633)
10. F, (634)

## 16.3 KNOW THE TERMS

1. bereavement (636)
2. grief (636)
3. mourning (636)
4. grief work (638)
5. anniversary reaction (639)
6. grief work as rumination (640)

## 16.3 KNOW THE DETAILS OF THE GRIEVING PROCESS

1. F, (636)
2. F, (636)
3. F, (636)
4. T, (637)
5. T, (637)
6. T, (638)

| 7. T, (638) | 10. T, (639) | 13. F, (642) |
| 8. T, (638) | 11. F, (639) | 14. T, (642) |
| 9. F, (638) | 12. T, (640) | 15. T, (643) |

# 16.4 KNOW THE DETAILS OF DYING AND BEREAVEMENT EXPERIENCES

| 1. T, (643) | 7. T, (646) | 13. F, (649) |
| 2. T, (644) | 8. T, (646) | 14. T, (649) |
| 3. T, (644) | 9. T, (646) | |
| 4. T, (644) | 10. T, (647) | |
| 5. F, (644) | 11. T, (647) | |
| 6. F, (646) | 12. T, (649) | |

# SUMMARY

## 16.1 DEFINITIONS AND ETHICAL ISSUES

1. meanings (618); statistics (620); reward (620)
2. clinical (620); respiration (620); activity (621)
3. actively (621); withholding (623); living will (625)

## 16.2 THINKING ABOUT DEATH: PERSONAL ASPECTS

1. cheated (627); lived (627); accepting (627)
2. bargaining (629); rates (629); tasks (629); interpersonal attachments (629)
3. age (631); humor (631)
4. distribution (632); final scenario (632).
5. quality of life (633)

## 16.3 SURVIVING THE LOSS: THE GRIEVING PROCESS

1. reality (636); loosening ties (637); anticipatory (637)
2. 1 years (638).; sadness (638); anniversary (639)
3. changing representations (640) ; to increase (640)
4. traumatic distress (643); self-blame (643)

## 16.4 DYING AND BEREAVEMENT EXPERIENCES ACROSS THE LIFE SPAN

1. long-lasting (644)
2. severely (646); reluctant (646)
3. intense (647); mortality (648).
4. less (648)

# TEST YOURSELF

## MULTIPLE-CHOICE QUESTIONS

| 1. C, (620) | 4. A, (621) | 7. D, (627) |
| 2. B, (620) | 5. D, (623) | 8. C, (628) |
| 3. C, (621) | 6. C, (627) | 9. D, (628) |

| | | |
|---|---|---|
| 10. A, (629) | 15. A, (638) | 20. B, (644) |
| 11. C, (633) | 16. A, (640) | 21. C, (644) |
| 12. B, (636) | 17. D, (642) | 22. B, (646) |
| 13. D, (637) | 18. B, (642) | 23. A, (649) |
| 14. B, (638) | 19. D, (643) | 24. A, (649) |

## ESSAY QUESTIONS

1.  Deliberately ending someone's life by withholding treatment is known as passive euthanasia. In most jurisdictions in the United States euthanasia is illegal unless patients have made their wishes known. If your friend feels strongly about this issue, there are 2 things that he should do to make his wishes known. First, he should have a living will that states his wishes regarding life support and other medical interventions in case he cannot state them when the time comes. Second, he should have a durable power of attorney that names someone else to speak for him if he is unconscious or otherwise incapable of speaking for himself. Both of these documents can be used as the basis for a "Do Not Resuscitate" medical order. He should make sure that family members or friends know where these papers are kept so that they can act as his advocate if the need arises in the future. (625-626)

2.  According to Elisabeth Kübler-Ross, a Chicago physician, terminally ill people experience 5 stages as they approach death. The first stage, denial, can be seen when people are told that they are terminally ill. They may ask for second opinions or may want labs to rerun diagnostic tests. Anger occurs during the second stage. This anger may be directed at health care workers, family, and friends. People may be angry at the unfairness of an early death. The third stage, bargaining, can be seen when people try to find a way out of dying. People may promise to do a good deed if they don't die. Depression is characteristic of the fourth stage. During this stage people may mourn the losses that have occurred (e.g., loss of a limb, loss of strength) and the losses that will occur in the future. In the final stage, people accept and come to terms with death. People may be in more than one stage at a time, and they may not experience every stage, but this is a guide for your friend to use. (628-629)

3.  Both normal and traumatic grieving are characterized by guilt and sadness, but normal and traumatic grieving differ in the degree and intensity of those feelings. Traumatic grief involves both symptoms of separation distress such as preoccupation with the deceased that interferes with daily living, and symptoms of traumatic distress such as feelings of mistrust, anger, and detachment from others. The most common manifestations of abnormal grief are excessive guilt and self-blame. Brandon may be experiencing traumatic grieving because his grief is interfering with his daily functioning and he seems to be showing very high levels of guilt and self-blame. Brandon should seek professional help because people suffering from traumatic grief usually need professional help to deal with their feelings and to recover from their grief. (642-643)

4.  Your child's remark was typical of statements made by young children. Most young children do not realize that death is a permanent, irreversible state. Instead, they believe that death is magical and temporary like going away on a magical trip from which one will return. Most children don't understand the permanent, biological nature of death until 5 to 7 years of age. So, your child's attempt to comfort you was not inappropriate but was consistent with his conception of death as being temporary. (644)

5.  Most adolescents are particularly reluctant to talk about their grief, mainly because they do not want to appear different from their peers. This reluctance to discuss their grief may lead to psychosomatic symptoms like headaches and stomach pains. Even when adolescents want to talk about their grief, their friends often do not want to listen. So, you can tell your daughter that her friend's behavior is not unusual, but she should let her friend know that she is willing to talk to her about her grief. (646)

6.  Liz's former mother-in-law experienced what is generally thought to be the most traumatic type of loss there is -- the death of a child. Mourning for a child is always intense and some parents never recover or reconcile themselves to the death of a child. Even more than 30 years after the death of a child, most parents still feel a keen sense of loss and continued difficulty in coming to terms with the loss. This sense of loss may often be accompanied by a sense of guilt that the pain affected the parents' relationships with surviving children. Most parents expect their children to outlive them, so it is very difficult to accept when a child dies first. So, Liz should realize that it's not

uncommon for her former mother-in-law to want to remember her lost child, especially on the anniversary of his death, but at the same time Liz should not feel guilty about not wanting to dwell on the past herself. Maybe now that she has children of her own she can better empathize with her former mother-in-law's feelings. (646-649)